FERRIES 2004
BRITISH ISLES AND NORTHERN EUROPE

STENA ADVENTURER

ISBN 1 871947 76 6

Ferry Publications, PO Box 33,
Ramsey, Isle of Man IM99 4LP

Email: ferrypubs@aol.com   Website: www.ferrypubs.co.uk

europe's **leading** *guide to the ferry industry*

contents

Introduction	3
Foreword	4
A guide to using this book	6
Brittany Ferries' new *Pont-Aven*	12
Round Britain Review 2003	23
Scandinavian and Northern Europe Review 2003	36
Stena Line's Masterclass in Ro-Pax	45
P&O Ferries' Darwin Project	53
DFDS' *Dana Gloria* & *Dana Sirena*	60
GB & Ireland – International passenger operations	68
GB & Ireland – Domestic services	102
GB & Ireland – Freight-only ferries	128
GB & Ireland – Chain, cable etc ferries	161
GB & Ireland – Major passenger-only ferries	164
Northern Europe	168
Other vessels	212
Changes since 'Ferries 2003 – British Isles & Northern Europe'	214
Late news	218
Index	219

Tom Sawyer *(TT Line)*

europe's **leading** *guide to the ferry industry*

introduction

This is the seventeenth edition of this book, which first appeared in 1983 as the 24 page 'home published' *'Car Ferries from Great Britain and Ireland'*. The book aims to list every passenger/vehicle ferry in Great Britain and Ireland, ro-ro freight vessels which operate regular services between Great Britain and Ireland and to nearby continental destinations and major passenger/vehicle ferries in other parts of Northern Europe. The coverage of Northern Europe is not fully comprehensive (to make it so would probably triple the size of the book) and does not include freight-only operations and vessels- although for the first time some freight-only vessels have been included where the operators also run passenger services. Also, ro-ro vessels engaged in 'deep sea' and Mediterranean trade and those operated solely for the carriage of trade cars are not included.

Each operator is listed alphabetically within sections – international and Northern Ireland routes, domestic services, freight-only operations, chain, cable and float ferries, passenger only ferries, other North European passenger operators and vehicle/passenger vessels owned by companies not currently engaged in operating services. After details relating to each company's management, address, telephone numbers, email, web site and services, there is a fleet list with technical data and then a potted history of each vessel with previous names and dates.

The ferry industry continues to be influenced by a number of external factors – terrorism, the growth of low cost airlines, differential tax rates between various European Union nations and the expansion of the European Union – all having both negative and positive effects. But the industry continues to invest in new tonnage and we are pleased to cover five very different new and extensively rebuilt vessels in feature articles. More new vessels are due later this year – including Color Line's mega-ferry, the *Color Fantasy*, which we hope to cover next year. Whatever else happens, we can be sure there will be more changes and surprises to come.

Whitstable, Kent

Nick Widdows

May 2004

europe's **leading** *guide to the ferry industry*

foreword

I am delighted to provide a Foreword for this much-valued annual publication, which is such a useful work of reference to all concerned with the ferry industry. The industry continues to face new challenges and all operators have had to cope with market changes following both the tragic events of 9/11 and the huge impact on passenger carryings made by the low-cost airlines. Change is as inevitable in our industry as it is within other spheres of transport and the quest for speed has also played an interesting role in the last twenty years.

A number of operators were quick to follow the fast ferry option but experience has shown that there is an optimum convenience versus comfort range, which precludes many of the longer distance crossings that Brittany Ferries operate. Fast craft most certainly do reduce crossing times but all too often the total travel experience can be compromised in terms of overall passenger comfort and on board facilities such as choice of restaurants, entertainment and shopping opportunities.

David Longdon

Speed most certainly isn't everything and after thirty years in the cross-Channel ferry industry, we have come to realise that our customers expect a choice, including comfortable overnight sailings. It is also a moot point whether speed brings profits! Right from the start of our operations, when we traded with well-chosen second-hand tonnage, we attempted to create a special and unique atmosphere on board our ships. It was and remains important that our customers feel both relaxed and happy in an environment which is totally French, no matter where any of our ships is at any particular moment.

With the introduction of our purpose-built fleet of ferries, we have taken this concept one step further and created a uniquely French ambience on board. Positive public reaction to our product indicates that we have succeeded in achieving this aim but in order to stay ahead of our competitors, it was essential that we reassess the speed issue for classic ferries and how it could benefit our routes in the Western Channel.

The result of many hundreds of hours of meetings, discussions and negotiations has been the introduction of our new £100 million cruise ferry *Pont-Aven* which we believe sets a completely new standard for the rest of the European ferry industry to follow, not just in style but also in better scheduling using its 27 knot service speed to reduce crossing times whilst continuing to provide a special passenger experience. Built in Meyer's Papenburg yard, which has gained a reputation second to none for the unsurpassed luxury of its cruise liners, the company's expertise was directed towards the creation our own ship. The result is there for all to experience and we believe that our decision to build such a mould-breaking ferry as the *Pont-Aven* has been fully justified.

In conclusion, I hope that you will enjoy the 2004 edition of this book and, on behalf of Brittany Ferries, I look forward to welcoming readers on board our ships during the forthcoming year.

David Longdon, Managing Director UK & Ireland

a **guide** *to*
using this book

Sections Listing is in seven sections **Section 1** – Services from Great Britain and Ireland to the continent and between Great Britain and Ireland (including services to/from the Isle of Man and Channel Islands), **Section 2** – Domestic services within Great Britain and Ireland, **Section 3** – Freight only services from Great Britain and Ireland and domestic routes, **Section 4** – Minor vehicle ferries in Great Britain and Ireland (chain and cable ferries etc), **Section 5** – Major passenger only operators, **Section 6** – Major car ferry operators in Northern Europe, **Section 7** – Companies not operating regular services possessing vehicle ferries which may be chartered or sold to other operators.

Order The company order within each section is alphabetical. Note that the definite article and words meaning 'company' or 'shipping company' (eg 'AG', 'Reederei') do not count. However, where this is part of a ship's name it does count. Sorting is by normal English convention eg 'Å' is treated the same as 'A' and comes at the start, not as a separate character which comes the end of the alphabet as is the Scandinavian convention. Where ships are numbered, order is by number whether number is expressed in Arabic or Latin digits or words (eg SUPERSEACAT THREE comes before SUPERSEACAT FOUR).

Company information This section gives general information regarding to status of the company ie nationality, whether it is public or private sector and whether it is part of a larger group.

Management The managing director and marketing director or manager of each company are listed. Where these posts do not exist, other equivalent people are listed. Where only initials are given, that person is, as far as is known, male.

Address This is the address of the company's administrative headquarters. In the case of some international companies, a British and overseas address is given.

Telephone and Fax Numbers are expressed as follows + [*number*] (this is the international dialling code which is dialled in combination with the number dialled for international calls (00 in the UK, Ireland and most other European countries); it is not used for calling within the country), ([*number*]) (this is the number which precedes area codes when making long distance domestic calls – it is not dialled when calling from another country or making local calls (not all countries have this)), [*number*] (this is the rest of the number including, where appropriate, the area dialling code). In a few cases free or local call rate numbers are used for reservations; note that these are not available from overseas. Telex numbers are also included where applicable; it should be noted that many operators no longer use this service, its role having largely been taken over by fax and email.

Internet Email addresses and **Website** URLs are given where these are available; the language(s) used is shown. Note that use of the Internet is increasing quickly and new sites may come into use during the currency of this book. If a web site is not shown for a particular operator, it may be worth trying one or more search engines to see if a new site has opened. In a few cases **Email** facility is only available through the **Website**. To avoid confusion, there is no other punctuation on the Internet line. All these addresses can be accessed from www.ferriesoftheworld.com and this will be updated at regular intervals as new web sites come on line. It should be noted that some sites are not always up to date and it is disappointing that few operators use this facility for 'real time' data showing day by day service changes. However, the standard is generally much higher than a few years ago and many operators now allow on-line booking, often at a discount over other methods. It is also often possible to find times for freight only sailings.

Routes operated After each route there are, in brackets, details of *1* normal journey time, *2* regular vessel(s) used on the route (number as in list of vessels) and *3* frequencies (where a number per day is given, this relates to return sailings). In the case of freight-only sailings which operate to a regular schedule, departure times are given where they have been supplied. Please note that times are subject to quite frequent change and cancellation.

Winter and Summer In this book, winter generally means the period between October and Easter while summer means, Easter to October. The peak summer period is generally June, July and August. In Scandinavia, the summer peak ends in mid-August whilst in the UK it starts rather later and generally stretches into the first or second week of September. Dates vary according to operator.

Spelling The convention is used in respect of town and country names is that English names are used for towns and areas of countries where such names exist (eg Gothenburg rather than Göteborg) and English names for countries (eg Germany rather than Deutschland). Otherwise local names are used, accented as appropriate. In a few cases, English names have slipped out of common usage and the local name is more commonly used in Britain, ie Dunkerque not Dunkirk, Helsingør not Elsinore and Vlissingen not Flushing. Many towns in Finland have both Finnish and Swedish names; we have used the Finnish name except in the case of Åland which is a Swedish speaking area. In the case of Danish towns, the alternative use of 'å' or 'aa' follows local convention. For technical reasons it is not possible to express some Polish names with the correct accents. The following towns, islands and territories are expressed using their English names; the local name is shown following: Antwerp – Antwerpen/Anvers, Fyn – Funen, Genoa – Génova, Ghent – Gent, Gothenburg – Göteborg, Jutland – Jylland, Copenhagen – København, Ostend – Oostende, Oporto – Porto, Seville – Sevilla, Sealand – Sjælland, Venice – Venezia.

Terms The following words mean *'shipping company'* in various languages Redereja (Latvian), Rederi (Danish, Norwegian, Swedish), Rederij (Dutch), Reederei (German), Zegluga (Polish). The following words mean *'limited company'* AB – Aktiebolag (Swedish) (Finnish companies who use both the Finnish and Swedish terms sometimes express it as Ab), AG – Aktiengesellschaft (German), AS – Aksjeselskap (Norwegian), A/S – Aktie Selskabet (Danish), BV – besloten vennootschap (Dutch), GmbH – Gesellschaft mit beschränkter Haftung (German), NV – naamloze vennootschap (Dutch), Oy – (Finnish), Oyj – (Finnish (plc)), SA – Société Anonyme (French).

Types of Ferry

These distinctions are necessarily general and many ships will have features of more than one category.

Car Ferry Up until about 1970, most vehicle ferries were primarily designed for the conveyance of cars and their passengers and foot passengers. Little regard was paid to the conveyance of lorries and trailers, since this sort of traffic had not began to develop. Few vessels of this type are still in service.

Multi-purpose Ferry From about 1970 onwards vehicle ferries began to make more provision for freight traffic, sharing the same ship with passengers and cars. Features usually include higher vehicle decks, often with retractable mezzanine decks, enabling two levels of cars or one level of freight and coaches, and separate facilities (including cabins on quite short crossings) for freight drivers.

Cruise Ferry In the 1980s the idea of travelling on a ferry, not just to get from A to B, but for the pleasure of the travel experience became more and more popular and ferries were built with increasingly luxurious and varied passenger accommodation. Such vessels also convey cars and freight but the emphasis is on passenger accommodation with a high level of berths (sometimes providing berths for all passengers).

Ro-pax Ferry A vessel designed primarily for the carriage of freight traffic but also carry a limited number of ordinary passengers. Features generally include a moderate passenger capacity – up to about 500 passengers – and a partly open upper vehicle deck. Modern ro-pax vessels are becoming increasingly luxurious with facilities approaching those of a cruise ferry.

Ro-ro Ferry A vessel designed for the conveyance of road freight, unaccompanied trailers and containers on low 'Mafi' trailers. Some such vessels have no passenger accommodation but the majority can accommodate to 12 passengers – the maximum allowed without a passenger certificate. On routes where there is a low level of driver accompanied traffic (mainly the longer ones), ordinary passengers, with or without cars, can sometimes be conveyed. On routes with a high level of driver accompanied traffic, passenger capacity will sometimes be higher but facilities tend to be geared to the needs of freight drivers eg lounge with video, high level of cabins on routes of three hours or more. Technically such vessels are passenger ferries (having a passenger certificate) but are included in the freight section when exclusively or mainly conveying freight drivers.

Fast Ferry Streamlined vessel of catamaran or monohull construction, speed in excess of 30 knots, water jet propulsion, generally aluminium built but some have steel hulls, little or no freight capacity, no cabins.

Timescale Although the book goes to press April 2004, I have sought to reflect the situation as it will exist in summer 2004 with regard to the introduction of new ships or other known changes. Vessels due to enter service from September 2004 are shown as '**Under Construction**'. The book is updated at all stages of the production process where this is feasible – although major changes once the text has been paginated are not possible; there is also a 'Late News' section at the back for changes which cannot be incorporated into the text.

List of vessels

NO (A)		GROSS TONNAGE (B)		SERVICE SPEED (KNOTS)		NUMBER OF PASSENGERS				VEHICLE ACCESS DECK (D)	
|		|	|			|			|		
1	NAME	‡26433t	87	22k	150m	290P		650C	100L	BA2	UK
	|		|		|		|	|			|
	NAME		YEAR BUILT		LENGTH OVERALL		VEHICLE (C) DECK CAPACITY				FLAG (E)

(A) >> = fast ferry, • = vessel laid up, F = freight only vessel, p = passenger only vessel

(B) '‡' = not measured in accordance with the 1969 Tonnage Convention; c = approximate.

(C) C = Cars, L = Lorries (**15m**), T = Trailers (**13.5m**), r = can also take rail wagons, – = No figure quoted.

(D) B = Bow, A = Aft, S = Side, Q = Quarterdeck, R = Slewing ramp, 2 = Two decks can be loaded at the same time, C = Vehicles must be crane loaded aboard, t = turntable ferry.

(E) The following abbreviations are used:

AL	= Åland Islands	DK	= Denmark	LB	= Liberia	PO	= Poland
AT	= Antigua and	ES	= Estonia	LT	= Lithuania	RO	= Romania
	Barbuda	FA	= Faroes	LV	= Latvia	RU	= Russia
BB	= Barbados	FI	= Finland	LX	= Luxembourg	SI	= Singapore
BD	= Bermuda	FR	= France	MA	= Malta	SP	= Spain
BE	= Belgium	GI	= Gibraltar	NA	= Netherlands	SV	= St Vincent &
BS	= Bahamas	GR	= Greece		Antilles		Grenadines
BZ	= Belize	GY	= Germany	NL	= Netherlands	SW	= Sweden
CI	= Cayman Islands	IM	= Isle of Man	NO	= Norway	TU	= Turkey
CR	= Croatia	IT	= Italy	PA	= Panama	UK	= United
CY	= Cyprus	IR	= Irish Republic	PL	= Portugal		Kingdom

In the notes ships are in CAPITAL LETTERS, shipping lines and other institutions are in *italics*.

Capacity In this book, capacities shown are the maxima. Sometimes vessels operate at less than their maximum passenger capacity due to reduced crewing or to operating on a route on which they are not permitted to operate above a certain level. Car and lorry/trailer capacities are the maximum for either type. The two figures are not directly comparable; some parts of a vessel may allow cars on two levels to occupy the space that a trailer or lorry occupies on one level, some may not. Also some parts of a vessel with low headroom may only be accessible to cars. All figures have to be fairly approximate.

Ownership The ownership of many vessels is very complicated. Some are actually owned by finance companies and banks, some by subsidiary companies of the shipping lines, some by subsidiary companies of a holding company of which the shipping company is also a subsidiary and some by companies which are jointly owned by the shipping company and other interests like a bank, set up specifically to own one ship or a group of ships. In all these cases the vessel is technically chartered to the shipping company. However, in this book, only those vessels chartered from one shipping company to another or from a ship owning company unconnected with the shipping line, are recorded as being on charter. Vessels are listed under the current operator rather than the owner. Charter is 'bareboat' (ie without crew) unless otherwise stated. If chartered with crew, vessels are 'time chartered'.

Gross Tonnage This is a measure of enclosed capacity rather than weight, based on a formula of one gross ton = 100 cubic feet. Even small alterations can alter the gross tonnage. Under old measurement systems, the capacity of enclosed car decks was not included but, under a 1969 convention, all vessels laid down after 1982 have been measured by a new system which includes enclosed vehicle decks as enclosed space, thereby considerably increasing the tonnage of vehicle ferries. Under this convention, from 1st January 1995, all vessels were due to be re-measured under this system; despite there, there are a number of vessels which have either not been re-registered or the details of the new measurements were not obtainable. All vessels measured by the old system are indicated with a double dagger '‡'. Tonnages quoted here are, where possible, those given by the shipping companies themselves.

The following people are gratefully thanked for their assistance with this publication many people in ferry companies in the UK and abroad, Gary Andrews, Cees de Bijl, Dick Clague, Andrew Cooke, Erik B Jonsen, Ian McCrorie, William Mayes, Barry Mitchell, The Ostend Ferry Crew, Jack Phelan, Pekka Ruponen, Christian Schrandt, Michael Speckenbach (FERRYinformation), Henk van der Lugt, Ian Smith (The Camrose Organisation), Foto Flite, Haven Colourprint and Pat Somner (Ferry Publications).

Whilst every effort has been made to ensure that the facts contained here are correct, neither the publishers nor the writer can accept any responsibility for errors contained herein. We would, However, appreciate comments from readers, which we will endeavour to incorporate in the next edition which we plan to publish in spring 2005.

Pont-Aven *(Brian D. Smith)*

Brittany **Ferries'**
pont-aven

B elieve it or not, it has now been 10 years since the opening of the Channel Tunnel and experts everywhere were predicting the end of the ferry industry as we knew it. So how come we have just witnessed entry into service of the most expensively-built and luxuriously-appointed ferry of all time? It cannot be denied that, in some ways, the experts were right and the industry has without doubt changed beyond all recognition. Historical and much loved services such as Dover-Zeebrugge have closed and many cherished ships have been swept away, being considered too small, old or just too expensive to update with the latest passenger amenities and SOLAS regulations.

So what have the ferry companies done to survive the threat of the Tunnel and indeed construct an industry ready for the 21st century? Well, the more efficient procedures and staff cuts brought in by managements have been well documented. Occasionally there have been amalgamations between companies and tonnage has been upgraded and improved. However, one of the main reasons that the ferry industry is looking forward to the future with more confidence than before is that they realised that to compete with the Tunnel, and indeed more recently with low cost airlines, they must provide the customer with what they want and at a price that is acceptable. They must also be willing to provide facilities that make travelling a pleasure and that people will be willing to pay for. This includes well-appointed ships with modern facilities, such as fine restaurants with good cuisine, shopping malls, comfortable lounges and, on longer routes, health spas and en-suite cabins. Step forward Brittany Ferries and their new flagship the *Pont-Aven*.

Back in 1989, after the Tunnel had been announced, the Breton company introduced the stylish *Bretagne* on their Plymouth-Santander route. She was a vast improvement on anything serving the English Channel and made a bold declaration that Brittany Ferries were to be major players in the luxury ferry business. In fact, only Olau could offer the travelling public anything close to the style and amenities available on any sailing from the British Isles. With this investment the company saw a spectacular increase in custom on its Spanish and Irish services that totally justified the large outlay on the new ship.

Three years later, the company introduced the English Channel's first real ferry liner on its popular Portsmouth-Caen service. The £90 million pound *Normandie* again set new standards that the company's competitors just could not keep up with. Immediately being given 5 stars by the AA, she was an great success, increasing the company's gain of passengers to over 50% on the Western Channel services. Many people commented that watching the *Normandie* arriving simultaneously with a rival's ship was like watching a cruise-liner arrive with a troop carrier. More new tonnage was introduced on the Poole-Cherbourg service and a larger second-hand (but extensively refurbished) ferry bought for the Santander service. This allowed the *Bretagne* to move to the St Malo service, again with spectacular results. By now the company had invested over £300 million in new ships since the Tunnel was announced and now were without doubt market leaders in the luxury ferry market.

It cannot be denied that most ferry companies were affected by the devaluing of the pound in the mid-1990s and the down-turn caused by the British recession. Yet as soon as things improved, the stronger showed the way forward by investing in more new tonnage. At last the *Normandie* got a sister as we said hello to the *Mont St Michel* and goodbye to the *Quiberon*. P&O introduced the *Pride of Hull* and *Pride of Rotterdam* on their North Sea service. Stena Line took delivery of two

Le Flora Restaurant *(Brian D. Smith)*

Le Flora Restaurant *(Brian D. Smith)*

Deck 9 *(Brian D. Smith)*

Le Grand Pavois *(Brian D. Smith)*

super freighters on the Harwich-Hoek of Holland service and SeaFrance got in on the act ordering a new Finnish ship to go head to head with the Tunnel. However, none of these improvements generated as much excitement and anticipation as the new building about to be announced by Brittany Ferries.

In June 2002 the company announced that they had signed an order with the German shipyard Meyer Werft for a £100 million cruise ferry which would cross the Bay of Biscay in 18 hours. To be named the *Pont-Aven*, she would offer amenities such as an open-air swimming pool, balconied cabins, health spa, fitness centre, shopping mall and club class travel for the first time. Style comfort and speed were about to be raised to new levels. A letter of intent was accepted by the yard just after the launch of the *Mont St Michel* with the contract being signed in June of that year. Delivery was scheduled for March 2004.

The construction officially started on 9th April 2003 when the first of 24 large building blocks were laid by the yard in the presence of the yard's managing partner Bernard Mayer and Brittany Ferries' managing director Michel Maraval. Construction then continued at a very impressive pace until she was finally ready for "floating up" on 13th September.

In front of invited guests, Michel Maraval, Alexis Gourvennec and Henri-Jean Lebeau, Managing Directors of Brittany Ferries, opened the valves of the dock gates by pressing the buttons and one hundred million litres of water flowed into the building dock. The ferry was moved within the covered building hangar to her final fitting out position. After completion and extensive tests she was towed out into the open world at 16.45 on 3rd February before starting her passage down the River Ems at midnight on 7th February. Passing the famous Friesenbrücke railway bridge at 03.00 she continued on past the Jann-Berghaus-Brücke bridge at 06.00 and the small town of Leer. She was delayed slightly at the Ems river barrier at Gandersum owing to extremely strong winds. She eventually passed through the barrier at about 13.00 where a large crowd had gathered to see her off. Her destination was Emershaven, which was to be her home for three weeks during which she would be taken out into the North Sea for extensive sea trials. Finally she was handed over to Brittany Ferries on 29th February 2004, three days before her contracted date.

During her delivery she was diverted to Caen where she met up with the *Mont St Michel* and the *Bretagne*.

She arrived in Roscoff the following morning before going to Brest for final adjustments and crew training. Several events then took place, including her being displayed to members of the French media. Finally she came to Britain on 17th March, arriving in Plymouth Sound exactly as the *Val de Loire* was departing on her penultimate departure to Spain. A noisy and impressive display then took place as the two ferries passed close by in Plymouth Sound before the new ship was shown to invited guests and members of the press.

After much anticipation, the *Pont-Aven* entered service on the 23.15 service to Roscoff on 23rd March. She returned the following morning for her official Maiden Voyage to Spain on the 24th. On arrival in Santander she was dressed overall and a celebration took place on board for invited Spanish guests. She was taken out of service twice in April to allow both the French and British sides of Brittany Ferries to celebrate her entry into service with the official naming ceremony taking place in Roscoff on 26th April.

Externally the *Pont-Aven* is very long and graceful looking, with a beam of almost 31 metres and a length of 185 metres. She does not have an upper vehicle deck like most new ferries and this does add to her outline. In total she has eleven decks, including two full decks of cabins, three car decks (main deck, mezzanine on main deck and hold below) and a walkway that goes right round the exterior of the ship including fantastic forward observation above the bridge.

The ship is propelled by four engines with reduction gears and two controllable pitch propellers. The output of the flexible mounted engines (MAK 4-stroke diesels) is 14,700 HP each at 500 rpm. The engines have been designed to operate on heavy fuel oil. Electrical power is provided by three diesel generator sets with an output of 2,400 kW each at 750 rpm. In addition, one emergency generator was installed. Two bow and one stern thruster each with a total power of about 2000 kW give the ship optimum manoeuvrability whilst two Brown Brother fin stabilisers help keep the ship stable in rough seas. Heat for the ship is provided by a steam boiler system with two oil-

Pont-Aven *(Miles Cowsill)*

burning boilers. Her funnel appears small for the size of the ship but it is a more aesthetically pleasing centre feature rather than the unsightly twin formation. The *Pont-Aven* is fully compliant with the latest SOLAS and environmental regulations.

The moment you drive on board the massive car deck you feel as if you are on something out of the ordinary. Entry to the passenger areas are via large spacious lifts which can hold up to 20 people. Lift fittings are a mixture of brushed aluminium and lightwood with a marble floor. Soft music sooths you on your journey to the upper decks. Deck 5 is the first passenger deck and consists of a mixture of standard class, club class and crew cabins. All cabins are en-suite and finished with a dark wood and yellow carpet giving a very modern and warm feel to the cabin. Lighting is via several soft fittings, all individually controlled so you can set the lighting to your own personal taste. On the four berth cabins the top berths fold into the ceiling, like on the *Mont St Michel*, giving extra space. The bathrooms are an enlarged version of the Brittany Ferries design, which although almost unchanged in over 10 years, are very functional and easy to use. Each cabin has an internal radio and alarm clock, which plays music chosen by the crew rather than local radio. Club class cabins also get a flat screen television and various beverage-making facilities. All outside cabins have large round windows with a deep wood surround, giving a very light and airy feel to the cabin.

Moving up to Deck 6 you come to the reception area which is set off centre to the portside of the ship. This area is purposeful and would benefit from a feature such as *Normandie's* bronze statues to give the area a feel of being the centre of the ship where passengers come to for information and assistance. The ship also has several plasma screens giving information about facilities on board including menus, safety and promotions. Some of them are interactive and allow you to interrogate the system by touching the screen at given points during the display – a most useful function when the information desk is busy. Next to this are two cinemas seating 90 people and a further mixture of standard class and disabled cabins. There is also a walkway that goes through a glazed forward seating area giving marvellous views of the open sea.

Next to the information desk is the start of the ship's atrium. Rising through all five passenger decks with its glass lifts, it gives the ship a cruise-liner feel of luxury. Light pastel colours and marble floor are complemented with coloured neon lights, white wood and glass with each floor having its own identity. The main staircase is situated in front of the lifts and is finished in a yellow and black carpet with metal fittings and yellow neon lights hidden into the ensemble. Glass display cabinets with various statues and objets d'art add to the experience. Floor to ceiling windows on each level, combined with yet another glass ceiling, give lots of natural light and again fantastic views out to the ocean. Comfortable seating is also provided, allowing passengers to sit down and enjoy the spectacle of the open sea.

Walking up the staircase you come to Deck 7. At the rear of the deck is the "La Flora" waiter service restaurant and "Le Fastnet" piano bar. These are reached along an inspirational arcade, coloured in deep yellow and blue with plush carpets and wooden walkways. Stylish sofas face out towards the sea whilst large glass display cabinets adorn the walls and pillars. The bar is built with large green glass tiles and frosted tops and is furnished with deep white leather chairs and deep green sofas with seating for around 80 people. A large white grand piano sets off the décor whilst individually lit glass sculptures add to the ambience. To the right of the bar is the entrance to "La Flora", restaurant while a wooden walkway leads out to the rear open deck. A large glass divide separates the two areas. On entry to the restaurant you are immediately confronted with four striking cold food displays to whet your appetite. To the right is an open kitchen where you can see and smell all the wonderful French food being prepared. Surrounding the central food display is an oval area with seating on the outside. These have extremely high-backed chairs giving diners a degree of privacy from other guests. Bright Burgundy and green sofas with white leather chairs are the décor for the main restaurant, which is split into separate areas so the room doesn't appear as big as it is. Black marble floor tiles are interwoven with a plush biscuit coloured carpet and wooden floor panelling. Again on three sides you have large windows giving lots of natural light.

The "La Belle Angele" self service restaurant is situated in front of the main atrium and is set up with the kitchens on the port side and the seating on the starboard. Uniquely this restaurant has three different serving counters with a variety of hot dishes. Firstly you have the Grill, followed by

Le Grand Pavois *(Brian D. Smith)*

Les Finisteres *(Brian D. Smith)*

the Traditional counter and then the World counter. A Salad bar, drinks counter and dessert selection finish off the choices available. The seats are again yellow with a mixture of wood and glass giving a very pleasing dining atmosphere. Moving forward to the bow you come to "Le Café du Festival". Unusually, Brittany Ferries market this not as a 'salon de tea' but as a café/restaurant. It is a very large room with similar décor as the Belle Angele and superb forward views across the ship's bow. Adjacent to this are a children's play area and a freight drivers' restaurant.

On Deck 8 is the Commodore area, eighteen well appointed cabins each with their own private balcony reached through French windows. Deep colourful carpets, light wooden panelling and original works of art give these cabins a very plush feel. You also have access to the Commodore lounge situated right at the stern of the ship. Also here are sixteen deluxe cabins which are similarly appointed but with large floor to ceiling windows rather that a balcony. The colour scheme is more austere with a fashionable European flavour. These cabins are clearly aimed at the more up-market end of the accommodation but will no doubt prove to be very popular.

By the atrium is the main shop "Mont et Merveilles". This is the vessel's only shop and encompasses the duty free shop, wine cellar, boutique and newsagents. In front of this is the entrance to the "Le Grand Pavois", the main bar. This is a grand two-tiered bar with a fantastic sweeping staircase going up to the second level with a wonderful glass roof giving masses of natural light. The seating is almost metallic green in colour and without doubt resembles the décor from the *Radiance of the Seas* class of ship, built and designed by Meyer Werft. Clearly the shipyard has had an input to the design of this area as it does have a very American feel to it, something I am sure Brittany Ferries would not have designed on their own. Even the waiters' drinks trays have dazzling neon lights in them. Vibrantly coloured tables and seating are provided on both levels with a small dance floor on the ground level beside the staircase. A glass wall behind the staircase gives views into the swimming pool and Les Finisteres bar. Large French windows give access onto the top promenade deck that has screens fitted rather than rails, which give a very sheltered outside area in which to relax and enjoy ship life. The teenage Games Planet is also situated up here along with a private lounge of white leather and light blue carpets.

The *Pont-Aven* has now settled down on her intensively operated schedule, departing for Spain on Sundays and Wednesdays with two crossings to Roscoff on Tuesday and Friday. She also covers the Irish services at the weekend. She is without doubt a major investment for the company and one that will prove extremely successful. Not only is the *Pont-Aven* the fastest ever ferry crossing from the UK to the Iberian Peninsula and France but her superb facilities leave the competition so far behind they are going to find it very hard to do anything to compete on level terms. The impressive details of the *Pont-Aven* do not begin to portray the feeling you get by sailing on her. She is a very well-designed ship that is both luxurious and contemporary. Passengers and enthusiasts are going to love her. Standards and expectations have risen to a new level. It is going to take something unbelievable to beat her. Sailing to the continent has never been so much fun.

Brian David Smith

Commodore Class Lounge *(Brian D. Smith)*

Commodore Class Cabin - Deck 8 *(Miles Cowsill)*

SeaFrance Rodin *(Miles Cowsill)*

Pride of Bilbao*(Miles Cowsill)*

round britain
review 2003

EAST COAST

The main change on the Tyne has been the sale of DFDS's *Princess of Scandinavia* to Moby Lines of Italy in October and her replacement by the *Duke of Scandinavia*, the former *Dana Anglia*, which had left UK waters in October 2002 to inaugurate a new Copenhagen – Trelleborg – Gdansk service. The Newcastle – IJmuiden route, which only started in 1995 and is shared with the *Queen of Scandinavia*, is now DFDS's busiest passenger route in the North Sea. Fjord Line's *Jupiter* continued to maintain the Newcastle – Bergen – Stavanger service and looks like doing so throughout 2004 although there are rumours of a replacement for this now rather elderly vessel which has to operate an intensive service during the peak summer period.

Nexus, who operate the North Shields – South Shields ferry, have announced plans to replace the 1976 built *Shieldsman*, which acts as backup to the newer *Pride of the Tyne*.

On the Humber, P&O Ferries launched their refurbished *Norsun* and *Norsea* as the *Pride of Bruges* and *Pride of York* on the Hull – Zeebrugge route in January. Less happy was their decision to cut back on support staff at Hull and concentrate management and bookings work at Dover.

Over the river at Immingham, freight traffic and services continued to grow with Cobelfret Ferries' daily Zeebrugge service often supplemented by a third vessel operating three round trips per week. The recently acquired *Catherine*, used on the Rotterdam service, was chartered to the US Defense Department for the Iraq war and did not return until August. Her running mate, the *Louise Russ* continued to operate throughout the year, still in her original RoRo Express livery and decals and these were not removed when she went for refit in the autumn.

In October DFDS Tor Line introduced the first of their five new Flensburg built ships on their daily service from Immingham to Gothenburg. The *Tor Magnolia* introduced a new naming policy and will be followed by four more 'flower class' vessels for the Gothenburg and Esbjerg routes and the second, the *Tor Petunia* entered service in early January 2004. The new ships represent a 40% increase in capacity over the previous generation vessels.

From the river terminal in the suburb of Killingholme – the Simon Group owned Humber Sea Terminal – Seawheel boosted their service to Hamburg and Esbjerg with the charter of the *Pasewalk* to run along side the Polish owned *Zeran*. However, it was later decided that this route could best be handled by container ships running from Goole to Brunsbüttel at the mouth of the Elbe and the service closed at the end of the year. The Rotterdam service however continues and during the year Seawheel ceased to be part of the Simon Group, which continues to own the terminal. In early 2004 the *Seawheel Rhine* was taken out of service with serious mechanical problems and was replaced by the Polish vessel *Chodziez*. The terminal capacity relinquished by Seawheel has been taken up by Cobelfret Ferries, which launched a new Gothenburg service in January 2004, operated by the *Anna Oden* and *Britta Oden*, which were for many years part of the DFDS Tor Line fleet as the *Tor Flandria* and *Tor Scania* and associated mainly with the Gothenburg – Ghent route. Cobelfret Ferries purchased these ferries, along with the third sister, the *Eva Oden* (ex *Tor Belgia*) in October. Cobelfret plan to move their other Immingham services to this terminal later in 2004 when additional berths have been constructed.

Ostend operator Ferryways, running to Ipswich and Killingholme, renamed the former Dag Engstrom vessels *Rodona* and *Sapphire* the *Ipswich Way* and *Ostend Way* in July. The *Beatrixhaven*, which was chartered in April to provide relief cover, was subsequently taken on long-term charter and renamed the *Humber Way*. In September the company replaced the chartered *Vilja* with a sister vessel of the *Humber Way*, the *Calibur*. With six vessels they were able to operate four sailings per day to Ipswich and one overnight sailing on the longer route to Killingholme.

At Harwich, DFDS resumed the Harwich – Cuxhaven service in April with the *Duchess of Scandinavia*, the former *Bergen* of Fjord Line. Over the winter they had chartered the ro-ro *Nordic Link* to operate the service in freight only mode. In June they replaced the *Dana Gloria* with the *Dana Sirena*. Built as sister vessels, whereas the *Dana Gloria* (originally built in Szczecin, Poland for Lloyd Sardegna of Italy as the *Golfo Dei Coralli*) was in more or less 'as built' state, the *Dana Sirena* was substantially modified to increase passenger capacity from 308 to 600 and provide a more comfortable environment. Whilst the Harwich – Cuxhaven service is branded as DFDS Seaways, the Esbjerg service in under the DFDS Tor Line banner with less facilities than the German route.

Stena Line, which had introduced the new *Stena Britannica II* on the Hoek van Holland – Harwich service early in 2003, renamed her the *Stena Britannica* in March, following the sale of the 2001 built vessel of the same name to Finnlines. Over at Felixstowe, Finnlines sold their *Finnmerchant* and *Transbaltica* to Norwegian interests and chartered them back. Following this they were renamed the *Merchant* and the *Baltica*. During the year Finnlines changed their Belgian port for the Helsinki/Hamina/Hanko service from Antwerp to Zeebrugge; the former Transfennica Kemi/Oulu/Helsinki vessels continued to serve Antwerp.

THAMES AND MEDWAY

Dart Line services were considerably affected by the Iraq conflict when, in January, the *Dart 8* and *Dart 9* were chartered to the MoD, joining sister vessel *Dart 10* which had been on long-term charter since 2001. The Zeebrugge service was covered by three Bazias class vessels, including the *Bazias 1* which had been back with the company since the autumn of 2002. The Vlissingen and Dunkerque routes were covered by another Bazias vessel plus the chartered *Northern Star* (which finished her charter with P&O Irish Sea at the end of 2002) and the *Varbola* (which had just ended a charter with NorseMerchant Ferries). In May the *Varbola* – which had not performed well due to her poor internal layout for loading – was swapped with NorseMerchant Ferries for the *River Lune*, another Bazias class vessel. The *Dart 8* and *Dart 9* returned in September, preceded by the *Dart 10* which served for a few weeks in August and early September until both the regular ships were back in traffic. She was then chartered out again. Whilst the *Northern Star* was returned to her owners, the *River Lune* was retained in order to enable a second daily sailing to Dunkerque to be operated. The *Bazias 1* left the company just before Christmas and the *River Lune* in February 2004. Services were reduced to two daily sailings to Zeebrugge and one to Dunkerque.

Cobelfret Ferries transferred their Dagenham – Zeebrugge service operated for the Ford Motor Company to a new terminal at Vlissingen in May and upped the frequency from two to three sailings per day, utilising all four Chinese built ships on the route. The *Amandine* and *Loverval* were sold to a Belize based company and renamed the *Amanda* and *Marabou* respectively. They were both chartered back for an indefinite period. All other UK registered vessels were transferred to the Bahamian flag. In the autumn, Cobelfret Ferries purchased the three ex Tor Line ships *Anna Oden*, *Britta Oden* and *Eva Oden* from Bylock & Norsjöfrakt. During the autumn the latter two vessels operated on services to Purfleet whilst the first remained on charter elsewhere. In the new year the *Anna Oden* and *Britta Oden* were transferred to the new Immingham – Gothenburg service.

The Tilbury – Gravesend Ferry was suspended between 6th May and 21st June after the engine of the 1956 built *Duchess M* 'blew up'. The company was able to obtain a replacement MoD surplus Thorneycroft engine; later in the year the vessel was fitted with a modern Scania engine which should give her several years' more life.

The Woolwich ferry *James Newman* was damaged by fire caused by arsonists on 13th July and had to be sent away for repair. This was a further problem for an operation that tries to maintain a frequent two-ship service on a busy route, crying out for new investment, which has been further stalled by prospects for the new Thames Gateway Bridge between Beckton and Thamesmead.

Your first port of call

Take a short cut. Now everything you need to know about the Port of Dover is online, at the new-look official port website.

Use it to check the day's crossing conditions, news and ferry services.

So whatever you need to know about the Port of Dover, make www.doverport.co.uk your first port of call.

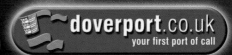

doverport.co.uk
your first port of call

EASTERN CHANNEL

January saw the introduction of the *Gardenia* (ex *European Endeavour*) on TransEuropa Ferries' Ostend – Ramsgate route. Although the *Begonia* (formerly *European Pathfinder*), was also acquired in 2002, she did not enter service until February 2004 after a lengthy 'do it yourself' refurbishment. The much forecast start of a passenger service one again never happened.

At Dover work began on constructing two new berths in the former trailer parking on the west side of the Eastern Docks. Plans for a new development on the Folkestone side of the Western Docks were shelved, although ferry activities in the Western Docks themselves are still on the cards, especially in the region of the hoverport, where the large concrete apron is not longer required.

P&O's *Pride of Provence* hit the Dover Southern Breakwater on 18th April, causing minor injuries to twenty-eight passengers and crew and damage to the ship. The subsequent enquiry revealed that it was due to poor planning by the master. The two 'Darwin Project' rebuilds of the *European Pathway* and *European Highway* as the *Pride of Canterbury* and *Pride of Kent* entered service in the early summer for P&O Ferries, replacing the *PO Canterbury* and *PO Kent*, which were both sold to GA ferries of Greece. As other ships returned from refit over the winter they received the new P&O Ferries livery and their new 'Pride of' names, replacing the interim 'PO' names (achieved by simply painting out '&' and 'SL' in 'P&OSL'). The new ships' unmodified sister *European Seaway* ran throughout the year between Dover and Calais in freight only mode but in December it was announced that in 2004 she would be withdrawn and the *Pride of Burgundy* would operate the freight service from March. This was combined with cutbacks on service provision during the night (including the non-acceptance of foot passengers) and involved nearly 500 redundancies.

SeaFrance reinstated the withdrawn *SeaFrance Renoir* and operated a four ship passenger service at many periods during the year. A second newbuilding was ordered for delivery in 2005 – this time from the Alsthom shipyard at St Nazaire. It was later announced that she would be called the *SeaFrance Berlioz*, this time being named after a composer rather than a visual artist.

After suspending their Dover – Ostend service for the winter at the end of the summer 2002 season, Hoverspeed announced that it would not resume in 2003 and only Dover – Calais sailings would operate. The service started the summer with three drive through 78m craft *SeaCat Danmark*, *SeaCat Scotland* and *Hoverspeed Great Britain* but in June the 'HGB' was withdrawn with a hull leak and replaced by the 81m *Diamant* – less suitable for the intensive Dover – Calais route due to her lack of a bow door and often the cause of delay to the other vessels. The Dover – Calais route was then suspended in mid December after the announcement that their operation would henceforth become seasonal, running March-December only.

Norfolkline continued to operate a three ship service but the *Dawn Merchant*, acquired in 2002, continued to operate in unmodified form with single deck loading and only able to use berth 1 at Dover. During the year an order was placed in Korea for two new, larger and faster ships for delivery in 2005, so it seems unlikely that the *Dawn Merchant* will ever be modified – although the new ships are to supposedly supplement the existing fleet rather than replace it. Her sister, the *Brave Merchant*, was also chartered at times to cover for refits. A third new ship was ordered in March 2004.

SpeedFerries' new Dover – Boulogne service, expected to start in May, did not materialise at all in 2003. It was found that a new pontoon was needed at Boulogne to accommodate the 91m *Mads Mols*, to be renamed the *Speed One* and by the time that this had been delivered it was decided it was too late to launch the service. Meanwhile, Mols Linien of Denmark pulled out of the venture (they had only ever been a shareholder, not sole owner as originally thought) and during the autumn negotiated a deal with P&O Ferries to charter the *Mads Mols'* sister, the *Max Mols* to P&O Ferries between Portsmouth and Cherbourg in 2004. This meant that the *Mads Mols* would not be available for charter and Speed Ferries instead is now due to start in May 2004 with the 85m craft, formerly *InCat 045*, also to be called the *Speed One*.

Operations at Newhaven continued much as in 2003 with Transmanche Ferries slowly building up traffic on their predominantly freight service – although several times running aground on the tricky approach channel to Newhaven. During the year it was announced that they were seeking quotes for a new ro-pax vessel to replace the chartered *Sardinia Vera*, which has too much passenger accommodation for the route. In February 2004 orders were placed for two vessels to replace both the *Sardinia Vera* and the *Dieppe*. Hoverspeed once again operated their seasonal Newhaven – Dieppe service with the *SuperSeaCat One*, their hopes that they might be allocated one of the last two such craft to be built and be enabled to convey coaches dashed when both the *SuperSeaCat Three* and *SuperSeaCat Four* were allocated to Silja Line for the Helsinki – Tallinn route.

WESTERN CHANNEL

There was much less change at Portsmouth in 2003 than in the previous year when both P&O and Brittany Ferries saw new craft. However, for P&O the impact of the formation of P&O Ferries as a single company began to be felt with the ships painted into the new livery (except the *Pride of Cherbourg*), P&O Dover 'brands' (inherited from P&O Stena Line) introduced onto the ships and onshore work and management moved from Portsmouth to Dover. Despite problems in previous years, P&O once again operated the 91m InCat *Catalonia* between Portsmouth and Cherbourg, this time as 'Express' rather than 'Portsmouth Express' and as a marketing name with no actual renaming of the vessel until November 2003. She spent the early winter laid up in Spain followed by a lot of work being done to improve her reliability rather than performing a stint in South America, but her performance was not a lot better than in 2002 and had to be withdrawn a few weeks early due to mechanical problems. She will return in March 2004 under the marketing name 'Cherbourg Express'. Additionally, P&O will operate a Portsmouth – Caen service with the chartered *Max Mols* as the 'Caen Express'.

A new rival to P&O's Portsmouth – Le Havre service was announced in the autumn. This was Channel Freight Ferries whose route was from Southampton to Radicatel, a completely new installation near the N178 bridge which crosses the River Seine east of Le Havre but actually part of the Port of Rouen. The company is owned by shipbrokers Clarkson plc. The service started in January 2004.

2004 looks to be a more eventful year with Brittany Ferries bringing up the *Val de Loire*, to share with the *Bretagne* the St Malo route and also a new Cherbourg route.

Channel Islands freight operator Commodore was 'rebranded' as Condor Ferries at the end of the year following a re-organisation of what was the Commodore Group and is now the Condor Ferries Group. The ro-pax *Commodore Clipper* and freight only *Commodore Goodwill* have been repainted into a new livery but will retain their 'Commodore' names.

In the Channel Islands, Condor Ferries, were, from April licensed by the island authorities to carry cars between St Malo and Jersey; previously they had been restricted to carrying passengers. Partly because of this new competition, Emeraude Lines had a difficult time and ran into serious financial problems by the end of the year. After services were suspended for a time the company was taken over by the Le Havre based Sogestram group. The *Solidor 5* will not operating in 2004 due to a dispute with the vessels' owners. Sea Containers' *Hoverspeed Great Britain* has been charted to operate their operations for 2004. Meanwhile Guernsey will no longer be served by Emeraude Lines and the *Solidor 4* was sold by the company to Senegal interests in the 2004, and renamed the *Aline*.

After Emeraude Lines withdrew its services to Normandy ports on the Cherbourg Peninsula at the end of the 2002 summer season and did not reintroduce them in 2003, there was a perceived gap in the market. Consequently the local authority purchased two Fjellstrand 35m FlyingCats, one from Norway and one from Tahiti. The operation of the service was put out to tender and won by Société de Navigation de Normandie, part of the Connex group, trading as Victor Hugo Express. Only one entered service in summer 2003, the *Victor Hugo*, formerly the *Salten*. The second, the *Marin Marie* (ex *Aremeti 3*) operated briefly in late October but all services were suspended on 1st November. It is planned that services will resume in spring 2004 and, for the first time for many years, a service from France to Alderney will be offered.

Red Funnel Ferries took delivery of the fourth fast ferry the *Red Jet 4* in May, the craft arriving from her Australian builders on a heavy lift ship. In the autumn and early winter they sent two of their 'Raptor Class' vessels – the *Red Falcon* followed by the *Red Osprey* – to Poland to have an additional vehicle deck added and for the ships to be lengthened. The rebuilding took place over winter 2003/4 and to cover the company purchased a second-hand ferry – the 1976 built *Nordhordland* from

Mont St Michel *(Miles Cowsill)*

Stena Explorer *(Miles Cowsill)*

Normandy *(Gordon Hislip)*

Ben-my-Chree *(Miles Cowsill)*

Bergen-Nordhordland Rutelag A/S of Norway. They renamed her the *Bergen Castle* and, whilst all ships should be back by the start of the summer period, she will be available for relief or cover purposes. The *Red Eagle* will go away next winter. A new 'Red Jet' passenger service between Gosport and Southampton was launched during the Southampton Boat Show in September and was so successful that it was decided to operate the service at weekends between 8th November and 4th January for Christmas and January sales shoppers.

Rival Isle of Wight operator Wightlink also tried new services, operating a Lymington – Cowes passenger service, initially during Cowes week at the beginning of August but extended until the August Bank Holiday Monday. A Ryde Pier Head – Southampton Ocean Village service was operated on Saturdays before Christmas and to 4th January 2004. Plans were also announced for a car ferry service between Portsmouth and Ryde Pier Head. This included the conversion of the closed tramway into a road. However, this has provoked opposition from some quarters due to the prospect of increased traffic in Ryde town centre. Work has yet to start.

North West Europe's only remaining hovercraft operator, Hovertravel of Ryde, Isle of Wight opened a new terminal on the island in August. Two of their craft were disposed of.

The Southampton – Hythe Ferry had an unexpected interruption on 1st November when the dredger *Donald Redford* crashed into the pier at Hythe. The service switched to the nearby marina, although smaller vessels had to be chartered for the first few days – the *Great Expectations* then resuming operations. The pier was re-opened on 6th January 2004 and the master of the dredger was later jailed.

During 2003 it was announced that the freight only Brittany Ferries service operated by the *Countances* from Poole to Cherbourg would cease when the new Portsmouth – Cherbourg service started in spring 2004. In conjunction with the passenger ship *Barfleur* a three sailings per day service for truckers is offered for most of the year, but a single ship service would have only offered three sailings every two days, which would have made the service much less attractive to regular shippers. However, early in 2004 it was announced the service would continue.

Plymouth saw Brittany Ferries service much as before, with the *Val de Loire* spending her last summer on the Santander and Cork roster before the arrival of the new *Pont-Aven* in March 2004. The *Duc de Normandie* spent her first full year based at the port and there are currently no plans to replace the 1978 built vessel.

Down in Cornwall, the family firm of C Toms and Son introduced a second home-built self propelled ferry on the 5 minute Fowey – Bodinnick crossing. The same length as the 2000 built *Jenack*, the *Gellan* is narrower with two rather than three traffic lanes.

IRISH SEA

When the *Stena Lynx III* finished her summer season on the Fishguard – Rosslare run, she resumed her previous name *Elite* and it looked as though this would be her last season. However in a surprise move, Stena Line purchased the craft and she will return once again as the *Stena Lynx III* in April 2004.

Stena Line's Korean built ro-pax the *Stena Adventurer* entered service on 1st July on the Holyhead – Dublin route. Because the new charterers of the *Stena Forwarder* needed delivery before the new ship was available, the older ship was withdrawn in April and the 74 passenger *Stena Transporter* was deployed from the Harwich – Rotterdam route to cover. Only freight was conveyed.

In April P&O and Stena Line signed a memorandum of understanding under which Stena Line would take over P&O's Fleetwood – Larne and Liverpool – Dublin routes and the vessels used on them. The Mostyn – Dublin route would cease and Stena Line would take the two vessels used – the *European Ambassador* and *European Envoy* – on charter. At a later date Stena Line would move their Stranraer – Belfast operation to P&O's port at Cairnryan and would give up plans to build their own facilities nearby. However, the plans (apart from the Cairnryan aspect) had to be referred to the Competition Commission and in the interim all services continued as before, including the loss-making Mostyn route. The Commission reported in February 2004 and refused to sanction Stena Line's take-over of the Liverpool – Dublin route, although not opposing the other changes. In March it was announced that Stena Line would take over the Fleetwood service and ships and the Mostyn route (including the weekend Dublin – Cherbourg service) would cease with the *European Ambassador* and *European Envoy* being purchased by Stena RoRo. P&O would continue to operate the Liverpool – Dublin route.

NorseMerchant Ferries' parent company Cenargo got into financial difficulties during the year and there were fears that the company's services could end. The group was restructured as Norse Merchant Group and the future of the company now looks more secure. Following the charter of the *Dawn Merchant* to Norfolkline in 2002, only those sailings on the Birkenhead – Dublin route operated by the *Brave Merchant* were available to car based and foot passengers. However, in February the *Brave Merchant* was chartered to the MoD and her replacement, the *Linda Rosa*, which had been operating additional sailings between Birkenhead and Belfast since autumn 2002, only took twelve passengers so the passenger service was suspended. The *Brave Merchant* returned in August but the passenger service was not restored. The *Linda Rosa* was retained and near sister *Norse Mersey* was the one whose charter was relinquished. In 2004 a passenger service on the *Brave Merchant* was resumed.

Early in the year, the Heysham – Belfast service was reduced to two sailings per day. The *Saga Moon* was moved to the Heysham – Dublin route, replacing the *Varbola*, whose charter was terminated. After her unsuccessful stint with Dart Line, she returned in May under an agreement which saw the *River Lune* moving to Dart Line. A three vessel service resumed in March 2004 following the return of the *River Lune*.

On 30th June, the Isle of Man Steam Packet Company was purchased from Sea Containers by Montagu Private Equity. In a rather complex deal, the new owners acquired the veteran *Lady of Mann*, the ro-pax *Ben-my-Chree* and the 78m InCat *SeaCat Isle of Man*. In addition they agreed to charter the *SuperSeaCat Two* and were licensed to continue to use the 'SeaCat' and 'SuperSeaCat' brands. They took on all the routes to the Isle of Man plus the summer only Liverpool – Dublin service. The Belfast – Troon route was to be managed by the newly independent company although profits and commercial risk remain with Sea Containers. It was decided before the sale that the Heysham – Belfast service would not resume and the craft used in 2002 – the former Dover – Ostend vessel *Rapide* – was moved to the Troon route, allowing the *SeaCat Scotland* to be transferred to Dover. When the *Ben-my-Chree* went for refit in early 2004, additional accommodation was fitted to improve passenger comfort when travelling at near her certified level of 500 passengers.

SCOTLAND

Caledonian MacBrayne introduced two new vessels during 2003. The first of these, the *Loch Portain*, replaced the *Loch Bhrusda* on the Leverburgh (Harris) – Berneray service in June, the latter vessel taking the Eriskay – Ard Mhor (Barra) service over from the Comhairle Nan Eilean Siar vessels *Eilean Bhearnaraigh* and *Eilean Na H-Oige*, which had inaugurated the new vehicle ferry service in 2002 (the service was actually taken over in April using the *Loch Linnhe).* In August the second new vessel, the *Coruisk*, entered service on the Mallaig – Armadale (Skye) service but after only a few days' service had to be withdrawn when she ran out of control and damaged her hull and one of her propulsion units. By the time she was ready the return to service, the route had reverted to the twice daily winter timetable (operated by the *Lochnevis*) and she was placed on the Gourock – Dunoon run, undertaking her winter role. Like many modern hi-tech ferries she is a vast improvement on her predecessors in terms of passenger comfort but seems plagued with teething troubles. These problems led to an extended season for the veteran *Pioneer* but in November she was finally laid up to await her fate. Also in October it was announced that the Scottish Executive would make funds available for a new ship for the Rothesay service. The project went out to tender at the end of the year and a contract was awarded to the Remontowa shipyard at Gdansk, Poland on 22nd March 2004.

The charter of the catamaran *Ali Cat* continued throughout the year on the Gourock – Dunoon route, providing peak hour extra sailings (the 1A roster previously operated by one of the 'Clyde Streakers') and occasionally having to step in when the *Coruisk* or a 'Streaker' had problems. The Gourock – Dunoon service was forced to go passenger only from the end of March until mid-June due to damage to the link span support structure at Dunoon. In the interim all vehicle traffic was diverted to Western Ferries.

BRITISH
ISLES

Scrabster
Stornoway
Ullapool
Aberdeen
Castlebay
Mallaig
Oban
Rosyth
Gourock
Largs
Troon
Cairnryan
Stranraer
Newcastle
Middlesbrough
Arranmore
Larne
Heysham
Belfast
Douglas
Fleetwood
Hull
Portaferry
Killingholme
Immingham
Warrenpoint
Holyhead
Liverpool
Mostyn
Dublin
Dun Laoghaire
Tarbert
Felixstowe
Rosslare
Fishguard
Harwich
Castletownbere
Passage East
Purfleet
Sheerness
Cork
Pembroke Dock
Dartford
Ramsgate
Dover
Southampton
Portsmouth
Weymouth
Poole
Newhaven
Fowey
Dartmouth
Penzance

In summer 2003 a third vessel was employed on the Oban based services – the first time since 1988. In addition a two ship Islay service was offered during the May -September period. In October the Tobermory – Kilchoan route was not suspended for the winter as happened in previous years but now operates all year.

Western Ferries also introduced a new ship in 2003. The new *Sound of Shuna* entered service on 7th October, joining her 2001 built sister *Sound of Scarba*. The 1961 built *Sound of Sleat* was then laid up for sale.

As mentioned above, Comhairle Nan Eilean Siar (Western Isles Council) ceased to be a ferry operator during 2003 and their two small ferries were disposed of.

Northlink's Scrabster – Stromness vessel, the *Hamnavoe* finally entered service in April, six month's after she had been delivered, following modifications to the old pier at Scrabster. Meanwhile work continued on the new pier and was fortunately completed by mid September, after when it could have been dangerous, in high winds, to have continued to berth such a large ship at the old pier. Caledonian MacBrayne's *Hebridean Isles* covered the route during the winter and seems likely to become the regular overhaul substitute on this route.

Meanwhile, NorthLink's Aberdeen ships *Hrossey* and *Hjaltland* performed well, although the service was spoiled to some degree by the temporary nature of the terminals, whose building was a little less expeditious than the ships.

Rival freight operator Norse Island Ferries ceased trading in June but their sole remaining vessel, the former P&O Scottish Ferries *St Rognvald*, (the *Merchant Venture* having been taken out of traffic at the end of 2002 due to mechanical failure) was immediately chartered to NorthLink and continued to operate much as before. In December she was replaced by the *Clare*, previously with Smyril Line, and was sold to Middle Eastern owners; she was subsequently scrapped. The *Clare* has now been chartered for 12 months with options to renew.

Pentland Ferries continued to operate the *Pentalina B* (ex *Iona*) between Gills Bay and St Margaret's Hope, offering a less luxurious but cheaper alternative to NorthLink. Their other vessel, the *Claymore*, remained laid up for most of the year due to lack of a passenger certificate. However, in November the *Pentalina B* suffered major engine failure and the *Claymore* replaced her in 12 passenger mode (the *Pentalina B* was by that time also operating in 12 passenger mode as her certificate for 250 passengers only applied between April and October). The *Claymore* was granted a certificate for 71 passengers in early 2004. The *Pentalina B* returned to the route in April.

Orkney Ferries' North Isles service was reduced to two ships from the end of 2003 until March 2004 following major engine damage to the *Earl Sigurd*. Orkney Islands Council have commissioned a study into a ferry replacement programme for the next twenty years.

The Shetland Islands Council introduced a second Polish built ferry for the Vidlin – Out Skerries route – the new *Filla*. The previous *Filla* was renamed the *Snolda* and was due to move to the West Burrafirth – Papa Stour route in 2004. Orders were placed at the same yard for two ferries for the busy Yell Sound route. The new ships – the *Daggri* and *Dagalien* – which will enter service in 2004, are named after the Old Norse words for dusk and dawn – names suggested by a Fair Isle schoolgirl in a competition. During 2003 work proceeded on the Toft and Ulsta terminals to accommodate the new ships.

Faeroese Smyril Line – now 25% owned by the Shetland Development Corporation – introduced their new *Norröna* in April. The service now calls twice weekly at Lerwick. The old *Norröna* was renamed the *Norröna I* and laid up in Denmark for sale. No buyers were forthcoming, which was fortuitous since, in January 2004 the new ship sustained hull and engine damage when entering Tórshavn harbour and had to be taken to Hamburg for repairs, expected to take up to three months. The *Norröna I* was hastily re-commissioned and placed on an emergency timetable. The freighter *Clare* served the company through the year until 18th September when it was decided that the *Norröna* had sufficient capacity to deal with all the freight during the winter months.

IRELAND

The new Lough Foyle Ferry company were able to return the *Carrigaloe* to her Cork owners in the spring when they acquired their own vessel – the former Shannon Ferries *Shannon Willow*, which had been laid up since 2000. They renamed her *Foyle Venture*. The company was selected by the Irish Government to inaugurate a new service across Lough Swilly between Buncrana and Rathmullan and although it was hoped it might be possible to launch this in autumn 2003, this did not happen as the vessel to be used – the *Stedingen* of Fähren Bremen-Stedingen GmbH to be renamed the *Foyle Rambler* – was not available and necessary dredging to start the service had not been completed.

Bere Island Ferries purchased the *Eilean Na H-oige* from Comhairle Nan Eilean Siar in autumn 2003 and in early 2004 sold their original car ferry, the Irish built *Misneach*, to Rex Lines (Offshore Work Boats) of Renfrew, Scotland.

Nick Widdows

scandinavia **&** *northern review*

review 2003

T he following geographical review again takes the form of a voyage along the coast of The Netherlands and Germany, round the southern tip of Norway, down the Kattegat, through the Great Belt and into the Baltic (with a side journey to the Øresund) then up to the Gulf of Finland and Gulf of Bothnia.

FRESIAN ISLANDS

Dutch operator Wagenborg Passagiersdiensten introduced a new ferry onto their Ameland – Holwerd route. The new *Oerd* is a sister to the 1995 built *Sier*. The 1985 built *Oerd* was rename the *Monnik* and moved to the Lauwersoog – Schiermonnikoog route.

Having introduced a freight carrying normal-speed catamaran, the *Noord-Nederland*, in 2002, Rederij Doeksen ordered a second in 2003 for general traffic. Unusually, they chose a Philippines yard to construct the FBMA Babcock Marine craft.

TESO chose the yard at Galatz, Romania to build the hull for their new vessel, the *Dokter Wagemaker*, which enters service in 2005. She will be fitted out at Vlissingen.

NORWEGIAN DOMESTIC

The plans by C G Brøvig & Partners Norske Ferger (Norwegian Ferries) to launch a new car and passenger service between Bergen and Stavanger at the end of June/early July using the 78 metre InCat *Thundercat II* came to nothing. It was later announced that Danish Mols-Linien had been given permission to operate a Stavanger – Bergen service although no information is yet available on when it will start. Bastø Fosen won the concession for the ferry service between Moss and Horten across the Oslofjord for another ten years from 2006. The company ordered a new ferry – to be built in Gdansk rather than Norway as expected – with a capacity for 212 cars to be delivered in 2004.

Troms Fylkes D/S introduced their new Hurtigruten vessel *Midnatsol* in April, replacing the similarly named 1982 built ship. Because of the large number of Germans who travel on the service she was taken to Hamburg the previous month to be named by the Norwegian born wife of the former German Chancellor, Willy Brandt. Partner OVDS announced plans for a further newbuilding as replacement for the 1964 built *Lofoten*. In contrast to the newbuildings delivered in 2002 and 2003, the ship would be smaller with a length of 100m and a capacity for 300 passengers. OVDS wants to be able to react to the lower capacity needs in the dead season and employ the larger vessels in other waters. Their *Nordnorge* spent winter 2003/2004 cruising in Chile and Antarctica and was substituted by the veteran *Lofoten*.

SKAGERAK AND KATTEGAT

Fjord Line introduced a new ship on their Bergen – Egersund – Hanstholm service in April to replace the *Bergen*, chartered to DFDS Seaways and renamed the *Duchess of Scandinavia*. The new *Fjord Norway*, as she was renamed, was bought from TT Line of Australia where she had operated as the *Spirit of Tasmania*. She was better known to Scandinavian passengers as TT-Line's *Peter Pan* of 1986.

In the autumn, Color Line announced that they were to charter the Rederi AB Gotland vessel *Thjelvar* to inaugurate a new service between Larvik and Hirtshals in spring 2004. The ship was transferred to Norwegian registry and renamed the *Color Traveller*. The new service has replaced the Larvik –

Peter Pan *(TT Line)*

Finnhans **Finnhansa** *(Finelines)*

Frederikshavn sailings of the ro-pax *Skagen* and this vessel has become spare. Rival operator Saga Lines' new Skagen – Moss service using the *Sagafjord* (ex *Sandefjord*) did not start in 2003 as they were unable to obtain certification for the ship. No more was heard of Langesund – Lysekil Line's plans to establish a new route between Sweden and Norway.

Color Line's new 74600t giant for the Oslo – Kiel route was, during 2003, named as the *Color Fantasy*. She will enter service in December 2004.

In the autumn, Stena Line announced that they were to replace the two freight ferries used on their overnight Gothenburg – Travemünde route in early 2004. There was some uncertainty about which ships they would use but in February 2004 they introduced the *Stena Foreteller* – on the of the three Chinese built Stena 4Runner Mark 2 class ships – onto the route. However, in March the long term replacements arrived. The first was the new *Stena Freighter*, second of the earlier Italian built Stena 4Runner Mark 1 class, on which work was abandoned in 1999 when the yard went bankrupt. The hull was purchased by Stena Line and completed in Croatia in 2003. The second vessel was the new *Stena Carrier*, also one of the earlier series, but this time completed in another Italian shipyard and then sold to Stena Line. She arrived as the *Stena Carrier II* and went direct to the Cityvarvet shipyard in Gothenburg for completion. The existing vessels were sold to Lillbacka Global Transports of Finland in December to open a new service, trading as Power Line, between Travemünde and Turku as the *Global Carrier* and *Global Freighter*. They were chartered back by Stena Line until the replacement tonnage arrived, the latter operating under her new name for several weeks before delivery to her new owners.

During the year the *Stena Saga*, used on the Oslo – Frederikshavn service, was upgraded to increase passenger accommodation from 1700 to 1900.

DANISH DOMESTIC

Prospects that Mols-Linien's would find a new permanent role for one of their 91m InCats (now needing only one for their own Oden – Århus service) rose in the spring with the announcement of the launch on Speedferries between Dover and Boulogne, using the *Mads Mols* as the *Speed One*. However, it was later decide to defer the new service until March 2004 and Mols-Linien pulled out of the venture. In December it was announced that their other 91m craft, the *Max Mols*, would be chartered to P&O Ferries to operate between Portsmouth and Caen. Prospects of a new, larger craft on their Odden – Ebeltoft route did not materialise but for most of the time only a single craft was used on the service.

ØRESUND

Norwegian company Moltzaus Tankrederi AS ordered two 400-passenger ferries for their passenger-only service between Helsingborg and Helsingør. The 56.2 metre vessels are being built by the Remontowa shipyard at Gdansk in Poland for delivery during May or June 2004.

Stena owned HH-Ferries, who operate on the same route, purchased a third Superflex ferry from DIFKO of Denmark. The *Gitte 3* had been laid up since she was withdrawn from the now defunct Easy Line service between Gedser and Rostock in August 1999, although she had undertaken brief periods on charter to *HH-Ferries*.

All operators on this route enjoyed a good year, despite the competition from the Øresundsbroen fixed link, especially after the Danes reduced alcohol taxes, further widening the gap in prices between Denmark and Sweden.

SOUTH BALTIC

Another Easy Line Superflex to make a return during 2003 was the Norwegian owned *Anja 11*, which, as the *Langeland*, reopened the service between Kiel and Bagenkop on the Danish island of Langeland in April. A new company, called Færgeruten Langeland-Kiel A/S, was formed and attracted investment from local people, aiming to attract Germans to visit Langeland, which was now much more difficult to get to following the ending of the direct link in 2000. Whilst targets in this respect were met, insufficient Danish people used the route, and, after a closure, supposedly just for the winter period, the company went into liquidation in November.

DFDS suspended their Copenhagen – Trelleborg – Gdansk service in November so that the vessel used, the *Duke of Scandinavia*, could be moved to the Newcastle – IJmuiden route to replace the *Prince of Scandinavia*. Although the route was earlier said to have met targets set, in February 2004 it was announced that the route had been permanently closed.

Scandlines announced a 60 million programme of investments in their vessels which operate between Denmark and Germany. On the Fehnmarnbelt, the four Rødby – Puttgarden vessels were to have a mezzanine car deck added on one side of the main vehicle deck to relieve overcrowding; this was done to all four ships between October 2003 and May 2004. On the Gedser – Rostock route, the former Great Belt train ferries *Kronpris Ferderik* and *Prins Joachim* were to be re-engined, enabling them to travel at 21 knots rather than their previous 19.5 knots, permitting a crossing time of 100 minutes and, with a turn-round time of just 20 minutes, a service every two hours – as is currently operated by three ships. This would enable the retirement of the 1973 built *Dronning Margrethe II*. This work is now likely to take place between August 2004 and February 2005.

During the year the concession to operate services to the Danish Island of Bornholm was advertised by the Danish Government. The specification called for a fast ferry, two ro-paxes and a conventional ferry during the peak season. Rederi Gotland AB, Mols-Linien A/S and Scandlines AG, all pre-qualified but only incumbent operator BornholmsTrafikken put forward a bid and, in March 2004, they were awarded the franchise. During the year BornholmsTrafikken replaced the freighter *Nordhav* on the Rønne – Køge service by the *Vilja*; this route will become the principal sea route between Sealand and Bornholm as the Rønne – Copenhagen route will no longer receive subsidy.

In September TT-Line launched a week-end one round trip service from Travemünde to Helsingborg in Sweden, operated by the ro-pax (or combicarrier as line calls them) *Nils Dacke* or *Robin Hood* in freight only mode.

Finnlines owned Nordö Link introduced a fourth ferry at the beginning of 2004 – the *Finnsailor*, which was transferred from Finnlines' FinnLink service between Sweden and Finland.

Polferries acquired two new vessels during the year. Firstly in April they chartered the *Kahleberg* to provide additional freight capacity on the Swinoujscie and Ystad route (she had previously been operating for Scandlines Amber Line between Karlshamn and Liepaja). Then they purchased the *Visborg* (formerly *Visby*) from Rederi AB Gotland and placed her on the Gdansk – Nynashamn route from 16th July. She was renamed the *Scandinavia* and replaced the *Silesia*, which was transferred to the Swinoujscie – Ystad route replacing the *Rogalin* which was sold for scrap.

The Scandlines Euroseabridge/Lisco Baltic Service 'Kiel-Klaìpeda-Express' service was revolutionised during 2003 by the introduction of two modern ro-pax vessels. In April, Scandlines introduced the *Svealand*, previously used by Scandlines AB between Trelleborg and Travemünde, replacing the *Petersburg*. In June Lisco Baltic Service brought into service the *Lisco Gloria*, introduced onto the DFDS Tor Lines' Esbjerg – Harwich service as the *Dana Gloria* in 2002. She replaced the *Vilnius*, *Kaunas* and *Palanga*. Under the new schedule, each ship operates three round trips per week with a crossing time of 21 hours – the older ships were only able to undertake two round trips per week. Thus with less ships the same number of sailings was maintained and with much greater capacity. The displaced ships all found new work quickly, the *Petersburg* moving to Scandlines Amber Line's Karlshamn – Liepaja service, the *Palanga* moving to Lisco Baltic Service's Klaìpeda – Karlshamn route and the *Vilnius* chartered to DFDS Tor Line to operate between Lübeck and Riga, followed by the *Kaunas* in 2004.

From 1st May, all sailings of the DFDS Tor Line and Latlines between Germany and Latvia were concentrated onto the port of Lübeck. Previously the service was split between Lübeck and Kiel. The two vessels used were the *Mermaid II* and the *Transparaden*. However, on 21st June the *Transparaden* was replaced by Lisco's *Vilnius*, displaced from the Kiel – Klaìpeda route by the *Lisco Gloria*. From 1st January 2004, the operation was merged, trading as DFDS Tor Line Hanse Bridge, with the *Mermaid II* replaced by Lisco Baltic Service's *Kaunus* in February.

Tor Petunia *(Cees de Bijl)*

Stena Freighter *(FERRYInformation)*

Scandlines AB's *Svealand*, transferred to the Kiel-Klaìpeda-Express in April, was replaced by Scandlines AG's *Ask* on the Swedish company's Trelleborg – Travemünde freight route. Scandlines AG's rebuilt *Mecklenburg-Vorpommern* returned to service on the Rostock – Trelleborg route on 10th March. The conversion of some passenger space to vehicle space raised her freight capacity to 3,200 lane metres.

Destination Gotland's new Chinese built *Visby* arrived at Visby on 28th February and entered service on the 24th March on the Nynäshamn – Visby route. The smaller 700 passenger fast ferry *Gotland* of 1999 was renamed the *Gotlandia* to release her former name for the second ship, which entered service in December. The introduction of these impressive high speed conventional craft was rather overshadowed by a bribery scandal involving some officials of Rederi AB Gotland and some of the suppliers of parts for the ship; although built in China, most of the equipment came from Western European manufacturers.

The Latvian port of Ventspils saw two changes during the year. Firstly Swedish VV-Line went into liquidation in April and their Ventspils – Nynäshamn route and vessel *Fellow* were, in July, taken over by Scandlines Amber Lines as part of Scandlines' policy of expansion into the Baltic. In June a new operator called Vent-Lines, owned by the recently privatised Latvian Shipping Company, established a route between Ventspils and Travemünde. Their vessel was the Turkish owned *Kaptan Burhanettin Isim* which in 2002 has been chartered to Latlines to operate between Lübeck and Riga.

CROSS BALTIC

After withdrawing the *Finnclipper* from the Travemünde – Helsinki route in late 2002, Finnlines found a replacement for 2003 in the form of the near sister *Stena Britannica*. Renamed the *Finnfellow*, she started operations on 2nd April. At the same time Finnlines sold the ro-ro ferry *Oihonna* to Stena RoRo. The *Finnfellow* moved to the FinnLink service at the beginning of 2004, again leaving the service in the hands of the four 'Hansa' class 90 passenger ro-pax ships. In February 2004 orders were placed with Fincantieri of Italy for three new, faster ships for the route with capacity for 500 passengers.

T&E ESCO RORO Line AS's freight only service between Rostock, Helsinki and Muuga was taken over by Scandlines AG in the spring, along with the two vessels used, the *Lembitu* and *Lehola*. Scandlines have said there is a possibility that the freighters will be replaced by ro-pax vessels in due course. Later in the year Scandlines introduced a third vessel onto their Rostock – Helsinki – Muuga freight service. The *Aurora*, which was previously used by Finnlines, was chartered for two years, and normally operates between Rostock and Helsinki only.

ESCO's other ro-ro service – operated by subsidiary ESCO Eurolines – was sold to Mann & Son Holdings of the UK – operators of Mann Lines. The company operated the *Rakvere* and the chartered *Hamburg* between Muuga and Kiel as well as Muuga and Århus in Denmark.

Two operators between Germany and Russia made a bid to boost their passenger carryings during the year. TransRussia Express, partly owned by Finnlines, whose route is Lübeck – Sassnitz – Baltijsk (Kaliningrad) – St Petersburg started marketing the sailings of the 80 passenger *Translubeca* more intensely whilst, in December, Russian SCF St Petersburg Line chartered the Engship owned 104 passenger *Transparaden* for their direct service between St Petersburg and Kiel. However, hopes that the initial six months charter could be renewed were dashed when, in January 2004, the vessel was purchased by Eckerö Line of Finland to boost freight capacity on their Helsinki – Tallinn route.

Silja Line operated the gas turbine *Finnjet* between Germany and Finland for the last time in summer 2003 and in the autumn she returned to Helsinki – Tallinn cruises. In summer 2004, after a major two month refit, she will operate on a new Rostock – Tallinn – St Petersburg service. Passengers are likely to be mainly doing cruises and most of the traffic on the vehicle deck will be freight. In anticipation of this, the vessel had a major refit during winter 2003/4.

Finnish freight operator Transfennica placed two of the AWSR Shipping ro-ros on their Hanko – Lübeck route. The *Longstone* and *Beachy Head* were two of six vessels built for the MoD's Strategic Sealift capability and are on time charter. In addition to these vessels, Transfennica also introduced two Stena 4Runner Mk II vessels – the 24,688t *Stena Forecaster* and *Stena Forerunner* – on the same route. The four ships are likely to be replaced by four new ships which were ordered from Szczecin in Poland for delivery in 2005 and 2006.

NORTH BALTIC

Heavy winter ice caused severe reductions in service. The RG Line service between Vaasa and Umeå was the most affected but SeaWind Line and Tallink who normally operate two round trips per day between Helsinki and Tallinn with their *Star Wind* and *Meloodia* respectively were forced to cut departures to one round trip per day. Fast ferry operations were planned to resume in April in time for the Easter holiday period but did not start until early May.

Silja Line doubled the number of departures on their fast ferry service between Helsinki and Tallinn through the introduction of a second 'SuperSeaCat'. They had operated the *SuperSeaCat Four* since her delivery from Italy in 1999 and, in 2003, she was joined by the *SuperSeaCat Three*. The second vessel enabled Silja Line to compete on more equal terms with competitors Tallink and Nordic Jet Line, both of whom operate two vessels.

In the autumn, Viking Line withdrew the *Cinderella* from Helsinki – Tallinn cruises. She was replaced by the *Rosella*, operating on a more conventional twice daily ferry schedule. The *Cinderella* took the *Rosella's* place on Stockholm – Mariehamn 22 hour cruises and switched to the Swedish flag; because there was already a Swedish ship of that name she was renamed the *Viking Cinderella*. The service was marketed as 'Cinderella Cruises' and the aim was to attract a more discerning clientele than patronised the *Rosella's* 'Dancing Queen' trips, which had acquired a reputation for wild behaviour.

Tallink's new Stockholm – Tallinn vessel, a near sister of the *Romantika*, was named the *Victoria I* in October. She entered service in March 2004 and runs with the *Regina Baltica*. From 1st May the service will call additionally at Mariehamn in order to preserve duty-free entitlement after Estonia enters the EU. The displaced *Fantaasia* now operates a new Helsinki – Tallinn – St Petersburg – Helsinki triangular route. With the *Meloodia* now operating two return journeys per day between Tallinn and Helsinki, only the *Romantika* remains operating 22 hour cruises. In December, Tallink purchased the ro-pax *Regal Star* from MCL of Italy and, during 2004 she will be placed on the Kapellskär – Paldiski route, replacing the *Kapella*, which will move to the Tallinn – Helsinki service to provide freight back-up to the passenger ships. In February 2004 Tallink purchased two additional fast ferries – the *Shannon Alexis* and *St Matthew* – from their Gibraltar owners.

Eckerö Line also announced increased freight capacity with their planned purchase of the *Transparaden* from Rederi AB Engship of Sweden in May 2004 when her charter to SCF St Petersburg Line finishes. Before the Sea Wind Line service started in 2002, *Silja Line* sold the freight capacity on the *Nordlandia* but since then Eckerö Line have established their own organisation. The *Nordlandia* operates day trips from Helsinki to Tallinn and will be less affected by the withdrawal of duty-free when Estonia enters the EU. Indeed, with the prospects of being able to buy much larger quantities of (lower) duty paid goods in Estonia, they foresee an increase in custom and, from 1st May will operate two round trips on Fridays.

Nick Widdows

Stena Adventurer and Ulysses *(Gordon Hislip)*

Rudi's Diner *(Miles Cowsill)*

Stena **Lines'**

masterclass in ro-pax

If the British love to see the underdog win through, then the British must love Stena Line. Barely two years ago, **Ferries 2002** celebrated the introduction of P&O's mighty *Pride of Rotterdam* and Irish Ferries' *Ulysses* in 2001. The subtext of these developments was of course, that Stena was declining and fast. The new giants immediately put Stena on the back foot on two of their key routes: Hook of Holland-Harwich and Holyhead-Dublin Bay. A fightback was needed and this continued in 2003 with the massive SeaMaster twins. The *Stena Britannica* and the *Stena Adventurer*, constructed by Hyundai Heavy Industries in South Korea, were introduced onto these two services in the first half of the year. Their arrival has created a large increase in capacity on each route and what many would say is the first decent passenger service provided by conventional tonnage on these routes since the mid 1990s when the HSS craft took over from older 1970s and 1980s-built tonnage.

The new vessels were, broadly speaking, design developments of the SeaPacer quartet which were completed between 1999 and 2000 from the Spanish AESA yard at Cadiz. But such is the improvement of their passenger areas over the rather spartan SeaPacers, in many ways they represent a rare marriage between the two design strands of Stena RoRo, that of high quality passenger vessel with massive and flexible freight configuration.

A DIFFICULT FEW YEARS

Although the introduction of the HSS of catamarans in 1996-7 could be viewed as huge success – certainly from a marketing perspective, if not from an operational perspective – since then, Stena Line has experienced something of a downward trend in the UK which has led some to speculate that in fact the company may eventually withdraw from the routes which were so dramatically wrested from Sea Containers in 1990.

One could not help forming the impression that the HSSs were going to be rather transient as no further ships were ordered following the first four – indeed a smaller class was actually cancelled. Therefore the decline of the traditional passenger services on many routes was interpreted in some quarters as selling off the family silver – the HSSs were untested and even at the time of their introduction it was not really obvious in what direction they would take their routes.

Profitability problems were encountered, and at the turn of the decade significant rationalisation was undertaken which effectively stripped away most UK head office functions and left routes as virtually independent entities reporting to Gothenburg.

Perhaps the most humiliating event was the merger with P&O on the Dover services in 1998. Although a rational move in the light of the Channel Tunnel, the merger gave the advantage to P&O and the Stena ships took on the nomenclature, (modified) livery and style of the P&O fleet. After four years the inevitable happened and P&O bought out the whole operation.

To be fair to Stena, the green shoots of life have been showing through for several years. First came the 2000 takeover of Scandlines of Sweden followed a couple of years later by a remarkable arrangement which saw P&O withdraw from the Southern North Sea in favour of Stena's Harwich services. This year sees a similar deal struck on the Irish Sea Fleetwood – Larne link.

Throughout this time, the one sign many industry observers had been seeking was a commitment that the HSS routes had a future that was not irredeemably tied to the fast craft. The arrival of the brand new 'SeaPacer' ro-paxes in 2000 enabled the Dutch service to breathe a little more easily once again. They also proved that if an operator invests in modern tonnage, the traffic is very likely to follow; the SeaPacers' witnessed a 9% increase in freight traffic in their first two years. The following year, something of an emergency arose on the Irish Sea with the sale of the *Stena Challenger* to the Canadian operator Marine Atlantic as the *Leif Ericson* and a charter of the *Stena Forwarder* was hastily arranged from the Visentini ro-pax production line. Whilst the ship was in no way a spiritual successor to the 1977-built stalwart *St Columba*, she did at least deliver a large increase in capacity which again brought the traffic along to match.

SEAMASTER PEDIGREE

Stena are known mainly for the large number of passenger ferries they have constructed since their first commission the *Stena Danica* in 1964. These vessels have supplied the second hand market of the ferry industry for four decades. What is often forgotten is the constant evolution of the company's freight ferry designs in the intervening years that has been, if anything, more innovative and prolific than the passenger vessels. A key factor in the success of the company's ship-building programme has been the separation between this element of the parent's operations from the day to day business of shipping services; Stena RoRo have become a world leader in ferry design, construction and chartering.

Stena's first ro-ro design was the four-strong 'Stena Runner' class constructed between 1970 and 1972, commencing with the *Stena Carrier*. Two of the class went to British Rail as the *Dalriada* and the *Anderida* and the *Stena Carrier* soon joined her sisters as the *Ulidia*. The success of these ships on the charter market paved the way for an upgraded design – a Dutch-built class, the second still in evidence today as Gothenburg – Frederikshavn's train ferry *Stena Scanrail*. The year 1975 saw a further design appear with the *Bison* leading a five-strong class.

The vast 'SeaRunner' class of 1977-1978 was perhaps the most acclaimed freight ferry design of a generation. Built at the same Hyundai Ulsan yard as the SeaMasters, eleven units spread forth from South Korea like the maritime equivalent of Swedish missionaries. It is perhaps something of a testament to the far reaching success of Stena's ferry designs that so many of their early ships have been "reabsorbed" into the fleet during their recent takeover spree.

What could be considered the true antecedent of the SeaMasters however, was the Bremerhaven-built 'Rickmers' quartet. Most passenger designs Stena tended to commission for their own services and then to release for charter once they were no longer useful. The 'Rickmers' vessels however were built purely for the charter market and were Stena's first attempt to graft a completely arranged passenger configuration onto a full sized freight deck. Most of the class found niches for themselves on short sea crossings such as Fishguard-Rosslare (*Stena Normandica*, the lead ship) or Ostend – Dover where their expansive facilities gave them the epithet of 'jumbo ferries' way before the first 20,000-tonners were taking to the waves. The 'Rickmers' class could carry 1,200 passengers and offered two full-height freight decks, a unique combination in those days when ferries were either 'passenger' or 'ro-ro'.

By the 1990s, Stena were fully occupied by the HSS project but as that was nearing completion, the company returned to the shipyards with their first true 'ro-pax' series in the SeaPacer class. The first pair of the quartet went straight to Finnlines as their *Finnclipper* and *Finneagle*. After much internal wrangling, the second pair went onto Stena's Hook of Holland – Harwich service in 2000, as the *Stena Britannica* (the fourth ship of this name) and the *Stena Hollandica*. This 'Mark II' design had an additional 419 metre freight deck. There was much relief at Harwich that these vessels had been secured as it was widely regarded that the route had suffered somewhat since the ending of conventional passenger services in 1997 and the arrival of the HSS *Stena Discovery*. This was despite gallant attempts to provide a shadow of a passenger service with the elderly trio *Stena Seatrader*, *Stena Searider* and *Rosebay*, which were in any case capacity-constrained on their freight decks.

Both SeaPacers proved immensely popular on the service and enabled Stena to adapt timetables to better suit the freight companies bringing fresh Dutch produce to the UK markets.

Lounge Area *(Miles Cowsill)*

Stena Plus Lounge *(Miles Cowsill)*

FROM SEAPACER TO SEAMASTER

Such was the success with the SeaPacer class – both on their own routes and also on the second-hand market – that Stena RoRo quickly placed an order for a much expanded version of the design with Hyundai. The pair would be one of the world's top ten largest ferries and the largest ro-pax vessels (if one contends that the *Pride of Rotterdam* and *Pride of Hull* are cruise ferries). The design measured 210.8 metres in length, 29.3 metres beam with a draft of 6.3 metres and a service speed of 22 knots. The three freight decks would total 3,400 lane metres whilst there would be passenger accommodation for 900, with 198 2-berth and 51 4-berth cabins. Construction on the first $90million vessel commenced on 4th February 2002 and she left the shipyard on her delivery voyage eleven months later.

In 2002 it was announced that the first vessel would be chartered to Stena Line BV for service between Hook of Holland and Harwich, replacing the third SeaPacer and taking her name *Stena Britannica*. Although at one stage the outgoing *Stena Britannica* was due to be redeployed at Harwich in place of the *Stena Forwarder*, Finnlines snapped up the vessel to join her two sisters in the Baltic as the *Finnfellow*.

It therefore made sense that the second SeaMaster would be sent to Holyhead and this was announced towards the end of the same year. Although originally ordered as a pair of identical, vessels the very different requirements of the Holyhead and Hook of Holland operations meant that significant alterations would have to be made to create one day ferry and one overnight ro-pax vessel. Interestingly, although the higher passenger capacity of the second Holyhead vessel was incorporated during construction, the internal layout of all other areas was fixed and would be rectified during the ships' delivery voyages.

However, such deployments were not foregone conclusions; the ships were available for charter on the open market and it is perhaps testament to the success of Stena UK and Stena BV's operations that they were able to secure the vessels from Stena RoRo. The first vessel entered service as the *Stena Britannica II* with the 2200 departure from Hook of Holland on 25th February 2003 but was formally named the fifth *Stena Britannica* a month later. Her twin entered service between Holyhead and Dublin on July 1st as the *Stena Adventurer* – reviving the final name carried by the *St Columba* during her 19-year reign on the route to Dun Laoghaire.

One of the key intentions behind the vessels' positioning was their ability to provide much needed backup to the HSS craft on each route. It has long been a criticism of the company that whilst the HSS may well be fast, convenient and even exciting vessels on which to travel, they are very vulnerable to weather disruptions. Given the strategic nature of their routes as the traditional railway services from London to Dublin and Amsterdam, the desire to provide alternative cover in the event of disruption was understandable. It could also be argued that the five-year delay in providing such cover was a political move in order demonstrate faith in the craft in the face of operational reality and common sense.

ONBOARD THE SEAMASTERS

To any traveller familiar with the *Stena Britannica* and the *Stena Adventurer's* SeaPacer predecessors, the most obvious difference is the scope and far higher quality of their passenger areas. Externally, the vessels look broadly similar to the Spanish pair but internally they represent the elevation of the design from common-or-garden ro-pax vessel to a full-blown passenger ferry.

Indeed, the *Stena Britannica* (4) and *Stena Hollandica* are typical of their genre with one main lounge/bar/cafeteria area stretching the full width of the forward section behind which lies other facilities such as a casino, cinema and shop. It is a pattern repeated on most similar vessels such as Merchant Ferries' 'Racehorse' quartet, Scandlines' *Mecklenburg-Vorpommern* and *Skåne*, P&O's *European Ambassador* and many more.

But whilst the SeaMasters retain the key principles of this design on their main passenger deck, further passenger facilities are spread out over decks eight and nine and the layout and quality of finish create an onboard ambience comparable to the many 'conventional' multi-purpose vessels introduced in the last decade or so.

The main passenger deck (seven) comprises the large 450m^2 Globetrotter Restaurant at the front stretching virtually the full width of the deck. On the *Stena Britannica*, the 175m^2 servery area is located midships at the back of the restaurant, with an easy walk-through arrangement either side of the bar facing out onto the seating area. The area is very open plan reflecting the fact that all meals are complementary. On the *Stena Adventurer*, the area is of a different design, with passengers paying to enter the servery, which occupies a more central location. The provision of a 'buffet' style restaurant is rather unusual on a short-sea ferry.

On both ships, the spacious Globetrotter Restaurant offers a variety of seating types from individual chairs around small tables to large wrap-around sofas with tables for around eight people. Flooring throughout is a mixture of wooden laminate, blue carpeting and grey tiling, whilst the furniture comprises green and red leather-effect seating on the edges with individual chairs in cream and orange. The restaurant seating area is broken up with waist-height divisions longitudinally.

Additionally, intimacy is enhanced in what is a fairly vast area through the creation of an area of bar seating forward with large floor-to-ceiling panoramic windows. To starboard, the ships again differ. On the *Stena Britannica* a totally separate non smoking area has been established along almost the full depth of the cafeteria and there is also a children's play area forward. This has been achieved by removing the shop that is found in this space on the *Stena Adventurer*. Both the *Stena Britannica's* side seating area and the bar seating at the front on both ships benefit from a slightly different colour scheme predominently in red.

Astern of the restaurant/bar area on the port side lies the information desk and bureau de change followed by an open-plan casino area suffering from a rather un-casino-like ambience. The walkway then leads to a large Truckers' Lounge on the *Stena Adventurer* which comprises a dining area and a TV lounge – with a servery nearest the galley – and affording excellent views through the large picture windows. Stena BV opted to convert this area into the shop in lieu of the starboard area of the Globetrotter as there was no need for a separate truckers' area on an essentially truckers' ship. The 105m^2 shop is extremely spacious and well appointed, offering the full range of onboard retail opportunities. However, it is rather curious that the Dutch service has ended up with a larger and superior shop. A passageway to the port side of the Truckers' Lounge/shop leads to the open decks.

The main feature of deck eight is the 'Food City' forward, in essence a similar but smaller (380m^2) version of the 'Globetrotter' restaurant below. This is decorated in a rather more minimalist style with much use of laminate wood flooring, beige or wood-effect walls and mint-coloured seating. On the *Stena Britannica*, this space is unused unless the HSS is off service or when there is a conference booking on board and in many ways just serves to demonstrate the fact that the ship is most definitely not purpose built for the Dutch service. On the *Stena Adventurer*, the area is normally used although she differs slightly from her sister in that the catering is more of a quick-snack variety and equipment has been tailored to this.

It is astern of the 'Food City' on deck eight where the greatest difference is seen between the vessels. The original design – which the *Stena Britannica* adheres to – dictated 98 well appointed two-berth cabins, attractively decorated and with much use made of wood-effect and including a number of luxury cabins. Prior to construction, the design for the *Stena Adventurer* was altered with large picture windows replacing the cabin windows externally whilst the interior would remain empty pending fit out during delivery. The ship now offers a 419-seat multi-purpose area featuring a Rudi's Diner fast food outlet and C.View Bar. However, this remains closed on all crossings except when the HSS passengers (and crew) are diverted.

The highest passenger deck is nine and on the starboard side houses the conference area. This attractive area opens onto a cocktail bar with numerous conference rooms then leading off a main passageway. Included in this area is the cinema. Although the ships hold very few conferences (and on the *Stena Britannica* they are usually hosted in the 'Food City' if they require catering), the cinema is as a rule in use on all crossings. Decor throughout is bright with full height glass panelling with sailing ship motifs interspersed with wood-effect. The port side of this deck is taken up with further cabins on the *Stena Britannica* which stretch astern to the freight decks.

Perhaps the most important aspect of the design is the four freight decks. These comprise the seven lane wide main deck (three) and upper deck (five) with 2,475 metres almost equally divided between the two and with a hoistable car deck on deck three providing an additional 925 metres. A further full height deck of 415m lies on deck one below the main freight deck and a second upper deck with 510 metres is on deck seven aft of the main passenger deck. The main deck is linked to shore with an 18 metre ramp at the bow and a 15 metre ramp at the stern and a tiltable ramp links deck three to five and a hoistable ramp links five to seven. On the *Stena Adventurer*, the upper deck also has bow and stern access to shore and brand new double-deck linkspans have been provided at both Holyhead and Dublin in order to maximise benefit from this facility.

Crew accommodation, mostly on deck ten, is spacious and comfortable – equal in standard to the passenger areas and there are 63 crew berths in 57 cabins. The crew also have the benefit of a sauna. The vast full-width bridge on deck eleven provides the very latest in technological innovation and 360 degree views around the ship.

The story behind the SeaMasters is a fascinating insight into the economics of modern ferry design and building. Two vast ships, built principally for the charter market and adapted prior to entering service on two very different routes are enabling their operators to regain significant lost ground against the competition.

It is likely that given the significant increase in capacity over their predecessors, both ships will be around for several years, particularly the *Ulysses*-challenging *Stena Adventurer*. The *Stena Britannica* however may potentially be rather short-lived on the Dutch service in that much of her accommodation is virtually unused. It would not be too surprising if at some stage in the future, a more needy service – such as Fishguard-Rosslare – was to end up with the vessel, whilst a future newbuilding with less passenger capacity took over at the Hook. Of course, another possible scenario is that with these ships Stena have the basis for proper replacements for the HSS and that they were simply economical opportunities to create suitable vessels and to wait until such a time as they come into their own, further expanding their accommodation in true Stena fashion.

Matthew Punter

Stena Britannica (*John Bryant*)

Globetrotter Buffet *(Miles Cowsill)*

Upper Freight Deck - Stena Adventurer *(Miles Cowsill)*

Caffe Oliveto *(P&O Ferries)*

Langan's Brasserie *(P&O Ferries)*

P&O Ferries' darwin project

The genesis of the Darwin Project coalesced from a number of events. First P&O Ferries (or P&O Stena Line as it was at the time) needed both to modernise its Dover fleet and to meet continuing traffic growth on the Dover – Calais route. At the same time, the Dover – Zeebrugge route was becoming increasingly difficult to maintain, following the opening of the new motorway along the north coast of France and Belgium. From the Zeebrugge turn off near Bruges, Calais was only about an hour further away than Zeebrugge, yet the sea journey took three hours longer. Coupled with increased competition from the lower cost base TransEuropa Ferries service at Ostend and Norfolkline at Dunkerque, it was clear by the end of 2001 that the future of the route was limited.

The route was served by three ships built in 1991 and 1992 to carry a mix of accompanied and unaccompanied freight on two decks, the upper of which was partly open, and up to 200 drivers in very comfortable conditions. Work started on a fourth ship of the series but before launch it was decided to finish her as a full passenger ship. So the ship laid down as the *European Causeway* was delivered as the *Pride of Burgundy*. The three ships operated two round trips per day, providing a four hour frequency (although initially an older ship ran with them giving a ship every three hours). In 2001 the 08.30 from Dover and 15.30 sailing from Zeebrugge were withdrawn. Instead, *European Seaway* performed two round trips to Calais – something that had previously happened occasionally on an ad hoc basis. The Zeebrugge service was thrown open to cars and car based passengers. However, in spring 2003 it was announced that the route would close by the end of the year as part of a package of changes which also involved Stena Line pulling out of the P&O Stena Line joint venture and P&O closing its Felixstowe – Zeebrugge freight service and transferring its Felixstowe – Rotterdam freight service to Stena Line.

Being built specifically for the Dover – Zeebrugge route, with double deck loading and shore link spans landing on the deck of the ferry rather than ship ramps landing on the link spans, the ships were not easy to deploy on other routes. Two ships in the passenger fleet – the *P&OSL Canterbury* and the *P&OSL Kent* – dated from the early 1980s and were due for replacement. In addition, at the time traffic was buoyant and additional capacity was required; in marketing terms new tonnage to set against SeaFrance's new *SeaFrance Rodin* was also a plus. It was thus decided that the optimum solution to solve all these problems was to convert two of the Zeebrugge ships – which were barely 10 years old – into full passenger ships to operate between Dover and Calais.

Planning work on what was dubbed the 'Darwin Project' (the implication being that the ships were evolving to meet changed circumstances) began on a speculative basis in early 2002. However it was not until the spring, when the various route changes were announced, that the project was started formally and made public. The two younger ships *European Highway* and *European Pathway* were selected for conversion, with the older third ship, the *European Seaway* remaining in freighter form to operate between Dover and Calais to deal with the traffic which it was hoped would switch from the Belgian to the French port.

Although there had been a precedent for converting a ship of this class in the building of the *Pride of Burgundy*, this had been done rather quickly as a change in plan during the build programme and the aim of Project Darwin was to produce ships with larger passenger capacity, better facilities and an altogether more radical change from the freighter layout. As will be seen below, whilst the basic deck layout has remained the same, the overall result has been to create ships which are fundamentally different and, from the passenger perspective, completely new.

Quotes for the conversion work were sought from a number of shipyards, with delivery dates seen as crucial as well as price. In the end, the yard which originally built the ships – Schichau Seebeckwerft (SSW) in Bremerhaven, Germany – was chosen to do the work and a letter of intent signed in August 2002. Whilst they were not the cheapest, they offered better completion dates and, from experience, were known to be reliable and produce work of high quality. After the signature of letters on intent, SSW were taken over by Lloyd Werft, also of Bremerhaven, who decided that the work would be undertaken at their own yard. The conversion contract was subsequently signed with Lloyd Werft. However, these changes did not seriously affect the process as many of the team who had been working on the project were transferred to the once rival company. The new steelwork sections for the ships were still built at the SSW yard and transferred to Lloyd Werft by barge.

P&O Stena Line appointed Three Quays Marine Services – who had worked on a number of P&O projects including the *Pride of Hull* and *Pride of Rotterdam* on the Hull – Rotterdam service – to carry out the project definition design work. They appointed FCG as interior designers to develop the company's 'BrandWorld' corporate scheme for passenger facilities. Under the co-ordination of the owner's naval architect, the consultant naval architect, interior designers and P&O onboard services people worked closely together to achieve the optimum mix of efficiency, easy to use customer facilities and aesthetics.

The *European Pathway* was the first ship to leave the Zeebrugge route, arriving at Bremerhaven on 1st December 2002. The *European Highway* closed the service on 15th December and arrived at Bremerhaven a couple of days later, although not formally handed over until 2nd January 2003. However, work had been continuing all through the autumn building new sections for the ships, which were then welded onto the two ships through the winter months of 2003. The 'Pathway' returned as the *Pride of Canterbury* on 5th May and 'Highway' as the *Pride of Kent* on 7th June. Shortly after Stena Line left the venture in mid 2002, all the passenger ships were renamed and had their prefix 'P&OSL' changed to 'PO' by the simple expedient of painting out the characters '&' and 'SL'. Although they were referred to as 'Pride of' publicly, they did not receive their final names until they emerged from refit in the early months of 2003. The soon to be withdrawn *PO Canterbury* and *PO Kent* were not renamed and this was fortunate because, for a variety of reasons it was necessary to run both the old *PO Canterbury* and the new *Pride of Canterbury* together for several days.

In theory, the rebuilding of these two ships was simple. As freighters they had two passenger decks which originally ran for about 1/3 of the length of the ship. The simple requirement for the project was to extend these two decks aft so they covered about 2/3 of the ship and to outfit them for a passenger "day" service. And that basically was it. But of course it was much more complicated and there were few parts of the ship which were unaffected by the rebuild.

Because the rebuilt ships had much more superstructure, they had greater windage, affecting manoeuvring in port. Ironically both the ships they replaced had been rebuilt and both had experienced manoeuvring problems following the rebuild. The old *PO Canterbury*, rebuilt in 1990 by Sea Containers as the *Fantasia* from the freighter *Tzarevetz*, had had to have her bow thrusters enhanced early in her career and the *PO Kent*, lengthened in 1992, had always suffered from underpowered thrusters in windy weather. To avoid making the same mistakes, P&O carried out manoeuvring simulations using BMT SeaTech's Rembrandt program to investigate upgrade alternatives. A similar exercise had been carried out in 1999 prior to the very successful manoeuvrability enhancement of *Pride of Provence* (formerly the *Stena Empereur*).

As a result of the simulations, the two bow thrusters were uprated from 1200 kW to 2000 kW each. The two 1450 kW shaft alternators were replaced with 2220 kW units to produce the necessary electrical power, fed at 6.6 kV to minimise the new cable installation. The high voltage switchboard is independent of other ship electrical supplies and enables either thruster to be run from either shaft. The additional hotel load electrical requirements are satisfied by the installation of a new Wartsila 1440 kW alternator unit.

The simulations showed also that the original two rudders, whilst designated of a high lift type, developed inadequate lift for the required berthing manoeuvres. As for *Pride of Provence*, flap rudders were retro-fitted. This design option introduces a conflict between the proven reliability of the conventional horn-hung mariner rudder and the potential vulnerability of the more complex spade arrangement. The superior performance of the flap rudders prevailed and two Barker-Meyer rudders were fitted.

Club Class Lounge *(P&O Ferries)*

Harbour Coffee Company *(P&O Ferries)*

The deadweight of the ships as-built was designed in excess of that necessary for general passenger service operation. This margin permitted the conversion to go ahead without hull modifications such as sponsons. However, in the course of the design, weight estimates suggested that additional draught might be required to ensure adequate vehicle carrying capability. As built, the ships had a subdivision draught of 6.25m but a scantling draught of 6.40m. Damaged stability analysis showed that the approval criteria could be satisfied at the deeper draught. The subdivision draught was increased as a precaution although a target design limitation of 6.25m was imposed.

Consequently, although it might be thought that all the additional accommodation and consequent weight would need extra engine power, this is not the case. The design draught of the ships when built was 6.0 m. The hydrodynamic efficiency of the hull and bulbous bow coupled with the efficiency of the bow-thrusters and propellers at this draught was predicted to compensate for the additional weight. So it has proved in service. The converted ships manoeuvre well and have no problem in meeting the Dover – Calais schedule which varies between 75 and 90 minutes depending on the ship used.

A limiting factor for the accommodation design was the trim of the ships. As built, most of the accommodation was forward and the hull design compensated for this. By extending the accommodation aft, this balance was disturbed and so every effort was made to install additional weight forward wherever possible. Consequently two large fresh water tanks were built forward and the aft tank opened up for high voltage switchboard room. Two new sewage tanks and all the new refrigeration plant was installed forward. The shop and catering stores are arranged forward.

A design complication of such a conversion is that whilst unchanged features of the ship are allowed to meet the standards prevalent at the time the ships were built, any new features must comply with newer, more stringent requirements. This is particularly apparent for access to and from the main vehicle deck, affecting the design of the two new staircases and two new lifts.

So how much has changed and how much of the old ship remains? From the bottom up:

Deck 1 (Tank-Top originally)

- uprated bowthrust units

- conversion of one void to additional forward machinery room – installation of additional chiller plant and sewage units

- conversion of one void to catering/shop store

- two new fresh water tanks

- new auxiliary generator

- refurbishment of main gearboxes (part of the annual refit work carried out consecutive with the conversion)

- uprated shaft alternators

Deck 2 (H-Deck originally)

New features include:

- creation of catering/shop store by building new flat in two former voids and the former forward machinery room

- additional auxiliary boiler

- high voltage electrical switchboard room

Deck 3 This is the lower of the two vehicles decks (G-Deck originally), which is fully enclosed and watertight. This has not been changed and remains mainly used by trucks and coaches. (Deck 4 exists only as flats within the various casings.). Change are:

- two new stair towers to passenger accommodation

- new lift to passenger accommodation

- three new stores elevators to deck below

Deck 5 The upper vehicle deck – the 'weather deck' (E-Deck) was, as built, about 2/3 open. With the additional accommodation above only about 1/5 is open aft, plus the f'c'sle area forward. A retractable mezzanine deck (Deck 6) has been installed on the starboard side, with half width ramps leading up to it fore and aft, allowing simultaneous loading of both the mezzanine and main decks. This permits the optimisation of loading high and low headroom vehicles without compromising the aim of first on-first off which is important for passenger goodwill. Other features are:

■ the two new stair towers serve this deck also

■ the original open stair to this deck is enclosed

■ a second new lift to passenger accommodation

■ one lift and two stair towers serve the mezzanine deck

■ installation of two rescue boats

Deck 7 The lower passenger deck (D-Deck) was originally drivers' cabins plus a small reception area and outside deck. All these facilities were literally bulldozed away (a small bulldozer was used in the initial clearance) and the accommodation extended to the rear, increasing the enclosed area by about 200%. On this deck are the retail outlets, the Horizon Lounge (a family lounge bar), Silverstones (a "pub" lounge/bar) and Caffé Oliveto, a new catering development serving Italian food in a bar type environment. The accommodation was also extended forward to give a distinctive 'bay window' effect and all windows were replaced by large full height ones, which gives a light, airy effect, especially in the Horizon Lounge which has great forward views on a route where there are always plenty of other ships to see. Another new development is the provision of cooked food in the Horizon Lounge; food is ordered at the bar but served to people's tables, a system common in many pub-restaurants in the UK. Like the Caffé Oliveto it provides a facility which lays some way between the two main restaurants in terms of style. (Both the two food outlets have their own small food preparation areas.) Other features on this deck are:

■ information office

■ bureau de change

■ game machine area

■ six MarinArk marine escape systems

■ two rescue boats

■ foot passenger access to Calais linkspan – midships, starboard

■ foot passenger access to Dover linkspan via enclosed walkway over aft open vehicle deck

Deck 8 The upper passenger deck (C-Deck) originally included the galley, passenger lounge, restaurant, bar and small shop. This is now the main catering deck, including the self service International Food Court (separate serveries for different types of food with common pay points and seating area), Langan's Brasserie à la carte restaurant, Routemasters freight driver restaurant and Harbour Coffee Company snack bar. Also on this deck and above the Horizon Lounge lies the Club Class Lounge, which enjoys the same forward views. The main galley is also on this deck, serving the three passenger catering outlets and also the crew mess on the deck above by way of two 'dumb waiters'. There is a small sheltered open area at the rear of this deck with ready wheelchair access.

Deck 9 The lower crew deck (B-deck) has also been extended to take into account the much larger crews now carried to serve the 2000 (rather than 200) passengers. Accommodation for crew who live aboard for a week consists of six single petty officer cabins with private facilities and twenty-six single cabins for crew. These latter cabins have a shower/toilet unit shared one between two cabins with a door from each. In order to overcome the obvious problems of people remembering to lock and unlock two doors, the locking mechanisms are electronically interlinked so that locking and unlocking one door will do the same to the other. Live aboard crew have their own dayrooms. A separate dayroom and three changing areas with showers are provided for those staff who work single day or night shifts. There is a common smoking room. To the rear of these facilities is an open deck area for passenger use and there are also wide open decks along each side of the accommodation block. Use of these decks by passengers has proved problematic for those crew asleep and whilst the glazing of cabins is sufficient to shut out the noise of anyone just walking up and down, it cannot cope with people skateboarding and banging on windows – which, unfortunately, some people are prone to do. Lift access to this deck is through crew accommodation only and therefore not generally wheelchair accessible for passengers. Two air conditioning plant and a new crew laundry occupy the remainder of the new accommodation.

Deck 10 The bridge deck (A-deck) is perhaps the least affected part of the ship. No particular changes have been made to the bridge other than the upgrading of equipment which has been going on continuously since the ships were new. The accommodation – which consists mainly of officers' cabins – has been extended by about 80% but is just over half the length of Deck 9. In it there are:

- 11 single officer cabins

- 2 single cadet cabins with shared facilities

- a crew training/conference room

- air conditioning and ventilation spaces

The funnel is in the same position as she was before but looks very different. Instead of coming out of the weather deck, it comes out of Deck 9 and is thus much higher up. It has been completely rebuilt and given a new modern, streamlined look. The exhaust uptakes have been extended and a new eco-friendly 'scrubbing' system installed on the second ship to reduce SOx and particulate emissions. P&O Ferries are pioneering new technical abatement equipment as an alternative to the use of low sulphur fuels.

The two ships are the first large passenger ships to be certificated without lifeboats. Evacuation of all passengers and crew may be achieved through the use of RFD Marin-Ark escape chutes and inflatable life rafts. There are six blocks of four life rafts, three blocks on each side, accessed from Deck 7. Each block can accommodate 430 people. The law now requires every ship to have a high speed rescue boat but these ships have four. There are two in the distinctive 'pods' at the front on each side (the port side one is the designated "fast" rescue boat) and two slightly different models further back accessed from Deck 7.

Un-rebuilt sister ship *European Seaway* was withdrawn at the end of 2003 following a decision of P&O Ferries to reduce the number of passenger ferries on the route from seven to six and to use the near sister *Pride of Burgundy* as the freighter. Modifications are being investigated to increase her flexibility – a new external stern ramp for use on single deck link spans at ports other than Dover, Calais or Zeebrugge and an internal tilting ramp to facilitate vehicle transfer between the two vehicle decks. She will then be either sold, chartered out or used on another P&O route.

The 'Darwin Project' rebuilding exercise is unlikely to be repeated and there are no plans to earmark the *European Seaway* for this purpose. P&O see a need to replace the oldest ship in the fleet, the ex-Stena Line *Pride of Provence* and the chartered *Pride of Aquitaine* in a few years time. What their replacements will be like is as yet unknown. Double ended ships (like those used between Puttgarden and Rødby) and pod propulsion have their attraction and bow rudders might make a comeback even if conventional ships are built (they allow ships to reverse out of Calais and clear the berths for incoming ships much quicker). But these features make for more expensive construction and the balance against the potential of reduced operating costs needs careful assessment. They are unlikely, however, to be much faster; raising speed from 21 knots to 25 knots doubles fuel consumption and P&O do not see this as justified at the present time. Whatever happens though, we can be sure there are many interesting developments to come.

I would like to thank Brian Rees and Simon Pollard of P&O Ferries for their assistance in compiling this article.

Nick Widdows

International Food Court *(P&O Ferries)*

Pride of Canterbury *(FotoFlite)*

DFDS'

Dana Gloria & Dana Sirena

When the *Dana Sirena* entered service between Harwich and Esbjerg on 17th June 2003 she represented as significant a change in direction for the route as did the *England* almost 40 years earlier. DFDS (Det Forende Dampskibs-Selskab A/S – in English The United Steamship Company), formed from the merger of three of the largest Danish shipping companies in 1866 operated occasional services to London from Copenhagen from the beginning, but it was not until 1875, two years after the opening of the port of Esbjerg that services from there to England commenced. At the beginning, the English terminal was at Thameshaven, but by 1880 the company's vessels were calling instead at Harwich on the weekly service to Denmark. In February 1883 the Great Eastern Railway Company opened Parkeston Quay, named after the then chairman of the Company. By the summer of that year DFDS had transferred to the new facility and second ship entered the trade. The Danish company has continued to serve the Essex railway port for more than 120 years.

The early vessels were predominantly cattle carriers with some passenger accommodation. The *Riberhuus*, dating from 1875 and the new *Koldinghuus* provided more frequent sailings in a service that was nearing the end of its first phase. With the introduction of refrigeration in the 1889-built *Kasan*, the emphasis switched from live animals to farm products, and in 1896 three sisters joined her on the route, each with large refrigerated holds and accommodation for 76 passengers.

It was not until 1901 that the first pure passenger ship, the *J C La Cour*, with luxuriously appointed spaces for 112 passengers, was introduced onto the route. By this time there were three sailings each week, increased to four from 1904. Two years later the 180-passenger *Dronning Maud* arrived, followed in 1913 by the beautifully proportioned 218-passenger *A P Bernstorff*. The First World War terminated the service, and delayed the completion of a sister to the 'Bernstorff', but sailings resumed in the autumn of 1919.

The first of four modern diesel-engined ships (the *Parkeston*) joined the route in 1925. Her sisters were the *Jylland*, the *Esbjerg* and the *England*. The service became daily except for Sundays, but in 1938 and 1939 extra Sunday sailings were operated in the peak summer period. In 1938 the Company carried more than 48,000 passengers on the Esbjerg to Harwich service.

Sailings were again suspended for the duration of the Second World War, with Parkeston Quay under British Admiralty requisition. On 6th December 1945 the only surviving member of the quartet of motor ships, the *Parkeston*, re-opened the route but with sailings reduced in frequency to weekly.

By the summer of 1949 a pair of immensely elegant and fast vessels was serving the route, with a service frequency that had reverted to six times weekly. The first of these, the *Kronprins Frederik*, had been laid-down in 1939 and launched the following year. She was delivered to DFDS in 1941 and immediately laid-up in an out of the way part of Copenhagen's harbour system, with some vital engine parts removed. Re-delivered to the Company in 1946 following final fitting out at the Elsinore Shipyard, she was immediately placed on the Harwich to Esbjerg service, where she continued until the summer of 1964. Her sister, the *Kronprinsesse Ingrid* was delivered to the company by the Elsinore Shipyard in June 1949, and together these 4,000 gross ton ships served the route for 15 years. They each carried 294 passengers and had storage space for 33 crane-loaded cars.

By now DFDS had developed its own style of elegance in the appearance of all of its passenger vessels, so the new 8,200 gross ton *England* in 1964 and her near sister the *Winston Churchill* of 1967 created no surprise in their looks. The *England* was, in her own way, a radical departure from previous ships as

Dana Sirena *(DFDS)*

The Columbus Lounge *(Miles Cowsill)*

she was the first drive-on ferry for the Harwich to Esbjerg service. Up to 100 cars could be carried, loaded through side doors, and her passenger capacity was 467. She also had 45,000 cubic feet of cargo space, of which most was refrigerated. Much of this cargo space was replaced by cabins in 1972, increasing her passenger capacity to 668. With her grey hull, tiered after decks and fine lines she was one of the most beautiful ships ever to have plied the North Sea. The *England* was partnered by the *Kronprinsesse Ingrid* until the arrival in 1967 of the *Winston Churchill*, slightly larger than the *England* at 8,600 tons and very different in that she was fitted with bow and stern visors and ramps and had a capacity for 180 cars. Her 464 passengers were accommodated in two classes, as they were on most DFDS passenger ships. In 1970 all DFDS ships became one-class and three years later she followed the lead of her near sister in having her cargo hold replaced by passenger cabins.

The 1960s also saw the arrival of the first dedicated ro-ro freighters to serve the route; the *Suffolk* and *Sussex* of 1966 were followed by the *Stafford* in 1967.

In 1974 the first of the next generation of Esbjerg ferries arrived at Harwich for the first time. The 12,000 ton *Dana Regina* was a big step upwards in terms of capacity. She carried 1,000 passengers and had space for 370 cars. Her arrival saw the transfer to Newcastle of the *England*. The appearance of the *Dana Regina*, whilst not as elegant the ship she replaced, can be considered an evolution from previous designs. However the next new vessel for the Harwich to Esbjerg service was externally more revolutionary. The largest passenger and car ferry to regularly ply between Harwich and Esbjerg was also to be the last, although no-one could have foreseen that at the time. The *Dana Anglia* was delivered in 1978 and carried 1,249 passengers and 470 cars. She was named in the Upper Pool of London and was, at the time (and probably still) the largest ship to enter the Upper Pool. Her exhausts had to be removed to enable her passage under Tower Bridge. The *Dana Anglia* did not have the elegant appearance of those ships that preceded her, but with her immensely tall funnel she was instantly recognisable at great distance. Her arrival in May 1978 displaced the *Winston Churchill* to Newcastle, from where she continued to operate to Esbjerg, although she did relieve at Harwich in May of each of the years 1979 to 1983. The *Dana Anglia* almost exclusively served the route for which she was built from 1978 until the autumn of 2002.

Putting matters in perspective, during the late 1970s and early 1980s there were four modern car ferries running between the UK and Denmark. In those days the emphasis was on passengers and their cars, with freight representing an opportunity to fill space on these ships. Most of the freight was then carried on dedicated freight ships. In 2002, however, with declining passenger numbers due to changes in travelling patterns and methods it was decided by the company that the future of the Harwich to Esbjerg service would be freight based. In the summer of that year DFDS successfully acquired two ro-pax ferries, the order having been cancelled by an Italian ship-owner, from the yard where they were being built.

It was as early as 1999 that Lloyd Sardegna ordered a pair of ships for its service from the Italian Mainland to the island of Sardinia, from the Stocnia Szczecinska Shipyard at Stettin, Poland. Delays, caused in part by financial problems at the shipyard resulting in its eventual bankruptcy, led to the order being cancelled in early 2002, long after both ships should have been delivered. DFDS had already announced the redeployment of the *Dana Anglia* away from the route and were seeking something suitable as a replacement in the light of the altered requirements for the route. The Company saw an opportunity to buy the ships from the mortgage-holding bank in the summer of that year.

The first of the new ships became the *Dana Gloria*. She was to have been Lloyd Sardegna's *Golfo Dei Coralli* and entered service with DFDS on the Harwich to Esbjerg route in freight mode on 10th August, little changed from her original configuration and with some signage still in Italian. The 'Dana' name and her DFDS Ro-Pax livery were designed to show the travelling public that she wasn't a so-called cruise ferry, but offered a rather more basic way of travelling. At 20,140 gross tons she was the largest DFDS ship to date to serve the passenger route to Esbjerg, a role that she took over from the *Dana Anglia* in November 2002.

The *Dana Gloria* is an impressive freight carrier with three full height freight decks and passenger accommodation on the two decks above. She can carry almost 200 trailers, and as much of her traffic is unaccompanied a good deal of 300 berths on Deck 7 and Deck 8 are available for passenger use. Her public areas on Deck 7 comprise an extremely pleasant lounge and bar at the forward end, aft of which is the galley on the starboard side and the restaurant on the port side. A fixed waiter-service menu together with a limited buffet is offered in the evening. Behind this room is a small family room with seating, tables, a television and some toys. This appeared to be in its original form, whereas the

DURASTIC

Durastic Ltd is one of the world's leading suppliers and installers of marine deck covering systems offering a wide range of specifications.

From primary underlays; including Durastic's lightweight underlay, to weatherdecks, sound reduction and A60 Solas rated materials; all with associated finishes such as carpets, vinyls and epoxy resins.

A full specification service and experienced, supervised contract teams ensure the best deck coverings are installed to the highest standards. Durastic's products are covered by International Certifications and produced at its ISO 9002 Quality Assured manufacturing facility.

UNIT 47	
CUTHBERT COURT	
BEDE INDUSTRIAL ESTATE	
JARROW	T: +44(0)191 483 2299
TYNE & WEAR	F: +44(0)191 483 2295
NE32 3HG	E: john.english@rigblast.com
UNITED KINGDOM	W: www.durastic-ltd.com

Branch Offices in Glasgow, Liverpool, Southampton & Jarrow.

Durastic is a member of the Rigblast Group

restaurant had certainly been re-styled to suit DFDS. Cabin accommodation is reasonably spacious and very tastefully completed with a good amount of wood finish in evidence. There is a small reception area at the after end of the Deck 7 passenger facilities. The sun deck on Deck 9 affords a good viewing platform for both departure and arrival, but can be a bit breezy as the ship slices through the North Sea at 22 knots. She has a long and low profile, emphasising her 200 metre length. Unusually, her beam doesn't reach its maximum until the upper trailer deck, and that level also has side walkways outside the width of the ship leading from the passenger accommodation to the stern. These were for use in the Mediterranean where berthing stern on to the quayside (the so-called 'Mediterranean Moor') is the norm.

The *Dana Gloria* (now the *Lisco Gloria* running in the Baltic for DFDS subsidiary LISCO) served the company well until June 2003, when she was replaced by her former sister the *Dana Sirena*, laid down as the *Golfo dei Delfini* but now much altered. The 'Sirena' was less complete when acquired by DFDS and it was not until October 2002 that she was at a suitable stage to be handed over. She was then moved to the Remontowa yard at Gdansk for major alteration, under the direction of Steen Friis Design of Denmark. She has been designed primarily as a freight carrier, but is also finished internally to a very high standard, making her a very comfortable passenger ship

Starting with Deck 6, a total of 31 cabins were installed along the sides of what was previously the upper trailer deck. These include 14 3-berth, 1 4-berth and 16 2-berth units. The upper part of what was previously Deck 6 has now become Deck 7 with 47 mainly 2- and 4-berth cabins along the sides, and at the front, the shop selling the usual range of merchandise, and the lighthouse café – a snack and coffee bar by day and night club later.

The new Deck 8 (formerly 7) has undergone the most radical change internally. Whilst the Columbus Lounge at the forward end remains unaltered, aft of this the superstructure has been extended to the sides of the ship thus raising the lifeboats by one deck. Within this enlarged area the elegant 48 seat Blue Riband à la carte restaurant and extended galley on the starboard side, and a new 172 seat Seven Seas buffet on the port side have been created. The buffet now extends though the original restaurant to meet the Blue Riband. Through the centre of the buffet area runs the main access to the Columbus Lounge, which is the only real drawback of the current layout on this deck. Aft of the Restaurant, where the family room was previously, the reception desk and office can now be found. The superstructure on this deck has been extended aft by the equivalent of five cabin widths, thus providing 25 extra rooms, 4- and 6-berth, in this area.

Deck 9 was previously Deck 8. On this deck the area that is occupied by crew cabins on the *Dana Gloria* is now filled with 30 passenger cabins. The outer cabins on this deck were initially marketed as Commodore, but are now sold as Sirena Class. The after end of the accommodation is now given over to crew cabins, with, unusually a block of eight that can be allocated to passengers or crew.

Deck 10 was the open sun deck (9) on the *Dana Gloria*. This area now carries some of the most luxurious accommodation on the North Sea and comprises 18 Commodore de-luxe mini suites with the use of an exclusive Commodore Lounge complete with private balcony (described as a sun deck but not really big enough).

Externally, there is a small amount of open deck at the after end of the passenger accommodation on Deck 8 that can be accessed either from that deck or from semi-open stairs from decks 6 and 7. There are some side deck areas on Deck 9 and Deck 10, and a small area around the after end of Deck 9. The after end of Deck 10 is the Commodore Balcony.

The 22,382 ton *Dana Sirena* can carry around 600 passengers, but the ship could feel very crowded with anything approaching that number of passengers. However, each of the reasonably sized and comfortably appointed cabins has a television and can receive around eight channels via satellite. Other channels are available on payment of a small fee, giving a total of up to 20, so there is entertainment away from the public areas of the ship.

The *Dana Sirena* is a totally different type of ship from those that preceded her on the Esbjerg route. That said, she is comfortable, tastefully fitted out, maintains the DFDS tradition of excellent service and good food, but most importantly is there, providing a service that DFDS could so easily have converted to a full freight role.

William Mayes

The Lighthouse Cafe *(Miles Cowsill)*

The Seven Seas Buffet Restaurant *(Miles Cowsill)*

FINLAND

Rauma

Naantali
Turku
Kotka
ÅLAND
Helsinki
Mariehamn Långnäs

Oslo SWEDEN Hanko
Kapellskär Tallinn
Moss Paldiski
Södertälje Stockholm
Strömstad Nynäshamn ESTONIA

R

othenburg Västervik

Oskarshamn Visby Ventspils Riga
avn Varberg GOTLAND LATVIA

oft ÖLAND Liepaja
Helsingborg
ingør Karlskrona
Karlshamn Klaipeda
Malmö
penhagen Ystad LITHUANIA
Trelleborg Rønne
ars BORNHOLM
Gedser Sassnitz Gdynia
en Rostock Gdansk
vemünde BYEL A
eck Swinoujscie

POLAND

UKR

CZECH

SLOVAKIA

section **I**

gb & ireland

BRITTANY FERRIES

THE COMPANY *Brittany Ferries* is the trading name of *BAI SA*, a French private sector company and the operating arm of the *Brittany Ferries Group*. The UK operations are run by *BAI (UK) Ltd*, a UK private sector company, wholly owned by the *Brittany Ferries Group*.

MANAGEMENT Group Managing Director Michel Maraval, **Managing Director UK & Ireland** David Longden.

ADDRESS Millbay Docks, Plymouth, Devon PL1 3EW.

TELEPHONE Administration *Plymouth* +44 (0)8709 010500, ***Portsmouth*** +44 (0)8709 011300, **Reservations *All Services*** +44 (0)8705 360360.

FAX Administration & Reservations +44 (0)8709 011100.

INTERNET Website www.brittanyferries.com *(English, French, Spanish, German)*

ROUTES OPERATED Conventional Ferries *All year* Plymouth – Roscoff (6 hrs (day), 6 hrs – 7 hrs 30 mins (night); *(3,6)*; up to 3 per day (summer), 1 per day (winter)), Portsmouth – St Malo (8 hrs 45 mins (day), 10 hrs 30 mins – 11 hrs 30 mins (night); *(2,7)*; 1/2 per day), Portsmouth – Caen (Ouistreham) (6 hrs (day), 6 hrs 15 mins – 8 hrs (night); *(4,5)*; 3 per day), Portsmouth – Cherbourg (4 hrs 30 mins; *(2,7)*; 4 per week), Plymouth – Santander (Spain) (18 hrs; *(6)*; 2 per week (March – November)), Poole – Cherbourg (4 hrs 15 mins; *(1)*; up to 2 per day), ***Summer only*** Cork – Roscoff (14 hrs; *(6)*; 1 per week), ***Winter only*** Plymouth – St Malo (8 hrs; *(7)*; 1 per week, Plymouth – Cherbourg (10 hrs; *(3)*; 1 per week). **Fast Ferry** Poole – Cherbourg (2 hrs 15 mins; *(CONDOR VITESSE of Condor Ferries)*; 1 per day). **Note** The Poole – Cherbourg fast ferry service is operated from May to September by *Condor Ferries* jointly with *Brittany Ferries*.

1	BARFLEUR	20133t	92	19.3k	158.0m	1212P	590C	112T	BA	FR
2	BRETAGNE	24534t	89	21.0k	151.0m	1926P	580C	84T	BA	FR
3	DUC DE NORMANDIE	13505t	78	19.0k	131.0m	1500P	354C	38T	BA	FR
4	MONT ST MICHEL	35592t	02	21.5k	173.0m	2200P	880C	166T	BA2	FR
5	NORMANDIE	27541t	92	20.5k	161.0m	2120P	600C	126T	BA2	FR
6	PONT-AVEN	41700t	04	27.0k	184.3m	2400P	650C	85L	BA	FR
7	VAL DE LOIRE	31788t	87	20.0k	162.0m	2140P	600C	104T	BA	FR

BARFLEUR Built at Helsinki for the *Truckline* Poole – Cherbourg service to replace two passenger vessels and to inaugurate a year round passenger service. In 1999 the *Truckline* branding was dropped for passenger services and she was repainted into full *Brittany Ferries* livery.

BRETAGNE Built at St Nazaire for the Plymouth – Santander and Cork – Roscoff services (with two sailings per week between Plymouth and Roscoff). In 1993 she was transferred to the Portsmouth – St Malo service. In 2004 also to operate between Portsmouth and Cherbourg.

DUC DE NORMANDIE Built at Heuseden, Netherlands as the PRINSES BEATRIX for *Stoomvaart Maatschappij Zeeland (Zeeland Steamship Company)* of The Netherlands for their Hoek van Holland – Harwich service. In September 1985 sold to *Brittany Ferries* and chartered back to *SMZ*, continuing to operate for them until the introduction of the KONINGIN BEATRIX (see STENA BALTICA) in May 1986. In June 1986 delivered to *Brittany Ferries* and inaugurated the Portsmouth – Caen service. From July 2002 she moved to the Plymouth – Roscoff route replacing the QUIBERON (11813t, 1975).

Miles better for
France & Spain
More ships - more routes - more convenience

Brittany Ferries' magnificent new £100 million flagship, Pont-Aven, is one of seven conventional ferries, plus a high speed service between Poole and Cherbourg, which together provide by far the **largest choice of routes from the UK** to France and Spain.

Pont-Aven, plus the £80 million Mont St Michel launched in 2002, are just part of an investment programme aimed at ensuring that we continue to provide the very finest service available for all our passengers.

Call **0870 366 9706**
or visit **www.brittanyferries.com**

Brittany ≈ Ferries

MONT ST MICHEL Built at Krimpen aan den IJssel, Rotterdam for *Brittany Ferries* to replace the DUC DE NORMANDIE on the Portsmouth – Caen route.

NORMANDIE Built at Turku, Finland for the Portsmouth – Caen route.

PONT-AVEN Built at Papenburg, Germany to operate on the Plymouth – Roscoff, Plymouth – Santander and Cork – Roscoff routes.

VAL DE LOIRE Built at Bremerhaven, Germany as the NILS HOLGERSSON for *Rederi AB Swedcarrier* of Sweden for their service between Trelleborg and Travemünde, joint with *TT-Line* of Germany (trading as *TT-Line*). In 1992 purchased by *Brittany Ferries* for entry into service in spring 1993. After a major rebuild, she was renamed the VAL DE LOIRE and introduced onto the Plymouth – Roscoff, Plymouth – Santander and Cork – Roscoff routes. In 2004 transferred to the Portsmouth – St Malo and Portsmouth – Cherbourg services.

CONDOR FERRIES

THE COMPANY *Condor Ferries Ltd* is a Channel Islands private sector company owned by the *Condor Group*, Guernsey which is owned by jointly by *ABN AMRO Capital Ltd* and the management.

MANAGEMENT Managing Director Robert Provan, **Operations Director** Jeff Vidamour, **General Manager, Sales & Marketing** Nicholas Dobbs.

ADDRESS Head Office PO Box 10, New Jetty Offices, White Rock, St Peter Port, Guernsey GY1 3AF, Sales and Marketing Condor House, New Harbour Road South, Hamworthy, POOLE BH15 4AJ.

TELEPHONE Administration *Guernsey* +44 (0)1481 728620, *Poole* +44 (0)1202 207207, **Reservations** +44 (0)845 345 2000.

FAX Administration *Guernsey* +44 (0)1481 728521, *Poole* +44 (0)1202 685184, **Reservations** +44(0)1305 760776.

INTERNET Email reservations@condorferries.co.uk **Website** www.condorferries.com *(English)*

ROUTES OPERATED Conventional Ferry *All year* Portsmouth – St Peter Port (Guernsey) (6 hrs 30 mins) – St Helier (Jersey) (10 hrs 30 mins) – Portsmouth (8 hrs 30 mins) (return Guernsey via Jersey, 12 hrs 30 mins); *(1)*; 6 per week, *Summer only* Portsmouth – Cherbourg (France) (5 hrs; *(1)*; 1 per week). **Fast Ferries** *Winter Only* Weymouth – St Peter Port (Guernsey) (2 hrs) – St Helier (Jersey via Guernsey) (3 hrs 20 mins); *(3)*; twice weekly, *Spring and Autumn* Weymouth – St Peter Port (Guernsey) (2 hrs) – St Helier (Jersey via Guernsey) (3 hrs 20 mins); *(3)*; 1 per day, Poole – St Peter Port (Guernsey) (2 hrs 30 mins) – St Helier (Jersey via Guernsey) (3 hrs 50 mins); *(3)*; daily, *Summer* Weymouth – St Peter Port (Guernsey) (2 hrs) – St Helier (Jersey via Guernsey) (3 hrs 20 mins); *(3)*; 1 per day, Poole – St Peter Port (Guernsey) (2 hrs 30 mins) – St Helier (via Guernsey 3 hrs 50 mins, direct 3 hrs) – St Malo (4 hrs 35 min) ; *(3,4)*; up to 2 per day to Jersey and Guernsey, 1 per day to St Malo (*Note* Poole – St Malo service operates via either Guernsey or Jersey), St Malo – St Peter Port (Guernsey) (2hrs 55 mins via Jersey, 1hr 45 mins direct; *(2)*; 2 per day), St Malo – St Helier (Jersey) (1 hr 10 mins; *(2)*; 1 per day – no cars conveyed on this service), Poole – Cherbourg (2 hrs 15 mins; *(4)*; 1 per day (service operated jointly with *Brittany Ferries)*).

1	COMMODORE CLIPPER	14000t	99	18.25.0k	129.1m	500P	100C	92T	A	BS
2»	CONDOR 10	3241t	93	37.0k	74.3m	580P	80C	-	BA	SI
3»	CONDOR EXPRESS	5005t	96	39.0k	86.6m	774P	185C	-	A2	BS
4»	CONDOR VITESSE	5005t	97	39.0k	86.6m	774P	185C	-	A2	BS

COMMODORE CLIPPER Ro-pax vessel built as the at Krimpen aan den IJssel, Rotterdam for *Commodore Ferries* to operate between Portsmouth and the Channel Islands. She replaced the ISLAND COMMODORE, a freight only vessel. Her passenger capacity is normally restricted to 300 but is increased to 500 when the fast ferries are unable to operate.

CONDOR 10 InCat 74m catamaran. Built at Hobart, Australia for the *Holyman Group* for use by *Condor Ferries*. In summer 1995 she was chartered to *Viking Line* to operate between Helsinki and Tallinn under the name 'VIKING EXPRESS II' (although not officially renamed). In summer 1996 she

was chartered to *Stena Line* to operate between Fishguard and Rosslare. During northern hemisphere winters she served for *TranzRail* of New Zealand for the service between Wellington (North Island) and Picton (South Island). In May 1997 she was transferred to *Holyman Sally Ferries* and inaugurated a new Ramsgate – Dunkerque (Est) service, replacing the Ramsgate – Dunkerque (Ouest) service of *Sally Ferries*. After further service in New Zealand during winter 1997/98, in summer 1998 she was due to operate between Weymouth, Guernsey and St Malo, but, in the event, the CONDOR VITESSE was chartered for that route and she was laid up in Australia. Refurbished during 2001, she returned to the UK in spring 2002 replacing the passenger-only CONDOR 9 between St Malo and Guernsey and Jersey.

CONDOR EXPRESS InCat 86m catamaran built at Hobart, Tasmania, Australia. She was delivered December 1996 and entered service in 1997.

CONDOR VITESSE InCat 86m catamaran built at Hobart. Built speculatively and launched as the INCAT 044. Moved to Europe in summer 1997 and spent time in the both the UK and Denmark but was not used. In 1998, she was chartered to *Condor Ferries* and renamed the CONDOR VITESSE. During winter 1999/2000 she was chartered to *TranzRail* of New Zealand. Returned to UK in spring 2000.

DFDS SEAWAYS

THE COMPANY *DFDS Seaways* is the passenger division of the *DFDS A/S*, a Danish private sector company. *DFDS Seaways Ltd* is a UK subsidiary.

MANAGEMENT Managing Director DFDS A/S Ole Frie, **Director DFDS Seaways** Thor Johannesen, **Managing Director DFDS Seaways Ltd** John Crummie.

ADDRESS Scandinavia House, Parkeston, Harwich, Essex CO12 4QG.

TELEPHONE Administration +44 (0)1255 243456, **Reservations** *National* 08705 333000 (from UK only), *Harwich* +44 (0)1255 240240, *Newcastle* +44 (0)191-293 6283.

FAX Administration & Reservations *Harwich* +44 (0)1255 244370, *Newcastle* +44 (0)191-293 6245.

INTERNET Email john.crummie@dfds.co.uk **Website** www.dfdsseaways.co.uk *(English)* www.dfdsseaways.com *(Danish, Dutch, German, Norwegian, Swedish)*

ROUTES OPERATED *All year* Harwich – Esbjerg (Denmark) (17 hrs; *(1)*; 3 per week), Kristiansand (Norway) – Gothenburg (Sweden) (7 hrs (day), 13 hrs 30 min (night); *(4)*; 1 per week (spring, summer and autumn), 3 per week (winter)), Harwich – Cuxhaven (Germany) (16 hrs; *(2)*; 3 per week (winter, spring, autumn), alternate days (summer)), Newcastle (North Shields) – IJmuiden (near Amsterdam, Netherlands) (15 hrs; *(3,5)*; daily). *Spring, Summer and Autumn only* Newcastle – Kristiansand – Gothenburg (25 hrs; *(4)*; 2 per week).

1	DANA SIRENA	22400t	03	22.5k	199.4m	600P	316C	154T	A	DK
2	DUCHESS OF SCANDINAVIA	16794t	93	19.0k	134.4m	882P	350C	46T	BA	DK
3	DUKE OF SCANDINAVIA	19589t	78	20.5k	152.9m	1120P	375C	56T	BA	DK
4	PRINCESS OF SCANDINAVIA	22528t	76	26.0k	184.6m	1620P	365C	32T	AS	DK
5	QUEEN OF SCANDINAVIA	34093t	81	21.0k	169.0m	1638P	360C	70T	BA	DK

DANA SIRENA Built in Szczecin, Poland for *Lloyd Sardegna* of Italy as the GOLFO DEI DELFINI for service between Italy and Sardinia. However, due to late delivery the order was cancelled. In 2002 purchased by *DFDS Seaways*, and, during winter 2002/3, passenger accommodation was enlarged and refitted, increasing passenger capacity from 308 to 600. In June 2003, renamed the DANA SIRENA, she replaced unmodified sister vessel, the DANA GLORIA (now with *Lisco Baltic Services* – see Section 6), on the Esbjerg – Harwich service. She is branded *DFDS Tor Line*.

DUCHESS OF SCANDINAVIA Built at Rissa, Norway as the BERGEN for *Rutelaget Askøy-Bergen* and used on the *Fjord Line* Bergen (Norway) – Egersund (Norway) – Hanstholm (Denmark) service. In 2003 chartered to *DFDS* and in April 2003, renamed the DUCHESS OF SCANDINAVIA and, after modifications, introduced onto the Harwich – Cuxhaven service.

Commodore Clipper *(Miles Cowsill)*

Ulysses *(Miles Cowsill)*

DUKE OF SCANDINAVIA Built at Aalborg, Denmark as the DANA ANGLIA for the Harwich – Esbjerg service and seldom operated elsewhere. In autumn 2002, renamed the DUKE OF SCANDINAVIA and inaugurated a new Copenhagen – Trelleborg – Gdansk service. In 2003 moved to the Newcastle – IJmuiden service.

PRINCESS OF SCANDINAVIA Built at Lübeck, Germany as the TOR SCANDINAVIA for *Tor Line* of Sweden for their Amsterdam – Gothenburg and Felixstowe – Gothenburg services. In 1979 she was used on a world trade cruise and was temporarily renamed the HOLLAND EXPO. Similar exercises were undertaken in 1980, 1982 and 1984, but on these occasions her temporary name was the WORLD WIDE EXPO. She was acquired by *DFDS* in 1981 and subsequently re-registered in Denmark. She has also operated on the Harwich – Esbjerg service. Between 1989 and 1993 she also operated Newcastle – Esbjerg and Amsterdam – Gothenburg services. In 1991, following a major refurbishment, she was renamed the PRINCESS OF SCANDINAVIA. Since 1994, she generally operated on the Harwich – Gothenburg and Newcastle – Gothenburg routes. During winter 1998/1999 she had major modifications made at Gdansk and during winter 1999/2000 she had a major engine rebuild. She now operates between Newcastle and Gothenburg via Kristiansand.

QUEEN OF SCANDINAVIA Built at Turku, Finland as the FINLANDIA for *EFFOA* of Sweden for *Silja Line* services between Helsinki and Stockholm. In 1990 she was sold to *DFDS*, renamed the QUEEN OF SCANDINAVIA and introduced onto the Copenhagen – Helsingborg – Oslo service. In 2001 transferred to the Newcastle – IJmuiden route.

EMERAUDE JERSEY FERRIES

THE COMPANY *Emeraude Jersey Ferries* is a French private sector company, owned by *Sogestran* of France. It was, until 2004, called *Emeraude Lines*.

MANAGEMENT Channel Islands Manager Gordon Forrest, **Brittany and Normandy Office Manager** Vacant.

ADDRESS Terminal Ferry du Naye, PO Box 16, 35401, St Malo Cedex, France.

TELEPHONE Administration & Reservations *St Malo* +33 (0)2 23 180 180, *Jersey* +44 (0)1534 766566.

FAX Administration & Reservations *St Malo* +33 (0) 2 23 181 500, *Jersey* +44 (0)1534 768741.

INTERNET Email sales@emeraude.co.uk **Website** www.emeraude.co.uk *(English)*

ROUTES OPERATED Fast Ferries St Malo (France) – St Helier (Jersey) (1 hr 10 mins; *(1)*; up to 3 per day).

1»	HOVERSPEED GREAT BRITAIN	3000t	90	37.0k	74.3m	577P	80C	-	BA	UK

HOVERSPEED GREAT BRITAIN InCat 74m catamaran built at Hobart, Tasmania. Launched as the CHRISTOPHER COLUMBUS but renamed before entering service. During delivery voyage from Australia, she won the Hales Trophy for the 'Blue Riband' of the Atlantic. She inaugurated a car and passenger service between Portsmouth and Cherbourg, operated by *Hoverspeed*. This service was suspended in early 1991 and later that year she was, after modification, switched to a new service between Dover (Eastern Docks) and Boulogne/Calais, replacing hovercraft. In 1992 operated on Channel routes, including services from Folkestone. During winter 1992/3 she was chartered to *Ferry Lineas* of Argentina, operating between Buenos Aires (Argentina) and Montevideo (Uruguay). In summer 1993 she was used to provide additional sailings on the Belfast - Stranraer route, transferring back to the channel later that year. Following the ending of the Folkestone - Boulogne service in autumn 2000, she was transferred to the Dover - Calais route. In summer 2001 she operated between Heysham and Belfast; in summer 2002 she operated between Dover and Calais and this was repeated in 2003 until mid summer when she was replaced by the DIAMANT due to structural problems. Laid up. In 2004 chartered to *Emeraude Jersey Ferries*.

FJORD LINE

THE COMPANY *Fjord Line* is a Norwegian company, 100% owned by *Bergen-Nordhordland Rutelag AS (BNR)*. It took over the Newcastle – Norway service from *Color Line* in December 1998.

MANAGEMENT Managing Director (UK) Dag Romslo, **Sales Director (UK)** Mike Wood.

ADDRESS Royal Quays, North Shields NE29 6EG.

TELEPHONE Administration +44 (0)191-296 1313, **Reservations** +44 (0)191-296 1313.

FAX Administration & Reservations +44 (0)191-296 1540, Telex 537275.

INTERNET Email fjordline.uk@fjordline.com **Website** www.fjordline.co.uk *(English)*

ROUTES OPERATED Bergen (Norway) – Haugesund (Norway) – Stavanger (Norway) – Newcastle – Bergen (triangular route), Bergen – Haugesund – Stavanger – Newcastle (Bergen – Stavanger (via 6 hrs), Stavanger – Newcastle (direct 18 hrs 30 mins, via Bergen 29 hrs 30 mins), Bergen – Newcastle (21 hrs 15 mins); *(1)*; 3 sailings Norway – Newcastle per week).

Fjord Line also operates between Norway and Denmark; see Section 6.

1	JUPITER	20581t	75	21.0k	175.3m	1250P	285C	40T	BA	NO

JUPITER Built at Nantes, France as the WELLAMO for *EFFOA* of Finland for *Silja Line* services between Helsinki and Stockholm. In 1981 sold to *DFDS*, renamed the DANA GLORIA and placed onto the Gothenburg – Newcastle and Esbjerg – Newcastle services. In 1983 she was moved to the Copenhagen – Oslo service. In 1984 she was chartered to *Johnson Line* of Sweden for *Silja Line* service between Stockholm and Turku and renamed the SVEA CORONA – the name previously born by a sister vessel, which had been sold. This charter ended in 1985 and she returned to the Copenhagen – Oslo service and resumed the name DANA GLORIA. During winter 1988/89 she was lengthened in Papenburg, Germany and in early 1989 she was renamed the KING OF SCANDINAVIA. She returned to the Copenhagen – Oslo route; in 1990 a Helsingborg call was introduced. In 1994 she was sold to *Color Line* and renamed the COLOR VIKING. In 1998 she was sold to *Fjord Line* and renamed the JUPITER.

IRISH FERRIES

THE COMPANY *Irish Ferries* is an Irish Republic private sector company, part of the *Irish Continental Group*. It was originally mainly owned by the state owned *Irish Shipping* and partly by *Lion Ferry AB* of Sweden. *Lion Ferry* participation ceased in 1977 and the company was sold into the private sector in 1987. Formerly state owned *B&I Line* was taken over in 1991 and from 1995 all operations were marketed as *Irish Ferries*.

MANAGEMENT Group Managing Director Eamon Rothwell, **Group Marketing Director** Tony Kelly.

ADDRESS 2 Merrion Row, Dublin 2, Republic of Ireland.

TELEPHONE Administration +353 (0)1 855 2222, **Reservations Dublin** +353 (0)1 638 3333, **Cork** +353 (0)21 455 1995, **Rosslare Harbour** +353 (0)53 33158, **Holyhead** 0990 329129 (from UK only), **Pembroke Dock** 0990 329543 (from UK only), **National** 08705 171717 (from UK only), **24 hour information** +353 (0)1 661 0715.

FAX Administration & Reservations Dublin +353 (0)1 661 0743, **Cork** +353 (0)21 450 4651, **Rosslare** +353 (0)53 33544.

INTERNET Email *Britain* info@irishferries.co.uk ***Elsewhere*** info@irishferries.com **Website** www.irishferries.com *(English)*

ROUTES OPERATED Conventional Ferries Dublin – Holyhead (3 hrs 15 mins; *(4)*; 2 per day), Rosslare – Pembroke Dock (3 hrs 45 mins; *(1)*; 2 per day), Rosslare – Cherbourg (France) (17 hrs 30 mins; *(3)*; 1 or 2 per week), Rosslare – Roscoff (France) (16 hrs; *(3)*; 1 or 2 per week). **Note** the

SECTION I – GB & IRELAND PASSENGER OPERATIONS

Rosslare – Cherbourg/Roscoff service operates on a seasonal basis. **Fast Ferry** Dublin – Holyhead (1 hr 49 min; *(2)*; up to 4 per day). Marketed as 'DUBLIN*Swift*'.

1	ISLE OF INISHMORE	34031t	97	21.5k	182.5m	2200P	802C	152T	BA2	IR
2»	JONATHAN SWIFT	5989t	99	39.5k	86.6m	800P	200C	-	BA	IR
3	NORMANDY	24872t	82	19.0k	149.0m	1526P	420C	62L	BA2	IR
4	ULYSSES	50938t	01	22.0k	209.0m	1875P	1342C	300T	BA2	IR

ISLE OF INISHMORE Built at Krimpen aan den IJssel, Rotterdam for *Irish Ferries* to operate on the Holyhead – Dublin service. In 2001 replaced by the ULYSSES and moved to the Rosslare – Pembroke Dock route. She also relives on the Dublin – Holyhead route when the ULYSSES receives her annual overhaul.

JONATHAN SWIFT Austal Auto-Express 86 catamaran built at Fremantle, Australia for *Irish Ferries* for the Dublin – Holyhead route.

NORMANDY Built at Gothenburg, Sweden. One of two vessels ordered by *Göteborg-Frederikshavn-Linjen* of Sweden (trading as *Sessan Linjen*) before the take over of their operations by *Stena Line AB* in 1981. Both were designed for the Gothenburg – Frederikshavn route (a journey of about three hours). However, *Stena Line* decided in 1982 to switch the first vessel, the KRONPRINSESSAN VICTORIA (now the STENA EUROPE of *Stena Line AB*), to their Gothenburg – Kiel (Germany) route since their own new tonnage for this route, being built in Poland, had been substantially delayed. She was modified to make her more suitable for this overnight route. Work on the second vessel – provisionally called the DROTTNING SILVIA – was suspended for a time but she was eventually delivered, as designed, in late 1982 and introduced onto the Gothenburg – Frederikshavn route on a temporary basis pending delivery of new *Stena Line* ordered vessels. She was named the PRINSESSAN BIRGITTA, the existing ex *Sessan Linjen* vessel of the same name being renamed the STENA SCANDINAVICA. In early 1983 she was substantially modified in a similar way to her sister. In June 1983 she was renamed the ST NICHOLAS, re-registered in Great Britain and entered service on five year charter to *Sealink UK* on the Harwich – Hoek van Holland route. In 1988 she was purchased and re-registered in The Bahamas. In 1989 she was sold to *Rederi AB Gotland* of Sweden and then chartered back. In 1991 she was renamed the STENA NORMANDY and inaugurated a new service between Southampton and Cherbourg. She was withdrawn in December 1996, returned to *Rederi AB Gotland* and renamed the NORMANDY. In 1997 she was chartered to *Tallink* and operated between Helsinki and Tallinn; this charter ended at the end of the year. In 1998 she was chartered to *Irish Ferries*. She briefly operated between Rosslare and Pembroke Dock before switching to the their French services. In 1999 she was purchased by *Irish Ferries*. She also operates between Rosslare and Pembroke Dock when the regular vessel is away on overhaul.

ULYSSES Built at Rauma, Finland for *Irish Ferries* for the Dublin – Holyhead service.

ISLE OF MAN STEAM PACKET COMPANY

THE COMPANY The *Isle of Man Steam Packet Company Limited*, trading as *Steam Packet Company*, is an Isle of Man registered company owned by *Montagu Private Equity Limited* of the UK. It was purchased from *Sea Containers Ferries Ltd* in 2003.

MANAGEMENT Managing Director Hamish Ross, **Operations Director** Mark Woodward.

ADDRESS Imperial Buildings, Douglas, Isle of Man IM1 2BY.

TELEPHONE Administration +44 (0)1624 645645, **Reservations** *From UK* 08705 523523, *From elsewhere* +44 (0)1624 661661.

FAX Administration +44 (0)1624 645609.

INTERNET Email spc@steam-packet.com **Website** www.steam-packet.com *(English)*

ROUTES OPERATED Conventional Ferries *All year* Douglas (Isle of Man) – Heysham (3 hrs 30 mins; *(1,2 (during TT races only))*; up to 2 per day), **Winter only** Douglas – Liverpool (4 hrs; *(2)*; winter), **Fast Ferries** Douglas – Liverpool (2 hrs 30 mins; *(3,4)*; up to 3 per day), Douglas – Belfast

Duke of Scandinavia *(Miles Cowsill)*

SuperSeaCat Two *(Goprdon Hislip)*

FAST AND COMFORTABLE

The only way to cross the Irish Sea.

(2 hrs 45 mins; *(3)*; up to 3 per week), Douglas – Dublin (2 hrs 45 mins; *(3)*; up to 3 per week), Douglas – Heysham (2 hrs; *(3)*; occasional), Liverpool – Dublin; (3 hrs 45 mins; *(4)*; 1/2 per day).

1	BEN-MY-CHREE	12504t	98	19.0k	124.9m	500P	-	90T	A	IM
2	LADY OF MANN	4482t	76	21.0k	104.5m	800P	130C	0T	S	IM
3»	SEACAT ISLE OF MAN	3003t	91	37.0k	74.3m	500P	80C	-	BA	UK
4»	SUPERSEACAT TWO	4462t	97	38.0k	100.0m	782P	175C	-	A	UK

BEN-MY-CHREE Built at Krimpen aan den IJssel, Rotterdam for the *IOMSP Co* and operates between Douglas and Heysham. Additional passenger accommodation was added at her Spring 2004 refit.

LADY OF MANN Built at Troon, UK for the *IOMSP Co*. Cars and small vans are side loaded but no ro-ro freight is conveyed. In 1994 replaced by the SEACAT ISLE OF MAN and laid up for sale. She was used in 1995 during the period of the 'TT' motor cycle races between 26th May to 12th June. Later in 1995 she was chartered to *Porto Santo Line* of Madeira for a service from Funchal to Porto Santo. In 1996 she operated throughout the summer, as no SeaCat was chartered. In 1997, she operated for the TT races and then inaugurated a new Liverpool – Dublin service in June, with a weekly Fleetwood – Douglas service until replaced by the SUPERSEACAT TWO in March 1998. In summer 1998, 2000, 2002 and 2003 she operated during the TT race period, plus a number of special cruises and was then chartered to *Acor Line* for service in the Azores. In 2001 the TT was cancelled, as were her extra sailings and cruises, but the charter went ahead. During winter 1998/99 she provided back-up to the fast ferries on the Liverpool – Dublin and Douglas – Liverpool routes. Between November 2000 and February 2001 she operated on the Liverpool – Douglas route and this was repeated between and the same periods 2001/2, 2002/3 and 2003/4. In summer 2002 she was again chartered to *Acor Line*. This was repeated in 2003 and is likely to happen again in 2004.

SEACAT ISLE OF MAN InCat 74m catamaran built at Hobart, Tasmania, Australia. Built as the HOVERSPEED FRANCE, the second SeaCat. She inaugurated Dover – Calais/Boulogne service in 1991. In 1992 she was chartered to *Sardinia Express* of Italy and renamed the SARDEGNA EXPRESS; she did not operate on the Channel that year. This charter was terminated at the end of 1992 and in 1993 she was renamed the SEACAT BOULOGNE and operated on the Dover – Calais and Folkestone – Boulogne services. In 1994 she was chartered to *IOMSP Co*, renamed the SEACAT ISLE OF MAN and replaced the LADY OF MANN on services between Douglas (Isle of Man) and Britain and Ireland. During winter 1994/5 operated for *SeaCat Scotland* between Stranraer and Belfast. She returned to *IOMSP Co* in June 1995. During spring 1995 she was chartered to *Condor Ferries*; she then was chartered again to *IOMSP Co* and returned to *Sea Containers* in the autumn. In 1996 she was chartered to *ColorSeaCat KS*, renamed the SEACAT NORGE and inaugurated a new service between Langesund (Norway) and Frederikshavn (Denmark). During winter 1996/97 she operated between Dover and Calais. In early 1997 she was again renamed the SEACAT ISLE OF MAN. During summer 1997 she operated for *IOMSP Co*, serving on Liverpool, Dublin and Belfast seasonal services to Douglas (May to September) plus a weekly Liverpool – Dublin service when the LADY OF MANN operated from Fleetwood. In late 1997 she was transferred to the *Hoverspeed* Dover – Calais route and operated on this route throughout 1998. In 1999 she operated between Douglas and Liverpool and Douglas and Dublin for *IOMSP Co*. In 2000, 2001 and 2002 she also operated between Douglas and Belfast and Douglas and Heysham (plus provide some additional sailings between Liverpool and Dublin in 2002). In early 2003 she replaced the SEACAT SCOTLAND on the Belfast – Troon service. Returned to Isle of Man services in March 2003. In 2003 transferred to the *IOMSP Co*.

SUPERSEACAT TWO Fincantieri MDV1200 monohull vessel built at Riva Trigoso, Italy. Built for *Sea Containers*. In 1997 operated on the *Hoverspeed* Dover – Calais route. She was withdrawn from this route at the end of 1997 and in March 1998, she inaugurated a Liverpool – Dublin fast ferry service, operated by *IOMSP Co*. In summer 1999 she operated for *Hoverspeed* between Newhaven and Dieppe. In 2000 she returned to the Irish Sea, operating on the Belfast – Heysham service. In summer 2001 she operated between Dover and Calais and Dover and Ostend. In 2002 she was laid up for sale or charter. Since 2003 she has been on charter to the *IOMSP Co*, operating on the Liverpool and Douglas and Liverpool and Dublin services.

NORFOLKLINE

THE COMPANY *Norfolkline* (before 1st January 1999 *Norfolk Line*) is a Dutch private sector company owned by *A P Møller Finance* of Denmark.

MANAGEMENT Managing Director Thomas Woldbye, **Deputy Managing Director** J Al-Erhayem, **Director Ferry Division** Kell Robdrup, **Manager Dover-Dunkerque** Wayne Bullen, **Manager Scheveningen-Felixstowe** Marc Lagrand.

ADDRESS *Netherlands* Kranenburgweg 180, 2583 ER Scheveningen, Netherlands. *UK* Norfolk House, The Dock, Felixstowe, Suffolk IP11 8UY, *Dover* Export Freight Plaza, Eastern Docks, Dover, Kent CT16 1JA.

TELEPHONE Administration *Netherlands* +31 (0)70 352 74 00, *UK* +44 (0)1394 673676, **Reservations** +44 (0)1304 225151.

FAX Administration & Reservations *Netherlands* +31 (0)70 352 74 35, *Felixstowe* +44 (0)1394 603673, *Dover* +44 (0)1304 208517.

INTERNET Email info@norfolkline.com   dover@norfolkline.com   dunkerque@norfolkline.com **Website** www.norfolkline.com *(English)*

ROUTE OPERATED Dover – Dunkerque (France) (2 hrs; *(1,2,3)*; up to 10 per day).

1	DAWN MERCHANT	22152t	98	22.5k	180.0m	250P	-	144T	BA	UK
2	MIDNIGHT MERCHANT	22152t	00	22.5k	180.0m	300P	-	144T	BA2	UK
3	NORTHERN MERCHANT	22152t	00	22.5k	180.0m	250P	-	144T	BA2	UK

DAWN MERCHANT Built at Seville, Spain for parent company *Cenargo* and chartered to *Merchant Ferries*. On delivery in autumn 1998, chartered to *UND RoRo Isletmeri* of Turkey to operate between Istanbul and Trieste. Returned to *Merchant Ferries* in late 1998 and in February 1999, inaugurated a new service between Liverpool and Dublin. In 2002 chartered to *Norfolkline*.

MIDNIGHT MERCHANT Built at Seville, Spain for *Cenargo* (owners of *NorseMerchant Ferries*). On delivery, chartered to *Norfolkline* to operate as second vessel on the Dover – Dunkerque (Ouest) service. In 2002 modified to allow two deck loading.

NORTHERN MERCHANT Built at Seville, Spain for *Cenargo* (owners of *NorseMerchant Ferries*). On delivery, chartered to *Norfolkline* to inaugurate a Dover – Dunkerque (Ouest) service in March 2000. In 2002 modified to allow two deck loading.

Under Construction

4	MAERSK DOVER	34500t	05	25.0k	187.0m	780P	200C	120L	BA2	UK
5	MAERSK DUNKERQUE	34500t	05	25.0k	187.0m	780P	200C	120L	BA2	UK
6	NEWBUILDING 3	34500t	06	25.0k	187.0m	780P	200C	120L	BA2	UK

MAERSK DOVER, MAERSK DUNKERQUE, NEWBUILDING 3 Under construction at Ulsan, South Korea for *Norfolkline* to operate between Dover and Dunkerque. Journey time will reduce to 1 hr 50 mins.

NORSEMERCHANT FERRIES

THE COMPANY *NorseMerchant Ferries* is a British private sector company, owned by *Norse Merchant Group Limited*. In 1999 the operations of *Belfast Freight Ferries* were integrated into *Merchant Ferries plc* and *Norse Irish Ferries Ltd* was acquired. In January 2001 *Merchant Ferries plc* and *Norse Irish Ferries Ltd* started trading as *NorseMerchant Ferries*.

MANAGEMENT CEO Norse Merchant Group Derek Sloan, **Managing Director** Philip Shepherd, **Freight Sales Director** Declan Cleary.

ADDRESS Twelve Quays Terminal, BIRKENHEAD, Merseyside.

TELEPHONE *Administration* +44 (0)151 906 2700, *Reservations UK* 08706 004321, *Irish Republic* +353 (0)1 819 2999.

FAX Administration +44 (0)28 9078 1599.

INTERNET Email enquiries@norsemerchant.com **Website** www.norsemerchant.com *(English)*

ROUTES OPERATED Port of Liverpool (Twelve Quays River Terminal, Birkenhead) – Belfast (8 hrs; *(2,3)*; 1 per day (Sun, Mon), 2 per day (Tue-Sat)). Port of Liverpool (Twelve Quays River Terminal, Birkenhead) – Dublin (8 hrs; *(1)*; 1 per day (other daily service currently operated by freight only vessel)). *NorseMerchant Ferries* also operate a freight-only services between Heysham and Dublin and Heysham and Belfast; see Section 3.

1	BRAVE MERCHANT	22046t	98	22.5k	180.0m	250P	-	144T	BA	UK
2	LAGAN VIKING	21856t	97	24.0k	186.0m	340P	100C	170T	A	IT
3	MERSEY VIKING	21856t	97	24.0k	186.0m	340P	100C	170T	A	IT

BRAVE MERCHANT Built at Seville, Spain for parent company *Cenargo* and chartered to *Merchant Ferries*. In February 1999 she inaugurated a new service between Liverpool and Dublin. In 2003 chartered to the *British MoD* to convey equipment to the Persian Gulf. In autumn 2003 returned to the Liverpool – Dublin route but no longer conveying passengers – only freight drivers. Passenger service restored March 2004.

LAGAN VIKING, MERSEY VIKING Built at Donada, Italy for *Levantina Trasporti* of Italy and chartered to *Norse Irish Ferries*, operating between Liverpool and Belfast. to In 1999 charter was taken over by *Merchant Ferries*. Purchased by *NorseMerchant Ferries* in 2001. In 2002 service transferred to Twelve Quays River Terminal, Birkenhead.

P&O FERRIES

THE COMPANY *P&O Ferries Ltd* is a private sector company, a subsidiary of the *Peninsular and Oriental Steam Navigation Company* of Great Britain. In autumn 2002 *P&O North Sea Ferries*, *P&O Portsmouth* and *P&O Stena Line* (*Stena Line* involvement having ceased) were merged into a single operation.

MANAGEMENT Managing Director Russ Peters, **Commercial Director Tourist Services** John Govett, **Communications Director** Chris Laming, **Commercial Director Freight Services** Brian Cork.

ADDRESSES *Head Office and Dover Services* Channel House, Channel View Road, Dover, Kent CT17 9TJ, *Portsmouth* Peninsular House, Wharf Road, Portsmouth PO2 8TA, *Hull* King George Dock, Hedon Road, Hull HU9 5QA, *Rotterdam* Beneluxhaven, Rotterdam (Europoort), Postbus 1123, NL-3180 Rozenburg, Netherlands, *Zeebrugge* Leopold II Dam 13, Havendam, B-8380 Zeebrugge, Belgium.

TELEPHONE Administration *UK* +44 (0)1304 863000, **Reservations** *Passenger* *UK* 08705 202020, *France* +33 (0)1 55 69 82 28, *Belgium* +32 (0)2 710 6444, *Netherlands* +31 (0)20 20 13333, *Spain* +34 (0)91 270 2332,

Freight (Dover) +44 (0)1304 863344.

FAX *UK Passenger* +44 (0)1304 863464, **Telex** 965104, *Freight (Dover)* +44 (0)1304 862577, **Telex** 96316. *Netherlands* +31 (0)118 1225 5215, *Belgium* +32 (0)50 54 71 12.

INTERNET Email customer.services@poferries.com **Website** www.poferries.com *(English)*

ROUTES OPERATED Dover – Calais (1 hr 15 mins – 1 hr 30 mins; *(3,6,7,8,10,12,15)*; up to 30 per day), Hull – Zeebrugge (Belgium) (from 12 hrs 30 mins; *(5,17)*; 1 per day), Hull – Rotterdam (Beneluxhaven, Europoort) (Netherlands) (from 10 hrs; *(11,16)*; 1 per day), Portsmouth – Cherbourg (from 4 hrs 45 mins up to 5 hrs 30 mins; *(4,9 (4 once weekly))*; 2 per day), Portsmouth – Le Havre (from 5 hrs 30 mins (day) up to 8 hrs (night); *(13,14)*; 2 day crossings, one night crossing per day), Portsmouth – Bilbao (Santurzi) (35 hrs (UK – Spain), 29 hrs (Spain – UK); *(5)*; 2 per week). **Fast Ferries** *Summer only* Portsmouth – Cherbourg (2 hrs 45 mins; *(1)*; 2 per day), Portsmouth – Caen (2 hrs 45 mins; *(2)*; 2 per day),

Pride of Calais *(Miles Cowsill)*

Pride of Le Havre *(Miles Cowsill)*

1»	EXPRESS	5902t	98	41.0k	91.3m	920P	225C	-	A	BS
2»	MAX MOLS	5617t	98	43.0k	91.3m	800P	220C	-	A	DK
3	PRIDE OF AQUITAINE	28833t	91	21.0k	163.6m	2000P	600C	100L	BA2	UK
4	PRIDE OF BILBAO	37583t	86	22.0k	177.0m	2553P	600C	77T	BA	UK
5	PRIDE OF BRUGES	31598t	87	18.5k	179.0m	1000P	850C	166T	A	NL
6	PRIDE OF BURGUNDY	28138t	93	21.0k	179.7m	1420P	600C	120L	BA2	UK
7	PRIDE OF CALAIS	26433t	87	22.0k	169.6m	2290P	650C	100L	BA2	UK
8	PRIDE OF CANTERBURY	30365t	92	21.0k	179.7m	2000P	650C	120L	BA2	UK
9	PRIDE OF CHERBOURG	22635t	95	22.0k	181.6m	1650P	600C	130T	BA	UK
10	PRIDE OF DOVER	26433t	87	22.0k	163.5m	2290P	650C	100L	BA2	UK
11	PRIDE OF HULL	59925t	01	22.0k	215.1m	1360P	250C	240T	AS	UK
12	PRIDE OF KENT	30635t	92	21.0k	179.7m	2000P	650C	120L	BA2	UK
13	PRIDE OF LE HAVRE	33336t	89	21.0k	161.2m	1600P	575C	91T	BA	UK
14	PRIDE OF PORTSMOUTH	33336t	90	21.0k	161.2m	1600P	575C	91T	BA	UK
15	PRIDE OF PROVENCE	28559t	83	19.0k	154.9m	2036P	550C	85L	BA2	UK
16	PRIDE OF ROTTERDAM	59925t	01	22.0k	215.1m	1360P	250C	240T	AS	NL
17	PRIDE OF YORK	31785t	87	18.5k	179.0m	1000P	850C	166T	A	UK

EXPRESS InCat 91m catamaran. Built at Hobart, Australia for *Buquebus* of Argentina as the CATALONIA 1 and used by *Buquebus España* on their service between Barcelona (Spain) and Mallorca. In April 2000 chartered to *P&O Portsmouth* and renamed the PORTSMOUTH EXPRESS. During winter 2000/2001 she operated for *Buquebus* between Buenos Aires (Argentina) and Piriapolis (Uruguay) and was renamed the CATALONIA. Returned to *P&O Portsmouth* in spring 2001 and was renamed the PORTSMOUTH EXPRESS. Returned to *Buquebus* in autumn 2001 and then returned to *P&O Portsmouth* in spring 2002. Laid up during winter 2002/3 and renamed the CATALONIA. Returned to *P&O Ferries* in spring 2003 operating under the marketing name 'Express'. In November 2003 renamed the EXPRESS. In 2004 she will operate as the 'Cherbourg Express'.

MAX MOLS InCat 91 metre catamaran, built speculatively at Hobart, Tasmania, Australia. In spring 1998, following *InCat's* acquisition of a 50% share in *Scandlines Cat-Link A/S, She* was sold to that company and named the CAT-LINK IV. In 1999 purchased by *Mols-Linien* and renamed the MAX MOLS. In 2000 chartered to *Marine Atlantic* of Canada to operate between Port aux Basques (Newfoundland) and North Sydney (Nova Scotia). Returned to *Mols-Linien* in autumn 2000. In summer 2002 chartered to *Riga Sea Lines* to operate between Riga and Nynäshamn. Returned to *Mols-Linien* in autumn 2002. In 2004 chartered to *P&O Ferries* to operate between Portsmouth and Caen. Operates under the marketing name, the 'Caen Express'.

PRIDE OF AQUITAINE Built at Temse, Belgium as the PRINS FILIP for *Regie voor Maritiem Transport (RMT)* of Belgium for the Ostend – Dover service. Although completed in 1991, she did not enter service until May 1992. In 1994 the British port became Ramsgate. Withdrawn in 1997 and laid up for sale. In 1998 she was sold to *Stena RoRo* and renamed the STENA ROYAL. In November 1998 she was chartered to *P&O Stena Line* to operate as a freight only vessel on the Dover – Zeebrugge route. In spring 1999 it was decided to charter the vessel on a long term basis and she was repainted into *P&O Stena Line* colours and renamed the P&OSL AQUITAINE. In autumn 1999 she was modified to make her suitable to operate between Dover and Calais and was transferred to that route, becoming a passenger vessel again. In 2002 renamed the PO AQUITAINE and in 2003 the PRIDE OF AQUITAINE.

PRIDE OF BILBAO Built at Turku, Finland as the OLYMPIA for *Rederi AB Slite* of Sweden for *Viking Line* service between Stockholm and Helsinki. In 1993 she was chartered to *P&O European Ferries* to inaugurate a new service between Portsmouth and Bilbao. During the summer period she also operates, at weekends, a round trip between Portsmouth and Cherbourg. In 1994 she was purchased by the *Irish Continental Group* and re-registered in the Bahamas. *P&O* have since entered her into the British bareboat register. In 2002 her charter was extended for a further five years.

PRIDE OF BRUGES Built as the NORSUN at Tsurumi, Japan for the Hull – Rotterdam service of *North Sea Ferries*. She was owned by *Nedlloyd* and was sold to *P&O* in 1996 but retains Dutch crew and registry. In May 2001 replaced by the PRIDE OF ROTTERDAM and in July 2001, after a major refurbishment, she was transferred to the Hull – Zeebrugge service, replacing the NORSTAR (26919t, 1974). In 2003 renamed the PRIDE OF BRUGES.

PRIDE OF BURGUNDY Built at Bremerhaven, Germany for *P&O European Ferries* for the Dover – Calais service. When construction started she was due to be a sister vessel to the EUROPEAN HIGHWAY, EUROPEAN PATHWAY and EUROPEAN SEAWAY (see Section 3) called the EUROPEAN CAUSEWAY and operate on the Zeebrugge freight route. However, it was decided that she should be completed as a passenger/freight vessel (the design allowed for conversion) and she was launched as the PRIDE OF BURGUNDY. In 1998, transferred to *P&O Stena Line*. In 1998 renamed the P&OSL BURGUNDY. In 2002 renamed the PO BURGUNDY and in 2003 renamed the PRIDE OF BURGUNDY. In 2004 to operate in freight-only mode although may operate in passenger mode during 2004/5 overhaul period..

PRIDE OF CALAIS Built at Bremerhaven, Germany for *European Ferries* as the PRIDE OF CALAIS for the Dover – Calais service. In 1998, transferred to *P&O Stena Line*. In 1999 renamed the P&OSL CALAIS. In 2003 renamed PO CALAIS and in 2003 renamed the PRIDE OF CALAIS.

PRIDE OF CANTERBURY Built at Bremerhaven, Germany for *P&O European Ferries* as the EUROPEAN PATHWAY for the Dover – Zeebrugge freight service. (Sister vessel EUROPEAN SEAWAY is shown in Section 3). In 1998 transferred to *P&O Stena Line*. In 2001 car/foot passengers were again conveyed on the route. In 2002/3 rebuilt as a full passenger vessel and renamed the PRIDE OF CANTERBURY; now operates between Dover and Calais.

PRIDE OF CHERBOURG Built at Krimpen aan den IJssel, Rotterdam as the ISLE OF INNISFREE for *Irish Ferries* to operate on the Holyhead – Dublin service. In 1997 transferred to the Rosslare – Pembroke Dock service; for a short period, before modifications at Pembroke Dock were completed, she operated between Rosslare and Fishguard. In spring 2001 she was replaced by the ISLE OF INISHMORE and laid up. In July 2002 she was chartered to *P&O Portsmouth* for 5 years and renamed the PRIDE OF CHERBOURG. Entered service in October 2002.

PRIDE OF DOVER Built at Bremerhaven, Germany for *European Ferries* as the PRIDE OF DOVER for the Dover – Calais service. In 1998, transferred to *P&O Stena Line*. In 1999 renamed the P&OSL DOVER. In 1999 renamed the P&OSL CALAIS. In 2002 renamed PO DOVER and in 2003 renamed the PRIDE OF DOVER.

PRIDE OF HULL Built at Venice, Italy for *P&O North Sea Ferries* to replace (with the PRIDE OF ROTTERDAM) the NORSEA and NORSUN plus the freight vessels NORBAY and NORBANK on the Hull – Rotterdam service.

PRIDE OF KENT Built at Bremerhaven, Germany for *P&O European Ferries* as the EUROPEAN HIGHWAY for the Dover – Zeebrugge freight service. In 1998 transferred to *P&O Stena Line*. In summer 1999 she operated full time between Dover and Calais. She returned to the Dover – Zeebrugge route in the autumn when the P&OSL AQUITAINE was transferred to the Dover – Calais service. In 2001 car/foot passengers were again conveyed on the route. In 2002/3 rebuilt as a full passenger vessel and renamed the PRIDE OF KENT; now operates between Dover and Calais.

PRIDE OF LE HAVRE, PRIDE OF PORTSMOUTH Built at Bremerhaven, Germany as the OLAU HOLLANDIA and OLAU BRITANNIA for *TT-Line* of Germany, to operate for associated company *Olau Line*. In 1994 chartered to *P&O European Ferries*, re-registered in the UK and renamed the PRIDE OF LE HAVRE and PRIDE OF PORTSMOUTH. After a brief period on the Portsmouth – Cherbourg service became a regular vessels on the Portsmouth – Le Havre service from June 1994.

PRIDE OF PROVENCE Built at Dunkerque, France as the STENA JUTLANDICA for *Stena Line* for the Gothenburg – Frederikshavn service. In 1996 she was transferred to the Dover – Calais route and renamed the STENA EMPEREUR. In 1998, transferred to *P&O Stena Line*. Later in 1998 renamed the P&OSL PROVENCE. In 2002 renamed the PO PROVENCE and in 2003 renamed the PRIDE OF PROVENCE.

PRIDE OF ROTTERDAM Built at Venice, Italy. Keel laid as the PRIDE OF HULL but launched as the PRIDE OF ROTTERDAM. Further details as the PRIDE OF HULL.

Max Mols as the **Caen Express** *(Miles Cowsill)*

SeaFrance Manet *(Miles Cowsill)*

PRIDE OF YORK Built as the NORSEA at Glasgow, UK for the Hull – Rotterdam service of *North Sea Ferries* (jointly owned by *P&O* and *The Royal Nedlloyd Group* of The Netherlands until 1996). In December 2001, she was replaced by the new PRIDE OF HULL and, after a two month refurbishment, in 2002 transferred to the Hull – Zeebrugge service, replacing the NORLAND (26290t, 1974). In 2003 renamed the PRIDE OF YORK.

P&O IRISH SEA

THE COMPANY *P&O Irish Sea* is the trading name of *P&O European Ferries (Irish Sea) Ltd*, a British private sector company and a subsidiary of the *Peninsular and Oriental Steam Navigation Company*. It was formed in 1998 by the merger of the shipping activities *Pandoro Ltd* and the Cairnryan – Larne services of *P&O European Ferries (Felixstowe) Ltd*.

MANAGEMENT Chairman Russ Peters, **Managing Director** J H Kearsley, **Passenger Services – Sales and Marketing Manager** James Esler.

ADDRESS Compass House, Dock Street, Fleetwood, Lancashire FY7 6HP.

TELEPHONE Administration +44 (0)1253 615700, **Reservations UK** 08702 424777, *Irish Republic* 1 800 409 049.

FAX Administration & Reservations +44 (0)1253 615740.

INTERNET Website www.poirishsea.com *(English)*

ROUTES OPERATED Conventional Ferries Cairnryan – Larne (1 hr 45 min; *(1,2)*; 7 per day). **Fast Ferry** (April – September) Cairnryan – Larne (1 hr; *(3)*; 2 per day), Troon – Larne (1 hr 49 min; *(3)*; 2 per day). Passengers are also conveyed on the Liverpool – Dublin freight service – see Section 3.

1	EUROPEAN CAUSEWAY	20800t	00	23.0k	159.5m	410P	375C	107T	BA2	BS
2	EUROPEAN HIGHLANDER	20800t	02	23.0k	159.5m	410P	375C	107T	BA2	BS
3»	SUPERSTAR EXPRESS	5517t	97	36.0k	82.3m	900P	175C	-	A	BS

EUROPEAN CAUSEWAY Built at Shimonoeki, Japan for *P&O Irish Sea* for the Cairnryan – Larne service.

EUROPEAN HIGHLANDER Built at Shimonoeki, Japan for *P&O Irish Sea* for the Cairnryan – Larne service.

SUPERSTAR EXPRESS Austal Ships 82 catamaran, built at Fremantle, Australia for *Star Cruises* of Malaysia for their service between Butterworth and Langkawi. Built as the SUPERSTAR EXPRESS, she was renamed the SUPERSTAR EXPRESS LANGKAWI later in 1997. She was due, in 1998, to circumnavigate the world and to seek to take the Hales Trophy from HOVERSPEED GREAT BRITAIN. However, these plans did not materialise and instead she was chartered to *P&O European Ferries (Portsmouth)* and placed on the Portsmouth – Cherbourg route. She resumed the name SUPERSTAR EXPRESS. In April 2000 she was transferred to *P&O Irish Sea*. She is chartered during the summer period. In 2003 began a Larne – Troon service.

SEA CONTAINERS FERRIES

THE COMPANY *Sea Containers Ferries Ltd* is a British private sector company, part of the *Sea Containers Group*.

MANAGEMENT Senior Vice President, Passenger Transport David Benson.

ADDRESS Sea Containers House, 20 Upper Ground, London SE1 9PF.

TELEPHONE Administration +44 (0)20 7805 5000.

FAX Administration +44 (0)20 7805 5900.

INTERNET Email info@seacontainers.com **Website** www.seacontainers.com *(English)*

Ferry services in the UK are operated through two subsidiaries – *Hoverspeed Ltd* and *Sea Containers Ferries Scotland Ltd* (trading as *SeaCat*). See also *Silja Line* in Section 6.

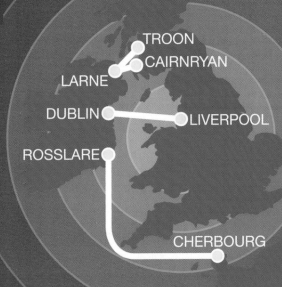

HOVERSPEED

THE COMPANY *Hoverspeed Ltd* is a British private sector company. It was formed in October 1981 by the merger of *Seaspeed*, a wholly owned subsidiary of the *British Railways Board*, operating between Dover and Calais and Dover and Boulogne and *Hoverlloyd*, a subsidiary of *Broström AB* of Sweden, operating between Ramsgate (Pegwell Bay) and Calais. The Ramsgate – Calais service ceased after summer 1982. In early 1984 the company was sold by its joint owners to a management consortium. In 1986 the company was acquired by *Sea Containers*.

MANAGEMENT Managing Director Geoffrey Ede.

ADDRESS The International Hoverport, Marine Parade, DOVER, Kent CT17 9TG.

TELEPHONE Administration +44 (0)1304 865000, **Reservations** 08705 240241 (from UK only).

FAX Administration +44 (0)1304 865087, **Reservations** +44 (0)1304 240088.

INTERNET Email info@hoverspeed.co.uk **Website** www.hoverspeed.co.uk *(English)*

ROUTES OPERATED *March-December* Dover – Calais (55 mins; *(1,4*,5)*; up to 15 per day), *April-October* Newhaven – Dieppe (2 hrs; *(6)*; up to 3 per day). *subject to confirmation.

SEA CONTAINERS FERRIES SCOTLAND

THE COMPANY *Sea Containers Ferries Scotland Ltd* is a subsidiary of *Sea Containers Ferries Ltd*. The service is operated under contract by the *Isle of Man Steam Packet Company*.

MANAGEMENT Chief Operating Manager John Burrows, **General Manager, Sales and Marketing**, Diane Poole.

ADDRESS SeaCat Terminal, Troon Harbour, Troon, Ayrshire KA10 6DX.

TELEPHONE Administration +44 (0)1292 319103, **Reservations** *From UK* 08705 523523, *From elsewhere* +44 (0)28 9031 3543.

FAX Administration +44 (0)1292 319108.

INTERNET Email spc@steam-packet.com **Website** www.seacat.co.uk *(English)*

ROUTES OPERATED Troon – Belfast (2 hrs 30 mins; *(3)*; 3 per day).

1»	DIAMANT	3454t	96	37.0k	81.1m	654P	140C	-	A	BS
2»	PESCARA JET	3003t	91	37.0k	74.3m	432P	80C	-	BA	PA
3»	RAPIDE	4112t	96	37.0k	81.1m	654P	140C	-	A	LX
4»•	SEACAT FRANCE	3012t	90	35.0k	74.3m	350P	80C	-	BA	BS
5»	SEACAT SCOTLAND	3003t	91	37.0k	74.3m	450P	80C	-	BA	UK
6»	SUPERSEACAT ONE	4462t	97	38.0k	100.0m	782P	175C	-	BA	IT
7»•	THE PRINCESS ANNE	-	69	50.0k	56.4m	360P	55C	-	BA	UK
8»•	THE PRINCESS MARGARET	-	68	50.0k	56.4m	360P	55C	-	BA	UK

DIAMANT InCat 81m catamaran built at Hobart, Tasmania, Australia. Ordered by *Del Bene SA* of Argentina. In 1996, before completion, purchased by the *Holyman Group* of Australia and named the HOLYMAN EXPRESS. In 1997 she was renamed the HOLYMAN DIAMANT, transferred to *Holyman Sally Ferries* and in March was introduced onto the Ramsgate – Ostend route. In March 1998 transferred to the Dover – Ostend route, operating for the *Hoverspeed – Holyman (UK)* joint venture, and renamed the DIAMANT. In 1999 this became a 100% *Hoverspeed* operation and in 2000 *Sea Containers* purchased her. During winter 1999/2000 she also operated between Dover and Calais at times. During summer 2001 she operated between Newhaven and Dieppe; in summer 2002 she operated between Dover and Ostend and Dover and Calais. In summer 2003 replaced the HOVERSPEED GREAT BRITAIN on the Dover – Calais route after a period of lay-up.

PESCARA JET InCat 74m catamaran built at Hobart, Tasmania, Australia. Christened in 1991 as the HOVERSPEED BELGIUM and renamed HOVERSPEED BOULOGNE before leaving the builders yard. She was the third SeaCat, introduced in 1992 to enable a three vessel service to be operated by

Hoverspeed across the Channel, including a new SeaCat route between Folkestone and Boulogne (replacing the *Sealink Stena Line* ferry service which ceased at the end of 1991). With the HOVERSPEED FRANCE (now SEACAT ISLE OF MAN) and the HOVERSPEED GREAT BRITAIN she operated on all three Channel routes (Dover – Calais, Dover – Boulogne and Folkestone – Boulogne). In 1993 she was transferred to *SeaCat AB* and renamed the SEACATAMARAN DANMARK and inaugurated a new high-speed service between Gothenburg and Frederikshavn. For legal reasons it was not possible to call her the SEACAT DANMARK as intended but in 1995 these problems were resolved and she was renamed the SEACAT DANMARK. From January 1996 transferred to the new joint venture company *ColorSeaCat KS*, jointly with *Color Line* of Norway. During winter 1996/97 she operated on the Dover – Calais route. *ColorSeaCat* did not operate in 1997 and she again operated for *SeaCat AB*. In autumn 1997 she replaced the SEACAT SCOTLAND on the Stranraer – Belfast route. During summer 1998, she operated for the *IOMSP Co*. In 1999 operated for *Sea Containers Ferries Scotland* between Belfast and Heysham and Belfast and Douglas. In 2000 she was transferred to *SeaCat AB* to operate between Gothenburg, Frederikshavn and Langesund under the *Silja Line SeaCat* branding. In August 2000 moved to the Dover – Calais service. In 2004 transferred to a *SNAV/Sea Containers* joint venture between Pescara (Italy) and Split (Croatia) and renamed PESCARA JET.

RAPIDE InCat 81m catamaran built at Hobart, Tasmania, Australia. Built for the *Holyman Group* as the CONDOR 12. In summer 1996 operated by *Condor Ferries* (at that time part owned by the *Holyman Group*). In 1997 she was renamed the HOLYMAN RAPIDE, transferred to *Holyman Sally Ferries* and in March was introduced onto the Ramsgate – Ostend route. In March 1998 transferred to the Dover – Ostend route, operating for the *Hoverspeed – Holyman (UK)* joint venture, and renamed the RAPIDE. In 1999 this became a 100% *Hoverspeed* operation and in 2000 *Sea Containers* purchased her. During winter 1999/2000 she also operated between Dover and Calais at times. In summer 2001, she operated between Liverpool and Dublin and Liverpool and Douglas; in summer 2002 she operated between Heysham and Belfast. In 2003 she operated between Troon and Belfast. From 2003 she has been managed by the *Isle of Man Steam Packet Company*.

SEACAT FRANCE Built at Hobart, Tasmania as the SEACAT TASMANIA for *Sea Containers* subsidiary *Tasmanian Ferry Services* of Australia to operate between George Town (Tasmania) and Port Welshpool (Victoria). In 1992 chartered to *Hoverspeed* to operate Dover – Calais and Folkestone – Boulogne services. Returned to Australia after the 1992 summer season but returned to Britain in summer 1993 to operate Dover – Calais and Folkestone – Boulogne services during the summer. She was repainted into *Hoverspeed* livery and renamed the SEACAT CALAIS. In 1994 chartered for five years (with a purchase option) to *Navegacion Atlantida* for *Ferry Linas Argentinas AS* of Uruguay service between Montevideo (Uruguay) – Buenos Aires (Argentina) service and renamed the ATLANTIC II. The purchase option was not taken up and in 1999 she was returned to *Sea Containers* and operated for Hoverspeed between Dover and Calais. In 2000 she was chartered to *SNAV Aliscafi* of Italy to operate between Ancona (Italy) and Split (Croatia) in a joint venture with *Sea Containers* and renamed the CROATIA JET. This operation was repeated in 2001. In 2002 renamed the SEACAT FRANCE and transferred to operate between Dover and Calais. At the end of the 2002 summer period laid up for sale or charter in Birkenhead. Due to operate Dover-Calais in 2004.

SEACAT SCOTLAND InCat 74m catamaran built at Hobart, Tasmania, Australia, the fifth SeaCat to be constructed. In 1992 she inaugurated a new high-speed car and passenger service for *SeaCat Scotland* on the Stranraer – Belfast route. In autumn 1994 she was chartered to *Q-Ships* of Qatar for services between Doha (Qatar) and Bahrain and Dubai and renamed the Q-SHIP EXPRESS. In spring 1995 she returned to the Stranraer – Belfast service and resumed the name SEACAT SCOTLAND. In autumn 1997 chartered to *Navegacion Atlantida SA* of Uruguay for service between Colonia (Uruguay) and Buenos Aires (Argentina). She returned to the UK in spring 1998 and operated on to the Stranraer – Belfast route. In 1999 and 2000 she operated for *Sea Containers Ferries Scotland* between Stranraer and Belfast (service now ended) and Troon and Belfast. This was repeated in 2001 and 2002. In 2003 to operate between Dover and Calais.

SUPERSEACAT ONE Fincantieri MDV1200 monohull vessel built at La Spézia, Italy. Built for *Sea Containers*. Between 1997 and 1999 operated for *SeaCat AB* on the Gothenburg – Frederikshavn route. In 2000 transferred to *Hoverspeed* to operate on the Newhaven – Dieppe service. In summer

2001 she operated between Dover and Ostend and Dover and Calais. Since 2002 she has operated on the summer service between Newhaven and Dieppe.

THE PRINCESS ANNE, THE PRINCESS MARGARET British Hovercraft Corporation SRN4 type hovercraft built at Cowes, UK for *Seaspeed*. Built at to Mark I specification. In 1978/1979 respectively lengthened to Mark III specification. They underwent complete refurbishment at the beginning of 1999. Withdrawn 2000 and laid up at the Hovercraft Museum at Lee on Solent.

SEAFRANCE

THE COMPANY SeaFrance SA (previously *SNAT* (*Société Nouvelle Armement Transmanche*)) is a French state owned company. It was originally jointly owned by *Société Nationale des Chemins de fer Français* (*French Railways*) and *Compagnie Générale Maritime Français* (*French National Shipping Company*). *SNAT* was established in 1990 to take over the services of *SNCF Armement Naval*, a wholly owned division of *SNCF*. At the same time a similarly constituted body called *Société Proprietaire Navires (SPN)* was established to take over ownership of the vessels; *Sealink British Ferries* (and later *Stena Line Ltd*) also had involvement in this company. Joint operation of services with *Stena Line* ceased at the end of 1995 and *SeaFrance SA* was formed. *Stena Line* involvement in *SPN* ended in 1999. In 2000, *SeaFrance* became 100% owned by *SNCF* (*French Railways*). At the same time, *SeaFrance* absorbed *SPN* and took over the ownership of its vessels.

MANAGEMENT Président du Directoire Eudes Riblier, **Directeur Sealink Calais** Gérard Jachet, **Managing Director (UK)** Robin Wilkins.

ADDRESS *France* 1 Avenue de Flandre, 75019 Paris, France, *UK* Whitfield Court, Honeywood Close, Whitfield, Dover, Kent CT16 3PX.

TELEPHONE Administration *France* +33 1 53 35 11 00, *UK* +44 (0)1304 828300, **Reservations *France*** +33 3 21 46 80 00, , *UK (Passenger)* 08705 711711 (from UK only), *UK (Freight)* +44 (0)1304 203030.

FAX Administration *France* +33 1 53 35 11 76, *UK* +44 (0)1304 828384.

INTERNET Email *France* sfadmin@seafrance.fr *UK* admin@seafrance.fr

Website www.seafrance.com *(English, French)*

ROUTE OPERATED Calais – Dover (1 hr 10 mins – 1 h 30 mins; *(1,2,3,4)*; up to 20 per day).

1	SEAFRANCE CEZANNE	25122t	80	19.5k	163.5m	1800P	600C	66L	BA2	FR
2	SEAFRANCE MANET	15093t	84	18.0k	130.0m	1800P	330C	43L	BA2	FR
3	SEAFRANCE RENOIR	15612t	81	18.0k	130.0m	1600P	330C	43L	BA2	FR
4	SEAFRANCE RODIN	34000t	01	25.0k	185.0m	1900P	700C	133L	BA2	FR

SEAFRANCE CEZANNE Built at Malmö, Sweden as the ARIADNE for *Rederi AB Nordö* of Sweden. Renamed the SOCA before entering service on *UMEF* freight services (but with capacity for 175 drivers) in the Mediterranean. In 1981 she was sold to *SO Mejdunaroden Automobilen Transport (SOMAT)* of Bulgaria and renamed the TRAPEZITZA. She operated on *Medlink* services between Bulgaria and the Middle East. In 1988 she was acquired by *Sealink British Ferries*, re-registered in the Bahamas and in 1989 renamed the FANTASIA. Later in 1989 she was modified in Bremerhaven, renamed the CHANNEL SEAWAY and, in May, she inaugurated a new freight-only service between Dover (Eastern Docks) and Calais. During winter 1989/90 she was modified in Bremerhaven to convert her for passenger service. In spring 1990 she was renamed the FIESTA, transferred to *SNAT*, re-registered in France and replaced the CHAMPS ELYSEES (now the SEAFRANCE MANET) on the Dover – Calais service. In 1996 she was renamed the SEAFRANCE CEZANNE.

SEAFRANCE MANET Built at Nantes, France for *SNCF* as the CHAMPS ELYSEES to operate Calais – Dover and Boulogne – Dover services, later operating Calais – Dover only. In 1990 transferred to the Dieppe – Newhaven service. Chartered to *Stena Sealink Line* in June 1992 when they took over the operation of the service. She was renamed the STENA PARISIEN and carried a French crew. In 1997 the charter was terminated; she returned to *SeaFrance* and was renamed the SEAFRANCE MANET.

SEAFRANCE RENOIR Built at Le Havre, France for *SNCF* as the COTE D'AZUR for the Dover – Calais service. She also operated Boulogne – Dover in 1985. In 1996 she was renamed the SEAFRANCE RENOIR. Following the delivery of the SEAFRANCE RODIN she became the reserve vessel. During summer 2002 she operated her own roster at peak periods with reduced passenger facilities. During summer 2003 she operated a full roster to enable 20 passenger sailings per day to operate. This will happen again in summer 2004.

SEAFRANCE RODIN Built at Rauma, Finland for *SeaFrance*.

Under construction

5	SEAFRANCE BERLIOZ	-	05	25.0k	186.0m	1900P	900C	120L	BA2	FR

SEAFRANCE BERLIOZ Under construction at St Nazaire for *SeaFrance*.

SMYRIL LINE

THE COMPANY *Smyril Line* is a Faroe Islands registered company.

MANAGEMENT Managing Director Niels Kreutzmann, **Financial Manager** Joannes A Vali.

ADDRESS Jonas Bronksgöta 37, PO Box 370, FO-100 Tórshavn, Faroe Islands.

TELEPHONE Administration +298-345900, **Reservations** Faroe Islands +298-345900, *UK* +44 (0)1595 690845 (Smyril Line Shetland).

FAX Administration & Reservations +298-343950.

INTERNET Email office@smyril-line.fo **Website** www.smyril-line.com *(English, Danish, German, Faroese, Icelandic, Norwegian)*

ROUTES OPERATED Tórshavn (Faroes) – Hanstholm (Denmark) (31 hrs; *(1)*; 1 per week), Tórshavn – Lerwick (Shetland) (12 hrs; *(1)*; 1 per week) – Bergen (Norway) (via Lerwick) (24 hrs – 27 hrs 30 mins; *(1)*; 1 per week), Tórshavn – Seydisfjordur (Iceland) (15 hrs – 18 hrs; *(1)*; 1 per week). Note: Lerwick sailings ceased after the 1992 season but resumed in 1998. The service now operates all year round except that Seydisfjordur is not served in the winter.

1	NORRÖNA	36000t	03	21.0k	164.0m	1482P	800C	134T	BA	FA

NORRÖNA Built at Lübeck, Germany for *Smyril Line*, to replace the existing NORRÖNA. Originally due to enter service in summer 2002, start of building was delayed by financing difficulties. Originally to have been built at Flensburg, Germany but delays led to change of shipyard.

SPEEDFERRIES

THE COMPANY *SpeedFerries Ltd* is a UK company wholly owned by *SpeedFerries A/S* of Denmark. Operations started in May 2004.

MANAGEMENT Managing Director Curt Stavis, **Marketing Manager** Marianne Illum.

ADDRESS 209 East Camber Office Building, Eastern Docks, Dover, Kent CT16 1JA.

TELEPHONE Administration +44 (0)1304 203000, **Reservations** +44 (0)1304 203000.

FAX +44 (0)1304 208000.

INTERNET Email mail@speedferries.com **Website** www.speedferries.com *(English)*

ROUTE OPERATED Dover – Boulogne (50 mins; *(1)*; 5 per day).

1	SPEED ONE	5007t	97	45.0k	86.1m	776P	200C	-	A	PL

SPEED ONE InCat 86m catamaran built at Hobart, Tasmania, Australia as the INCAT 045. Chartered to *Transport Tasmania* of Australia and operated between Melbourne (Victoria) and Devonport (Tasmania). In 1999 she was chartered to the *Royal Australian Navy*, renamed the HMAS JERVIS BAY and took part in moving Australian troops from Darwin to Dili (East Timor) as part of the United

Nations operation. She operated over 75 trips between the two points carrying personnel and equipment for the United Nations Transitional Administration in East Timor (UNTAET). The charter ended in Many 2001 and she was renamed the INCAT 045 and laid up. In spring 2003 she was chartered to *Traghetti Isole Sarde (TRIS)* of Italy, rename the WINNER and operated between Genoa and Palau (Sardinia). In autumn 2003 the charter ended, she resumed the name INCAT 045 and was laid up at Portland, Dorset. In 2004 chartered to *SpeedFerries* and renamed the SPEED ONE.

STENA LINE

THE COMPANY *Stena Line Limited* is incorporated in Great Britain and registered in England and Wales. *Stena Line bv* is a Dutch company. The ultimate parent undertaking is *Stena AB* of Sweden.

MANAGEMENT Route Director – Hoek van Holland – Harwich Pim de Lange. **Route Director – Fishguard – Rosslare** Vic Goodwin. **Route Director – Holyhead – Dun Laoghaire/Dublin** Vic Goodwin. **Route Director – Stranraer – Belfast** Alan Gordon.

ADDRESS *UK* Charter House, Park Street, Ashford, Kent TN24 8EX, *Netherlands* PO Box 2, 3150 AA, Hoek van Holland, Netherlands. **Note** The Ashford office is to close later in 2004; most functions will transfer to Holyhead.

TELEPHONE Administration *UK* +44 (0)1233 647022, *Netherlands* +31 (0)174 389333, **Reservations** *UK* 08075 707070 (from UK only), *Netherlands* +31 (0)174 315811.

FAX Administration & Reservations *UK* +44 (0)1233 202349, *Netherlands* +31 (0)174 387045, Telex 31272.

INTERNET Email info@stenaline.com **Website** www.stenaline.com *(English, Swedish)*

ROUTES OPERATED Conventional Ferries Stranraer – Belfast (3 hrs 15 mins; *(4)*; 2/3 per day), Holyhead – Dublin (3 hrs 15 mins; *(1)*; 2 per day), Fishguard – Rosslare (3 hrs 30 mins; *(5)*; 2 per day). **Ro-pax Ferries** Harwich – Hoek van Holland (Netherlands) (7 hrs 30 mins; *(3,7)*; 2 per day) (car passengers only conveyed – no foot passengers). **Fast Ferries** Stranraer – Belfast (1 hr 45 mins; *(9)*; up to 5 per day), Holyhead – Dun Laoghaire (1 hr 39 mins; *(6)*; up to 4 per day), Fishguard – Rosslare (Summer Only) (1 hr 50 mins; *(8)*; up to 4 per day), Harwich – Hoek van Holland – (3 hrs 40 mins; *(4)*; 2 per day.

1	STENA ADVENTURER	44000t	03	22.0k	210.8m	1500P	-	250T	BA2	UK
2	STENA BRITANNICA	44000t	02	22.0k	210.8m	900P	-	250T	BA2	UK
3	STENA CALEDONIA	12619t	81	19.5k	129.6m	1000P	280C	56L	BA2	UK
4»	STENA DISCOVERY	19638t	97	40.0k	126.6m	1500P	375C	50L	A	NL
5	STENA EUROPE	24828t	81	19.0k	149.0m	2076P	456C	60T	BA2	UK
6»	STENA EXPLORER	19638t	96	40.0k	126.6m	1500P	375C	50L	A	UK
7	STENA HOLLANDICA	33796t	01	22.0k	188.3m	380P	-	216T	BA	NL
8»	STENA LYNX III	4113t	96	35.0k	81.1m	620P	181C	-	A	UK
9»	STENA VOYAGER	19638t	96	40.0k	126.6m	1500P	375C	50L	A	UK

STENA ADVENTURER Ro-pax vessel built at Ulsan, South Korea, for *Stena RoRo* and chartered to *Stena Line* to operate between Holyhead and Dublin.

STENA BRITANNICA Ro-pax vessel built at Ulsan, South Korea, for *Stena RoRo*. Launched and delivered as the STENA BRITANNICA II. Chartered to *Stena Line* for use on the Hoek van Holland – Harwich service, replacing the 2000 built STENA BRITANNICA, now the FINNFELLOW of *FinnLink*. A month after delivery renamed the STENA BRITANNICA.

STENA CALEDONIA Built at Belfast, UK for *Sealink* as the ST DAVID for the Holyhead – Dun Laoghaire and Fishguard – Rosslare services. It was originally planned that she would replace the chartered STENA NORMANDICA (5607t, 1975) but it was subsequently decided that an additional large vessel was required for the Irish Sea routes. Until 1985 her normal use was, therefore, to substitute for other Irish Sea vessels as necessary (including the Stranraer – Larne route) and also to operate additional summer services on the Holyhead – Dun Laoghaire route. During the spring of 1983 she operated on the Dover – Calais service. From March 1985 she operated between Dover

Stena Line – when you need a shortcut to the world.

With 18 routes around Scandinavia and the UK, Stena Line offers convenient and time efficient shortcuts when travelling in northern Europe. But, travelling with us is more than just getting from A to B. On our ferries it's all about avoiding the usual hassles and instead having a good time onboard. That's why you, after an easy check-in, can enjoy good food, good shopping and relax in a truly maritime environment. No matter how you travel or where you're going, we are there to make sure you are making good time. And arrive refreshed and ready for whatever lies ahead.

www.stenaline.com

Stena Line

Making good time™

and Ostend, a service which ceased in December 1985 with the decision of *RMT* to link up with *Townsend Thoresen*. During the early part of 1986 she operated between Dover and Calais and then moved to the Stranraer – Larne route (later Stranraer – Belfast) where she became a regular vessel. In 1990 she was renamed the STENA CALEDONIA. In September 1996 she became mainly a freight-only vessel but passengers were carried on certain sailings and when the STENA VOYAGER was unavailable; cars and passengers are now conveyed on all sailings.

STENA DISCOVERY Finnyards HSS1500 ('High-speed Sea Service') built at Rauma, Finland for *Stena Line* to replace two vessels on the Harwich – Hoek van Holland service.

STENA EUROPE Built at Gothenburg, Sweden as the KRONPRINSESSAN VICTORIA for *Göteborg-Frederikshavn-Linjen* of Sweden (trading as *Sessan Linjen*) for their Gothenburg – Frederikshavn service. Shortly after delivery, the company was taken over by *Stena Line* and services were marketed as *Stena-Sessan Line* for a period. In 1982 she was converted to an overnight ferry by the conversion of one vehicle deck to two additional decks of cabins and she was switched to the Gothenburg – Kiel route (with, during the summer, daytime runs from Gothenburg to Frederikshavn and Kiel to Korsør (Denmark)). In 1989 she was transferred to the Oslo – Frederikshavn route and renamed the STENA SAGA. In 1994, transferred to *Stena Line bv*, renamed the STENA EUROPE and operated between Hoek van Holland and Harwich. She was withdrawn in June 1997, transferred to the *Lion Ferry* (a *Stena Line* subsidiary) Karlskrona – Gdynia service and renamed the LION EUROPE. In 1998 she was transferred back to *Stena Line* (remaining on the same route) and renamed the STENA EUROPE. In early 2002 the cabins installed in 1982 were removed and other modifications made and she was transferred to the Fishguard – Rosslare route.

STENA EXPLORER Finnyards HSS1500 built at Rauma, Finland for *Stena RoRo* and chartered to *Stena Line*. Operates on the Holyhead – Dun Laoghaire route.

STENA HOLLANDICA Ro-pax ferry built at Cadiz, Spain for *Stena RoRo* and chartered to *Stena Line bv* to operate between Hoek van Holland and Harwich.

STENA LYNX III InCat 81m catamaran built at Hobart, Tasmania, Australia. Chartered new by *American Fast Ferries* of Argentina to *Stena Line* in June 1996 and named the STENA LYNX III. Initially used on the Dover – Calais service. From summer 1997 until autumn 1998 she operated between Newhaven and Dieppe. In March 1998 she was transferred to *P&O Stena Line* and renamed the ELITE. She was then renamed the P&O STENA ELITE (although only carrying the name ELITE on the bow). In late 1998 she was transferred back to *Stena Line* and renamed the STENA LYNX III. In 1999 she was placed on the Fishguard – Rosslare service, replacing the STENA LYNX (3231t, 1993). The charter ended in autumn 2000 but was immediately renewed as a summer only operation (with winter lay up). The charter ended again in autumn 2003 and she resumes the name ELITE. Later in 2003 purchased by *Stena Ropax*. In 2004 renamed the STENA LYNX III and resumed service on the Fishguard – Rosslare route, marketed as the 'Stena Express'.

STENA VOYAGER Finnyards HSS1500 built at Rauma, Finland for *Stena RoRo* and chartered to *Stena Line*. Operates on the Stranraer – Belfast route.

SUPERFAST FERRIES

THE COMPANY *SuperFast Ferries* is a Greek company, owned by *Attica Enterprises*.

MANAGEMENT Managing Director Alexander P Panagopulos, **Corporate Marketing Director** Yannis B Criticos, **Manager, Superfast Ferries Scotland** Denise Holmes.

ADDRESS *Greece* 157 Alkyonidon Avenue, Voula, GR-16673 Athens, Greece, ***UK*** Superfast Ferries, The Terminal Building, Port of Rosyth, Fife KY11 2XP, ***Belgium*** Superfast Ferries, Terminal A, Port of Zeebrugge, Doverlaan 7, Box 14, 8380 Zeebrugge, Belgium.

TELEPHONE Administration *Greece & Scotland* +30 (0)210 8919500, ***Belgium*** +32 (0)50 252211, **Reservations *UK*** 0870 234 0870, ***Belgium*** +32 (0)50 252252.

FAX Administration *Greece & Scotland* +30 (0)210 8919509.

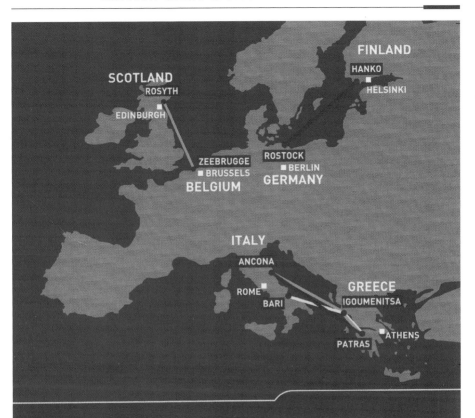

INTERNET Email criticos@superfast.com **Website** www.superfast.com *(English, German, Dutch, French)*

ROUTES OPERATED Rosyth (Scotland) – Zeebrugge (Belgium) (17 hrs 30 mins; *(1,2)*; 1 per day). Service started in May 2002.

| 1 | SUPERFAST IX | 30285t | 01 | 29.2k | 203.3m | 717P | 661C | 140T | BA2 | GR |
| 2 | SUPERFAST X | 30285t | 02 | 29.2k | 203.3m | 717P | 661C | 140T | BA2 | GR |

SUPERFAST IX and SUPERFAST X Built at Kiel, Germany for *Attica Enterprises* for use by *SuperFast Ferries*. SUPERFAST IX operated between Rostock and Södertälje from January until April 2002. In May 2002 both began operating between Rosyth and Zeebrugge.

SWANSEA CORK FERRIES

THE COMPANY *Swansea Cork Ferries* is a company established in 1987 to re-open the Swansea – Cork service abandoned by *B&I Line* in 1979. It was originally jointly owned by *West Glamorgan County Council, Cork Corporation, Cork County Council* and *Kerry County Council*. The service did not operate in 1989 but resumed in 1990. In 1993 the company was acquired by *Strintzis Lines* of Greece. In 1999 it was purchased from *Strintzis Lines* by a consortium of Irish businessmen.

MANAGEMENT Managing Director Thomas Hunter McGowan, **Sales Manager** *IR* Simone Collins, *UK* John Doonican.

ADDRESS *IR* 52 South Mall, Cork, Republic of Ireland, *UK* Kings Docks, Swansea SA1 1SF.

TELEPHONE Administration *Head Office* +353 (0)21 427 6000, *Cork Ferry Port* +353 (0)21 437 8036, **Reservations** *IR* +353 (0)21 427 1166, *UK* +44 (0)1792 456116.

FAX Administration *IR* +353 (0)21 427 5814, *UK* +44 (0)1792 644356, **Reservations** *IR* +353 (0)21 427 5061, *UK* +44 (0)1792 644356.

INTERNET Email info@swanseacorkferries.com **Website** www.swanseacorkferries.com *(English)*

ROUTE OPERATED *March – January* Cork – Swansea (10 hrs; *(1)*; 1 per day or alternate days, according to season. Due to tidal restrictions at Swansea, the service operates to Pembroke Dock on a few days each year.

| 1 | SUPERFERRY | 15127t | 72 | 21.0k | 137.8m | 1100P | 300C | 45L | BA2 | SV |

SUPERFERRY Built at Hashihama, Japan as the CASSIOPEIA for *Ocean Ferry KK* of Japan. In 1976 the company became *Ocean Tokyu Ferry KK* and she was renamed the IZU NO 3. She was used on the service between Tokyo (Honshu) – Tokushima (Shikoko) – Kokura (Kyshu). In 1991 she was sold to *Strintzis Lines* and briefly renamed the IONIAN EXPRESS. Following major rebuilding, she was renamed the SUPERFERRY and used on their services between Greece and the Greek islands. In 1993 time chartered to *Swansea Cork Ferries*. The charter continued following the sale of *SCF* by *Strintzis Lines*. In winter she used to return to *Strintzis Lines* in Greece for refit and also operated for them on Mediterranean routes. The charter was not renewed for 2001 and she remained in the Mediterranean, operating for *Strintzis Lines* under the *Blue Ferries* name (following the reorganisation of the company after its acquisition by *Attica Enterprises*). She was renamed the BLUE AEGEAN. In 2002 she was sold to *Swansea Cork Ferries* and renamed the SUPERFERRY.

TRANSMANCHE FERRIES

Transmanche Ferries is a French company, controlled by the *Syndicat Mixte de L'Activité Transmanche*.

ADDRESS Transmanche Ferries, Quai Gaston Lalitte, 76200 Dieppe, France.

TELEPHONE Administration +33 02 32 14 52 03, **Reservations** *UK* 0800 917 1201, *France* 0800 650 100.

FAX Administration +33 02 32 14 52 00.

INTERNET Website www.transmancheferries.com *(English, French)*

ROUTE OPERATED Newhaven – Dieppe (4 hrs; *(1,2)*; 4 per day).

1	DIEPPE	17672t	81	19.0k	145.9m	250P	-	140T	BA	FR
2	SARDINIA VERA	11637t	75	18.5k	120.8m	700P	479C	58T	BA	IT

DIEPPE Built at Kalmar, Sweden as the SAGA STAR for *TT-Saga-Line* and, from 1982, used on freight services between Travemünde and Trelleborg/Malmö. (Originally ordered by *Rederi AB Svea* as the SAGALAND). In 1989 sold to *Cie Meridonale* of France, renamed the GIROLATA and used on *SNCM* (later *CMR*) services in the Mediterranean. In 1993 she was chartered back to *TT-Line*, resumed her original name and was used on the Travemünde – Trelleborg service. Following delivery of the ROBIN HOOD and the NILS DACKE in 1995, she was transferred to the Rostock – Trelleborg route. In July 1997 she was purchased by *TT-Line* and in 1998 passenger facilities were completely renovated to full ro-pax format; following the delivery of the TOM SAWYER she was transferred back to the Travemünde – Trelleborg route, operating additional freight sailings. Briefly transferred back to Rostock – Trelleborg when the charter of the TT-TRAVELLER ended. Withdrawn in 2002, sold to *Transmanche Ferries* and renamed the DIEPPE.

SARDINIA VERA Built at Bremerhaven, Germany for *Stena Line* of Sweden. Laid down as the STENA ATLANTICA but launched as the MARINE ATLANTICA. On delivery, chartered to *CN Marine* (from 1986 *Marine Atlantic*) of Canada for service between North Sydney (Nova Scotia) and Port-aux-Basques (Newfoundland). In 1986 she was sold to *Tourship Co AS* of Italy (parent company of *Corsica Ferries*) and, in 1987, renamed the CORSICA VERA. Later in 1987 renamed the SARDINIA VERA. Used on services between Italy and France and Corsica and Sardinia. In 2001 chartered to the *Transmanche Ferries*.

Under Construction

3	NEWBUILDING 1	-	05	22.0k	112.0m	600P	-	62L	BA	FR
4	NEWBUILDING 2	-	06	22.0k	112.0m	600P	-	62L	BA	FR

NEWBUILDING 1, NEWBUILDING 2 Under construction in Vigo, Spain to replaced the DIEPPE and SARDINIA VERA.

Superfast X *(Superfast)*

Dawn Merchant *(D.J.Walter)*

section **2** *domestic services*

gb & ireland

ARGYLL AND BUTE COUNCIL

THE COMPANY *Argyll and Bute Council* is a British local government authority.

MANAGEMENT Director of Operations Andrew Law.

ADDRESS Manse Brae, Lochgilphead, Argyll PA31 8RD.

TELEPHONE Administration +44 (0)1546 604657.

FAX Administration +44 (0)1546 606618.

INTERNET Email andrew.law@argyll-bute.gov.uk **Website** www.argyll-bute.gov.uk *(English)*

ROUTES OPERATED Vehicle ferries Seil – Luing (5 mins; *(1)*; approx half hourly), Port Askaig (Islay) – Feolin (Jura) (5 mins; *(3)*; approx hourly). **Passenger only ferries** Port Appin – Lismore (10 mins; *(4)*; approx half hourly), Ellenabeich – Easdale (5 mins; *(2)*; as required).

1	BELNAHUA	35t	72	8.0k	17.1m	40P	5C	1L	BA	UK
2p	EASDALE	-	93	6.5k	6.4m	11P	0C	0L	-	UK
3	EILEAN DHIURA	86t	98	9.0k	25.6m	50P	13C	1L	BA	UK
4p	LISMORE	12t	88	8.0k	9.7m	20P	0C	0L	-	UK

BELNAHUA Built at Campbeltown, UK for *Argyll County Council* for the Seil – Luing service. In 1975, following local government reorganisation, transferred to *Strathclyde Regional Council*. In 1996, transferred to *Argyll and Bute Council*.

EASDALE Built for *Strathclyde Regional Council* for the Ellenabeich – Easdale passenger only service. In 1996, following local government reorganisation, transferred to *Argyll and Bute Council*.

EILEAN DHIURA Built at Bromborough, Birkenhead, UK for *Argyll and Bute County Council* to replace the *Western Ferries (Argyll)* SOUND OF GIGHA on the Islay – Jura route. *Serco-Denholm Ltd* manage and operate this vessel on behalf of the *Argyll and Bute Council*.

LISMORE Built for *Strathclyde Regional Council* for the Port Appin – Lismore passenger only service. In 1996, following local government reorganisation, transferred to *Argyll and Bute Council*.

ARRANMORE ISLAND FERRY SERVICES

THE COMPANY *Arranmore Island Ferry Services* is an Irish Republic company, supported by *Údarás na Gaeltachta (The Gaeltacht Authority)*, a semi-state owned body responsible for tourism and development in the Irish speaking areas of The Irish Republic. The operation is also known as *Maoin-Na-Farraige* (literally 'sea treasure' or 'sea wealth').

MANAGEMENT Managing Director Cornelius Bonner.

ADDRESS Bridge House, Leabgarrow, Arranmore, County Donegal, Republic of Ireland.

TELEPHONE Administration & Reservations +353 (0)7595 20532.

FAX Administration & Reservations + 353 (0)7595 20750.

INTERNET Email: arranmoreferry@arainnmhor.com

Website www.arainnmhor.com/visit/howtogethere/theboat.htm *(English)*

Saturn *(Colin Smith)*

Isle of Cumbrae *(Colin Smith)*

ROUTE OPERATED Burtonport (County Donegal) – Leabgarrow (Arranmore Island) (20 mins; *(1,2,3)*; up to 8 per day (summer), 5 per day (winter)) (Note only one vessel is generally in use at any one time).

1	ÁRAINN MHÓR	64t	72	8.0k	23.8m	138P	6C	-	B	IR
2	COLL	69t	74	8.0k	25.3m	152P	6C	-	B	IR
3	RHUM	69t	73	8.0k	25.3m	164P	6C	-	B	IR

ÁRAINN MHÓR Built at Port Glasgow, UK as the KILBRANNAN for *Caledonian MacBrayne*. Used on a variety of routes until 1977, she was then transferred to the Scalpay (Harris) – Kyles Scalpay service. In 1990 she was replaced by the CANNA and, in turn, replaced the CANNA in her reserve/relief role. In 1992 sold to *Arranmore Island Ferry Services* and renamed the ÁRAINN MHÓR. She was subsequently sold to *Údarás na Gaeltachta* and leased back to *Arranmore Island Ferry Services*.

COLL Built at Port Glasgow, UK for *Caledonian MacBrayne*. For several years she was employed mainly in a relief capacity. In 1986 she took over the Tobermory (Mull) – Kilchoan service from a passenger only vessel; the conveyance of vehicles was not inaugurated until 1991. In 1996 she was transferred to the Oban – Lismore route. In 1998 she was sold to *Arranmore Island Ferry Services*.

RHUM Built at Port Glasgow, UK for *Caledonian MacBrayne*. Until 1987, she was used primarily on the Claonaig – Lochranza (Arran) service. After that time she served on various routes. In 1994 she inaugurated a new service between Tarbert (Loch Fyne) and Portavadie. In 1997 operated between Kyles Scalpay and Scalpay until the opening of the new bridge on 16th December 1997. In 1998 she was sold to *Arranmore Island Ferry Services*.

BERE ISLAND FERRIES

THE COMPANY *Bere Island Ferries Ltd* is an Irish Republic private sector company.

MANAGEMENT Operator Colm Harrington.

ADDRESS Ferry Lodge, West End, Bere Island, County Cork, Republic of Ireland.

TELEPHONE Administration +353 (0)27 75009, **Reservations** Not applicable.

INTERNET Email info@bereislandferries.com **Website** www.bereislandferries.com *(English)*

ROUTE OPERATED Castletownbere (County Cork) – Bere Island (10 mins; *(2,3)*; up to 10 per day).

1•	F.B.D. DUNBRODY	139t	60	8.0k	39.6m	107P	18C	-	BA	IR
2	MORVERN	64t	73	8.0k	23.8m	138P	6C	-	B	IR
3	OILEAN NA H-OIGE	69t	80	7.0k	18.6m	35P	4C	-	B	IR

F.B.D. DUNBRODY Built at Hamburg, Germany as the BERNE-FARGE for the service between Berne and Farge, across the River Weser in Germany. Subsequently she was sold to *Elbe Clearing* of Germany, renamed the ELBE CLEARING 12 and used as a floating platform for construction works in the Elbe. In 1979 she was sold to *Passage East Ferry Company* and renamed the F.B.D. DUNBRODY. Withdrawn in January 1998 and became a spare vessel. Later in 1998 she was sold to *Bere Island Ferries* and replaced the MISNEACH as main vessel. In 2000 badly damaged when she broke loose during a gale and laid up. Since then her condition has deteriorated and she will eventually be scrapped.

MORVERN Built at Port Glasgow, UK for *Caledonian MacBrayne*. After service on a number of routes she was, after 1979, the main vessel on the Fionnphort (Mull) – Iona service. In 1992 replaced by the LOCH BUIE and became a spare vessel. In 1995 sold to *Arranmore Island Ferry Services*. In 2001 sold to *Bere Island Ferries*.

OILEAN NA H-OIGE Built at Stornoway, UK as the EILEAN NA H-OIGE for *Western Isles Islands Council* (from 1st April 1996 the *Western Isles Council* and from 1st January 1998 *Comhairle Nan Eilean Siar*) for their Ludaig – Eriskay service. From 2000 operated from temporary slipway at the Eriskay causeway. This route ceased in July 2001 following the opening of a causeway and she was laid up. In 2002 she started operating between Eriskay and Barra. In 2003 replaced by the LOCH BHRUSDA of *Caledonian MacBrayne* and laid up. Later sold to *Bere Island Ferries* and renamed the OILEAN NA H-OIGE (same name in Irish rather than Scots Gaelic).

CALEDONIAN MACBRAYNE

THE COMPANY *Caledonian MacBrayne Limited* is a British state owned company, the responsibility of the First Minister of Scotland. Until 1990 it was part of the state owned *Scottish Transport Group* (formed in 1969). *Caledonian MacBrayne Limited* as such was formed in 1973 by the merger of the *Caledonian Steam Packet Company Ltd* (which had been formed in 1889) and *David MacBrayne Ltd* (whose origins go back to 1851). The company has more vessels sailing under the British flag than any other.

MANAGEMENT Managing Director Lawrie Sinclair, Head of Marketing Hugh D MacLennan.

ADDRESS The Ferry Terminal, Gourock PA19 1QP.

TELEPHONE Administration +44 (0)1475 650100, **Vehicle Reservations** +44 (0)8705 650000.

FAX Administration +44 (0)1475 637607, **Vehicle Reservations** +44 (0)1475 635235.

INTERNET Email hugh.maclennan@calmac.co.uk **Website** www.calmac.co.uk *(English)*

ROUTES OPERATED All year vehicle ferries (frequencies are for summer) Ardrossan – Brodick (Arran) (55 mins; *(3)*; up to 6 per day), Largs – Cumbrae Slip (Cumbrac) (10 mins; *(16,24)*; every 30 or 15 mins), Wemyss Bay – Rothesay (Bute) (35 mins; *(14,15,31)*; up to 18 per day), Colintraive – Rhubodach (Bute) (5 mins; *(19)*; frequent service), Tarbert (Loch Fyne) – Portavadie (20 mins; *(11)*; up to 12 per day), Gourock – Dunoon (23 mins; *(14,15,31)*; hourly service), Kennacraig – Port Ellen (Islay) (2 hrs 20 mins; *(8)*; up to 3 per day), Kennacraig – Port Askaig (Islay) (2 hrs 5 mins *(8,10)*; 1 or 2 per day), Tayinloan – Gigha (20 mins; *(23)*; up to 10 per day), Oban – Lismore (50 mins; *(7)*; up to 4 per day), Oban – Colonsay (2 hrs 15 mins; *(5,8,13,28)*; 5 per week), Oban – Craignure (Mull) (45 mins; *(13)*; up to 7 per day), Oban-Coll-Tiree (2 hrs 45 min direct to 4 hrs 20 min via other island); *(5,28)*; 1 per day), Oban – Castlebay (Barra) (5 hrs (direct); *(5,28)*; 1 per day), Oban – Lochboisdale (South Uist) (5 hrs (if direct), 7 hrs (via Barra); *(5,28)*; 4 per week), Leverburgh (Harris) – Berneray (1 hr 10 mins; *(22)*; 3-4 per day), Lochaline – Fishnish (Mull) (15 mins; *(20)*; up to 14 per day), Tobermory (Mull) – Kilchoan (35 mins; *(21)*; up to 7 per day), Eriskay – Ard Mhor (Barra) (40 mins; *(17)*; up to 5 per day), Mallaig – Armadale (Skye) (23 mins; *(6* (summer), *27*(winter)); up to 9 per day (2 in winter)), Sconser (Skye) – Raasay (15 mins; *(25)*; up to 11 per day), Uig (Skye) – Tarbert (Harris) (1 hr 40 mins; *(9)*; 1 or 2 per day), Uig (Skye) – Lochmaddy (North Uist) (1 hr 45 mins; *(9)*; 1 or 2 per day), Ullapool – Stornoway (Lewis) (2 hrs 45 mins; *(12)*; up to 3 per day). **All year passenger and restricted vehicle ferries** (frequencies are for summer) Fionnphort (Mull) – Iona (5 mins; *(18)*; frequent), Ballycastle (Northern Ireland) – Rathlin Island (40 mins; *(4)*; 4 per day), Mallaig – Eigg – Muck – Rum – Canna – Mallaig (round trip 7 hrs (all islands); *(27)*; at least 1 sailing per day – most islands visited daily). **Note** although these services are operated by vehicle ferries, special permission is required to take a vehicle and tourist cars are not normally conveyed. **Summer only vehicle ferries** Claonaig – Lochranza (Arran) (30 mins; *(26)*; up to 9 per day), Kennacraig – Port Askaig – Colonsay – Oban (3 hrs 35 mins; *(10)*; 1 per week). **Winter only vehicle ferry** Tarbert (Loch Fyne) – Lochranza (Arran) (1 hr; *(varies)*; 1 per day). **All year passenger only ferry** Gourock – Dunoon (20 mins; *(1)*; 3 per day).

1p	ALI CAT	74t	99	-	19.8m	250P	0C	0L	-	UK
2	BRUERNISH	69t	73	8.0k	22.5m	121P	6C	-	B	UK
3	CALEDONIAN ISLES	52211t	93	15.0k	93.5m	1000P	120C	10L	BA	UK
4	CANNA	69t	73	8.0k	22.5m	140P	6C	-	B	UK
5	CLANSMAN	5400t	98	16.5k	99.0m	638P	90C	6L	BA	UK
6	CORUISK	c1100t	03	14.0k	60.0m	250P	40C	-	BA	UK
7	EIGG	69t	75	8.0k	22.5m	75P	6C	-	B	UK
8	HEBRIDEAN ISLES	3040t	85	15.0k	85.1m	494P	68C	10L	BAS	UK
9	HEBRIDES	5299t	00	16.5k	99.0m	612P	110C	6L	BA	UK
10	ISLE OF ARRAN	3269t	84	15.0k	85.0m	446P	68C	8L	BA	UK
11	ISLE OF CUMBRAE	201t	77	8.5k	32.0m	139P	18C	-	BA	UK
12	ISLE OF LEWIS	6753t	95	18.0k	101.2m	680P	123C	10L	BA	UK
13	ISLE OF MULL	4719t	88	15.0k	90.1m	962P	80C	20L	BA	UK

14	JUNO	854t	74	12.0k	69.0m	381P	40C	-	AS	UK
15	JUPITER	848t	74	12.0k	69.0m	381P	40C	-	AS	UK
16	LOCH ALAINN	396t	98	10.0k	41.0m	150P	24C	-	BA	UK
17	LOCH BHRUSDA	246t	96	8.0k	30.0m	150P	18C	-	BA	UK
18	LOCH BUIE	295t	92	9.0k	30.2m	250P	9C	-	BA	UK
19	LOCH DUNVEGAN	549t	91	9.0k	54.2m	200P	36C	-	BA	UK
20	LOCH FYNE	549t	91	9.0k	54.2m	200P	36C	-	BA	UK
21	LOCH LINNHE	206t	86	9.0k	30.2m	199P	12C	-	BA	UK
22	LOCH PORTAIN	c800t	03	11.0k	50.0m	200P	32C	-	BA	UK
23	LOCH RANZA	206t	86	9.0k	30.2m	199P	12C	-	BA	UK
24	LOCH RIDDON	206t	86	9.0k	30.2m	199P	12C	-	BA	UK
25	LOCH STRIVEN	206t	86	9.0k	30.2m	199P	12C	-	BA	UK
26	LOCH TARBERT	211t	92	9.0k	30.2m	149P	18C	-	BA	UK
27	LOCHNEVIS	941t	00	9.0k	49.1m	190P	14C	-	A	UK
28	LORD OF THE ISLES	3504t	89	16.0k	84.6m	506P	56C	16L	BAS	UK
29•	PIONEER	1071t	74	16.0k	67.4m	218P	33C	-	AS	UK
30	RAASAY	69t	76	8.0k	22.5m	75P	6C	-	B	UK
31	SATURN	851t	78	12.0k	69.0m	381P	40C	-	AS	UK

ALI CAT Catamaran built for *Solent & White Line Cruises* of Ryde, Isle of Wight. Operated a passenger service between Cowes to Hamble and Warsash and cruises from Cowes. At times chartered to *Wightlink* to cover for the fast catamarans when there were only two in their fleet. In 2002 chartered to *Red Funnel Ferries* who had contracted with *Caledonian MacBrayne* to operate passenger only services between Gourock and Dunoon in the morning and evening peaks. In April 2003 this contract was extended by another year.

BRUERNISH Built at Port Glasgow, UK. Until 1980 she served on a variety of routes. In 1980 she inaugurated ro-ro working between Tayinloan and the island of Gigha and served this route until June 1992 when she was replaced by the LOCH RANZA and became a relief vessel. In summer 1994 she operated as secondary vessel on the Tobermory (Mull) – Kilchoan service for one season only. In December 1996 she started a vehicle ferry service between Ballycastle (on the North West coast of Northern Ireland) and Rathlin Island under charter; the route became a *Caledonian MacBrayne* operation in April 1997 – see the CANNA. In 1997 she operated on the Tarbert – Portavadie service and in 1998 on the Oban – Lismore service. Since 1999 she has been a spare vessel.

CALEDONIAN ISLES Built at Lowestoft, UK for the Ardrossan – Brodick (Arran) service.

CANNA Built at Port Glasgow, UK. She was the regular vessel on the Lochaline – Fishnish (Mull) service. In 1986 she was replaced by the ISLE OF CUMBRAE and until 1990 she served in a relief capacity in the north, often assisting on the Iona service. In 1990 she replaced the KILBRANNAN (see the ÁRAINN MHÓR, *Arranmore Island Ferry Services*) on the Kyles Scalpay (Harris) – Scalpay service (replaced by a bridge in autumn 1997). In spring 1997 she was transferred to the Ballycastle – Rathlin Island route.

CLANSMAN Built at Appledore, UK to replace the LORD OF THE ISLES on the Oban – Coll and Tiree and Oban – Castlebay and Lochboisdale service in the summer. She also serves as winter relief vessel on the Stornoway, Tarbert, Lochmaddy, Mull/Colonsay, Islay and Brodick routes.

CORUISK Built at Appledore, UK to replace the LORD OF THE ISLES on the Mallaig – Armadale route during the summer. She operates on the Upper Clyde during the winter.

EIGG Built at Port Glasgow, UK. Since 1976 she was employed mainly on the Oban – Lismore service. In 1996 she was transferred to the Tobermory (Mull) – Kilchoan route, very occasionally making special sailings to the Small Isles (Canna, Eigg, Muck and Rum) for special cargoes. In 1999 her wheelhouse was raised to make it easier to see over taller lorries and she returned to the Oban – Lismore route.

HEBRIDEAN ISLES Built at Selby UK for the Uig – Tarbert/Lochmaddy service. She was used initially on the Ullapool – Stornoway and Oban – Craignure/Colonsay services pending installation of linkspan facilities at Uig, Tarbert and Lochmaddy. She took up her regular role in May 1986. Since May 1996 she no longer operated direct services in summer between Tarbert and Lochmaddy, this role being taken on by the new Harris – North Uist services of the LOCH BHRUSDA. In 2001 replaced by the HEBRIDES and transferred to the Islay service. In autumn 2002 she operated between Scrabster and Stromness for *NorthLink Orkney and Shetland Ferries* before port modifications at Scrabster enabled the HAMNAVOE to enter service in spring 2003. She then returned to the Islay service. She also relieved on the Pentland Firth in 2004.

HEBRIDES Built at Port Glasgow, UK for the Uig – Tarbert and Uig – Lochmaddy services.

ISLE OF ARRAN Built at Port Glasgow, UK for the Ardrossan – Brodick service. In 1993 transferred to the Kennacraig – Port Ellen/Port Askaig service, also undertaking the weekly Port Askaig – Colonsay – Oban summer service. From then until 1997/98 she also relieved on the Brodick, Coll/Tiree, Castlebay/Lochboisdale, Craignure and Tarbert/Lochmaddy routes in winter. In 2001 replaced by the HEBRIDEAN ISLES and is now reserve for the larger vessels. She has operated on the two-ship Islay service in summer since 2003.

ISLE OF CUMBRAE Built at Troon, UK for the Largs – Cumbrae Slip (Cumbrae) service. In 1986 she was replaced by the LOCH LINNHE and the LOCH STRIVEN and transferred to the Lochaline – Fishnish (Mull) service. She used to spend most of the winter as secondary vessel on the Kyle of Lochalsh – Kyleakin service; however this ceased following the opening of the Skye Bridge in 1995. In 1997 she was transferred to the Colintraive – Rhubodach service. In summer 1999 she was transferred to the Tarbert – Portavadie service.

ISLE OF LEWIS Built at Port Glasgow, UK for the Ullapool – Stornoway service.

ISLE OF MULL Built at Port Glasgow, UK for the Oban – Craignure (Mull) service. She also operates the Oban – Colonsay service and until 1997/98 was the usual winter relief vessel on the Ullapool – Stornoway service. She has also deputised on the Oban – Castlebay/Lochboisdale and Oban – Coll/Tiree routes.

JUNO, JUPITER, SATURN Built at Port Glasgow, UK for the Gourock – Dunoon, Gourock – Kilcreggan and Wemyss Bay – Rothesay services. The JUPITER has been upgraded for a while to Class III standard for the Ardrossan – Brodick service. Before 1986, the JUNO and JUPITER operated mainly on the Gourock – Dunoon and Gourock – Kilcreggan (now withdrawn) services and the SATURN on the Wemyss Bay – Rothesay service. Since 1986 they have usually rotated on a three weekly basis on the three services; until 2000 this, in summer, included Clyde cruising but this was not repeated in 2001.

LOCH ALAINN Built at Buckie, UK for the Lochaline – Fishnish service. Launched as the LOCH ALINE but renamed the LOCH ALAINN before entering service. After a brief period on the service she was built for, she was transferred to the Colintraive – Rhubodach route. In summer 1998 she was transferred to the Largs – Cumbrae Slip service.

LOCH BHRUSDA Built at Bromborough, Birkenhead, UK to inaugurate a new Otternish (North Uist) – Leverburgh (Harris) service. In 2001 the service became Berneray – Leverburgh. In 2003 moved to the Eriskay – Barra service, previously operated by *Comhairle Nan Eilean Siar* vessels. Note 'Bhrusda' is pronounced "Vroosta".

LOCH BUIE Built at St Monans, UK for the Fionnphort (Mull) – Iona service to replace the MORVERN (see *Arranmore Island Ferry Services*) and obviate the need for a relief vessel in the summer. Due to height restrictions, loading arrangements for vehicles taller than private cars are bow only. Only islanders' cars and service vehicles (eg mail vans, police) are carried; no tourist vehicles are conveyed.

LOCH DUNVEGAN Built at Port Glasgow, UK for the Kyle of Lochalsh – Kyleakin service. On the opening of the Skye Bridge in October 1995 she was withdrawn from service and put up for sale. In autumn 1997, returned to service on the Lochaline – Fishnish route. In 1998 she was due to be transferred to the Colintraive – Rhubodach route but this was delayed because of problems in providing terminal facilities. She operated on the Clyde and between Mallaig and Armadale during the early summer and spent the rest of the summer laid up. In 1999 she was transferred to the Colintraive – Rhubodach route.

Loch Tarbert *(Colin Smith)*

Sound of Sanda *(Colin Smith)*

LOCH FYNE Built at Port Glasgow UK for the Kyle of Lochalsh – Kyleakin service (see the LOCH DUNVEGAN). In autumn 1997, she also served on the Lochaline – Fishnish route and was transferred to this route as regular vessel in 1998.

LOCH LINNHE Built at Hessle, UK. Until 1997 she was used mainly on the Largs – Cumbrae Slip (Cumbrae) service and until winter 1994/95 she was usually used on the Lochaline – Fishnish service during the winter. Since then she had relieved on various routes in winter. In summer 1998 she operated mainly on the Tarbert – Portavadie route. In 1999 she was transferred to the summer only Tobermory – Kilchoan service. In 2003 she launched the new Sound of Barra before delivery of the LOCH PORTAIN allowed the LOCH BHRUSDA to be moved to that route.

LOCH PORTAIN Built at Bromborough, Birkenhead, UK (hull constructed in Poland) to replace the LOCH BHRUSDA on the Berneray – Leverburgh service.

LOCH RANZA Built at Hessle, UK for the Claonaig – Lochranza (Arran) seasonal service and used a relief vessel in the winter. In 1992 she was replaced by the LOCH TARBERT and transferred to the Tayinloan – Gigha service.

LOCH RIDDON Built at Hessle, UK. Until 1997 she was used almost exclusively on the Colintraive – Rhubodach service. In 1997, she was transferred to the Largs – Cumbrae Slip service and is often to be found on the Tarbert-Portavadie/Lochranza service in winter.

LOCH STRIVEN Built at Hessle, UK. Used mainly on the Largs – Cumbrae Slip service until 1997. In winter 1995/6 and 1996/67 she was used on the Tarbert – Portavadie and Claonaig – Lochranza routes. In 1997 she took over the Sconser – Raasay service.

LOCH TARBERT Built at St Monans, UK for the Claonaig – Lochranza service. She has been the winter relief vessel on the Largs – Cumbrae Slip route since winter 1994/5 and is also the winter relief vessel for the Otternish – Leverburgh route.

LOCHNEVIS Built at Troon, UK to replace the LOCHMOR on the Mallaig – Small Isles service and the winter Mallaig – Armadale service. Although a vehicle ferry, cars are not normally carried to the Small Isles; the ro-ro facility is used for the carriage of agricultural machinery and livestock and it is possible to convey a vehicle on the ferry from which goods can be unloaded directly on to local transport rather than transhipping at Mallaig. Ramps are being provided at each island and, when complete, the practice of tendering at Eigg, Muck and Rum will cease, the LAIG BAY (the Eigg tender) being disposed of. The slipway on Rum will be available for use in 2004.

LORD OF THE ISLES Built at Port Glasgow, UK to replace the CLAYMORE on the Oban – Castlebay and Lochboisdale services and also the COLUMBA (1420t, 1964) on the Oban – Coll and Tiree service. She took over Mallaig – Armadale and Mallaig – Outer Isles service in July 1998 but returned to her previous routes during the winter period. In spring 2003 the Mallaig – Armadale service was taken over by the PIONEER standing in for the new CORUISK and she operated services from Oban to South Uist and Barra.

PIONEER Built at Leith, UK to operate on the West Loch Tarbert – Port Ellen service (see the PENTALINA B, *Pentland Ferries*). When the IONA was at last able to operate this service in 1978 (following the move to Kennacraig) the PIONEER was transferred to the Mallaig – Armadale service, operating as a relief vessel in the winter on Upper Clyde and Small Isles routes. In 1989 she was replaced at Mallaig by the IONA and became the company's spare vessel, replacing the GLEN SANNOX (1269t, 1957). Since summer 1995 she has undertaken Wemyss Bay – Rothesay and until 1998 Rothesay – Largs – Brodick sailings. She served as a Clyde and Small Isles relief vessel in the winter replacing the JUNO, JUPITER, SATURN and LOCHNEVIS for annual overhaul. In 1998 she opened the Mallaig – Armadale/Outer Isles service and temporarily operated between Oban and Craignure before returning to the Clyde in July. In summers 1999 and 2000 she operated on the Wemyss Bay – Rothesay route. Following the demise of Clyde Cruising she was from 2001 restricted to a supplementary service between Gourock and Dunoon. In 2003 she operated on the Mallaig – Armadale service until the delivery of the CORUISK in August 2003. She was sent back to Gourock but returned to the route when the CORUISK had to be taken out of service for repairs shortly after delivery. In autumn 2003 she was laid up in Greenock and had been mothballed by the end of the year.

RAASAY Built at Port Glasgow, UK for and used primarily on the Sconser (Skye) – Raasay service. In 1997 she was replaced by the LOCH STRIVEN and became a spare/relief vessel and inaugurated in October 2003 the winter service between Tobermory (Mull) and Kilchoan (Ardnamurchan).

SATURN Built at Troon, UK. As the JUNO and JUPITER. In earlier days operated mainly on the Wemyss Bay – Rothesay service.

Under Construction

| 32 | NEWBUILDING | - | 05 | 14.0k | 70.0m | 450P | 62C | - | BAS | UK |

NEWBUILDING Under construction at Gdansk, Poland. To operate mainly on the Wemyss Bay – Rothesay service and replace the JUPITER, JUNO or SATURN.

Caledonian MacBrayne also operates the LAIG BAY, an 8k, 10.5m motor vessel built in 2000 and carrying up to 28 passengers. She tenders to the LOCHNEVIS at Eigg. She will be withdrawn and sold when a ramp is built on the island later in 2003.

CROMARTY FERRY COMPANY

THE COMPANY The *Cromarty Ferry Company* operate under contract to *The Highland Council.*

MANAGEMENT Managing Director Mr John Henderson.

ADDRESS Udale Farm, Poyntzfield, BY DINGWALL, IV7 8LY.

TELEPHONE +44 (0)1381 610269, Mobile +44 (0)7768 653674.

FAX +44 (0)1381 610408.

INTERNET Email john@udalefarm.com **Website** www.cromarty-ferry.co.uk *(English)*

ROUTE OPERATED *June-October* Cromarty – Nigg (Ross-shire) (10 mins; *(1)*; half hourly – 0800 to 1800 ex Cromarty (19.00 in July and August)).

| 1 | CROMARTY ROSE | 28t | 87 | 8.0k | 14.0m | 50P | 2C | - | B | UK |

CROMARTY ROSE Built at Ardrossan, UK for *Seaboard Marine (Nigg) Ltd* who operated the service until 2001, supported by *The Highland Council.* In 2002, after a tendering exercise held in 2001, the contract was awarded to the *Cromarty Ferry Company.* The new company purchased the CROMARY ROSE from *Seaboard Marine (Nigg) Ltd.*

CROSS RIVER FERRIES

THE COMPANY *Cross River Ferries Ltd* is an Irish Republic company, jointly owned by *Marine Transport Services Ltd* of Cobh and *Arklow Shipping Ltd* of Arklow, County Wicklow.

MANAGEMENT Operations Manager Eoin O'Sullivan.

ADDRESS Westlands House, Rushbrooke, Cobh, County Cork, Republic of Ireland.

TELEPHONE Administration +353 (0)21 481 1223, **Reservations** Not applicable.

FAX Administration +353 (0)21 481 2645, **Reservations** Not applicable.

ROUTE OPERATED Carrigaloe (near Cobh, on Great Island) – Glenbrook (Co Cork) (4 mins; *(1,2)*; frequent service 07.00 – 00.15 (one or two vessels used according to demand)).

| 1 | CARRIGALOE | ‡225t | 70 | 8.0k | 49.1m | 200P | 27C | - | BA | IR |
| 2 | GLENBROOK | ‡225t | 71 | 8.0k | 49.1m | 200P | 27C | - | BA | IR |

CARRIGALOE Built at Newport (Gwent) UK as the KYLEAKIN for *Caledonian Steam Packet Company* (later *Caledonian MacBrayne*) for the Kyle of Lochalsh – Kyleakin service. In 1991 sold to *Marine Transport Services Ltd* and renamed them the CARRIGALOE. She entered service in March 1993. In summer 2002 chartered to the *Lough Foyle Ferry Company,* returning in spring 2003.

GLENBROOK Built at Newport (Gwent) UK as the LOCHALSH for *Caledonian Steam Packet Company* (later *Caledonian MacBrayne*) for the Kyle of Lochalsh – Kyleakin service. In 1991 sold to *Marine Transport Services Ltd* and renamed the GLENBROOK. She entered service in March 1993.

GLENELG – KYLERHEA FERRY

THE COMPANY The *Glenelg – Kylerhea Ferry* is privately operated.

MANAGEMENT Ferry Master R MacLeod.

ADDRESS Corriehallie, Inverinate, Kyle IV40 8HD.

TELEPHONE Administration & Reservations +44 (0)1599 511302.

FAX Administration & Reservations +44 (0)1599 511477.

INTERNET Email roddy@skyeferry.co.uk **Website** www.skyeferry.co.uk *(English)*

ROUTE OPERATED *Easter – October only* Glenelg – Kylerhea (Skye) (10 mins; *(1)*; frequent service).

1	GLENACHULISH		44t	69	9.0k	20.0m	12P	6C	-	BSt	UK

GLENACHULISH Built at Troon, UK for the *Ballachulish Ferry Company* for the service between North Ballachulish and South Ballachulish, across the mouth of Loch Leven. In 1975 the ferry was replaced by a bridge and she was sold to *Highland Regional Council* and used on a relief basis on the North Kessock – South Kessock and Kylesku – Kylestrome routes. In 1984 she was sold to the operator of the Glenelg – Kylerhea service. She is the last turntable ferry in operation.

THE HIGHLAND COUNCIL

THE COMPANY The *Highland Council* (previously *Highland Regional Council*) is a British local government authority.

MANAGEMENT Area Transport, Environment & Community Works Services Manager James C Tolmie, **Ferry Manager** J McAuslane.

ADDRESS *Area Office* Lochybridge Depot, Carr's Corner Industrial Estate, Fort William PH33 6TQ, *Ferry Office* Ferry Cottage, Ardgour, Fort William.

TELEPHONE Administration *Area Office* +44 (0)1397 709000, *Corran* +44 (0)1855 841243, *Camusnagaul* +44 (0)1397 772483, **Reservations** Not applicable.

FAX Administration *Area Office* +44 (0)1397 705735, *Corran* +44 (0)1855 841243, **Reservations** Not applicable.

INTERNET Email tecs@highland.gov.uk **Website** lochabertransport.org.uk/corranferry.html *(English – external site reproducing official ferry leaflet)*

ROUTES OPERATED Vehicle Ferries Corran – Ardgour (5 mins; *(2,3)*; half hourly), **Passenger Only Ferry** Fort William – Camusnagaul (10 mins; *(1)*; Frequent).

1p	CAILIN AN AISEAG	-	80	7.5k	9.8m	26P	0C	0L	-	UK
2	CORRAN	351t	01	10.0k	42.0m	150P	30C	2L	BA	UK
3	MAID OF GLENCOUL	‡166t	75	8.0k	32.0m	116P	16C	1L	BA	UK

CAILIN AN AISEAG Built at Buckie, UK for *Highland Regional Council* and used on the Fort William – Camusnagaul service.

CORRAN Built at Hull, UK for *The Highland Council* to replace the MAID OF GLENCOUL as main vessel.

MAID OF GLENCOUL Built at Ardrossan, UK for *Highland Regional Council* for the service between Kylesku and Kylestrome. In 1984 the ferry service was replaced by a bridge and she was transferred to the Corran – Ardgour service. In April 1996, ownership transferred to *The Highland Council*. In 2001 became the reserve vessel.

ISLES OF SCILLY STEAMSHIP COMPANY

THE COMPANY *Isles of Scilly Steamship Company* is a British private sector company.

MANAGEMENT Chief Executive J Marston, **Marketing Manager** L Ramzan.

ADDRESS *Scilly* PO Box 10, Hugh Town, St Mary's, Isles of Scilly TR21 0LJ, *Penzance* Steamship House, Quay Street, Penzance, Cornwall, TR18 4BZ.

TELEPHONE Administration & Reservations *Scilly* +44 (0)1720 424220, *Penzance* +44 (0)1736 334220.

FAX Administration & Reservations *Scilly* +44 (0)1720 422192, *Penzance* +44 (0)1736 351223.

INTERNET Email sales@islesofscilly-travel.co.uk **Website** www.ios-travel.co.uk *(English)*

ROUTES OPERATED Penzance – St Mary's (Isles of Scilly) (2 hrs 40 mins; *(1,3)*; 1 per day), St Mary's – Tresco/St Martin's/St Agnes/Bryher; *(2)*; irregular).

1	GRY MARITHA	590t	81	10.5k	40.3m	6P	5C	1L	C	UK
2	LYONESSE LADY	40t	91	9.0k	15.5m	12P	1C	0L	AC	UK
3	SCILLONIAN III	1256t	77	15.5k	67.7m	600P	5C	-	C	UK

GRY MARITHA Built at Kolvereid, Norway for *Gjofor* of Norway. In design she is a coaster rather than a ferry. In 1990 sold to *Isles of Scilly Steamship Company*. She operates a freight and passenger service all year (conveying most goods to and from the Islands). During the winter she provides the only sea service to the islands, the SCILLONIAN III being laid up.

LYONESSE LADY Built at Fort William UK, for inter-island ferry work.

SCILLONIAN III Built at Appledore, UK for the Penzance-St Mary's service. She operates from late March to November and is laid up in the winter. Last major conventional passenger/cargo ferry built for UK waters and probably Western Europe. Extensively refurbished during winter 98/99. She can carry cars in her hold and on deck, as well as general cargo/perishables, boats, trailer tents and passenger luggage.

IT FERRIES

THE COMPANY *It Ferries* is an Alderney registered company

MANAGEMENT Managing Director not known, **Marketing Manager** not known.

ADDRESS It ferries, Braye Harbour, Alderney, Channel Islands.

TELEPHONE Administration and Reservations +44 (0)1481 825555.

FAX Administration and Reservations - not known.

INTERNET Email - not known.

Website - not known.

ROUTE OPERATED Braye Harbour (Alderney) – St Peter Port (Guernsey), Braye Harbour – Diellete (France). Operations are due to start in 2004. No other details are avaiable at the time of going to press.

1	BRAYE SPIRIT	-	04	20k	16.0m	12P	4C	1L	B	UK

BRAYE SPIRIT Catamaran built in Newcastle, UK for *It Ferries*.

Hamnavoe *(Miles Cowsill)*

Thorsvoe *(Miles Cowsill)*

KERRERA FERRY

THE COMPANY The *Kerrera Ferry* is privately operated.

MANAGEMENT Ferry Master Duncan MacEachen.

ADDRESS The Ferry, Isle of Kerrera, By Oban PA34 4SX.

TELEPHONE Administration +44 (0)1631 563665.

ROUTE OPERATED Gallanach (Argyll) – Kerrera (5 mins; *(1)*; on demand 10.30 – 12.30 and 14.00 – 18.00, Easter – October, other times by arrangement).

1	GYLEN LADY		9t	99	8.0k	10.0m	12P	1C	-	B	UK

GYLEN LADY Built at Corpach, UK to inaugurate a vehicle ferry service to the Isle of Kerrera, replacing open passenger boat.

LOUGH FOYLE FERRY COMPANY

THE COMPANY *Lough Foyle Ferry Company Ltd* is an Irish Republic Company.

MANAGEMENT Managing Director: Jim McClenaghan.

ADDRESS The Pier, Greencastle, Co Donegal, Republic of Ireland.

TELEPHONE Administration +353 (0)74 93 81901.

FAX Administration: +353 (0)74 93 81903.

INTERNET Email: info@loughfoyleferry.com **Website:** www.loughfoyleferry.com *(English)*

ROUTES OPERATED *Lough Foyle Service* Greencastle (Inishowen, Co Donegal, Republic of Ireland) – Magilligan (Co Londonderry, Northern Ireland) (10 mins; *(1)*; about every 20 mins), *Lough Swilly Service (1st April – 30th September)* Buncrana (Inishowen, Co Donegal) – Rathmullan (Co Donegal) (20 mins; *(2)*; hourly) **Note:** This service is due to start in May 2004.

1	FOYLE RAMBLER	190t	72	10.0k	35.0m	100P	20C	-	BA	IR
2	FOYLE VENTURE	360t	78	10.0k	47.9m	300P	44C	-	BA	IR

FOYLE VENTURE Built at Bowling, Dumbarton, UK as the SHANNON WILLOW for *Shannon Ferry Ltd*. In 2000 replaced by the SHANNON BREEZE and laid up for sale. In 2003 sold to the *Lough Foyle Ferry Company Ltd* and renamed the FOYLE VENTURE.

FOYLE RAMBLER Built in Germany as the STEDINGEN for *Fähren Bremen-Stedingen GmbH* to operate across the River Weser. In 2004 sold to the *Lough Foyle Ferry Company Ltd* and renamed the FOYLE RAMBLER.

MURPHY'S FERRY SERVICE

THE COMPANY *Murphy's Ferry Service* is privately operated.

MANAGEMENT Operator Patrick Murphy, **Finance/Marketing** Carol Murphy.

ADDRESS Anchorage, Lawrence Cove, Bere Island, Co Cork, Republic of Ireland.

TELEPHONE Administration +353 (0)27 75014 **Mobile** +353 (0)87 2386095.

FAX Administration +353 (0)27 75014.

INTERNET Email info@murphysferry.com **Website** www.murphysferry.com *(English)*

ROUTE OPERATED Castletownbere (Pontoon – 3 miles to east of town centre) – Bere Island (Lawrence Cove, near Rerrin) (20 mins ; *(1)*; up to 8 per day).

1	IKOM K		55t	99	10.0k	16.0m	60P	4C	1L	B	IR

IKOM K Built at Arklow, Irish Republic for *Murphy's Ferry Service*.

NORTHLINK ORKNEY AND SHETLAND FERRIES

THE COMPANY *NorthLink Orkney and Shetland Ferries Ltd* is a Scottish company jointly owned by *Caledonian MacBrayne* and *The Royal Bank of Scotland*. It took over the service from Scotland to Orkney and Shetland from *P&O Scottish Ferries* in October 2002.

MANAGEMENT Chief Executive Bill Davidson, **Commercial Director** Gareth Crichton.

ADDRESS Kiln Corner, Ayre Road, Kirkwall, Orkney KW15 1QX.

TELEPHONE Administration +44 (0)1856 885500, **Reservations** +44 (0)845 6000 449.

FAX Administration +44 (0)1856 879588.

INTERNET Email info@northlinkferries.co.uk **Website** www.northlinkferries.co.uk *(English)*

ROUTES OPERATED Scrabster – Stromness (Orkney) (1 hr 30 min; *(1)*; up to 3 per day), Aberdeen – Lerwick (Shetland) (direct) (12 hrs; *(2,3)*; 3 northbound/4 southbound per week), Aberdeen – Kirkwall, Hatston New Pier (Orkney) (5 hrs 45 mins) – Lerwick (14 hrs) (*(2,3)*; 4 northbound/3 southbound per week).

1	HAMNAVOE	8600t	02	19.0k	112.0m	600P	95C	20L	BA	UK
2	HJALTLAND	12000t	02	24.0k	125.0m	600P	150C	30L	BA	UK
3	HROSSEY	12000t	02	24.0k	125.0m	600P	150C	30L	BA	UK

HAMNAVOE Built at Rauma, Finland for *NorthLink Orkney and Shetland Ferries Ltd* to operate on the Scrabster – Stromness route. Did not enter service until spring 2003 due to late completion of work at Scrabster to accommodate the ship. *Caledonian MacBrayne's* HEBRIDEAN ISLES covered between October 2002 and spring 2003.

HJALTLAND, HROSSEY Built at in Rauma, Finland for *NorthLink Orkney and Shetland Ferries Ltd* to operate on the Aberdeen – Kirkwall – Lerwick route when services started in 2002.

ORKNEY FERRIES

THE COMPANY *Orkney Ferries Ltd* (previously the *Orkney Islands Shipping Company*) is a British company, owned by *The Orkney Islands Council*.

MANAGEMENT Operations Director N H Mills, **Ferry Services Manager** A Henderson.

ADDRESS Shore Street, Kirkwall, Orkney KW15 1LG.

TELEPHONE Administration +44 (0)1856 872044, **Reservations** +44 (0)1856 872044.

FAX Administration & Reservations +44 (0)1856 872921, Telex 75475.

INTERNET Email info@orkneyferries.co.uk **Website** www.orkneyferries.co.uk *(English)*

ROUTES OPERATED Kirkwall (Mainland) to Eday (1 hr 15 mins), Rapness (Westray) (1 hr 25 mins), Sanday (1 hr 25 mins), Stronsay (1 hr 35 mins), Papa Westray (1 hr 50 mins), North Ronaldsay (2 hrs 30 mins) ('North Isles service') (timings are direct from Kirkwall – sailings via other islands take longer; *(1,2,9)*; 1/2 per day except Papa Westray which is twice weekly and North Ronaldsay which is weekly), Pierowall (Westray) – Papa Westray (25 mins; *(4)*; up to six per day (passenger only)), Kirkwall – Shapinsay (25 mins; *(7)*; 6 per day), Houton (Mainland) to Lyness (Hoy) (35 mins; *(6)*; 5 per day), and Flotta (35 mins; *(6)*; 4 per day) ('South Isles service') (timings are direct from Houton – sailings via other islands take longer), Tingwall (Mainland) to Rousay (20 mins; *(3)*; 6 per day), Egilsay (30 mins; *(3)*; 5 per day) and Wyre (20 mins; *(3)*; 5 per day) (timings are direct from Tingwall – sailings via other islands take longer), Stromness (Mainland) to Moaness (Hoy) (25 mins; *(5)*; 2/3 per day) and Graemsay (25 mins; *(5)*; 2/3 per day) (passenger/cargo service – cars not normally conveyed).

1	EARL SIGURD	771t	90	12.0k	45.4m	190P	26C	-	BA	UK
2	EARL THORFINN	771t	90	12.0k	45.4m	190P	26C	-	BA	UK
3	EYNHALLOW	79t	87	9.5k	26.2m	95P	8C	-	BA	UK

4p	GOLDEN MARIANA	33t	73	9.5k	16.2m	40P	0C	-	-	UK
5	GRAEMSAY	82t	96	10.0k	17.1m	73P	1C	-	C	UK
6	HOY HEAD	358t	94	9.8k	39.6m	125P	18C	-	BA	UK
7	SHAPINSAY	199t	89	9.5k	30.2m	91P	12C	-	BA	UK
8	THORSVOE	400t	91	10.5k	35.1m	96P	16C	-	BA	UK
9	VARAGEN	950t	89	12.0k	50.0m	144P	33C	5L	BA	UK

EARL SIGURD, EARL THORFINN Built at Bromborough, Birkenhead, UK to inaugurate ro-ro working on the 'North Isles' service (see above).

EYNHALLOW Built at Bristol, UK to inaugurate ro-ro services from Tingwall (Mainland) to Rousay, Egilsay and Wyre. In 1991 she was lengthened by 5 metres, to increase car capacity.

GOLDEN MARIANA Built at Bideford, UK. Passenger only vessel. Generally operates feeder service between Pierowall (Westray) and Papa Westray.

GRAEMSAY Built at Troon UK to operate between Stromness (Mainland), Moaness (Hoy) and Graemsay. Designed to offer an all year round service to these islands, primarily for passengers and cargo.

HOY HEAD Built at Bideford, UK to replace the THORSVOE on the 'South Isles' service (see above).

SHAPINSAY Built at Hull, UK for the service from Kirkwall (Mainland) to Shapinsay.

THORSVOE Built at Campbeltown, UK for the 'South Isles' service (see above). In 1994 replaced by new HOY HEAD and became the main reserve vessel for the fleet.

VARAGEN Built at Selby, UK for *Orkney Ferries*, a private company established to start a new route between Gills Bay (Caithness, Scotland) and Burwick (South Ronaldsay, Orkney). However, due to problems with the terminals it was not possible to maintain regular services. In 1991, the company was taken over by *OISC* and the VARAGEN became part of their fleet, sharing 'North Isles' services with the EARL SIGURD and the EARL THORFINN and replacing the freight vessel ISLANDER (494t, 1969).

PASSAGE EAST FERRY

THE COMPANY *Passage East Ferry Company Ltd* is an Irish Republic private sector company.

MANAGEMENT Managing Director Derek Donnelly, **Operations Manager** Conor Gilligan.

ADDRESS Barrack Street, Passage East, Co Waterford, Republic of Ireland.

TELEPHONE Administration +353 (0)51 382480, **Reservations** Not applicable.

FAX Administration +353 (0)51 382598, **Reservations** Not applicable.

INTERNET Email passageferry@eircom.net **Website** www.passageferry.com *(English)*

ROUTE OPERATED Passage East (County Waterford) – Ballyhack (County Wexford) (7 mins; *(1)*; frequent service).

1	EDMUND D	300t	68	9.0k	45.1m	143P	30C	-	BA	IR

EDMUND D Built at Dartmouth UK as the SHANNON HEATHER for *Shannon Ferry Ltd* and used on their service between Killimer (County Clare) and Tarbert (County Kerry). Withdrawn from regular service in 1996 and, in 1997, sold to *Passage East Ferry* and renamed the EDMUND D. She entered service in January 1998.

PENTLAND FERRIES

THE COMPANY *Pentland Ferries* is a UK private sector company.

MANAGEMENT Managing Director Andrew Banks, **Marketing Manager** Linda Knott.

ADDRESS Pier Road, St Margaret's Hope, South Ronaldsay, Orkney KW172SW.

TELEPHONE Administration & Reservations +44 (0)1856 831226.

FAX Administration & Reservations +44 (0)1856 831614.

INTERNET Email sales@pentlandferries.co.uk **Website** www.pentlandferries.com *(English)*

ROUTE OPERATED Gills Bay (Scotland) – St Margaret's Hope (South Ronaldsay, Orkney) (1 hr; *(1,2)*; 3 per day).

1	CLAYMORE	1871t	78	14.0k	77.2m	71P	50C	8T	AS	UK
2	PENTALINA B	1908t	70	16.0k	74.3m	250P	46C	7L	BAS	UK

CLAYMORE Built at Leith, UK for *Caledonian MacBrayne* for the Oban – Castlebay/Lochboisdale service, also serving Coll and Tiree between October and May, replacing the IONA (see the PENTALINA B, *Pentland Ferries*). In 1989 she was transferred to the Kennacraig – Port Ellen/Port Askaig (Islay) route, again replacing the IONA. In summer she also operated a weekly service from Port Askaig (Islay) to Colonsay and Oban. She relieved on the Ardrossan – Brodick service during winter 1990. In autumn 1993 she was replaced by the ISLE OF ARRAN and became a spare vessel. Her summer duties in 1994, 1995 and 1996 included Saturday sailings from Ardrossan to Douglas (Isle of Man), returning on Sundays plus standby duties and charter to the *Isle of Man Steam Packet Company* to provide extra sailings between Heysham and Douglas during the TT Season. During the winter she was general relief vessel, spending several months on Islay sailings. In 1997 she was sold to *Sea Containers* to operate for *Sea Containers Ferries Scotland Ltd* (trading as the *Argyll and Antrim Steam Packet Company*) between Campbeltown (Scotland) and Ballycastle (Northern Ireland) (summer only). During the winter she has been chartered back to *Caledonian MacBrayne* to cover during the refit period. The Campbeltown – Ballycastle service did not resume in 2000 and during the summer she was chartered to *Strandfaraskip Landsins* of the Faroe Islands and used on the Tórshavn – Suderoy service. She was then laid up for sale. In 2002 she was sold to *Pentland Ferries* and inaugurated a new Invergordon – St Margaret's Hope service. This service was withdrawn after a short period and she was laid up until the summer period when it was planned she would operate along-side the PENTALINA B. However, a passenger certificate was not granted until 2004 so at times she operated only 12 passengers were allowed.

PENTALINA B Built at Troon, UK as the IONA for *David MacBrayne*. She was built to operate the Islay service. However, shortly after the order was placed, plans to build a new pier at Redhouse, near the mouth of West Loch Tarbert, were abandoned, so she was not able to operate on this route until *Caledonian MacBrayne* acquired the *Western Ferries'* pier in deeper water at Kennacraig in 1978. She operated on the Gourock – Dunoon service in 1970 and 1971, between Mallaig and Kyle of Lochalsh and Stornoway in 1972 and between Oban and Craignure in 1973. From 1974 until 1978 she operated mainly on the Oban to Castlebay/Lochboisdale service and in addition the winter Oban – Coll/Tiree route. From 1978 until 1989 she operated mainly on the Islay service. In 1989 she was replaced by the CLAYMORE and then replaced the PIONEER as the summer Mallaig – Armadale vessel. Full ro-ro working was introduced on the route in 1994 and she also operated a twice weekly sailing between Mallaig, Lochboisdale and Castlebay and, in 1997, a weekly Mallaig – Coll and Tiree sailing. She was withdrawn in October 1997 and sold to *Pentland Ferries*. In 1998 she was renamed the PENTALINA B. In spring 1998 she was chartered back to *Caledonian MacBrayne* to operate between Oban and Craignure following the breakdown of the ISLE OF MULL. *Pentland Ferries* services started in summer 2001.

Linga *(Miles Cowsill)*

God Met Ons III *(FERRYInformation)*

RED FUNNEL FERRIES

THE COMPANY *Red Funnel Ferries* is the trading name of the *Southampton, Isle of Wight and South of England Royal Mail Steam Packet Public Limited Company*, a British private sector company. The company was acquired by *JP Morgan International Capital Corporation* in 2000.

MANAGEMENT Managing Director A M Whyte, **Marketing Director** Ms O H Glass.

ADDRESS 12 Bugle Street, Southampton SO14 2JY.

TELEPHONE Administration +44 (0)870 444 8889, **Reservations** +44 (0)870 444 8898.

FAX Administration & Reservations +44 (0)870 444 8897.

INTERNET Email post@redfunnel.co.uk **Website** www.redfunnel.co.uk *(English)*

ROUTES OPERATED Conventional Ferries Southampton – East Cowes (55 mins; *(1,2,3,8)*; hourly). **Fast Passenger Ferries** Southampton – Cowes (22 mins; *(1,2,3,4)*; every half hour), Southampton – Gosport (35 mins; *(1,2,3,4)*; 4 per day (Sats and Suns at certain times only)).

1	BERGEN CASTLE	1220t	76	-	66.0m	250P	80C	8L	BA	SV
2	RED EAGLE	3028t	96	13.0k	83.6m	895P	140C	16L	BA	UK
3	RED FALCON	3953t	94	14.0k	93.2m	895P	200C	18L	BA	UK
4»p	RED JET 1	168t	91	34.0k	31.5m	138P	0C	0L	-	UK
5»p	RED JET 2	168t	91	34.0k	31.5m	138P	0C	0L	-	UK
6»p	RED JET 3	213t	98	34.0k	32.9m	190P	0C	0L	-	UK
7»p	RED JET 4	345t	03	35.0k	39.0m	277P	0C	0L	-	UK
8	RED OSPREY	3953t	94	14.0k	93.2m	895P	200C	18L	BA	UK

BERGEN CASTLE Built at Lø/lan, Norway as the NORDHORDLAND for *Bergen-Nordhordland Rutelag A/S* of Norway to operate services in the Bergen area. In 2003 purchased by *Red Funnel Ferries* to cover for the three car ferries during the period of their lengthening (autumn 2003 – early 2005 but no lengthening during summer 2004).

RED EAGLE Built at Port Glasgow, UK for the Southampton – East Cowes service. During winter 2004/5 to be stretched by 10 metres and height raised by 3 metres at Gdansk, Poland.

RED FALCON Built at Port Glasgow, UK for the Southampton – East Cowes service. In 2004 stretched by 10 metres and height raised by 3 metres at Gdansk, Poland.

RED JET 1, RED JET 2, RED JET 3 FBM Marine catamarans built at Cowes, UK for the Southampton – Cowes service.

RED JET 4 North West Bay Ships Pty Ltd catamaran built in Hobart, Tasmania, Australia for the Southampton – Cowes service.

RED OSPREY Built at Port Glasgow, UK for the Southampton – East Cowes service. In 2003 stretched by 10 metres and height raised by 3 metres at Gdansk, Poland.

SHANNON FERRY LTD

THE COMPANY *Shannon Ferry Ltd* is an Irish Republic private company owned by six families on both sides of the Shannon Estuary.

MANAGEMENT Managing Director J J Meehan.

ADDRESS Ferry Terminal, Killimer, County Clare, Republic of Ireland.

TELEPHONE Administration +353 (0)65 9053124, **Reservations** Not applicable.

FAX Administration +353 (0)65 9053125, **Reservations** Not applicable.

INTERNET Email enquiries@shannonferries.com **Website** www.shannonferries.com *(English, German, French, Italian)*

ROUTE OPERATED Killimer (County Clare) – Tarbert (County Kerry) (20 mins; *(1,2)*; hourly (half hourly during June, July, August and September). The company is also planning to establish a new service been Headford and Oughterard in Country Galway, across Lake Corrib. The vessel would be cable operated and accommodate up to 24 cars. It is unlikely to start before 2005/6.

| 1 | SHANNON BREEZE | 611t | 00 | 10.0k | 80.8m | 350P | 60C | - | BA | IR |
| 2 | SHANNON DOLPHIN | 501t | 95 | 10.0k | 71.9m | 350P | 52C | - | BA | IR |

SHANNON BREEZE, SHANNON DOLPHIN Built at Appledore, UK for *Shannon Ferry Ltd.*

SHETLAND ISLANDS COUNCIL

THE COMPANY *Shetland Islands Council* is a British Local Government authority.

MANAGEMENT Divisional Manager – Ferry Services Ken Duerden, **Marine Superintendents** Capt William MacTear and Capt William Clark.

ADDRESS Port **Administration** Building, Sella Ness, Mossbank, Shetland ZE2 9QR.

TELEPHONE Administration +44(0)1806 244262, 244252, **Reservations/Voicebank**

Bressay Not Bookable/+44 (0)7626 980317, *Fair Isle* +44 (0)1595 760222/+44 (0)7626 986763 *Foula* +44 (0)1595 753226/+44 (0)7626 986763, *Papa Stour* +44 (0)1595 810460/+44 (0)7626 986763, *Skerries* +44 (0)1806 515226/+44 (0)7626 983633, *Whalsay* +44 (0)1806 566259/+44 (0)7626 983633, *Yell, Unst, Fetlar* +44 (0)1957 722259/+44 (0)7626 980735/980209.

FAX +44 (0)1806 244232.

INTERNET Emails Ken.Duerden@sic.shetland.gov.uk   William.MacTear@sic.shetland.gov.uk, Bill.Clark@sic.shetland.gov.uk

Website: www.shetland.gov.uk/ferryinfo/ferry.htm *(English)*

ROUTES OPERATED Toft (Mainland) – Ulsta (Yell) (20 mins; *(1,2,3,10)*; up to 26 per day), Gutcher (Yell) – Belmont (Unst) (10 mins; *(5,6)*; 30 per day), Gutcher – Oddsta (Fetlar) (25 mins; *(5,6)*; 6 per day), Lerwick (Mainland) – Maryfield (Bressay) (5 mins; *(12)*; 19 per day), Laxo/Vidlin (Mainland) – Symbister (Whalsay) (30-45 mins; *(7,10,13)*; 17 per day), Lerwick (Mainland) – Out Skerries (3 hrs; *(4)*; 2 per week), Vidlin (Mainland) – Skerries (1 hr 30 mins; *(4)*; 7 per week), Grutness (Mainland) – Fair Isle (3 hrs; *(8)*; 2 per week), West Burrafirth (Mainland) – Papa Stour (40 mins; *(11,15)*; 7 per week), Walls/Scalloway (Mainland) – Foula (3 hrs; *(14)*; 2 per week).

1	BIGGA	274t	91	11.0k	33.5m	96P	21C	4L	BA	UK
2	DAGGRI	1850t	04	12.0k	61m	145P	30C	4L	BA	UK
3	DAGALIEN	1850t	04	12.0k	61m	145P	30C	4L	BA	UK
4	FILLA	351t	03	12.0k	35.5m	30P	10C	2L	BA	UK
5	FIVLA	230t	85	11.0k	29.9m	95P	15C	4L	BA	UK
6	FYLGA	147t	75	8.5k	25.3m	93P	10C	2L	BA	UK
7	GEIRA	226t	88	10.8k	29.9m	95P	15C	4L	BA	UK
8	GOOD SHEPHERD IV	76t	86	10.0k	18.3m	12P	1C	0L	C	UK
9•	GRIMA	147t	74	8.5k	25.3m	93P	10C	2L	BA	UK
10	HENDRA	225t	82	11.0k	33.8m	100P	18C	4L	BA	UK
11	KOADA	35t	69	8.0k	14.6m	12P	1C	0L	C	UK
12	LEIRNA	420t	92	9.0k	35.1m	100P	20C	4L	BA	UK
13	LINGA	400t	01	11.0k	35.8m	100P	16C	2L	BA	UK
14	NEW ADVANCE	25t	96	8.7k	9.8m	12P	1C	0L	C	UK
15	SNOLDA	130t	83	9.0k	24.4m	12P	6C	1L	A	UK
16•	THORA	147t	75	8.5k	25.3m	93P	10C	2L	BA	UK

BIGGA Built at St Monans, UK. Used on the Toft – Ulsta service. In 2004 to be replaced by new vessels DAGGRI and DAGALIEN and become a spare vessel.

DAGGRI Built at Gdansk, Poland to replace (with sister vessel the DAGALIEN) the BIGGA and HENDRA on Yell Sound. Enters service in June 2004.

DAGALIEN Built at Gdansk, Poland to replace (with sister vessel the DAGGRI) the BIGGA and HENDRA on Yell Sound. Enters service in August 2004.

FILLA Built at Gdansk, Poland for the Lerwick /Vidlin – Out Skerries service.

FIVLA Built at Troon, UK. Used on the Gutcher – Belmont/Oddsta service.

FYLGA Built at Tórshavn, UK. Used on the Gutcher – Belmont/Oddsta service. To be withdrawn and sold during 2004.

GEIRA Built at Hessle, UK. Used on the Laxo – Symbister route. To be replaced by the HENDRA in 2004.

GOOD SHEPHERD IV Built at St Monans, UK. Used on the service between Grutness (Mainland) and Fair Isle. Vehicles conveyed by special arrangement and generally consist of agricultural vehicles. She is pulled up on marine slip on Fair Isle at the conclusion of each voyage.

GRIMA Built at Bideford, UK. Used on the Lerwick (Mainland) – Maryfield (Bressay) service until 1992 when she was replaced by the LEIRNA and became a spare vessel. To be withdrawn and sold in 2004.

HENDRA Built at Bromborough, Birkenhead, UK for the Laxo – Symbister service. In 2002 transferred to the Toft – Ulsta service. In 2004 to be replaced by new vessels DAGGRI and DAGALIEN and to return to the Laxo – Symbister service as second vessel.

KOADA Built at Bideford, UK. Built as an inshore trawler and bought by the shareholders on Fair Isle to operate to Shetland and named the GOOD SHEPHERD III. In 1986 the service was taken over by *Shetland Islands Council* and she was replaced by GOOD SHEPHERD IV. She was however acquired by the *Shetland Islands Council* and renamed the KOADA. Until 2004 she operated between West Burrafirth (Mainland) and Papa Stour (operation to Foula having ceased following the delivery of the NEW ADVANCE). Car carrying capacity used occasionally. Later in 2004 to be replaced by the SNOLDA and laid up.

LEIRNA Built at Port Glasgow, UK. Used on the Lerwick – Maryfield (Bressay) service.

LINGA Built at Gdansk, Poland. Used on the Laxo – Symbister service.

NEW ADVANCE Built at Penryn, UK for the Foula service. Although built at Penryn, she was completed at Stromness in Orkney. She has a Cygnus Marine GM38 hull and is based on the island where she can be lifted out of the water. Vehicle capacity is to take new vehicles to the island – not for tourist vehicles. Mainland ports used are Walls and Scalloway.

SNOLDA Built at Flekkefjord, Norway as the FILLA. Used on the Lerwick (Mainland) – Out Skerries and Vidlin (Mainland) – Out Skerries services. At other times she operates freight and charter services around the Shetland Archipelago. She resembles a miniature oil rig supply vessel. Passenger capacity was originally 20 from 1st April to 31st October inclusive but is now 12 all year. In 2003 renamed the SNOLDA; replaced by the new FILLA, and transferred to the West Burrafirth – Papa Stour route, replacing the KOADA.

THORA Built at Tórshavn, Faroe Islands. Sister vessel to the FYLGA and the GRIMA. After a period as a spare vessel, in 1998 she took over the Laxo – Symbister service from the withdrawn KJELLA. Withdrawn in 2001 and became a spare vessel.

SECTION 2 – DOMESTIC SERVICES

STRANGFORD LOUGH FERRY SERVICE

THE COMPANY The *Strangford Lough Ferry Service* is operated by the *DRD (Department for Regional Development)*, a Northern Ireland Government Department (formerly operated by *DOE (Northern Ireland)*).

MANAGEMENT Ferry Manager D Pedlow.

ADDRESS Strangford Lough Ferry Service, Strangford, Co Down BT30 7NE.

TELEPHONE Administration +44 (0)28 4488 1637, **Reservations** Not applicable.

FAX Administration +44 (0)28 4488 1249, **Reservations** Not applicable.

ROUTE OPERATED Strangford – Portaferry (County Down) (10 mins; *(1,2)*; half hourly).

| 1 | PORTAFERRY II | 312t | 01 | 12.0k | 38.2m | 260P | 28C | - | BA | UK |
| 2 | STRANGFORD FERRY | 186t | 69 | 10.0k | 32.9m | 263P | 20C | - | BA | UK |

PORTAFERRY II Built at Bromborough, Birkenhead, UK for *DRD (Northern Ireland)*.

STRANGFORD FERRY Built at Cork, Irish Republic for *Down County Council*. Subsequently transferred to the *DOE (Northern Ireland)* and then the *DRD (Northern Ireland)*. Following delivery of the PORTAFERRY II, she became reserve ferry.

C TOMS & SON LTD

THE COMPANY *C Toms & Son Ltd* is a British private sector company.

MANAGEMENT Managing Director Mr Allen Toms.

ADDRESS East Street, Polruan, Fowey, Cornwall PL23 1PB.

TELEPHONE Administration +44 (0)1726 870232.

FAX Administration +44 (0)1726 870318.

ROUTE OPERATED Fowey – Bodinnick (Cornwall) (5 mins; *(1,2)*; frequent).

1	GELLAN	50t	03	4.5k	36.0m	50P	10C	-	BA	UK
2	JENACK	60t	00	4.5k	36.0m	50P	15C	-	BA	UK
3•	NO 4	-	75	-	15.8m	48P	8C	-	BA	-

GELLAN, JENACK Built at Fowey, UK by *C Toms & Sons Ltd*. Self propelled and steered.

NO 4 Built at Fowey, UK by *C Toms & Son Ltd*. Float propelled by motor launch. No longer used.

VALENTIA ISLAND FERRIES

THE COMPANY *Valentia Island Ferries Ltd* is an Irish Republic private sector company.

MANAGEMENT Manager Richard Foran.

ADDRESS Valentia Island, County Kerry, Republic of Ireland.

TELEPHONE Administration +353 (0)66 76141, **Reservations** Not applicable.

FAX Administration +353 (0)66 76377, **Reservations** Not applicable.

INTERNET Email reforan@indigo.ie **Website** www.kerrygems.ie/valentiaferry/ *(English)*

ROUTE OPERATED Reenard (Co Kerry) – Knightstown (Valentia Island) (5 minutes; *(1)*; frequent service, 1st April – 30th September).

| 1 | GOD MET ONS III | 95t | 63 | - | 43.0m | 95P | 18C | - | BA | IR |

GOD MET ONS III Built at Millingen, Netherlands for *FMHE Res* of the Netherlands for a service across the River Maas between Cuijk and Middelaar. In 1987 a new bridge was opened and the service ceased. She was latterly used on contract work in the Elbe and then laid up. In 1996 acquired by *Valentia Island Ferries* and inaugurated a car ferry service to the island. Note: this island never had a car ferry service before. A bridge was opened at the south end of the island in 1970; before that a passenger/cargo service operated between Reenard Point and Knightstown.

WESTERN FERRIES

THE COMPANY *Western Ferries (Clyde) Ltd* is a British private sector company.

MANAGEMENT Managing Director Gordon Ross.

ADDRESSES Hunter's Quay, Dunoon PA23 8HJ.

TELEPHONE Administration +44 (0)1369 704452, **Reservations** Not applicable.

FAX Administration +44 (0)1369 706020, **Reservations** Not applicable.

INTERNET Email enquiries@western-ferries.co.uk **Website** www.western-ferries.co.uk *(English)*

ROUTE OPERATED McInroy's Point (Gourock) – Hunter's Quay (Dunoon) (20 mins; *(1,2,3,4)*; half hourly).

1	SOUND OF SANDA	403t	64	10.0k	48.4m	220P	37C	4/5L	BA	UK
2	SOUND OF SCALPAY	403t	61	10.0k	48.4m	220P	37C	4/5L	BA	UK
3	SOUND OF SCARBA	489t	01	11.0k	49.5m	220P	40C	4/5L	BA	UK
4	SOUND OF SHUNA	489t	03	11.0k	49.5m	220P	40C	4/5L	BA	UK
5•	SOUND OF SLEAT	466t	61	10.0k	39.9m	296P	30C	4/5L	BA	UK

SOUND OF SANDA Built at Walsum, Germany as the G24 for *Amsterdam City Council* and operated from Centraal Station to the other side of the River IJ. In 1996 purchased by *Western Ferries* and renamed the SOUND OF SANDA.

SOUND OF SCALPAY Built at Arnhem, Netherlands as the G23 for *Amsterdam City Council*. In 1995 sold to *Western Ferries* and renamed the SOUND OF SCALPAY.

SOUND OF SCARBA Built at Port Glasgow, UK for *Western Ferries*.

SOUND OF SHUNA Built at Port Glasgow, UK for *Western Ferries*.

SOUND OF SLEAT Built at Hardinxveld, Netherlands as the DE HOORN for the service between Maassluis and Rozenburg, across the 'Nieuwe Waterweg' (New Waterway) in The Netherlands. In 1988 she was purchased by *Western Ferries* and renamed the SOUND OF SLEAT. In 2003 laid up for sale.

SECTION 2 – DOMESTIC SERVICES

WIGHTLINK

THE COMPANY *Wightlink* is a British private sector company, owned by the management. The routes and vessels were previously part of *Sealink* but were excluded from the purchase of most of the *Sealink* operations by *Stena Line AB* in 1990. They remained in *Sea Containers'* ownership until purchased by *CINVen* Ltd, a venture capital company in 1995. The company was the subject of a management buy-out in 2001.

MANAGEMENT Chairman Michael Aiken, **Marketing Director** Janet Saville.

ADDRESS PO Box 59, Portsmouth PO1 2XB.

TELEPHONE Administration +44 (0)23 9281 2011, **Reservations** 08705 827744 (from UK only), +44 (0)23 9281 2011 (from overseas).

FAX Administration & Reservations +44 (0)23 9285 5257, **Telex** 86440 WIGHTLG.

INTERNET Email info@wightlink.co.uk **Website** www.wightlink.co.uk *(English)*

ROUTES OPERATED Conventional Ferries Lymington – Yarmouth (Isle of Wight) (approx 30 mins; *(1,2,3)*; half hourly), Portsmouth – Fishbourne (Isle of Wight) (approx 35 mins; *(8,9,10,11,12)*; half hourly or hourly depending on time of day). **Fast Passenger Ferries** Portsmouth – Ryde (Isle of Wight) (passenger only) (approx 15 mins; *(4,5,6,7)*; half hourly/hourly).

1	CAEDMON	764t	73	9.5k	57.9m	512P	58C	6L	BA	UK
2	CENRED	761t	73	9.5k	57.9m	512P	58C	6L	BA	UK
3	CENWULF	761t	73	9.5k	57.9m	512P	58C	6L	BA	UK
4»p	FASTCAT RYDE	478t	96	34.0k	40.0m	361P	0C	0L	-	UK
5»p	FASTCAT SHANKLIN	478t	96	34.0k	40.0m	361P	0C	0L	-	UK
6»p	OUR LADY PAMELA	312t	86	28.5k	29.5m	395P	0C	0L	-	UK
7»p	OUR LADY PATRICIA	312t	86	28.5k	29.5m	395P	0C	0L	-	UK
8	ST CATHERINE	2038t	83	12.5k	77.0m	771P	142C	12L	BA	UK
9	ST CECILIA	2968t	86	12.5k	77.0m	771P	142C	12L	BA	UK
10	ST CLARE	3500t	01	13.0k	86.0m	818P	186C	-	BA	UK
11	ST FAITH	3009t	90	12.5k	77.0m	771P	142C	12L	BA	UK
12	ST HELEN	2983t	83	12.5k	77.0m	771P	142C	12L	BA	UK

CAEDMON Built at Dundee, UK for *Sealink* for the Portsmouth – Fishbourne service. In 1983 transferred to the Lymington – Yarmouth service.

CENRED, CENWULF Built at Dundee, UK for *Sealink* for the Lymington – Yarmouth service.

FASTCAT RYDE Kværner Fjellstrand Flyingcat 40m built at Singapore as the WATER JET 1 for *Waterjet Netherlands Antilles* and operated in the Philippines. In 1999 renamed the SUPERCAT 17. In summer 2000 sold to *Wightlink* and renamed the FASTCAT RYDE. After modifications, entered service on the Portsmouth – Ryde route in autumn 2000.

FASTCAT SHANKLIN Kværner Fjellstrand Flyingcat 40m built at Singapore as the WATER JET 2 for *Waterjet Netherlands Antilles* and operated in the Philippines. In 1999 renamed the SUPERCAT 18. In summer 2000 sold to *Wightlink* and renamed the FASTCAT SHANKLIN. After modifications, entered service on the Portsmouth – Ryde route in autumn 2000.

OUR LADY PAMELA, OUR LADY PATRICIA InCat 30 m catamarans built at Hobart, Tasmania, Australia for *Sealink* for the Portsmouth – Ryde service.

ST CATHERINE, ST HELEN Built at Leith, UK for *Sealink* for the Portsmouth – Fishbourne service.

ST CECILIA, ST FAITH Built at Selby, UK for *Sealink* for the Portsmouth – Fishbourne service.

ST CLARE Built at Gdansk, Poland for *Wightlink* for the Portsmouth – Fishbourne service. She is a double ended ferry with a central bridge.

WOOLWICH FREE FERRY

THE COMPANY The *Woolwich Free Ferry* is operated by the *London Borough of Greenwich*, a British municipal authority on behalf of *Transport for London*.

MANAGEMENT Ferry Manager Capt P Deeks.

ADDRESS New Ferry Approach, Woolwich, London SE18 6DX.

TELEPHONE Administration +44 (0)20 8921 5786, +44 (0)20 8921 5967, **Reservations** Not applicable.

FAX Administration +44 (0)20 8316 6096, **Reservations** Not applicable.

INTERNET Email peter.deeks@greenwich.gov.uk

Website www.greenwich.gov.uk/Greenwich/Travel/LocalTravelServices/WoolwichFerry.htm
(English)

ROUTE OPERATED Woolwich – North Woolwich (free ferry) (5 mins; *(1,2,3)*; every 9 mins (weekdays – two ferries in operation), every 16 mins (weekends – one ferry in operation)). Note: one ferry is always in reserve/under maintenance.

1	ERNEST BEVIN	738t	63	8.0k	56.7m	310P	32C	6L	BA	UK
2	JAMES NEWMAN	738t	63	8.0k	56.7m	310P	32C	6L	BA	UK
3	JOHN BURNS	738t	63	8.0k	56.7m	310P	32C	6L	BA	UK

ERNEST BEVIN, JAMES NEWMAN, JOHN BURNS Built at Dundee, UK for the *London County Council* who operated the service in 1963. In 1965 ownership was transferred to the *Greater London Council*. Following the abolition of the *GLC* in April 1986, ownership was transferred to the *Department of Transport* and in 2001 to *Transport for London*. The *London Borough of Greenwich* operate the service on their behalf. An alternative loading is 6m x 18m articulated lorries cars and 14 cars; lorries of this length are too high for the nearby northbound Blackwall Tunnel.

St Catherine *(Miles Cowsill)*

Gardenia *(FotoFlite)*

section 3 freight only services
gb & ireland

AWSR SHIPPING

THE COMPANY *AWSR Shipping Limited* is a UK private sector company jointly owned by *Bibby Line, James Fisher, Houlder Hadley* and *Andrew Weir.*

MANAGEMENT Managing Director Max J Gladwyn.

ADDRESS Dexter House, 2 Royal Mint Court, London EC3N 4XX

TELEPHONE Administration +44 (0)20 7480 4140.

FAX Administration +44 (0)20 7481 9940.

INTERNET Email max.gladwyn@awsr.co.uk **Website** www.awsr.co.uk *(English)*

ROUTES OPERATED No routes are operated. The ships are for charter to the UK *Ministry of Defence* for their Strategic Sealift capability. Normally two of the ships are chartered commercially but can be recalled in times of emergency.

1	ANVIL POINT	23235t	03	18.0k	193.0m	12P	-	180T	A	UK
2	BEACHY HEAD	23235t	03	21.0k	193.0m	12P	-	180T	A	UK
3	EDDYSTONE	23235t	02	21.0k	193.0m	12P	-	180T	A	UK
4	HARTLAND POINT	23235t	03	18.0k	193.0m	12P	-	180T	A	UK
5	HURST POINT	23235t	02	18.0k	193.0m	12P	-	180T	A	UK
6	LONGSTONE	23235t	03	21.0k	193.0m	12P	-	180T	A	UK

ANVIL POINT, HARTLAND POINT Built at Belfast, UK for *AWSR Shipping.*

BEACHY HEAD, LONGSTONE Built at Flensburg, Germany for *AWSR Shipping.* Currently on charter to *Transfennica* and operating between Hanko (Finland) and Lübeck (Germany).

EDDYSTONE, HURST POINT Built at Flensburg, Germany for *AWSR Shipping.*

BRITTANY FERRIES

THE COMPANY *See section 1.* The freight division of *Brittany Ferries* traded as *Truckline Ferries* until 2002.

MANAGEMENT Managing Director David Longden, **Freight Director** John Clarke.

ADDRESS New Harbour Road, POOLE, Dorset BH15 4AJ.

TELEPHONE Administration & Enquiries +44 (0)8709 013300, **Reservations** +44 (0)8709 040200.

FAX Administration & Reservations +44 (0)1202 679828, **Telex** 41744, 41745.

INTERNET Website www.brittanyferriesfreight.co.uk *(English)*

ROUTES OPERATED Cherbourg (*Winter* dep: 09.30 Wed, Fri, Sun, 18.30 Tue, Thu, Sat, 23.45 Mon, Wed, Fri, Sun, **Summer** 02.00 Mon, Sat, Sun, 09.30 Tue, Thu, 14.30 Fri, Sat, Sun, 18.30 Mon, Wed, 23.45 Tue, Thu) – Poole (**Winter** dep: 16.00 Mon, Wed, Fri, Sun, 08.30, 23.45 Tue, Thu, Sat, **Summer** dep: 16.00 Tue, Thu, 08.30, 23.45 Mon, Wed, 07.30, 23.45 Fri, Sat, Sun) (4 hrs 30 mins; (1); 1/2 per day). Note Operates with the passenger vessel BARFLEUR to provide three or four sailings every 24 hrs.

Eva Oden *(Robert de Visser)*

Countances *(Kevin Mitchell)*

SECTION 3 – FREIGHT ONLY FERRIES

| 1 | COUTANCES | 6507t | 78 | 17.0k | 125.2m | 58P | - | 58T | BA | FR |

COUTANCES Built at Le Havre, France for *Truckline Ferries* for their Cherbourg – Poole service. In 1986 lengthened to increase vehicle capacity by 34%.

CALEDONIAN MACBRAYNE

THE COMPANY, MANAGEMENT , ADDRESS , TELEPHONE & INTERNET See section 2.

ROUTE OPERATED Ullapool – Stornoway (Lewis) (3 hours; *(1)*; 1 per day) (no fixed schedule – run according to demand).

| 1 | MUIRNEAG | 5801t | 79 | 15.5k | 105.6m | 0P | - | 54T | AS | UK |

MUIRNEAG Built at Frederikshavn, Denmark as the MERCANDIAN CARRIER II for *Mercandia* of Denmark and used on a variety of services. In 1983 she was briefly renamed ALIANZA and between 1984 and 1985 she carried the name CARRIER II. In 1985 sold to *P&O*, renamed the BELARD and used on *Northern Ireland Trailers* services between Ardrossan and Belfast (later Larne), subsequently becoming part of *Pandoro*. In 1993 she was chartered to *IOMSP* subsidiary *Mannin Line* to inaugurate a new service between Great Yarmouth and IJmuiden. In 1994 she was purchased by *IOMSP*; however, in 1995 the *Mannin Line* service ceased and she was chartered back to *Pandoro*. At the end of 1995 she was returned to *IOMSP*. In 1996, after deputising for the PEVERIL, she was briefly chartered to *Exxtor Ferries* (operating between Immingham and Rotterdam) and then laid up. In 1997, she again deputised for the PEVERIL, followed by a short period of charter to *P&O European Ferries*. In 1997 she returned to *IOMSP* and replaced the PEVERIL as the main freight vessel. In 1998 she was sold to the *Aabrenaa Rederi* and operated between Åbenrå and Klaìpeda. This service ended in 199 and she was used on a number of short term charters. In spring 2002 chartered to *Ferryways* and operated between Ipswich and Ostend. In autumn 2002 she was chartered to *Caledonian MacBrayne*, renamed the MUIRNEAG and placed on the Ullapool – Stornoway service, replacing the HASCOSAY (see *NorthLink*).

CHANNEL FREIGHT FERRIES

THE COMPANY *Channel Freight Ferries Ltd* is a UK private sector company, wholly owned by *Clarkson plc*.

MANAGEMENT Managing Director Simon Taylor, **General Manager – UK** Kevin Miller.

ADDRESS *UK* 30 Berth, European Way, Eastern Docks, Southampton SO14 3XD, *France*

Quai de Radicatel, Saint-Jean-de-Folleville, 76170 Lillebonne.

TELEPHONE Administration & Reservations *UK* +44 (0)2380 205 900, *France* +33 2 35 39 01 01.

FAX Administration & Reservations *UK* +44 (0)2380 205 901, *France* +33 2 35 39 39 70

INTERNET Email info@channelfreight.com **Website** www.channelfreight.com *(English, French)*

ROUTE OPERATED Southampton *(dep: 20.30 Daily))* – Radicatel (Port of Rouen) *(dep: 21.30 Daily)* (9 hrs; *(1,2)*; 1 per day).

| 1 | CFF SEINE | 9071t | 84 | 15.0k | 121.5m | 12P | - | 90T | A | RO |
| 2 | CFF SOLENT | 9983t | 84 | 15.5k | 138.5m | 12P | - | 69T | A | RO |

CFF SEINE Built at Galatz, Romania as the BALDER FJORD for *K/S A/S Balder RO/RO No 2* of Norway. In 1986 acquired by *Navrom* of Romania and renamed the BAZIAS 1. In 1990 transferred to *Romline* of Romania and subsequently sold to *Octogon Shipping* of Romania. In 1996 chartered to *Ignazio Messina* of Italy and later renamed the JOLLY ARANCIONE. In late 1997 chartered to *Dart Line* and renamed the DART 1. In late 1999 charter ended, and she was briefly chartered to *Merchant Ferries*, although she was taken back on short term charter by *Dart Line* in February 2000. In 2001 renamed the BAZIAS 1 and in April chartered to *Cobelfret Ferries* to operate between Rotterdam and Purfleet. In autumn she transferred to the Zeebrugge -Purfleet service. In March

2002 chartered to *Dart Line* to operate between Dartford and Dunkerque (not inter-worked with the Vlissingen service). In summer 2002 charter ended. Re-chartered in autumn 2002 and worked additional sailings from Dartford to Zeebrugge. From November 2002 she has operated a triangular Dartford – Dunkerque – Zeebrugge – Dartford service. From January 2003 resumed service between Dartford and Zeebrugge only. In 2004 chartered to *Channel Freight Ferries* and renamed the CFF SEINE.

CFF SOLENT Built at Wismar, East Germany. Launched as the RITZBERG for *DDR RoRo* of East Germany, but delivered to *NavRom* of Romania and renamed the TUTOVA; she was used for charter to many operators. In 1996 sold to *Octogon Shipping* of Romania and renamed the OCTOGON 3. In November she was chartered to *East Coast Ferries* and placed on their Hull – Dunkerque service. This service ceased in January 1999. Later in 1999 she was renamed the TANGO; she was engaged in a number of short term charters. In 2002 she entered service with *Ferryways* on their Zeebrugge – Killingholme service. In 2004 chartered to *Channel Freight Ferries* and renamed the CFF SOLENT.

COBELFRET FERRIES

THE COMPANY *Cobelfret Ferries nv* is a Belgian private sector company, a subsidiary of *Cobelfret nv* of Antwerp.

MANAGEMENT Operations Manager (Belgium) Marc Vandersteen, **UK *Purfleet and Dagenham services*** Cobelfret Ferries UK Ltd – **General Manager, Line & Agency Division** Nick Kavanagh, ***Immingham Services*** Cobelfret Ferries UK Ltd (Immingham Branch) – **General Manager** Peter Kirman.

ADDRESS *Belgium* B-8380 Zeebrugge, Belgium, **UK *Purfleet*** Purfleet Thames Terminal, London Road, Purfleet, Essex RM19 1RP, **UK *Immingham*** Cobelfret Ferries UK Ltd (Immingham Branch), Manby Road, Immingham, South Humberside DN40 3EG.

TELEPHONE Administration & Reservations *Belgium* +32 (0)50 502243, **UK *(Purfleet)*** +44 (0)1708 891199, ***(Immingham)*** +44 (0)1469 573115.

FAX Administration & Reservations *Belgium* +32 (0)50 502219, **UK *(Purfleet)*** +44 (0)1708 890853, ***(Immingham)*** +44 (0)1469 573739.

INTERNET Email *Zeebrugge* pur.cobzee@cobelfretferries.be

Purfleet nick.kavanagh@cobelfretfrerries.co.uk **Website:** www.cobelfret.com *(English)*

ROUTES OPERATED Zeebrugge *(dep: 04.00 Tue-Fri, 10.00 Mon-Fri, 16.00 Mon-Fri, 22.00 Mon-Fri)* – Purfleet *(dep: 06.00 Tue-Fri, 12.00 Mon-Fri, 18.00 Mon-Fri, 23.00 Mon-Fri (Note: weekend service run subject to demand and are liable to vary))* (9 hrs; *(5,10,12,19,20)*; 4 per day), Vlissingen *(dep: 02.00 Tue-Fri, 10.00 Mon-Fri, 18.00 Mon-Fri)* – Dagenham *(dep: 01.00 Tue-Fri, 09.00 Mon-Fri, 17.00 Mon-Fri)* (contract service for Ford Motor Company) (11 hrs; *(8,9,17,18)*; 3 per day), Rotterdam (Brittanniehaven) *(dep: 17.00 Sat, 20.00 Mon-Fri)* – Purfleet *(dep: 16.00 Sat, 19.00 Mon-Fri)* (14 hrs; *(1,11)*; 1 per day), Zeebrugge *(dep: 17.00 Sat, 19.00 Mon-Fri)* – Immingham *(17.00 Sat, 19.00 Mon-Fri)* (14 hrs; *(6,7)* (Sunday sailings as required)); 1/2 per day), Rotterdam (Brittanniehaven) *(dep: 17.30)* – Immingham *(dep: 17.30)* (14 hrs; *(4,13)*; 1 per day), Killingholme *(dep: Tue 01.00, Thu 10.00, Fri 11.00, Sun 22.00)* – Gothenburg *(dep: Tue 17.00, Wed 19.00, Sat 05.00, Sun 06.00)* (36 hrs; *(2,3)*; 4 per week), Zeebrugge *(dep: 06.00 Sun, 09.00 Mon, 12.00 Tue, 18.00 Wed, 18.00 Thu, 22.00 Fri)* – Gothenburg *(dep: 16.00 Sun, 00.01 Tue, 00.01 Wed, 04.00 Thu, 13.00 Fri, 13.00 Sat)* (33-38 hrs; *(14,15,16)*; 6 per week) (this service is operated by *Wagenborg* of the Netherlands for the *Stora-Enso* paper and board group, for the conveyance of their products. *Cobelfret Ferries* act as handling agents at Zeebrugge and market the surplus capacity on the vessels, which is available for general ro-ro traffic. Although this route is strictly outside the scope of this book it is included for the sake of completeness). The Dagenham – Zeebrugge service was moved to Vlissingen in spring 2003. Correct at 31st March 2004; ships are quite frequently moved between routes so the above may have changed by the time this book is published.

1	AMANDA	14715t	78	14.5k	172.9m	12P	-	133T	A	BZ
2	ANNA ODEN	16947t	78	15.0k	170.3m	12P	180C	160T	A	SW

3	BRITTA ODEN	16950t	79	15.0k	170.3m	12P	180C	160T	A	SW
4	CATHERINE	21287t	02	20.0k	182.2m	12P		200T	A2	LX
5	CELANDINE	23986t	00	18.0k	162.5m	12P	630C	157T	A	BS
6	CELESTINE	23986t	96	17.8k	162.5m	24P	630C	157T	A	BS
7	CLEMENTINE	23986t	97	17.8k	162.5m	24P	630C	157T	A	LX
8	CYMBELINE	11866t	92	14.5k	147.4m	8P	350C	100T	A2	LX
9	EGLANTINE	10035t	89	14.5k	147.4m	8P	350C	100T	A2	LX
10	EVA ODEN	16950t	79	15.0k	170.3m	12P	180C	160T	A	SW
11	LOUISE RUSS	18400t	00	23.5k	174.0m	12P	-	171T	A	GI
12	MARABOU	10931t	78	17.0k	161.4m	12P	-	102T	A2	BZ
13	MELUSINE	23987t	99	18.0k	162.5m	12P	630C	157T	A	LX
14	SCHIEBORG	21005t	00	17.0k	183.4m	12P	-	180T	A	NL
15	SLINGEBORG	21005t	00	17.0k	183.4m	12P	-	180T	A	NL
16	SPAARNEBORG	21005t	00	17.0k	183.4m	12P	-	180T	A	NL
17	SYMPHORINE	10030t	88	14.5k	147.4m	8P	350C	100T	A2	LX
18	UNDINE	11854t	91	14.5k	147.4m	8P	350C	100T	A2	LX
19	VALENTINE	23987t	99	18.0k	162.5m	12P	630C	157T	A	BS
20	VICTORINE	23987t	00	18.0k	162.5m	12P	630C	157T	A	BS

AMANDA Built at Kiel, Germany as the MERZARIO PERSIA for *Merzario Line* of Italy and used on services between Italy and the Middle East. In 1986 she was chartered to *Grimaldi* of Italy and renamed the PERSIA, continuing on Middle East services. In 1988 she was sold to *Eimskip* of Iceland and renamed the BRUARFOSS. She was used on their service between Reykjavik, Immingham, Hamburg and Rotterdam. In 1996, the ro-ro service was replaced by a container only service and she was withdrawn. She was renamed the VEGA and was placed a number of short term charters including *Suardiaz* of Spain and *Fred. Olsen Lines*. In 1998, she was sold to *Cobelfret* and renamed the AMANDINE. Used mainly on the Rotterdam – Immingham service until 2002 when she was transferred to the Rotterdam – Purfleet route. In 2003 sold and renamed the AMANDA. Chartered back.

ANNA ODEN Built as the ANNA ODEN for *AB Norsjöfrakt* of Sweden and chartered to *Oden Line* of Sweden for North Sea services, in particular associated with the export of Volvo cars and trucks from Göteborg. In 1980 *Oden Line* was taken over by *Tor Lloyd AB*, a joint venture between *Tor Line* and *Broströms AB* and the charter transferred to them, moving to *Tor Line* in 1981 when *DFDS* took over. In 1987 she was lengthened and on re-entry into service in early 1988 was renamed the TOR FLANDRIA and became regular vessel on the Göteborg – Ghent (Belgium) service, largely operated for Volvo. In 1999 the charter was ended and she was renamed the SOUTHERN CARRIER. She was chartered to a number of operators including *Cobelfret Ferries* and *Flota Suardiaz*. In 2002 she was renamed the ANNA ODEN. In 2003 she was sold to *Cobelfret Ferries*. In 2004 inaugurated a new Immingham – Gothenburg service.

BRITTA ODEN Built at Landskrona, Sweden as the BRITTA ODEN for *AB Norsjöfrakt* (later *Bylock & Norsjöfrakt*) of Sweden and chartered to *Oden Line* of Sweden for North Sea services, in particular associated with the export of Volvo cars and trucks from Göteborg. In 1980 *Oden Line* was taken over by *Tor Lloyd AB*, a joint venture between *Tor Line* and *Broströms AB* and the charter transferred to them, moving to *Tor Line* in 1981 when *DFDS* took over. In 1987 she was enlarged and on re-entry into service in early 1988 was renamed the TOR SCANDIA and became regular vessel on the Göteborg – Gent (Belgium) service. In 1998 renamed the BRITTA ODEN. In 1999 the charter was ended and she was chartered to *Flot Suardiaz*. In September 2003 she was chartered to *Cobelfret Ferries* and placed on the Rotterdam – Purfleet service. In October 2003 purchased by *Cobelfret Ferries*. In 2004 inaugurated a new Immingham – Gothenburg service.

CATHERINE Built as the ROMIRA at Zhonghua , China for *Dag Engström Rederi* of Sweden. For six months engaged on a number of short term charters, including *Cobelfret Ferries* who used her on both the Rotterdam – Immingham and Zeebrugge – Purfleet routes. In September 2002 purchased by *Cobelfret Ferries* and in November 2002, renamed the CATHERINE and started on the Rotterdam

– Immingham service. In spring 2003 chartered to the *US Defense Department* to convey materials to the Persian Gulf. Returned in late summer.

CELANDINE, VALENTINE, VICTORINE Built at Sakaide, Japan for *Cobelfret*. Similar to the CLEMENTINE. The CELANDINE was originally to be called the CATHERINE and the VICTORINE the CELANDINE. The names were changed before delivery. They are generally used on the Zeebrugge – Purfleet service.

CELESTINE Built at Sakaide, Japan as the CELESTINE. In 1996 chartered to the *British MoD* and renamed the SEA CRUSADER. She was originally expected to return to *Cobelfret Ferries* in early 2003 and resume the name CELESTINE; however the charter was extended because of the Iraq crisis. Returned in September 2003 and placed on the Zeebrugge – Immingham service.

CLEMENTINE Built at Sakaide, Japan for *Cobelfret*. Currently used on the Zeebrugge – Immingham service.

CYMBELINE, EGLANTINE, SYMPHORINE, UNDINE Built at Dalian, China for *Cobelfret*. Used on the Dagenham – Vlissingen route.

EVA ODEN Built at Landskrona, Sweden as the EVA ODEN for *AB Norsjöfrakt* (later *Bylock & Norsjöfrakt*) of Sweden and chartered to *Oden Line* of Sweden for North Sea services, in particular associated with the export of Volvo cars and trucks from Gothenburg. In 1980 *Oden Line* was taken over by *Tor Lloyd AB*, a joint venture between *Tor Line* and *Broströms AB* and the charter transferred to them, moving to *Tor Line* in 1981 when *DFDS* took over. In 1987 she was enlarged and on re-entry into service in early 1988 was renamed the TOR BELGIA and became regular vessel on the Gothenburg – Ghent (Belgium) service. In 1998 she was renamed the EVA ODEN and in 1999 the charter was terminated. In 2000 she was chartered to *Cobelfret Ferries*. Until 2003, generally used on the Zeebrugge – Purfleet service. In 2003 transferred to the Rotterdam – Immingham service, replacing the CATHERINE. In July 2003 transferred to the Rotterdam – Purfleet route. In September replaced by the BRITTA ODEN and, on return from refit placed on the Zeebrugge – Purfleet route. Currently operating on the Zeebrugge – Purfleet service.

LOUISE RUSS Launched at Hamburg, Germany as the LOUISE RUSS for *Ernst Russ* of Germany. On completion, renamed the PORTO EXPRESS and chartered to *ROROExpress* to operate between Southampton, Oporto and Tangier. The service ceased in autumn 2001 and she was returned to her owners and resumed the name LOUISE RUSS. In 2002 chartered to *Cobelfret Ferries* and placed on the Rotterdam – Immingham service, replacing the AMANDINE. In 2004 transferred to the Rotterdam – Purfleet service.

MARABOU Built at Lödöse, Sweden as the VALLMO for the *Johansson Group* of Sweden and undertook a variety of charters. In 1982 she was sold to *Cobelfret* and renamed the MATINA. In 1984 renamed the LOVERVAL. In recent years has been chartered out for periods. Currently used on the Zeebrugge – Purfleet service. In 2003 sold and renamed the MARABOU; chartered back.

MELUSINE Built at Sakaide, Japan for *Cobelfret*. Similar to the CLEMENTINE. Currently being used on the Rotterdam – Immingham service.

SCHIEBORG, SLINGEBORG, SPAARNEBORG Built at Lübeck, Germany for *Wagenborg* of The Netherlands and time chartered to *Stora-Enso* to operate between Zeebrugge and Gothenburg.

CONDOR FERRIES

THE COMPANY, MANAGEMENT & ADDRESSES See Section 1.

TELEPHONE Administration & Reservations +44 (0)1481 728620.

FAX Administration & Reservations +44 (0)1481 728521.

INTERNET Email jeff.vidamour@condorferries.co.uk **Website:** www.condorferries.co.uk

ROUTE OPERATED Portsmouth *(dep: 09.00*, 19.30)* – Guernsey *(dep: 04.00, 17.30*)* (6 hrs 30 min) – Jersey *(dep: 08.15, 21.30*)* (10 hrs 30 min; *(1)*; 2 per day) (*operated by ro-pax ferry COMMODORE CLIPPER – see Section 1), Guernsey *(dep: 07.00 Sat)* – Jersey *(dep: 11.00 Sat)* – St Malo *(arr: 14.00 Sat, dep: 17.00 Sat)* – Jersey *(arr: 06.00 Sun)* – Guernsey *(arr: 03.00 Mon)*; *(1)*; 1 per week).

1	COMMODORE GOODWILL	11166t	96	18.3k	126.4m	12P	-	92T	A	BS

COMMODORE GOODWILL Built at Vlissingen, Netherlands for *Commodore Ferries.*

DART LINE

THE COMPANY *Dart Line Ltd* is a British private sector company owned by *Bidcorp plc.* It took over the Dartford – Vlissingen service from *Sally Ferries* in 1996.

MANAGEMENT Managing Director Ron Herman, **Commercial Director** Ronny Daelman, **Continental Sales Director** Helmut Walgræve.

ADDRESS Crossways Business Park, Thames Europort, Dartford, Kent DA2 6QB.

TELEPHONE Administration & Reservations +44 (0)1322 281122.

FAX Administration & Reservations +44 (0)1322 281133.

INTERNET Email sales@dartline.co.uk **Website** www.dartline.co.uk *(English)*

ROUTES OPERATED Dartford *(dep: 07.30 Tue-Fri, 20.30 daily)* – Zeebrugge *(dep: 09.30 Tue-Fri, 20.30 Daily)* (8 hrs 30 mins; *(4,5)*; up to 3 per day), Dartford *(dep: 09.00 Tue-Fri, 20.00 Daily)* – Vlissingen *(dep: 09.00 Tue-Fri, 21.30 Daily)* (9 hrs 30 mins; *(2,3)*; 2 per day), Dartford *(dep: 05.00 Tue-Fri, 23.59 Sun)* – Dunkerque *(dep: 21.30 Mon-Fri)* *(Optional Saturday sailings depending on volumes))* (6 hrs 45 min; *(1)*; 1 per day).

1	DART 2	9082t	84	15.0k	121.5m	12P	-	90T	A	BD
2	DART 3	9088t	85	15.0k	121.5m	12P	-	90T	A	BD
3	DART 4	9088t	85	16.5k	121.5m	12P	-	90T	A	BD
4	DART 8	22748t	80	18.0k	178.5m	12P	-	155T	A	BS
5	DART 9	22748t	80	18.0k	178.5m	12P	-	155T	A	BD
6	MASSILIA	22748t	80	18.0k	178.5m	12P	-	155T	A	UK

DART 2 Built at Galatz, Romania as the BALDER HAV for *K/S A/S Balder RO/RO No 2* of Norway. In 1985 acquired by *Navrom* of Romania, renamed the BAZIAS 2 and used on Mediterranean services. In 1995 chartered to *Dart Line* and renamed the DART 2. Operations began in 1996. Later in 1996 she was sold to *Jacobs Holdings.* Currently operates on the Dartford – Dunkerque route.

DART 3 Built at Galatz, Romania as the BALDER STEN for *K/S A/S Balder RO/RO No 2* of Norway (part of the *Parley Augustsson* group). In 1995 acquired by *Navrom* of Romania and renamed the BAZIAS 3. In 1991 chartered to *Sally Ferries* for the Ramsgate – Ostend freight service and subsequently purchased by a joint *Sally Ferries/Romline* company. In 1993 renamed the SALLY EUROROUTE and re-registered in The Bahamas. In October 1996 she was chartered to *Belfast Freight Ferries* and renamed the MERLE. In 1997 *Sally Ferries'* interests in her were purchased by *Jacobs Holdings.* In January 2000 she joined *Dart Line* and was placed on the Vlissingen service, being renamed the DART 3. In autumn 2000 she was chartered to *NorseMerchant Ferries* and placed

Commodore Godwill *(Miles Cowsill)*

Dart 2 *(FotoFlite)*

again on the Heysham – Belfast service. In autumn 2001 returned to *Dart Line*. Currently operates on the Dartford – Vlissingen route.

DART 4 Built at Galatz, Romania as the BALDER BRE for *K/S A/S Balder RO/RO No 2* of Norway. Later in 1985 acquired by *Navrom* of Romania and renamed the BAZIAS 4. In 1991 chartered to *Sally Ferries* for the Ramsgate – Ostend freight service and subsequently purchased by *Rosal SA*, a joint *Sally Ferries/Romline* company. In 1993 renamed the SALLY EUROLINK and re-registered in The Bahamas. In 1997 *Sally Ferries'* interests in her were purchased by *Jacobs Holdings*. She was later transferred to *Dart Line* and renamed the DART 4. In 1998 she was chartered to *Belfast Freight Ferries*. She returned to *Dart Line* in February 1999 and operated on the Dartford – Vlissingen route. Currently operates on the Dartford – Vlissingen route.

DART 8 Built at Sakaide, Japan as the XI FENG KOU, a deep sea ro-ro/container ship for *China Ocean Shipping Company* of the People's Republic of China for service between the USA, Australia and New Zealand. In 1999, purchased by *Jacobs Holdings*. After delivery, she was converted in Nantong, China to short sea ro-ro specification, including the fitting of a stern ramp (replacing the quarter ramp) and luxury accommodation for 12 drivers and entered service in August 1999 on the Dartford – Zeebrugge service. In 2003 chartered to the *British MoD* for service in the Persian Gulf. Returned in September 2003 and resumed service on the Dartford – Zeebrugge route.

DART 9 Built at Sakaide, Japan as the GU BEI KOU. As the DART 8. She entered service in September 1999 on the Dartford – Zeebrugge service. In 2003 chartered to the *British MoD* for service in the Persian Gulf. Returned in September 2003 and resumed service on the Dartford – Zeebrugge route.

MASSILIA Built at Sakaide, Japan as the ZHANG JIA KOU. As the DART 8. Rebuilt as the DART 10. On completion of rebuilding, chartered to *Sudcargos* of France and renamed the MONT VENTOUX and operated between France and North Africa. In December 2000 the charter ended. In January 2001 she briefly ran on the Dartford – Zeebrugge route in place of the DART 8. After two brief charters to the *British MoD* she was refitted and renamed the DART 10. She then entered long term charter with the *British MoD*. Returned to *Dart Line* in August 2003 and operated between Dartford and Zeebrugge for about three weeks before going on another *MoD* charter to Iraq. She was then chartered to *CETAM* of France and renamed the MASSILIA.

DFDS TOR LINE

THE COMPANY *DFDS Tor Line* is primarily a ro-ro operator on the North Sea and Baltic Sea. It is part of *DFDS A/S* which was formed in 1866 and is today quoted on the Copenhagen Stock Exchange. The *DFDS A/S* group consists of companies in Denmark, Sweden, Norway, the United Kingdom, the Netherlands, Belgium, Germany and Lithuania. 1,200 people are employed at sea and ashore and ro-ro, lo-lo and ro-pax vessels are operated to 18 destinations.

MANAGEMENT Managing Director Ole Frie, **Managing Director UK** Ebbe K Pedersen.

ADDRESS *Denmark (Head Office)* Sankt Annæ Plads 30, DK-1295 Copenhagen K, Denmark, **UK** Nordic House, Western Access Road, Immingham Dock, Immingham, South Humberside DN40 2LZ.

TELEPHONE Administration & Reservations *Denmark (Head Office)* +45 33 42 33 00, **UK** +44 (0)1469 575231.

FAX Administration & Reservations *Denmark* +45 33 42 33 01, **UK** +44 (0)1469 552690.

INTERNET Email info@dfdstorline.com **Website** www.dfdstorline.com *(English)*

ROUTES OPERATED Esbjerg *(dep: 19.00 Tue, Thu, Sat)* - Harwich *(dep: 18.00 Sun, Wed, Fri)* (17hrs; *(Ro-pax vessel DANA SIRENA (see DFDS Seaways, Section 1)*; 3 per week, Esbjerg *(dep: 21.30 Mon-Sat)* - Immingham *(dep: 20.30 Mon-Sat)* (18 hrs)); *(5,21)*; 6 per week, Cuxhaven *(dep: 19.00 Mon, 19.00 Tue, 02.00 Thu, 19.00 Fri, 09.00 Sat)* - Immingham *(dep: 11.00 Sun, 22.30 Tue, 22.30 Wed, 04.30 Fri, 22.30 Sat)* (22 hrs; *(6,11,14)*; 9 per week), Gothenburg *(dep: 19.00 Tue, 16.00 Thu, 19.00 Sat)* - Harwich *(dep: 19.00 Tue, 12.00 Thu, 19.00 Sat)*; 38-52 hrs; *(3,16)*; 3 per week), Gothenburg *(dep: 19.00 Tue, 16.00 Thu)* - Rotterdam *(dep: 02.00 Fri, 05.00 Sat)*; 32-51 hrs; *(3,16)*; 3 per week), Gothenburg *(dep: 21.00 Sun-Fri, 18.00 Sat)* - Immingham *(dep: 04.00 Sun-Fri, 10.00 Sat)* - (26 hrs); *(13,17,18)*; 7 per week), Rotterdam (Maasvlakte) *(dep: 19.00 Mon, 18.00 Tue-*

Fri, 17.00 Sat) - Immingham *(dep: 18.15 Mon-Fri, 17.00 Sat)* (14 hrs 30 mins); *(12,15)*; 6 per week), Gothenburg *(dep: 03.00 Tue-Thu, 03.00 Sat, 23.00 Sat, 23.59 Sun)* - Brevik (Norway) *(dep: 10.00 Sun, 16.00, 15.00)* - Ghent (Belgium) *(dep:, 03.00 Tue-Sat (Brevik served Wed*, Fri and Sun)* 22.00 *Sat* (Gothenburg 42 hrs, Brevik 35 hrs; *(4,7,8,19)*; 6 per week) (*calls at Gothenburg before Brevik), Brevik *(dep: 03.00 Mon, 20.00 Thu)* - Kristiansand *(dep: 11.00 Mon, 02.30 Thu)* - Immingham *(dep: 20.30 Tue, 14.00 Sat)* (approx 27-29 hours Norwegian Port - Immingham; *(10)*; 2 per week) (Note Tue ex Immingham operates Immingham - Kristiansand - Brevik - Immingham, Sat ex Immingham operates Immingham - Brevik - Kristiansand - Immingham), Fredericia *(dep: 22.00 Tue, 02.30 Sat)* – Copenhagen *(dep: Wed 09.00, Sat 15.00)* - Klaìpeda (Lithuania) *(dep: 21.00 Sun, 13.00 Thu)* *(15)*; 3 per week), *(16)*; 2 per week).

DFDS Tor Line also operates a Ro-pax service between Lübeck and Riga. See Section 6.

Space is also used for freight on *DFDS Seaways/DFDS Tor Line* passenger vessels between Harwich and Esbjerg, Cuxhaven and Harwich (3 per week or alternate days during the summer), Gothenburg and Kristiansand/Newcastle (2-3 per week) and IJmuiden – Newcastle (daily).

Note Non-UK routes shown above are strictly outside the scope of this book but are shown for the sale of completeness.

1	STENA SHIPPER	12237t	79	19.0k	168.8m	12P	-	150T	A	UK
2	TOR ANGLIA	17492t	77	16.0k	171.9m	12P	-	180T	A	UK
3	TOR BALTICA	14374t	78	18.5k	163.6m	12P	-	184T	A	BZ
4	TOR BELGIA	21491t	78	19.5k	193.3m	12P	200C	194T	AS	SW
5	TOR BRITANNIA	24196t	00	21.1k	197.5m	12P	-	200T	A	DK
6	TOR CIMBRIA	12189t	86	17.0k	145.0m	12P	-	142T	A	UK
7	TOR DANIA	21491t	78	19.5k	193.3m	12P	200C	192T	AS	SW
8	TOR FLANDRIA	33652t	81	19.7k	193.6m	12P	300C	204T	A	SW
9	TOR FUTURA	18469t	96	18.5k	183.1m	12P	-	164T	AS	DK
10	TOR GOTHIA	12259t	71	16.0k	163.6m	12P	-	110T	A	NO
11	TOR HOLLANDIA	12259t	73	16.0k	163.6m	12P	-	110T	A	NO
12	TOR HUMBRIA	20165t	78	18.5k	183.1m	12P	-	154T	A	NO
13	TOR MAGNOLIA	32400t	03	22.5k	199.8m	12P	-	280T	AS	DK
14	TOR MAXIMA	17068t	78	17.5k	176.2m	12P	-	194T	A	NO
15	TOR MINERVA	32400t	03	22.5k	199.8m	12P	-	280T	AS	NO
16	TOR NERINGA	12494t	75	19.0k	168.0m	12P	-	122T	A	LT
17	TOR PETUNIA	32400t	04	22.5k	199.8m	12P	-	280T	AS	DK
18	TOR PRIMULA	32400t	04	22.5k	199.8m	12P	-	280T	AS	DK
19	TOR SCANDIA	33652t	81	19.5k	193.6m	12P	400C	206T	A	SW
20	TOR SELANDIA	24196t	98	21.1k	197.5m	12P	-	206T	A	SW
21	TOR SUECIA	24200t	99	21.1k	197.5m	12P	-	206T	A	SW

STENA SHIPPER Built at Papenburg, Germany as the NESTOR for *K R G Schepers* of Germany and chartered out. In 1984 she was renamed the NESTOR 1. Chartered to *Crowley Maritime Transport* of the USA for services between the USA and Caribbean. In 1985 she resumed the name NESTOR and operated between Gothenburg and Eemshaven for *EG-Line*. In 1987 she was renamed the AFRICAN GATEWAY and operated for *Nile Dutch Line* between Northern Europe and West Africa. In 1989 she was chartered to *Tor Line* and operated on their Harwich - Immingham - Helsingborg service. She was renamed the NESTOR. Later in 1989 she was chartered to *Stream Line* and renamed the CARIBBEAN STREAM, resuming the name NESTOR in 1991. In 1994 she was sold to *Stena Florida Line* and renamed the STENA SHIPPER. In 1995 she was chartered to *Cobelfret Ferries*, operating mainly on the Zeebrugge - Immingham route. In 2001 chartered to *CETAM* for service between France and Tunisia. In 2004 chartered to *DFDS Tor Line* and placed on the Frederica - Copenhagen - Klaìpeda service.

TOR ANGLIA Built at Kiel, Germany as the MERZARIO GALLIA and chartered to *Merzario Line* of Italy for services between Italy and Saudi Arabia. In 1981 she was chartered to *Wilhelmsen*, renamed the TANA and used between USA and West Africa. In 1983 she was chartered to *Salenia AB* of

Sweden and renamed the NORDIC WASA. In 1987 she had a brief period on charter to *Atlantic Marine* as the AFRICAN GATEWAY and in 1988 she was sold to *Tor Line* and renamed the TOR ANGLIA. In 1989 an additional deck was added. In recent years she operated on the Gothenburg – Ghent service but in late 1998 she was switched to the Immingham – Rotterdam service. In 2001 transferred back to the Gothenburg – Ghent service. In January 2003 chartered to the *British MoD* for three months. Later chartered to the *Danish MoD* for 36 months.

TOR BALTICA Built at Ulsan, South Korea as the ELK for *Stena Rederi* of Sweden and chartered to *P&O Ferrymasters* for use on services from Middlesbrough to Gothenburg and Helsingborg. Purchased by *P&O* in 1981 and lengthened in 1986; she was managed by *P&O North Sea Ferries Ltd.* In 2001 she was sold to *DFDS Tor Line*, who took over management of the vessel. *P&O Ferrymasters'* services ceased in May 2001. She was renamed the TOR BALTICA and transferred to the *DFDS Tor Line* Gothenburg – Harwich route. Now operates between Gothenburg and Harwich.

TOR BELGIA Built at Dunkerque, France as the VILLE DU HAVRE for *Société Française de Transports Maritimes* of France. Between 1979 and 1981 she was chartered to *Foss Line*, renamed the FOSS HAVRE and operated between Europe and the Middle East. In 1987 she was renamed the KAMINA. In 1990 she was chartered to *Maersk Line* of Denmark, renamed the MAERSK KENT and used on *Kent Line* services between Dartford and Zeebrugge. In 1992 she was chartered to and later purchased by *Tor Line*, placed on the Gothenburg – Immingham route and renamed the TOR BRITANNIA. In 1994 she was lengthened by 23.7m. In 1999 she was renamed the TOR BELGIA and was later transferred to the Gothenburg – Brevik -Ghent route. In 2003 she was sold to Norwegian interests and chartered back for four years.

TOR BRITANNIA Built at Ancona, Italy for *DFDS Tor Line*. Operated on the Gothenburg – Immingham route until 2004 when she was transferred to the Esbjerg – Immingham route.

TOR CIMBRIA Built at Frederikshavn, Denmark. Launched as the MERCANDIAN EXPRESS II and immediately bare-boat chartered to *DFDS* for their North Sea freight services, being renamed the DANA CIMBRIA. Purchased by *DFDS* in 1989. Until 1996, generally used on Immingham and North Shields – Esbjerg services; between 1996 and 1998 she operated between Immingham and Esbjerg. In 1998 she was transferred to the Immingham – Cuxhaven service. In 2001 renamed the TOR CIMBRIA. In 2002 sold to Norwegian interests and chartered back to *DFDS Tor Line*.

TOR DANIA Built at Dunkerque, France as the VILLE DE DUNKERQUE for *Société Française de Transports Maritimes* of France. Between 1979 and 1981 she was chartered to *Foss Line*, renamed the FOSS DUNKERQUE and operated between Europe and the Middle East. In 1986 she was chartered to *Grimaldi* of Italy and renamed the G AND C EXPRESS. In 1988 she was briefly chartered to *Elbe-Humber RoLine* and renamed the RAILRO. She was then chartered to *DFDS* where she was renamed the DANIA HAFNIA. The following year she was chartered to *Maersk Line* of Denmark, renamed the MAERSK ESSEX and used on *Kent Line* services between Dartford and Zeebrugge. In 1992 she was chartered to and later purchased by *DFDS* and renamed the TOR DANIA. In 1993 she was renamed the BRIT DANIA but later in the year reverted to her original name. She was generally used on the Harwich – Esbjerg service, working in consort with the passenger ferry DANIA ANGLIA (see *DFDS Seaways*). In 1994 she was lengthened by 23.7m. and chartered to *Tor Line* and placed on the Gothenburg – Immingham route. She now operates on the Gothenburg – Brevik – Ghent route. In 2003 she was sold to Norwegian interests and chartered back for four years.

TOR FLANDRIA Built at Malmö, Sweden as the FINNCLIPPER for the *Johansson Group* of Sweden and chartered out. In 1983 she was sold to *Zenit Shipping* and renamed the ZENIT CLIPPER. She was chartered to *Foss Line* and used on services between Northern Europe and the Middle East. In 1986 she was sold to *Crowley American Transport* of the USA and chartered to the US Military. She was renamed the AMERICAN FALCON and used for military transport purposes across the world. In 1998 sold to *Stena Rederi* and was renamed the STENA PARTNER. She was then chartered to *Tor Line* and renamed the TOR FLANDRIA; part of her charter conditions are that she be purchased at the end of the five year charter period; however, she was purchased in 2001. She is normally used on the Gothenburg – Brevik – Ghent route. In 2002 she was sold to *Norwegian Scandinavian Ro/Ro KS* and chartered back for 5.5 years.

TOR FUTURA Built at Donada, Italy as the DANA FUTURA for *DFDS*. In 2001 she was renamed the TOR FUTURA. Initially operated mainly between Esbjerg and Harwich, but latterly operated mainly between Esbjerg and Immingham. In 2004 chartered to *Toll Shipping* of Australia.

TOR GOTHIA Built at Sandefjord, Norway for *Tor Line*. Lengthened in 1977. She was usually used on the Immingham – Rotterdam service. In 1999 transferred to the Norway – UK service and in 2000 to the Norway – UK/Netherlands service. In 2001 she was moved to the Rotterdam – Immingham route. Now operates on the Immingham – Kristiansand – Brevik route.

TOR HOLLANDIA Built at Sandefjord, Norway as the TOR DANIA for charter to *Tor Line*. In 1975 she was chartered to *Salenrederierna* for service in the Middle East and renamed the BANDAR ABBAS EXPRESS. In 1977 she was lengthened and, in 1978, returned to *Tor Line* and resumed the name TOR DANIA. Purchased by *Tor Line* in 1986. In 1992 she was renamed the TOR DAN and in 1993 the TOR HOLLANDIA. She was usually used on the Immingham – Rotterdam service. In 1999 transferred to the Norway – UK/Netherlands services (Netherlands services ceased in 2001). In 2002 moved to the Norway – Immingham route. Now operates on other routes.

TOR HUMBRIA Built at Oskarshamn, Sweden as the EMIRATES EXPRESS for *A/S Skarhamns Oljetransport* of Norway and chartered to *Mideastcargo* for services between Europe and the Middle East. In 1981 chartered to *OT West Africa Line* for services between Europe and West Africa and renamed the ABUJA EXPRESS. In 1983 chartered to *Foss Line*, renamed the FOSSEAGLE and returned to Middle East service. In 1985 she was renamed the FINNEAGLE, chartered briefly to *Finncarriers* and then to *Fred. Olsen Lines*. In 1987 they purchased her and renamed her the BORAC. In 1999 purchased by *DFDS Tor Line* and renamed the TOR HUMBRIA. In 2000 she was chartered to *Costa Container Lines spa* of Italy, operating between Savano and Catania. This service ended in early 2001 and she was then chartered to *CoTuNav* of Tunisia. Returned in April 2001. In 2003 sold to Norwegian interests and chartered back. She currently operates on the Rotterdam – Immingham service.

TOR MAGNOLIA Built at Flensburg, Germany for *DFDS Tor Line* to operate on the Gothenburg – Immingham route.

TOR MAXIMA Built at Osaka, Japan as the DANA MAXIMA for *DFDS* for their North Sea services. Until 1996, generally used on the Esbjerg – Grimsby and North Shields services. In summer 1995 she was lengthened to increase trailer capacity. In December 2000 she was renamed the TOR MAXIMA. In December 2001 sold to *Per Sand* of Norway and chartered back for 3 years. She currently operates between Cuxhaven and Immingham.

TOR MINERVA Built at Oskarshamn, Sweden as the BANDAR ABBAS EXPRESS for *A/S Skarhamns Oljetransport* of Norway and chartered out. In 1980 renamed the SAUDI EXPRESS. During the early eighties she undertook a number of charters including *Mideastcargo* for services between Europe and the Middle East, *Atlanticargo* for services from Europe to USA and Mexico and *OT West Africa Line* from Europe to West Africa. In 1983 she was chartered to *Ignazio Messina* of Italy, renamed the JOLLY AVORIO and used on services from Italy to the Middle East. In 1986 this charter ended and she briefly reverted to the name the SAUDI EXPRESS before being chartered again to *OT West Africa Line* and renamed the KARAWA. In 1987 she was sold to *Fred. Olsen Lines* who renamed her the BORACAY; she operated between Norway and Northern Europe. In 1998 she was sold to *DFDS*, renamed the DANA MINERVA and placed on the Esbjerg – Immingham route. In 2001 she was renamed the TOR MINERVA. She now operates between Immingham and Rotterdam.

TOR NERINGA Built at Florø, Norway as the BALDUIN for *Fred. Olsen Lines*. In 1999 purchased by *DFDS Tor Line* and renamed the TOR NORVEGIA. Initially used on Norway – UK/Netherlands services; in 2001 moved to the Fredericia – Copenhagen – Klaìpeda (Lithuania) service. In 2001 December 2001 sold to *Lisco Baltic Service* of Lithuania, renamed the TOR NERINGA and chartered back to *DFDS Tor Line*. In 2004 moved to the Gothenburg-Harwich/Rotterdam route.

TOR PETUNIA Built at Flensburg, Germany for *DFDS Tor Line* to operate on the Gothenburg – Immingham route.

TOR PRIMULA Built at Flensburg, Germany for *DFDS Tor Line* to operate on the Gothenburg – Immingham route.

Hascosay *(Colin Smith)*

Tor Neringa *(FotoFlite)*

TOR SCANDIA Built at Malmö, Sweden as the KUWAIT EXPRESS for the *Johansson Group* of Sweden and chartered to *NYK Line* of Japan for services between Japan and the Arabian Gulf. In 1983 she was sold to *Zenit Shipping* and renamed the ZENIT EXPRESS. She was chartered to *Foss Line* and used on services between Northern Europe and the Middle East. In 1984 she was sold to *Crowley American Transport* of the USA and chartered to the US Military. She was reamed the AMERICAN CONDOR and used for military transport purposes across the world. In 1998 she was sold to *Stena Rederi* and renamed the STENA PORTER. Later she was sold to *Tor Line* and renamed the TOR SCANDIA. She is used on the Gothenburg – Brevik – Ghent route. In 2002 she was sold to Norwegian Scandinavian Ro/Ro KS and chartered back for 5.5 years.

TOR SELANDIA Built at Ancona, Italy for *DFDS Tor Line*. Operated on the Gothenburg – Immingham route until 2004. In spring 2004 replaced by the TOR PRIMULA. To be moved to another route.

TOR SUECIA Built at Ancona, Italy for *DFDS Tor Line*. Operated on the Gothenburg – Immingham route until 2004 when she was transferred to the Esbjerg – Immingham route.

Under Construction

22	TOR BEGONIA	32400t	04	22.5k	199.8m	12P	-	280T	AS	SW
23	TOR FRESIA	32400t	04	22.5k	199.8m	12P	-	280T	AS	SW
24	NEWBUILDING 6	32400t	06	22.5k	199.8m	12P	-	280T	AS	DK

TOR BEGONIA, TOR FREESIA & NEWBUILDING 6 Under construction at Flensburg, Germany for *DFDS Tor Line*.

FERRYWAYS

THE COMPANY *Ferryways nv* is a Belgian company.

MANAGEMENT Managing Director J Dewilde, **Marketing Manager** Filip Olde Bijvank.

ADDRESS *Ostend* Esplanadestraat 10, B-8400 Ostend, Belgium. *Ipswich* West Bank Terminal, Wherstead Road, Ipswich IP2 8NB.

TELEPHONE Administration & Reservations *Ostend* +32 (0)59 34 22 20, *Ipswich* +44 (0)1473 696200.

FAX Administration & Reservations *Ostend* +32 (0)59 34 22 29, *Ipswich* +44 (0)1473 696201.

INTERNET Email *Ostend* info@ferryways.com *Ipswich* **Website** www.ferryways.co.uk *(English)*

ROUTE OPERATED Ostend *(dep: 03.30 Tue-Sat, 11.00 Tue -Fri, 15.00 Sat, 17.00 Mon-Fri, 21.30 Sun, 22.00 Mon-Fri,)* – Ipswich *(dep: 03.00 Tue-Sat, 09.30 Tue-Fri, 10.00 Sat, 16.00 Mon-Fri, 21.30 Sun, 22.00 Mon-Fri)* (7 hrs; *(1,3,5,6)*; 4 per day), Ostend *(dep: 02.00 Tue-Sat, 22.00 Sat)* – Killingholme *(dep: 23.59 Mon-Sat)* (14/19 hrs; *(2,4)*; 1 per day.

1	ANGLIAN WAY	7635t	78	15.0k	141.3m	12P	55C	84T	A	PA
2	CALIBUR	9963t	76	16.0k	126.4m	12P	-	95T	A	MA
3	FLANDERS WAY	7628t	77	16.0k	141.3m	12P	55C	84T	A	PA
4	HUMBER WAY	9963t	76	16.0k	132.5m	12P	-	96T	A	MA
5	IPSWICH WAY	6568t	80	15.0k	136.0m	12P	-	84T	A	PA
6	OSTEND WAY	6568t	80	15.0k	136.1m	12P	-	84T	A	PA

ANGLIAN WAY Built at Bremerhaven, Germany as the THOMAS WEHR for *Wehr Transport* of Germany as THOMAS WEHR but on delivery chartered to *Wacro Line* and renamed the WACRO EXPRESS. In 1978 charter ended and she was renamed the THOMAS WEHR. Over the next few years she was chartered to several operators. In 1982 she was chartered to *Tor Lloyd* (later *Tor Line*) for North Sea service and renamed the TOR NEERLANDIA. In 1985 the charter was transferred to *DFDS* and she was renamed the DANA GERMANIA. This charter terminated in 1985 and she resumed her original name. In early 1986 she was chartered to *North Sea Ferries* for their Hull – Zeebrugge service. This charter ended in summer 1987. Subsequent charters included *Cobelfret* and *Elbe-Humber RoLine* and a twelve month period with *North Sea Ferries* again – this time on the Hull – Rotterdam and Teesport – Zeebrugge routes. In 1993 she was renamed the MANA, then the SANTA

MARIA and finally chartered to *TT-Line* and renamed the FULDATAL. 1994 she was chartered to *Horn Line* for service between Europe and the Caribbean and renamed the HORNLINK. Later that year she was chartered to *P&O European Ferries* for the Portsmouth – Le Havre freight service and resumed the name THOMAS WEHR. In late 1995 transferred to the Felixstowe – Zeebrugge freight service. In autumn 1999 the charter was ended. In 2000 she was chartered to *Ferryways*. In 2001 she was purchased by *Ferryways* and renamed the ANGLIAN WAY. Generally operates between Ostend and Ipswich.

CALIBUR Built at Brevik, Norway as the SEASPEED DANA for *Seaspeed Ferries* of Greece and chartered to *Fred. Olsen Seaspeed Ferries* for service in the Middle East. In 1979 chartered to *Roto Line* and used on services between Sweden and the UK. , renamed the DANA In 1983 she was sold to *Stena Line* and embarked on a number of charters, mainly in the Caribbean. In 1990 she was chartered to *CoTuNav* of Tunisia, renamed the SALAH L and used on services from Tunisia to Southern Europe. In 1993 she was chartered to *Olympic Ferries* of Greece, renamed the SENATOR, operating between Greece and Italy. In 1995 she was sold to *Exxtor Ferries* and renamed the EXCALIBUR. She operated between Immingham and Rotterdam. When the service was taken over by *Cobelfret Ferries* in 1997, the charter was ended. She was sold to *Kaliningrad Key Kine* of Malta, renamed the CALIBUR and placed on their Køge (Denmark) – Aabenraa (Denmark) – Kaliningrad service. In 1998 she was sold to *V Ships* of Monaco and placed on the charter market, undertaking a number of short charters. In 2003 she was chartered to *Ferryways* and placed on their Ostend – Killingholme service.

FLANDERS WAY Built at Bremerhaven, Germany as the GABRIELE WEHR for *Wehr Transport* of Germany and chartered to several operators. In 1982, chartered to *Tor Lloyd* (later *Tor Line*) for North Sea service and renamed the TOR ANGLIA. This charter terminated in 1985 when she resumed her original name and, in early 1986, she was chartered to *North Sea Ferries* for their Hull – Zeebrugge service. This charter ended in summer 1987 when the lengthened NORLAND and NORSTAR entered service. Subsequent charters included *Kent Line* and *Brittany Ferries*. In 1989 she was chartered to *P&O European Ferries* for the Portsmouth – Le Havre freight service. Her charter was terminated following the transfer of the EUROPEAN TRADER to the route in late 1992 but in 1993 it was renewed, following the transfer of the EUROPEAN CLEARWAY (now the EUROPEAN PATHFINDER) to *Pandoro*. In 1996, she was transferred to the Felixstowe – Zeebrugge service. In autumn 1999 the charter was ended. In 2000 she was chartered to *Ferryways*. In 2001 she was purchased by *Ferryways* and renamed the FLANDERS WAY. Generally operates between Ostend and Ipswich.

HUMBER WAY Built as the SEASPEED DORA for *Seaspeed Ferries* of Greece and chartered to *Fred. Olsen Seaspeed Ferries* for service in the Middle East. In renamed the INGER EXPRESS and in 1979 chartered to *Roto Line*, used on services between Sweden and the UK. In 1981 she was sold to *Cobelfret*, renamed the MARCEL C and used on their services between the UK and Belgium. In 1989 she was sold to *Bassro Star A/S* of the Bahamas and renamed the BASSRO STAR. She embarked on a series of charters including *Belfast Freight Ferries*, *North Sea Ferries* and a number of other operators. In 1995 she was sold to *Exxtor Ferries* and renamed the ENDEAVOUR. In 1997 she was sold to *Cobelfret*, when they took over the *Exxtor Ferries'* service, and renamed the MARCELINE. She continued to operate between Immingham and Rotterdam. In 1998 she was sold to *East West Mediterranean Ltd* of Malta (trading as *Van Uden RoRo*) and renamed the BEATRIXHAVEN. She operated between Europe and the Middle East plus undertaking a number of short term charters. In 2003 she was chartered to *Ferryways* and later renamed the HUMBER WAY. Generally operates between Ipswich and Killingholme.

IPSWICH WAY Built at Karslkrona, Sweden as the BALDER DONA for *Dag Engström Rederi* of Sweden and undertook a number of charters in the Caribbean and Mediterranean. In 1984 she was renamed the RODONA and chartered to *Seaboard Shipping* of the USA and used on Caribbean services. In 1987 she was chartered to the *Ford Motor Company* for conveyance of privately owned trailers between Dagenham and Zeebrugge. In 1995 *Cobelfret Ferries* took over the operation of this service and she was used on both the Purfleet – Zeebrugge and Dagenham – Zeebrugge services. In 1999 she was chartered to *P&O North Sea Ferries* to operate between Felixstowe and Zeebrugge. In 2002 this service ceased and she was chartered to *Ferryways*. In 2003 purchased by *Ferryways* and renamed the ISPWICH WAY. Generally operates between Ostend and Ipswich.

OSTEND WAY Built at Karlskrona, Sweden as the BALDER VINGA for *Dag Engström Rederi* of Sweden and undertook a number of charters in the Caribbean and Mediterranean. In 1984 she was renamed the ROVINGA and chartered to *Seaboard Shipping* of the USA and used on Caribbean services. In 1985 she was renamed the AZUA. In 1987 she briefly reverted to the name ROVINGA before being renamed the SAPPHIRE and chartered to the *Ford Motor Company* for conveyance of privately owned trailers between Dagenham and Zeebrugge. Since 1995, as the IPSWICH WAY. Normally operates on the Ipswich service. In 2003 purchased by *Ferryways* and renamed the OSTEND WAY.

FINNLINES

THE COMPANY *Finnlines PLC* is a Finnish private sector company. Services to the UK are marketed by *Finnlines UK Ltd*, a British private sector company. From 1st January 2001, *Finncarriers* was merged into the parent company, trading as *Finnlines Cargo Service*.

MANAGEMENT *Finnlines* President Antti Lageroos, **Vice-President** Simo Airas.

ADDRESS *Finnlines* PO Box 197, Salmisaarenkatu 1, FIN-00181 Helsinki, Finland, *Finnlines UK Ltd* 8 Heron Quay, London E14 4JB.

TELEPHONE Administration & Reservations *Finnlines* +358 (0)10 34350, *Finnlines UK Ltd* +44 (0)20 7519 7300.

FAX Administration *Finnlines* +358 (0)10 3435200, *Finnlines UK Ltd* +44 (0)20 7536 0255.

INTERNET Email *Finnlines* info@finnlines.fi *Finnlines UK Ltd* london@finnlines.co.uk

Websites www.finnlines.fi *(English, Finnish)*

ROUTES OPERATED Hanko *(dep: 11.00 Mon)* – Helsinki (Finland) *(arr: 16.00 Mon, dep: 22.00 Mon)* – Hamina (Finland) *(arr: 06.00 Tue, dep: 23.00 Tue)* – Felixstowe *(arr: 20.00 Fri, dep: 07.00 Sat)* – Zeebrugge *(arr: 12.00 Sat, 16.00 Sat)* – Helsinki *(arr: 11.00 Tue, dep: 21.00 Tue)* – Hamina *(arr: 06.00 Wed, dep: 20.00 Thu)* – Helsinki *(arr: 07.00 Fri, dep: 23.00 Fri)* – Zeebrugge *(arr: 14.00 Mon, dep: 18.00 Mon)* – Felixstowe *(arr: 08.00 Tue, dep: 18.00 Tue)* – Amsterdam *(arr: 08.00 Wed, dep 15.00 Thu)* – Zeebrugge *(arr: 04.00 Fri, dep: 12.00 Fri)* – Hanko *(arr: 07.00 Mon)* *(3,4,19)*; three ships operate on a three week cycle which gives two sailings per week between Finland and UK/Benelux), Kemi *(dep: 16.00 Mon)* – Oulu *(arr: 06.00 Tue, dep: 22.00 Tue)* – Felixstowe *(arr: 08.00 Sat, dep: 16.00 Sat)* – Antwerp *(arr: 08.00 Sun, dep: 16.00 Sun)* – Helsinki *(arr: 07.00 Wed, dep 11.00 Wed)* – Kemi *(arr: 16.00 Thu, dep: 23.00 Thu)* – Oulu *(arr: 06.00 Fri, dep: 22.00 Fri)* – Antwerp *(arr: 14.00 Tue, dep: 22.00 Tue)* – Felixstowe *(arr: 08.00 Wed, dep: 14.00 Wed)* – Helsinki *(arr: 07.00 Sat, dep: 12.00 Sat)* – Turku *(arr: 08.00 Sun, 11.00 Sun)* – Kemi *(arr: 08.00 Mon)(5,6,7)*; three ships operate on a three week cycle which gives two sailings per week between Finland and UK/Benelux), Hamina *(dep: 23.00 Thu)* – Helsinki *(arr: 07.00 Fri, dep: 15.00 Fri)* – Hull *(arr: 07.00 Mon, dep: 18.00 Mon)* – Hamina *(arr: 12.00 Thu)* (3 days; *(12)*; 1 per week), Rauma *(dep: 20.00 Wed)* – Hull *(arr: 07.00 Sat, dep: 20.00 Sat)* – Helsinki *(arr: 08.00 Tue, dep: 15.00 Tue)* – Rauma *(arr: 07.00 Wed)*, (3 days; *(16)*; 1 per week).

In view of the fact that ships are liable to be transferred between routes, the following is a list of all *Finnlines Cargo* ro-ro vessels, including those which currently do not serve the UK. Ro-pax vessels (none of which normally serve the UK) are listed in Section 6.

1	ANTARES	5989t	88	20.3k	157.6m	18P	-	154T	A	NO
2	ASTREA	7380t	91	15.0k	129.1m	0P	-	60T	A	FI
3	BALTIC EIDER	20865t	89	19.0k	157.7m	0P	-	160T	A	IM
4	BALTICA	21224t	90	19.0k	157.7m	0P	-	163T	A	CY
5	BIRKA CARRIER	12251t	98	20.0k	155.5m	12P	-	124T	A2	FI
6	BIRKA EXPRESS	12251t	97	20.0k	154.5m	12P	-	124T	A2	FI
7	BIRKA TRADER	12251t	98	20.0k	154.5m	12P	-	124T	A2	FI
8	FINNBIRCH	15396t	78	17.0k	155.9m	0P	-	155T	A	SW
9	FINNFOREST	15525t	78	17.0k	155.9m	0P	-	155T	A	SW

10	FINNHAWK	11530t	01	20.0k	162.2m	12P	-	140T	A	NO
11	FINNKRAFT	11530t	00	20.0k	162.2m	12P	-	140T	A	UK
12	FINNMASTER	11530t	00	20.0k	162.2m	12P	-	140T	A	UK
13	FINNMILL	11400t	02	20.0k	184.8m	12P	-	230T	A	UK
14	FINNOAK	7953t	91	16.5k	139.5m	0P	-	94T	A	FI
15	FINNPULP	11400t	02	20.0k	184.8m	12P	-	230T	A	UK
16	FINNREEL	11530t	00	20.0k	162.2m	12P	-	140T	A	UK
17	MERCHANT	21195t	82	17.0k	154.9m	12P	-	160T	A	FI
18	MIRANDA	10471t	99	20.3k	153.5m	12P	-	120T	A2	FI
19	NORCLIFF	8407t	94	14.5k	125.2m	0P	-	78T	A	NO
20	POLARIS	7944t	88	14.7k	122.0m	0P	500C	38T	A	GY
21	RIDER	20077t	84	18.9k	186.5m	12P	-	140T	A	GY
22	RUNNER	20729t	90	18.9k	189.7m	12P	-	144t	A	GY
23	VASALAND	20203t	84	14.0k	155.0m	0P	-	160T	A	SW

ANTARES Built at Gdansk, Poland as the FINNFORREST for *Neste* of Finland and chartered to *Finncarriers*. In 1988 renamed the ANTARES. In 2002 chartered to *Stena Line* to operate between Harwich and Rotterdam. In 2003 chartered to the *British MoD* for service to the Gulf. Current operates on the Uusi – Kaupunki – Rauma – Rostock – Lübeck – Travemünde route.

ASTREA Built at Tomrefjord, Norway for *Finncarriers*. Operates between Finland and Spain – Portugal via Antwerp.

BALTIC EIDER Built at Ulsan, South Korea for *United Baltic Corporation*. Used on the Helsinki – Hamina – Felixstowe – Amsterdam – Zeebrugge service.

BALTICA Built at Ulsan, South Korea as the AHLERS BALTIC the for *Ahlers Line* and chartered to *Finncarriers*. In 1995 acquired by *Poseidon Schiffahrt AG* of Germany and renamed the TRANSBALTICA. She continued to be chartered to *Finncarriers* and was acquired by them when they purchased *Poseidon Schiffahrt AG* (now *Finnlines Deutschland AG*) in 1997. In 2003 sold to Norwegian interests and chartered back. She was renamed the BALTICA. Currently operating on the Helsinki – Hamina – Felixstowe – Zeebrugge service.

BIRKA CARRIER, BIRKA EXPRESS, BIRKA TRADER Built at Rissa, Norway as the UNITED CARRIER, UNITED EXPRESS and UNITED TRADER for *United Shipping* (a subsidiary of *Birka Shipping*) of Finland and chartered to *Transfennica*. During 2000 they were used on their Kemi – Oulu – Antwerp – Felixstowe service. In 2001 the route was transferred to *Finnlines* and vessels used sub-chartered to them. In 2002 *United Shipping* was renamed *Birka Cargo* and the ships were renamed the BIRKA CARRIER, BIRKA EXPRESS and BIRKA TRADER.

FINNBIRCH Laid down at Ulsan, South Korea as the STENA PROSPER and completed as the ATLANTIC PROSPER for *Stena Rederi* and chartered to *ACL* of Great Britain for service between Britain and Canada. In 1981 chartered to *Merzario Line* of Italy for services between Italy and Saudi Arabia and renamed, initially, the STENA IONIA and then the MERZARIO IONIA. In 1982 she reverted to the name STENA IONIA and was chartered to *OT West Africa Line* for services between Europe and Nigeria. In 1985 she was renamed the STENA GOTHICA and used on *Stena Portlink* services. In 1988 she was chartered to *Bore Line* of Finland and renamed the BORE GOTHICA. In 1992 chartered to *Finncarriers*. In 1996 renamed the FINNBIRCH. In 1997 she began operating a service between Hull and Zeebrugge on charter to *P&O North Sea Ferries* in the course of her normal two week circuit from Finland. This ceased in 1999. In 2000 transferred to the Helsinki – Århus service.

FINNFOREST Laid down at Ulsan, South Korea as the STENA PROJECT and completed as ATLANTIC PROJECT for *Stena Rederi* and chartered to *ACL* (see above). In 1981 chartered to *Merzario Line* of Italy for services between Italy and Saudi Arabia and renamed the MERZARIO HISPANIA. In 1983 returned to *Stena Line* and renamed the STENA HISPANIA. In 1984 chartered to *Kotka Line* of Finland, renamed the KOTKA VIOLET and used on their services between Finland, UK and West Africa. This charter ended in 1985 and she was again named the STENA HISPANIA. In 1986 she was renamed the STENA BRITANNICA and used on *Stena Portlink* (later *Stena Tor Line*) service between Sweden and Britain. In 1988 she was chartered to *Bore Line* of Finland, renamed the BORE

BRITANNICA and used on services between Finland and Britain. In 1992 chartered to *Finncarriers*. In 1997 renamed the FINNFOREST. In 1997 she began operating a service between Hull and Zeebrugge on charter to *P&O North Sea Ferries* in the course of her normal two week circuit from Finland. This ceased in 1999. In 2000 transferred to the Helsinki – Århus service.

FINNHAWK Built at Nanjing, China for *Finnlines*. Currently operates on the Rauma – Lübeck – Helsinki – Travemünde route.

FINNKRAFT Built at Nanjing, China for *Forest Terminals* and chartered to *Finncarriers*. Currently operates on the Rauma – Lübeck – Helsinki – Travemünde route.

FINNMASTER Built at Nanjing, China for *Forest Terminals* and chartered to *Finncarriers*. Operates on Helsinki – Rauma – Hull route.

FINNMILL Built at Nanjing, China for *Forest Terminals* and chartered to *Finnlines*. Currently used on the Helsinki – Kotka – Rauma – Lübeck route.

FINNOAK Built at Rissa, Norway as the AHTELA for *Holming Shipping* of Finland and chartered to *Transfennica*. In 1997 renamed the FINNOAK and chartered to *Finncarriers*. Used on the *Polfin Line* service between Helsinki – Kotka and Gdynia – Szczecin (joint with *Euroafrica Shipping* of Poland).

FINNPULP Built at Nanjing, China for *Forest Terminals* and chartered to *Finnlines*. Currently used on the Helsinki – Kotka – Rauma – Lübeck service.

FINNREEL Launched as the FINNMAID but renamed before delivery. Built at Nanjing, China for *Forest Terminals* and chartered to *Finncarriers*. Currently operating on the Hamina – Helsinki – Hull service.

MERCHANT Built as the FINNMERCHANT at Rauma, Finland for *Finnlines*. In 2003 sold to subsidiary *Nordö-Link* and chartered back. Later sold to *Finn Ro Ro* of Norway and renamed the MERCHANT; charter continued. Currently operates on the Helsinki – Hamina – Felixstowe – Amsterdam – Zeebrugge service.

MIRANDA Built at Hamburg, Germany for *Godby Shipping A/S* of Finland. Initially chartered to *Transfennica*. In 2000 she was chartered to *Finnlines*. Currently used on the Turku – Kemi – Oulu – Lübeck – Travemünde route.

NORCLIFF Built at Trogir, Croatia for *Sea-Link AB* of Sweden but due to delays order cancelled before completion. On delivery, renamed the BRAVO and chartered to the *Stora Paper Group*. In 1995 chartered to *North Sea Ferries* and renamed the NORCLIFF. She became second vessel on the Middlesbrough – Rotterdam service. The charter ended in 1996 when the service reverted to a single ship operation. She kept her *NSF* name and was chartered to a number of operators including *Finnlines (Finncarriers)*. In 2001 again chartered to *Finnlines* and is currently used on the Finland to Spain – Portugal via Antwerp service.

POLARIS Built at Hamburg, Germany for *Pohl Shipping* and chartered to Finncarriers. Currently operating between Finland and Spain – Portugal via Antwerp.

RIDER Built at Bremerhaven, Germany as the RAILSHIP II for *Railship*, later taken over by Finnlines. In 2002 renamed the FINNRIDER. Operates between Travemünde and Turku.

RUNNER Built at Bremerhaven, Germany as the RAILSHIP III for *Railship*, later taken over by Finnlines. In 2002 role changed from rail ferry to truck and trailer ferry; renamed the FINNRUNNER. In 2003 sold to Norwegian interests and chartered back. In 2004 renamed the RUNNER. Operates between Travemünde and Turku.

VASALAND Built at Rauma, Finland as the OIHONNA for *Finncarriers*. In 2003 sold to *Stena RoRo*. Later sold to *Imperial RoRo*, chartered back to *Stena RoRo* and then time chartered to *Finnlines*. Currently operating on the Lübeck – Malmö – Hanko – Kotka – Rostock service.

MANN LINES

THE COMPANY *Mann Lines* is owned by *Mann & Son (London) Ltd* of Great Britain. It replaced in 2001 *ArgoMann Ferry Service*, a joint venture between *Argo Reederei* of Germany and *Mann & Son*.

MANAGEMENT Managing Director Bill Binks.

ADDRESS *UK* Mann & Son (London) Ltd, The Naval House, Kings Quay Street, Harwich CO12 3JJ, *Germany* Mann Lines GmbH, Birkenstrasse 15, 28195 Bremen.

TELEPHONE Administration & Reservations *UK* +44 (0)1255 245200, *Germany* +49 (0)421 163850.

FAX Administration & Reservations *UK* +44 (0)1255 245219, *Germany* +49 (0)421 1638520.

INTERNET Email enquiry@mannlines.co.uk **Website** www.mannlines.com *(English)*

ROUTE OPERATED Harwich (Navyard) *(dep: 19.00 Fri)* – Cuxhaven *(arr: 14.00 Sat, dep: 18.00 Sat)* – Paldiski *(arr: 16.00 Mon, dep: 23.00 Mon)* – Turku *(arr: 08.00 Tue, dep: 15.00 Tue)* – Bremerhaven *(arr: 12.00 Thu, dep: 17.00 Thu)* – Harwich *(arr: 11.00 Fri)*; *(1)*; one per week).

| 1 | ESTRADEN | 18205t | 99 | 20.0k | 162.7m | 12P | 130C | 170T | A | FI |
| 2 | HAMBURG | 8454t | 77 | 16.5k | 123.6m | 12P | - | 64T | A | MA |

ESTRADEN Built at Rauma, Finland as the ESTRADEN for *Rederi Ab Engship* of Finland and chartered to *ArgoMann*. Later in 1999 renamed the AMAZON. In 2001 charter was taken over by *Mann Lines* and later in the year she resumed the name ESTRADEN.

HAMBURG Built in Rauma, Finland as the MEKHANIK FEDOROV for *Latvian Shipping* of the former Soviet Union. In 1991 renamed the MEHANIKIS FJODOROVS (the same name but in Latvian rather than Russian). She was generally used on services from Latvia to North West Europe. In 1999 she was chartered to *CCTL*, renamed the CCTL HAMBURG and placed on their Hamburg – Hull service. Service switched to Killingholme in November 2000. In 2002 the charter ended, she was renamed the HAMBURG and she was employed on a number of short term charters. In 2003 chartered to *Mann Lines*. In 2004 chartered to *SCF St Peterburg Line*

NORFOLKLINE

THE COMPANY, MANAGEMENT, ADDRESS, TELEPHONE & INTERNET See Section 1.

ROUTES OPERATED Felixstowe *(dep: 00.30 Daily, 06.00 Tue-Fr, 12.00 Daily, 19.00 Mon-Fri)* – Scheveningen *(dep: 07.00 Tue-Fri, 14.30 Daily, 19.30 Mon-Sat, 22.00 Sun, 23.59 Mon-Fri)* (7 hrs; *(1,2,3,4)*; 4 per day), Immingham – Esbjerg (5 per week), Harwich – Esbjerg (6/7 per week). UK – Denmark services operated in conjunction with *DFDS Tor Line* who provide all vessels.

1	MAERSK ANGLIA	13017t	00	18.6k	142.5m	12P	-	114T	A	NL
2	MAERSK EXPORTER	13017t	96	18.6k	142.5m	12P	-	114T	A	NL
3	MAERSK FLANDERS	13073t	00	18.6k	142.5m	12P	-	114T	A	NL
4	MAERSK IMPORTER	13017t	96	18.6k	142.5m	12P	-	114T	A	NL

MAERSK ANGLIA Built at Guangzhou, China for *Norfolkline*. Entered service as the GUANGZHOU 7130011 (unofficially the 'China II') but renamed shortly afterwards. Operates on the Scheveningen – Felixstowe service.

MAERSK EXPORTER, MAERSK IMPORTER Built at Shimizu, Japan for *Norfolkline*. Used on the Felixstowe – Scheveningen service.

MAERSK FLANDERS Built at Guangzhou, China for *Norfolkline*. Used on the Felixstowe – Scheveningen service.

Norbank *(Miles Cowsill)*

Maersk Anglia *(Miles Cowsill)*

NORSEMERCHANT FERRIES

THE COMPANY, MANAGEMENT AND ADDRESS. See Section 1.

TELEPHONE Administration +44 (0)28 9077 9090, **Reservations** *Belfast (Liverpool service)* +44 (0)870 6099 299, *(Heysham service)* +44 (0) +44 (0)870 6099 299, *Liverpool (Belfast service)* +44 (0) +44 (0)870 6099 299, *(Dublin service)* +44 (0) +44 (0)870 6099 299, *Heysham* +44 (0)1524 865050, *Dublin* +353 (0)1 819 2955.

FAX Administration *Belfast* +44 (0)28 9077 1286, **Reservations** *Belfast (Liverpool service)* +44 (0)28 9077 5520, *(Heysham service)* +44 (0)28 9078 6073, *Heysham* +44 (0)1524 865070, *Liverpool (Belfast service)* 44 (0)151 906 2718, *(Dublin service)* 44 (0)151 906 2718, *Dublin* +353 (0)1 819 2941.

INTERNET Email enquiries@norsemerchant.com **Website** www.norsemerchant.com *(English)*

ROUTES OPERATED Port of Liverpool (Twelve Quays River Terminal, Birkenhead) *(dep: 10.45 Sun, Tue-Sat, 22.00 Daily*)* – Dublin *(dep: 10.00 Daily*, 22.00 Sun, 22.45 Mon-Sat)* (3 hrs; (**BRAVE MERCHANT (see Section 1), 1)*; 2 per day), Heysham *(dep: 09.00 Tue-Sat,19 21.00 Daily)* – Dublin *(dep: 09.00 Tue-Sat, 21.00 Daily)* (8 hrs; (2,4); 2 per day), Heysham *(dep: 09.00 Tue-Sat, 19.30 Tue-Sat, 23.30 Daily)* – Belfast *(dep: 07.30 Tue-Sat, 11.30 Tue-Sat, 21.00 Daily)* (7 hrs; (3,5,6); 3 per day.

NorseMerchant Ferries also operate passenger/freight services from Liverpool to Belfast. See Section 1.

1	LINDA ROSA	17428t	96	19.7k	183.1m	12P	-	144T	AS	IT
2	MERCHANT BRAVERY	9368t	78	17.0k	133.0m	12P	-	94T	A	BS
3	MERCHANT BRILLIANT	9368t	79	17.0k	133.0m	12P	-	94T	A	BS
4	RIVER LUNE	7765t	83	15.0k	121.4m	12P	-	90T	A	BS
5	SAGA MOON	7746t	84	15.0k	134.8m	12P	-	66T	A	GI
6	VARBOLA	7800t	98	17.0k	122.3m	12P	-	84T	A	ES

LINDA ROSA Built at Donanda, Italy for *Levantina Trasporti* of Italy. Chartered to *CoTuNav* of Tunisia for service between Tunisia and Italy. In 2002 chartered to *NorseMerchant Ferries* to operate additional sailings between Liverpool and Belfast. In 2003 transferred to the Birkenhead – Dublin service.

MERCHANT BRAVERY Built at Oslo, Norway. Launched as the STEVI for *Steineger & Wiik* of Norway and, on delivery, chartered to *Norient Line* of Norway, being renamed the NORWEGIAN CRUSADER. In 1980 chartered to *Ignazio Messina* of Italy for Mediterranean service and renamed the JOLLY GIALLO. In 1982 the charter ended and she was briefly renamed the NORWEGIAN CRUSADER before being purchased by *Ignazio Messina* and resuming the name JOLLY GIALLO. In 1993 sold to *Merchant Ferries*, renamed the MERCHANT BRAVERY and placed on the Heysham – Warrenpoint (Dublin since 1995) service. In 1999 transferred to *Belfast Freight Ferries'* Heysham – Belfast service. In 2004 moved to the Heysham – Dublin route.

MERCHANT BRILLIANT Built at Kyrksæterøra, Norway as the NORWEGIAN CHALLENGER *for Steineger & Wiik* of Norway and chartered to *Norient Line* of Norway. In 1982, chartered to *Ignazio Messina* of Italy for Mediterranean service and renamed the JOLLY BRUNO. Later in 1982 she was purchased by *Ignazio Messina*. In 1993 sold to *Merchant Ferries*, renamed the MERCHANT BRILLIANT and placed on the Heysham – Warrenpoint (Dublin since 1995) service. In 1999 transferred to *Belfast Freight Ferries'* Heysham – Belfast service.

RIVER LUNE Built at Galatz, Romania for *Almira Shipping* of Liberia (part of the Norwegian *Balder* group) as the BALDER VIK and initially used on services between Italy and the Middle East. Subsequently she was employed on a number of charters including *North Sea Ferries* and *Norfolk Line*. In 1986 she was acquired by *Navimpex* of Romania, renamed the BAZIAS 7 and initially used on Mediterranean and Black Sea services. In 1987 she was chartered to *Kent Line* for service between Chatham and Zeebrugge. In 1988 she was sold to *Stena Rederi AB* of Sweden and chartered for service between Finland and Germany. In 1989 she was briefly renamed the STENA TOPPER before being further renamed the SALAR. During the ensuing years she undertook a number of charters. In 1993 she briefly resumed the name STENA TOPPER before being chartered to *Belfast Freight Ferries* and renamed the RIVER LUNE. In October 1996 she was sold to *Belfast Freight Ferries*. In 1999 she was transferred to *Merchant Ferries'* Heysham – Dublin service. In 2000 she returned to the Heysham – Belfast route. In January 2003 replaced the VARBOLA on the Heysham – Dublin service. In summer 2003 chartered to *Dart Line*, replacing the VARBOLA which was sub-chartered to *NorseMerchant Ferries*. In March 2004 returned to the Heysham – Belfast service but later transferred to the Heysham – Dublin service.

SAGA MOON Built at Travemünde, Germany as the LIDARTINDUR for *Trader Line* of the Faroe Islands for services between Tórshavn and Denmark. In 1986 chartered to *Belfast Freight Ferries* renamed the SAGA MOON. In 1990 she was purchased by *Belfast Freight Ferries*. In 1995 she was lengthened by 18m to increase trailer capacity from 52 to 72 units and trade cars from 25 to 50; the lift was replaced by an internal fixed ramp. In 1998 she was transferred to *Merchant Ferries'* Heysham – Dublin service and in 2001 back to the Heysham – Belfast service. Resumed service between Heysham and Dublin in 2002. In 2004 transferred to the Heysham – Belfast service.

VARBOLA Built at Huelva, Spain as the VARBOLA for *Estonian Shipping Company*. On completion, chartered to *Dart Line* and placed on the Dartford – Vlissingen route. In 1999 she was renamed the DART 6. At the end of August 1999, the charter was terminated and she was renamed the VARBOLA. She undertook a number of short term charters, including *Merchant Ferries*. In 2000 long-term chartered to *Merchant Ferries* to operate between Heysham and Dublin. In 2003 the charter ended and she was chartered to *Dart Line* to replace the DART 9; she was placed initially on the Dartford – Vlissingen route but later transferred to the Dartford – Dunkerque route. Later sub-chartered to *NorseMerchant Ferries* and placed on the Heysham – Dublin route. In 2004 charter transferred to *NorseMerchant Ferries* and later transferred to the Heysham – Belfast service.

NORTHLINK ORKNEY AND SHETLAND FERRIES

THE COMPANY, MANAGEMENT, ADDRESS, TELEPHONE, FAX & INTERNET See Section 1.

ROUTES OPERATED Aberdeen *(dep: 18.00 Sun)* – Kirkwall (Orkney) *(dep: 18.00 Mon)* (8 hrs; *(1,2)*; 1 per week), Aberdeen *(dep: 18.00 Tue-Fri)* – Lerwick (Shetland) *(dep: 18.00 Tue-Fri)* (13 hrs; *(1,2)*; 4 per week).

| 1 | CLARE | 5617t | 72 | 17.0k | 114.9m | 12P | - | 62T | A | NO |
| 2 | HASCOSAY | 6136t | 71 | 17.0k | 118.4m | 12P | - | 50T | A | UK |

CLARE Built at Bremerhaven, Germany as the WESERTAL for *Reinecke* of Germany. After delivery she was renamed the MEYER EXPRESS and resumed the name WESERTAL in 1973. She was chartered out to a number of operators including *North Sea Ferries* and *Olau Line*. In 1998 she was briefly renamed the. In 1993 she was sold to Italian Interests and renamed the VINZIA E. She was chartered to *Stena Sealink Line* and operated between Newhaven and Dieppe. In 1994 she was chartered to DFDS subsidiary *Dan-Let Line* (later *DFDS Baltic Line*) and renamed the DANA BALTICA. She operated between Denmark and Lithuania. In 1996 she was renamed the CLARE and again placed on the charter market. 1997 she briefly served on *NorSea Link*, a joint venture between *Scandlines (DSB Rederi)* and *Norse Irish Ferries* between Kristiansand and Eemshaven in the north of the Netherlands. In 1998 she was again chartered to *DFDS* to institute freight only services between Newcastle and IJmuiden. After further brief charters she was, in 1999, briefly chartered to *CargoConnect Transport + Logistics* and placed on a new service between Hull and Hamburg. In 2001, she was chartered to *Smyril Line* to operate between Tórshavn and Hanstholm. In 2002, Lerwick was added to her winter itinerary. From September 2002 Aberdeen was added to a year round roster but dropped at the beginning of 2003. In autumn 2003, the charter was ended. In December 2003 chartered to *NorthLink*.

HASCOSAY Built Kristiansand, Norway as the JUNO. In 1979 sold to *Finnfranline* of France, renamed the NORMANDIA and chartered to *Finncarriers* for service between Finland and France. In 1982 chartered to *Sudcargo* and used on services between France and Algeria and the Middle East. In 1986 sold to *Mikkola* of Finland, renamed the MISIDIA and chartered to *Transfennica* for services between Finland and Northern Europe. In 1990 sold to *Kristiania Eiendom* of Norway and renamed the EURO NOR. In 1991 she was chartered to *Commodore Ferries* and renamed the COMMODORE CLIPPER. In 1996 she was replaced by the COMMODORE GOODWILL and renamed the SEA CLIPPER. She was placed on the charter market. In 1998 she was chartered to the *Estonian Shipping Company (ESCO)* and operated between Germany and Estonia; she was renamed the TRANSBALTICA. In 2001 she resumed the name SEA CLIPPER and chartered to *Fjord Line*. In 2002 she was sold to *NorthLink* and renamed the HASCOSAY. She was modified to enable her to accommodate *NorthLink's* cassette system for livestock transport in addition to commercial vehicles. She was chartered to *Caledonian MacBrayne* to operate between Ullapool and Stornoway during summer 2002. In October 2002 entered service with *NorthLink*.

P&O FERRIES

THE COMPANY, MANAGEMENT, ADDRESS, TELEPHONE See Section 1.

INTERNET Website www.poferriesfreight.co.uk *(English)*

ROUTES OPERATED Hull *(dep: 18.00 Thu (2), 21.00 Daily (passenger ship), 21.00 Wed (4))* – Rotterdam *(dep: 18.00 Wed (via Zeebrugge) (4), 21.00 Daily (passenger ship), 23.30 Wed (2))*, Hull *(dep: 17.00 Sat , 19.00* Daily, 21.00 Mon, Tue, Wed+, Fri)* – Zeebrugge *(dep: 19.00* Daily, 21.00 Tue, Sat, 22.00 Thu)* (13 hrs (+23 hrs via Rotterdam); *(2,*passenger vessels)*; 10 per week), Middlesbrough (Teesport) *(dep: 21.00 Mon-Wed, Fri, 17.00 Sat)* – Rotterdam (Beneluxhaven, Europoort) *(dep: 23.00 Mon-Tue, Thu-Fri, 19.00 Sat)* (15 hrs; *(3,4)*; 5 per week), Middlesbrough (Teesport) *(dep: 21.00 Mon-Fri, 17.00 Sat)* – Zeebrugge *(dep: 20.30 Mon-Sat)* (15 hrs; *(5,6)*; 6 per week).

1•	EUROPEAN SEAWAY	22986t	91	21.0k	179.7m	200P	-	120L	BA2	UK
2	NORCAPE	14807t	79	19.4k	151.0m	12P	-	124T	A	NL
3	NORKING	17884t	80	19.0k	170.9m	12P	-	155T	A	FI
4	NORQUEEN	17884t	80	19.0k	170.9m	12P	-	155T	A	FI
5	NORSKY	19992t	99	20.0k	180.0m	12P	-	194T	A	NL
6	NORSTREAM	19992t	99	20.0k	180.0m	12P	-	194T	A	NL

EUROPEAN SEAWAY Built at Bremerhaven, Germany for *P&O European Ferries* for the Dover – Zeebrugge freight service. In 2000 a regular twice daily freight only Dover-Calais service was established, using this vessel, which continued to operate to Zeebrugge at night. In 2001 passengers (not foot or coach passengers) began to be conveyed on the Dover – Zeebrugge service. In 2003 the Zeebrugge service ended and she now operates only between Dover and Calais in a freight only mode. In 2004 withdrawn and laid up.

NORCAPE Built at Tamano, Japan. Launched as the PUMA but, on completion chartered to *B&I Line* and renamed the TIPPERARY for their Dublin – Liverpool service. In 1989 sold to *North Sea Ferries*, renamed the NORCAPE and introduced onto the Ipswich – Rotterdam service. In 1995 that service ceased and she was moved to the Hull – Zeebrugge freight service. She retains Dutch crew and registry.

NORKING, NORQUEEN Built at Rauma, Finland as the BORE KING and the BORE QUEEN for *Bore Line* of Finland for Baltic services. In 1991 chartered to *North Sea Ferries* for their Teesport – Zeebrugge service and renamed the NORKING and NORQUEEN respectively. During winter 1995/96 they were lengthened by 28.8 metres and re-engined. In 1999 transferred to the Teesport – Rotterdam service.

NORSKY, NORSTREAM Built at Rauma, Finland for *Bore Line* of Finland and chartered to *P&O North Sea Ferries*. They operate on the Teesport – Zeebrugge service.

P&O IRISH SEA

THE COMPANY AND ADDRESS See Section 1.

MANAGEMENT Chairman Russ Peters, **Managing Director** J H Kearsley, **Commercial Manager** Philip Simpson.

TELEPHONE Administration +44 (0)1253 615700, **Reservations UK** 0870 6000 868, *Irish Republic* +353 (0)1 855 0522.

FAX Administration & Reservations *Cairnryan* +44 (0)1581 200282, *Larne* +44 (0)28 2827 2477, *Fleetwood* +44 (0)1253 615740.

INTERNET Website www.poisfreight.com *(English)*

PLEASE NOTE: The company reserves the right to alter sailing times without prior notice

ROUTES OPERATED Troon *(dep: 02.30 Mon-Sat, 12.00 Sun)* – Larne *(dep: 10.00 Sat, 19.00 Sun-Fri)* (4 hrs 30 mins; *(2)*; 1 per day), Liverpool *(dep: 10.00 Tue-Sat, 22.00 Daily)* – Dublin *(dep: 10.00 Tue-Sat, 22.00 Daily)* (8 hrs; *(3,4)*; 2 per day), Rosslare *(dep: 22.00 Tue, 21.30 Thu, 16.00 Sat)* – Cherbourg *(dep: 14.00 Sun, 22.00 Wed, 19.00 Fri)* (18 hrs; *(1)*; 3 per week). A limited number of private cars and their passengers is conveyed on the day sailings between Liverpool and Dublin and on all sailings between Rosslare and Cherbourg under the 'Value Route' branding.

1	EUROPEAN DIPLOMAT	16776t	78	17.0k	151.0m	74P	-	122T	A2	UK
2	EUROPEAN MARINER	5897t	77	15.0k	116.3m	12P	-	62T	A	BS
3	NORBANK	17464t	93	22.0k	166.7m	114P	-	150T	A	NL
4	NORBAY	17464t	94	22.0k	166.7m	114P	-	150T	A	UK

EUROPEAN DIPLOMAT Built at Ulsan, South Korea as the STENA TRANSPORTER, for *Stena Rederi* of Sweden. In 1979 she was renamed the FINNROSE and chartered to *Finnlines*. She later served with *Atlanticargo* on their service between Europe and USA/Mexico. In 1980 she returned to *Stena Line* and resumed her original name. Later in 1980 she was chartered to *European Ferries* for their Felixstowe – Rotterdam freight-only service and renamed the BALTIC FERRY. In 1982 she served in the Falkland Islands Task Force. In 1986 she was converted to ro-pax format and moved to the Felixstowe – Zeebrugge passenger service. In 1992 she was renamed the PRIDE OF SUFFOLK. In 1994 she was purchased by *P&O European Ferries*. In 1995 the Felixstowe – Zeebrugge passenger service ceased, most of her additional passenger accommodation was removed, passenger capacity was reduced and she was transferred to the Felixstowe – Rotterdam freight service. In 2001 transferred to the *P&O Irish Sea's* Liverpool – Dublin route and renamed the EUROPEAN DIPLOMAT. In 2002 transferred to the Rosslare – Cherbourg route.

EUROPEAN MARINER Built at Bremerhaven, Germany as the SALAHALA and chartered to *Gilnavi* of Italy for Mediterranean services. In 1990 she was purchased by *Cenargo* and chartered to *Merchant Ferries* who renamed her the MERCHANT VALIANT. She was used on their Fleetwood – Warrenpoint service until 1993 when she was chartered to *Pandoro* and placed on their Ardrossan – Larne service. Purchased by *P&O* in 1995 and renamed the LION. In early 1998 renamed the EUROPEAN HIGHLANDER. In July 2001, the service moved to Troon and she was renamed the EUROPEAN MARINER. In 2002 replaced by the EUROPEAN NAVIGATOR. After a brief charter to *Seatruck Ferries* she went on a two month charter to *Color Line*, operating between Kristiansand and Hirtshals. On return she went on a short charter to *Commodore Ferries* and in late September was transferred to the Larne – Troon route replacing the EUROPEAN NAVIGATOR. Later she was chartered to *Norse Island Ferries*; she returned to *P&O Irish Sea* in late 2002.

NORBANK Built at Krimpen aan den IJssel, Rotterdam, Netherlands for *North Sea Ferries* for the Hull – Rotterdam service. She was originally built for and chartered to *Nedlloyd* but the charter was taken over by *P&O* in 1966 and she was bought by *P&O* in 2003 and retains Dutch crew and registry. In May 2001 moved to the Felixstowe – Europoort route. In January 2002 transferred to *P&O Irish Sea* and operated on the Liverpool – Dublin route.

NORBAY Built at Krimpen aan den IJssel, Rotterdam, Netherlands for *North Sea Ferries* for the Hull – Rotterdam service. Owned by *P&O*. In January 2002 transferred to *P&O Irish Sea* and operated on the Liverpool – Dublin route.

SCA TRANSFOREST

THE COMPANY *SCA Transforest* is a Swedish company.

MANAGEMENT Managing Director (UK) Bo Frölander.

ADDRESS Interforest Terminal London Ltd, 44 Berth, Tilbury Dock, Essex RM18 7HR.

TELEPHONE Administration & Reservations +44 (0)1375 48 85 00.

FAX Administration & Reservations +44 (0)1375 48 85 03.

INTERNET Email bo.frolander@sca.com **Website** www.transforest.sca.se *(English)*

ROUTE OPERATED Umeå *(dep: 11.00 Mon, 16.00 Thu)* – Husum *(dep: 20.00 Mon, 22.00 Thu)* – Sundsvall *(dep: 12.00 Tue, 12.00 Fri)* – Iggesund *(dep: 19.00 Tue, 19.00 Fri)* – Tilbury *(arr: 11.00 Tue, 13.00 Sat, dep: 16.00 Tue, 18.00 Sat)* – Rotterdam (Eemhaven) *(dep: 13.00 Sun, 12.00 Wed)* – Helsingborg *(arr: 07.00 Fri)* (8/9 day round trip; *(1,2,3)*; 2 per week).

1	OBBOLA	20171t	96	16.0k	170.6m	0P	-	-	A	SW
2	ORTVIKEN	20171t	97	16.0k	170.4m	0P	-	-	A	SW
3	ÖSTRAND	20171t	96	16.0k	170.6m	0P	-	-	A	SW

OBBOLA, ORTVIKEN, ÖSTRAND Built at Seville, Spain for *Gorthon Lines* and chartered to *SCA Transforest*. They are designed for the handling of forest products in non-wheeled 'cassettes' but can also accommodate ro-ro trailers; however no trailer capacity is quoted. The ORTVIKEN was lengthened during autumn 2000 and the OBBOLA and ÖSTRAND were lengthened during 2001.

SEA-CARGO

THE COMPANY *Sea-Cargo AS* of Norway is a joint venture between *Nor-Cargo AS* (a Norwegian company jointly owned by *Ofotens og Vesteraalen Dampskipsselskab, Det Stavangerske Dampskipsselskab* and *Troms Fylkes Dampskipsselskab*) and *SeaTrans DS* of Norway.

MANAGEMENT *Sea-Cargo UK Ltd* **Managing Director** Barry Jenks.

ADDRESS *Norway* Sea-Cargo AS, PO Box 353, Nesttun, N-5853 Bergen, Norway, *Immingham* Sea-Cargo UK, West Riverside Road, Immingham Dock, Immingham DN40 2NT, *Aberdeen* Nor-Cargo Ltd, Matthews Quay, Aberdeen Harbour, Aberdeen, AB11 5PG.

TELEPHONE Administration & Bookings *Bergen* +47 55 10 84 84, *Immingham* +44 (0)1469 577119, *Aberdeen* +44 (0)1224 596481.

FAX Administration & Reservations *Bergen* +47 55 91 22 33, *Immingham* 44 (0)1469 577708, *Aberdeen* +44 (0)1224 582360.

INTERNET Email mail@ .no **Website** www.sea-cargo.no *(English, Norwegian)*

ROUTES OPERATED *Circuit 1* Bergen *(dep: Thu eve)* – Odda *(dep: Fri morn)* – Haugesund *(dep: Sat morn)* – Tanager *(dep: Sat)* – Immingham *(arr Mon morn, dep: Mon eve)* – Amsterdam *(arr Tue morn, dep: Tue eve)* – Tananger *(arr: Thu)* – Haugesund *(arr: Thu)* – Bergen *(arr: Thu)* (1 week; *(1)*; weekly), *Circuit 2* Bergen *(dep: Tue eve)* – Husnes *(dep: Wed)* – Haugesund *(dep: Wed)* – Kamøy *(dep: Wed)* – Tanager *(dep: Wed eve)* – Amsterdam *(arr Fri morn, dep: Fri eve)* – Immingham *(arr: Sat morn, dep: Sat eve)* – Tanager *(arr: Mon morn)* – Bergen *(arr: Mon noon)* (1 week; *(3)*; weekly), *Circuit 3* Trondheim *(dep: Wed eve)* – Kristiansund *(dep: Thu morn)* – Molde *(dep: Thu)* – Aalesund *(dep: Thu eve)* – Bergen *(dep: Fri eve)* – Haugesund *(dep: Sat morn)* – Tanager *(dep: Sat morn)* – Aberdeen *(arr: Sun morn, dep: Sun noon)* – Tanager *(arr: Mon morn)* – Haugesund *(arr: Mon)* – Bergen *(arr: Tue morn)* – Florø *(arr: Tue eve)* – Aalesund *(arr: Wed morn)* – Molde *(arr: Wed noon)* – Trondheim *(arr: Wed eve)* (1 week; *(2)*; weekly).

1	COMETA	4610t	81	16.0k	102.2m	0P	-	26T	AS	NO
2	SC ABERDEEN	4234t	79	15.5k	109.0m	0P	-	24T	AS	BS
3	TRANS CARRIER	8476t	93	14.5k	125.2m	0P	-	78T	A	BS

COMETA Built at Rissa, Norway for *Nor-Cargo*.

SC ABERDEEN Built at Rissa, Norway for *Nor-Cargo*. Launched as the ERIC JARL but renamed the ASTREA before entering service. In 1986 she sank and, after raising and refitting she was, in 1992, renamed the TUNGENES. In 2001 she was renamed the SC ABERDEEN.

TRANS CARRIER Built at Kraljevica, Croatia as the KORSNÄS LINK for *SeaLink AB* of Sweden and due to be time chartered to *Korsnäs AB*, a Swedish forest products company. However, due to the war in Croatia, delivery was seriously delayed and she was offered for sale. In 1994 sold to the *Swan Group* and renamed the SWAN HUNTER. She was placed on the charter market. In 1997 she was chartered to *Euroseabridge* and renamed the PARCHIM. In 1999 the charter ended and she resumed the name SWAN HUNTER. In 1999 she was sold to *SeaTrans* and renamed the TRANS CARRIER.

SEAFRANCE

THE COMPANY, MANAGEMENT & ADDRESS See Section 1.

TELEPHONE Reservations +44 (0)1304 203030.

FAX Reservations +44 (0)1304 212726

INTERNET Email freightdover@wanadoo.fr **Website** www.seafrancefreight.com *(English, French)*

ROUTE OPERATED Calais *(dep: 01.30 Mon-Sat, 09.30 Mon-Sat, 21.30 Sun-Fri)* – Dover *(dep: 02.30 Mon-Sat, 10.30 Mon-Sat, 22.30 Sun-Fri)* (1 hr 30 mins; *(1)*; 3 per day).

1	SEAFRANCE NORD PAS-DE-CALAIS	13727t	87	21.5k	160.1m	80P	-	102L	BA2	FR

SEAFRANCE NORD PAS-DE-CALAIS Built as the NORD PAS-DE-CALAIS at Dunkerque, France for *SNCF* for the Dunkerque (Ouest) – Dover train ferry service. Before being used on this service (which required the construction of a new berth at Dover (Western Docks)) in May 1988, she operated road freight services from Calais to Dover Eastern Docks. The train ferry service continued to operate following the opening of the Channel Tunnel in 1994, to convey road vehicles and dangerous loads which were banned from the tunnel. However, it ceased in December 1995 and, after a refit, in February 1996 she was renamed the SEAFRANCE NORD PAS-DE-CALAIS and switched to the Calais – Dover service, primarily for road freight vehicles and drivers but also advertised as carrying up to 50 car passengers. Since the entry into service of a third multi-purpose ferry, she has operated on a freight-only basis.

SEATRUCK FERRIES

THE COMPANY *Seatruck Ferries Ltd* is a British private sector company, owned by *Crescent plc*.

MANAGEMENT Managing Director Kevin Hobbs, **Sales Director** Alistair Eagles.

ADDRESS *Warrenpoint (HQ)* Seatruck House, The Ferry Terminal, Warrenpoint, County Down BT34 3JR. *Heysham* North Quay, Heysham Port, Heysham, Morecambe, Lancs LA3 2UL.

TELEPHONE Administration +44 (0)28 4175 4411, **Reservations** *Warrenpoint* +44 (0)28 4175 4400, *Heysham* +44 (0)1524 853512.

FAX Administration +44 (0)28 4175 4545, **Reservations** *Warrenpoint* +44 (0)28 4177 3737, *Heysham* +44 (0)1524 853549.

INTERNET Email alistair@seatruck-ferries.co.uk **Website** www.seatruckferries.com *(English)*

ROUTES OPERATED Heysham *(dep: 08.00 Tue-Sat, 21.00 Daily)* – Warrenpoint *(dep: 08.00 Tue-Sat, 17.00 Sun, 20.00 Mon-Sat)* (8 hrs; *(1,2)*; 2 per day).

1	MOONDANCE	5881t	78	15.0k	116.3m	12P	-	62T	A	BS
2	RIVERDANCE	6041t	77	15.0k	116.3m	12P	-	62T	A	BS

MOONDANCE Built at Bremerhaven, Germany as the EMADALA for *Emadala Shipping* and chartered to *Gilnavi Line* of Italy for Mediterranean service. In 1987 she was purchased by *Gilnavi Line*. In 1990 sold to *Cenargo* of Great Britain and chartered to *Merchant Ferries* for their Heysham – Warrenpoint service and renamed the MERCHANT VICTOR. She was withdrawn from that service in 1993 and was chartered out to a number of operators. In 1997 she was chartered to *Seatruck Ferries* and renamed the MOONDANCE. In 1998 she was purchased by *Seatruck Ferries*. Following collapse of ramp at Warrenpoint in January 2001, she briefly operated between Heysham and Larne.

RIVERDANCE Built at Bremerhaven, as the MASHALA for *Mashala Shipping* and chartered to *Gilnavi* of Italy for Mediterranean services. After a long period out of service in the mid-nineteen eighties, in 1987 she was sold, renamed the HALLA and chartered for Caribbean service. In 1988 she was renamed the TIKAL. In 1989 she was sold to *Schiaffino Line* of France, renamed the SCHIAFFINO and put into service between Ramsgate and Ostend. In 1990 the company was taken over by *Sally Ferries* and in 1991 she was chartered to *Belfast Freight Ferries*. In 1993 she was renamed the SALLY EUROBRIDGE. In January 1994, she was chartered to *North Sea Ferries* to operate between Hull and Zeebrugge and renamed the EUROBRIDGE. In summer 1994 she returned to *Sally Ferries*, resumed the name SALLY EUROBRIDGE and became the second vessel on the Ramsgate – Vlissingen service; in the autumn the British terminal was switched to Dartford. In 1995 she was chartered to *Norfolk Line*, renamed the EUROBRIDGE and also sold by *Sally Ferries*. In 1996 she was chartered to *Seatruck Ferries* and renamed the RIVERDANCE. In 1997 she was purchased by *Seatruck Ferries*. Following collapse of ramp at Warrenpoint in January 2001, she briefly operated between Heysham and Larne.

SEAWHEEL

THE COMPANY *Seawheel Ltd* is a UK company.

MANAGEMENT Managing Director Alan Jones, **Marketing Manager** Richard Beales, **Killingholme Manager** Robin Anson.

ADDRESS *Seawheel HO* Western House, Hadleigh Road, Ipswich, Suffolk IP2 0HB, *Local Office* Seawheel Limited, CCTL Division, Humber Sea Terminal, Clough Lane, North Killingholme, North Lincolnshire, DN40 3JP.

TELEPHONE *Seawheel HO* Administration and Reservations +44 (0)1473 222000, *Local Office* +44 (0)1469 540 689.

FAX *Seawheel HO* Administration & Reservations +44 (0)1473 230083, *Local Office* +44 (0)1469 540 687.

INTERNET Email RAnson@seawheel.com **Website** www.seawheel.com *(English)*

ROUTE OPERATED Killingholme *(dep: 20.30 or 21.00 Mon- Sat)* – Rotterdam (Prins Johan Frisohaven) *(dep: 20.30 or 21.00)* (14-15 hrs; *(1,2)*; 6 per week).

1	CHODZIEZ	15666t	89	14.5k	147.4m	12P	-	84T	A	MA
2	SEAWHEEL HUMBER	14738t	79	18.0k	137.5m	12P	-	116T	A	UK
3•	SEAWHEEL RHINE	10279t	77	17.5k	142.3m	8P	-	95T	A	SW

CHODZIEZ Built in Gdynia, Poland for *Polish Ocean Lines* and used on service from Poland to the Middle east. In 2004 chartered to *Seawheel* to replace the SEAWHEEL RHINE on the Killingholme – Rotterdam service.

SEAWHEEL HUMBER Built in Rauma, Finland as the BALTIC EAGLE for *United Baltic Corporation* and used on *Finanglia Ferries* services between the UK and Finland (joint with *Finncarriers*). In 1999 chartered to *Crowley American Transport Inc* for Caribbean service. In 2002 sold to *Jay Management Corporation* of the UK and renamed the OLYMPIC STAR. Later in 2002 chartered to *Seawheel* to inaugurate a Killingholme – Rotterdam service and renamed the SEAWHEEL HUMBER. Operates between Killingholme and Rotterdam.

SEAWHEEL RHINE Built at Naantali, Finland as the ROLITA for *Merivienti* of Italy. In 1979 chartered to *Finncarriers* of Finland, renamed the FINNFOREST and used on services between Finland and North West Europe. In 1982 sold to *EFFOA* of Finland and renamed the CANOPUS. In 1992 sold to *B&N* of Sweden and chartered to *Stora Line* for services from Sweden to NW Europe. She was renamed the CUPRIA. In 1995, chartered to *North Sea Ferries* to inaugurate a new service between Middlesbrough and Rotterdam and renamed the NORCOVE. In 1999 she was chartered to *Finncarriers* and renamed the CUPRIA. She was used on services from Finland to Spain via Antwerp. In 2001 she was chartered to *Cobelfret Ferries* for the Purfleet – Rotterdam service. In 2002 chartered to *SeaWind Line* to operate additional freight only sailings between Stockholm and Turku before the SKY WIND was delivered in September 2002. In September 2002 chartered to *Seawheel*, renamed the SEAWHEEL RHINE and placed on the Killingholme – Rotterdam service. In early 2004 suffered serious mechanical failure and laid up.

STENA LINE

THE COMPANY, MANAGEMENT, ADDRESS, TELEPHONE AND INTERNET See Section 1.

ROUTES OPERATED Harwich *(dep: 05.00 (Tue-Sat), 11.00 (Mon-Sat), 22.45 (Sun-Fri)* – Rotterdam *(dep: 11.30 (Mon-Sat), 19.00 (Mon-Fri), 23.45 (Sun-Fri))* (7 hrs 45 mins; *(2,7,8)*; 3 per day), Killingholme *(dep: 19.15)* – Hoek van Holland *(dep: 19.00)* (13 hrs; *(5,6)*; 1 per day), Fleetwood *(dep: 03.00 Mon-Sat, 10.00 Daily, 22.00 Daily)* – Larne *(dep: 10.00 Daily, 16.00 Sun, Mon-Fri, 22.00 Daily)* (7 hrs; *(1,3,4)*; 3 per day). **Note** The Fleetwood – Larne service was taken over from *P&O Irish Sea* in spring 2004. A limited number of cars and car passengers is carried on this service.

1	STENA LEADER	12879t	75	17.0k	157.2m	50P	-	114T	A	BD
2	STENA PARTNER	21162t	77	16.5k	184.6m	166P	-	180T	A2	UK
3	STENA PIONEER	14387t	75	17.7k	141.8m	76P	-	114T	A	BD
4	STENA SEAFARER	10957t	75	18.0k	141.8m	50P	-	80T	A	BD
5	STENA SEARIDER	21019t	69	17.0k	178.9m	120P	-	198T	AS2	IM
6	STENA SEATRADER	17991t	73	17.5k	181.6m	221P	-	174T	AS2	UK
7	STENA TRANSFER	21162t	77	16.5k	184.6m	166P	-	180T	A2	UK
8	STENA TRANSPORTER	16776t	78	17.0k	151.0m	74P	-	122T	A2	UK

STENA LEADER Built at Hamburg, Germany for *Stena AB* as the BUFFALO and due to be chartered to *P&O* for *Pandoro* Irish Sea services. Before completion she was purchased by *P&O*. In 1989 she was lengthened by 12.5m and in 1998 she was further lengthened by 15m and renamed the EUROPEAN LEADER. In 2004 sold to *Stena Line* and renamed the STENA LEADER. Used on the Fleetwood – Larne service.

STENA PARTNER Built at Ulsan, South Korea for *Stena Rederi* as the ALPHA ENTERPRISE and chartered to *Aghiris Navigation* of Cyprus. In 1979 she was renamed the SYRIA and chartered to *Hellas Ferries* for services between Greece and Syria. In 1981 she was lengthened by 33.6m. In 1982 she was chartered to *European Ferries* and used on freight services between Felixstowe and Rotterdam. In 1983 she was renamed the STENA TRANSPORTER and in 1986 the CERDIC FERRY. In 1992 she was renamed the EUROPEAN FREEWAY and, in 1994, purchased by *P&O European Ferries*. In 2002 sold to *Stena Line* and renamed the FREEWAY. She initially operated between Felixstowe and Rotterdam and later Harwich and Rotterdam. In early 2003 she was renamed the STENA PARTNER.

STENA PIONEER Built at Hamburg, Germany for *Stena AB* as the BISON and due to be chartered to *P&O* for *Pandoro* Irish Sea services. Before completion she was purchased by *P&O*. Between 1989 and 1993 she was operated by *B&I Line* of Ireland on a joint service with *Pandoro* between Dublin and Liverpool. An additional deck was added in 1995. In late 1997 she was renamed the EUROPEAN PIONEER. In 2004 sold to *Stena Line* and renamed the STENA PIONEER. Used on the Fleetwood – Larne service.

STENA SEAFARER Built at Hamburg, Germany. Ordered by *Stena AB* as the UNION TRADER but completed as the UNION MELBOURNE for the *Northern Coasters Ltd* of the UK and lengthened before entering service. Chartered to the *Union Steamship Company* of New Zealand and used on services

SECTION 3 – FREIGHT ONLY FERRIES

Stena Transfer *(Henk van de Lugt)*

SeaFrance Nord-pas-de-Calais *(Miles Cowsill)*

to Australia. In 1980 she was sold to another *P&O* subsidiary and renamed the PUMA. In early 1998 she was renamed the EUROPEAN SEAFARER. Used on the Fleetwood – Larne service in recent years, in 2001 she was transferred to the Rosslare – Cherbourg service. In 2002 replaced by the EUROPEAN DIPLOMAT and returned to the Fleetwood – Larne service. In 2004 sold to *Stena Line* and renamed the STENA SEAFARER.

STENA SEARIDER Built at Helsinki, Finland as the FINNCARRIER for *Finnlines* of Finland for service between Finland, Denmark and Germany. In 1975 renamed the POLARIS. In 1984 sold to *Rederi AB Nordö* of Sweden to operate between Malmö (Sweden) and Travemünde (Germany) and renamed the SCANDINAVIA. In 1987 she was rebuilt to increase capacity from 122 trailers to 200. In 1989 the name of the company was changed to *Nordö Link* and she was renamed the SCANDINAVIA LINK. In 1990 she was sold to *Stena Line*, renamed the STENA SEARIDER and used on their Gothenburg (Sweden) – Travemünde service. In 1991 she was chartered out for service in the Caribbean and renamed the SEARIDER. In 1992 she was chartered to *Norse Irish Ferries* and renamed the NORSE MERSEY. In 1995 she was replaced by a new vessel of the same name and returned to *Stena Line*, resumed the name STENA SEARIDER and resumed operating between Gothenburg and Travemünde and Gothenburg and Kiel. In May 1997, she was transferred to the Harwich – Hoek van Holland service. In autumn 2000 she inaugurated (with the chartered ROSEBAY – see the TRANSLANDIA, *Eckerö Line*) a new service from Hoek van Holland to Killingholme (near Immingham).

STENA SEATRADER Built at Nakskov, Denmark as the SVEALAND for *Lion Ferry AB* of Sweden and chartered to *Statens Järnvägar (Swedish State Railways)* for the train ferry service between Trelleborg (Sweden) and Sassnitz (Germany (DDR)). The charter ceased in 1980 and in 1982 she was sold to *Rederi AB Nordö* of Sweden. She was lengthened by 33.7 metres, renamed the SVEALAND AV MALMÖ and used on their lorry/rail wagon service between Malmö and Travemünde. In 1986 she was rebuilt with a higher superstructure and in 1987 she was renamed the SVEA LINK, the service being renamed *Nordö Link*. In 1990 she was sold to *Stena Line*, renamed the STENA SEATRADER and introduced onto the Hoek van Holland – Harwich service. In spring 2001 she replaced the chartered ROSEBAY (see TRANSPARADEN, *Eckerö Line*) on the Hoek van Holland – Killingholme service.

STENA TRANSFER Built at Ulsan, South Korea. Launched as the STENA RUNNER by *Stena Rederi* of Sweden. On completion, renamed the ALPHA PROGRESS and chartered to *Aghiris Navigation* of Greece. In 1979 renamed the HELLAS and operated by *Soutos-Hellas Ferry Services* on services between Greece and Syria. In 1982 she was lengthened by 33.6m. In 1982 she was chartered to *European Ferries* and used on freight services between Felixstowe and Rotterdam. The following year she was returned to *Hellas Ferries*. In 1985 she returned to *European Ferries* and the Rotterdam service. In 1986 she was renamed the DORIC FERRY. In 1992 she was renamed the EUROPEAN TIDEWAY and, in 1994, purchased by *P&O European Ferries*. In 2001 replaced by the NORBANK and laid up. In 2002 returned to the Felixstowe – Rotterdam route when the NORBANK was transferred to *P&O Irish Sea*. In 2002 sold to *Stena Line* and renamed the IDEWAY. She initially operated between Felixstowe and Rotterdam and later Harwich and Rotterdam. Later in 2002 she was renamed the STENA TRANSFER.

STENA TRANSPORTER Built at Ulsan, South Korea as the MERZARIO ESPANIA for *Stena Rederi* of Sweden and immediately chartered to *Merzario Line* for their service between Italy and Saudi Arabia. In the same year she was renamed the MERZARIO HISPANIA. In 1979 she was chartered to *European Ferries* for their ro-ro freight service between Felixstowe and Rotterdam and renamed the NORDIC FERRY. In 1982 she served in the Falkland Islands Task Force. In 1986 she was modified to carry 688 passengers and, with sister vessel the BALTIC FERRY (now the EUROPEAN DIPLOMAT), took over the Felixstowe – Zeebrugge passenger service. In 1992 she was renamed the PRIDE OF FLANDERS. In 1994, purchased by *P&O European Ferries*. In 1995 the Felixstowe – Zeebrugge passenger service ceased, her additional passenger accommodation was removed, passenger capacity was reduced and she was transferred to the Felixstowe – Rotterdam freight service. In 2002 sold to *Stena Line* and renamed the FLANDERS. She initially operated between Felixstowe and Rotterdam and later Harwich and Rotterdam. In autumn 2002 chartered to *Scandlines AB* of Sweden to operate between Travemünde and Trelleborg whilst the SVEALAND was undergoing a major rebuild. Later in 2002, after a refit, she returned to the Harwich – Rotterdam route and was renamed the STENA TRANSPORTER.

TRANSEUROPA FERRIES

THE COMPANY *TransEuropa Ferries NV* is a Belgian subsidiary of *TransEuropa Shipping Lines*, a Slovenian private sector company. Channel operations started in 1997, in conjunction with *Sally Ferries*, replacing them on November 1998. The company traded as *TransEuropa Shipping Lines (TSL)* until 2000. Note that all the owning companies listed here are associated companies of *TSL*.

MANAGEMENT *TransEuropa Shipping* **Managing Director** Stergulc Rihard, *TransEuropa Ferries NV*, **General Manager Belgium & UK** Mr Dominique Penel, **Sales Manger, Europe** Mr Peter Sys.

ADDRESS *TSL Slovenia* Vojkovo nabrezje 38, 6000 Koper, Slovenia, *TEF UK* Ferry Terminal, Ramsgate New Port, RAMSGATE, Kent CT11 8RP *TEF Belgium* Slijkensesteenweg 2, 8400 Ostend, Belgium.

TELEPHONE *TSL Slovenia* +386 (0)5 664 17 77, *TEF UK* +44 (0)1843 853833, *TEF Belgium* +32 (0)59 34 02 50.

FAX *TSL Slovenia* +386 (0)5 639 50 36, *TEF UK* +44 (0)1843 853668, *TEF Belgium* +32 (0)59 34 02 51.

INTERNET Website www.transeuropaferries.co.uk *(English)*

ROUTE OPERATED Ramsgate *(dep: 01.00 Sat, 01.30 Mon, 20.30 Tue-Thu, 03.30 Tue-Fri, 05.30 Tue-Thu, Sat, 06.30 Mon, 09.30 Tue-Thu, 10.00 Sun, 11.30 Mon, 13.00 Mon-Fri, 13.30 Sun, 15.00 Mon-Fri, 15.30 Sun, 18.30 Mon-Fri, 19.00 Sun, 20.30 Mon-Fri, 21.30 Sun, 22.00 Sat, 22.30 Mon-Fri, 23.59 Mon-Thu)* – Ostend (Belgium) *(dep: 01.00 Mon-Sat, 03.00 Tue-Thu, 05.00 Sun, Mon, 07.00 Tue-Thu, 07.30 Sun, 10.30 Tue-Fri, 11.00 Sun, 13.00 Tue-Fri, 13.30 Sun, Mon, 16.00 Mon-Thu, 17.30 Sun, 18.00 Mon-Sat, 20.00 Sun-Fri, 21.30 Sun, Mon-Thu, 23.00 Sun, Mon-Thu)* (4 hrs; *(1,2,3,4,5)*; up to 10 per day).

1	BEGONIA	8023t	76	18.5k	118.1m	105P	-	52L	BA	SV
2	EUROVOYAGER	12110t	78	22.0k	118.4m	1250P	348C	45L	BA2	CY
3	GARDENIA	8097t	78	18.4k	118.1m	105P	-	52L	BA2	CY
4	LARKSPUR	14458t	76	17.5k	143.8m	1150P	314C	55L	BA2	BS
5	OLEANDER	13728t	80	23.0k	132.5m	1326P	350C	44L	BA2	CY
6	PRIMROSE	12046t	75	22.0k	118.4m	1250P	348C	45L	BA2	CY

BEGONIA Built at Bremerhaven, Germany as the EUROPEAN CLEARWAY for *European Ferries* ro-ro freight services. She was used on freight services between Dover and Calais and Dover and Zeebrugge. In 1992 she was moved to the Portsmouth – Le Havre route. In 1993 she was transferred to *Pandoro* to inaugurate a new Cherbourg – Rosslare service. In 1996 she was renamed the PANTHER. In early 1998 she was renamed the EUROPEAN PATHFINDER. In 2001 she was moved to the Cairnryan – Larne service to replace the EUROPEAN TRADER. In 2002 sold *ERATO Shipping* and renamed the REGINA I. Before delivery, resold to *Abbey Trading SA Trust Co*, delivered to *TEF* and renamed the BEGONIA. In 2004 began operating for *TransEuropa Ferries*.

EUROVOYAGER Built at Hoboken, Belgium as the PRINS ALBERT for *RMT* of Belgium for the Ostend – Dover service. During 1986 she had an additional vehicle deck added. In 1994 the British port became Ramsgate. Withdrawn after 28th February 1997 and laid up. In 1998 she was sold to *Hawthorn Shipping Co Ltd*, renamed the EUROVOYAGER. In July, she was chartered to *Sally Freight*. In November the *Sally Freight* service ended and she immediately began operating for *TSL*.

GARDENIA Built at Bremerhaven, Germany as the EUROPEAN ENTERPRISE for *European Ferries*. In 1988 she was renamed the EUROPEAN ENDEAVOUR. She was used on freight services between Dover and Calais and Dover and Zeebrugge. If space was available, a small number of passengers was sometimes conveyed on the Zeebrugge service, although the sailings were not advertised for passengers. This ceased with the withdrawal of passenger services on this route at the end of 1991. During the summer period she provided additional freight capacity on the Dover – Calais service and has also served on other routes. In autumn 1995 she was transferred to the Cairnryan – Larne service. In 1998 accommodation was raised to provide extra freight capacity. In March 1999 began also operating from Larne to Ardrossan but this ceased later in the year. Withdrawn from service in July 2002 and sold to *Odyssy Maritime Co Ltd* and renamed the GARDENIA. In 2003 she began operating for *TEF* between Ramsgate and Ostend.

LARKSPUR Built at Bremerhaven, Germany as the GEDSER for *Gedser-Travemünde Ruten* of Denmark for their service between Gedser (Denmark) and Travemünde (Germany). In 1986 she was purchased by *Thorsviks Rederi A/S* of Norway and chartered to *Sally Ferries*, re-registered in the Bahamas, renamed the VIKING 2 and entered service on the Ramsgate – Dunkerque service. In early 1989 she was renamed the SALLY SKY and during winter 1989/90 she was 'stretched' to increase vehicle capacity. At the end of 1996 she was withdrawn from the Dunkerque service. In 1997 she was renamed the EUROTRAVELLER, transferred to *Holyman-Sally Ferries* and, in March, was introduced onto the Ramsgate – Ostend route. In 1998, when *Holyman-Sally Ferries* came to an end, she operated in a freight-only role for *Sally Line* under the *Sally Freight* name. Passenger services were resumed in May, under the name of *Sally Direct*. All *Sally Line* operations ended in November 1998 and she was withdrawn for sale and laid up. In 1999 sold to *Forsythia Maritime Co Ltd* and renamed the LARKSPUR. She was given a major refit at Dunkerque, including the provision of 60 drivers' cabins with private facilities. She entered service with *TEF* in August 2000.

OLEANDER Built at Bremerhaven, Germany for *European Ferries (Townsend Thoresen)* as the PRIDE OF FREE ENTERPRISE for the Dover – Calais service, also operating on the Dover – Zeebrugge service during the winter. In 1988 she was renamed the PRIDE OF BRUGES and, following the delivery of the new PRIDE OF CALAIS, she was transferred all year to the Dover – Zeebrugge service. In 1992, after the closure of that routes to passengers, she returned to the Dover – Calais route. Plans to operate her in a freight-only mode in 1997 were changed and she ran as a full passenger vessel. In 1998, transferred to *P&O Stena Line*; plans to transfer her to the Newhaven – Dieppe route were dropped and she remained at Dover. In 1999 renamed the P&OSL PICARDY. In early 2000 she was laid up for sale in Dunkerque. In 2001 she was sold to *Seaborne Navigation Co Ltd* and renamed the OLEANDER. Entered service with *TEF* in July 2002 after major renovation work in Dunkerque, including the provision of 60 drivers' cabins with private facilities.

PRIMROSE Built at Hoboken, Belgium as the PRINCESSE MARIE-CHRISTINE for *Regie voor Maritiem Transport* of Belgium for the Ostend – Dover service. During 1985 she had an extra vehicle deck added, increasing vehicle capacity. Passenger capacity was increased by 200 by the conversion of an upper deck 'garage' into passenger accommodation. In January 1994 the British port became Ramsgate. In 1994 chartered briefly to *Sally Ferries* and operated between Ramsgate and Dunkerque. Since then a spare vessel and withdrawn in early 1997. In 1998 sold to *Dianthus Maritime Co Ltd* of the UK and renamed the PRIMROSE. In 1999 she began operating for *TSL* between Ramsgate and Ostend after a major refit at Dunkerque.

TRANSFENNICA

THE COMPANY *Transfennica Ltd* is a Finnish private sector company.

MANAGEMENT President Rolf G W Eriksson, **Director (UK)** Jim Deeprose, **Operations Manager (UK)** Andrew Prior.

ADDRESS *Finland* Eteläranta 12, FIN-00130 Helsinki, Finland, *UK* Finland House, 47 Berth, Tilbury Freeport, Tilbury, Essex RM18 7EH.

TELEPHONE Administration & Reservations *Finland* +358 (0)9 13262, *UK* +44 (0)1375 363 900.

FAX Administration & Reservations *Finland* +358 (0)9 652377, *UK* +44 (0)1375 840 888.

INTERNET Email *Finland* info@transfennica.com *UK* info.uk@transfennica.com

Website www.transfennica.com *(English)*

ROUTES OPERATED *Circuit 1* – Hamina *(dep: 17.00 Thu)* – Hanko *(arr: 07.00 Fri, dep 14.00 Fri)* – Tilbury *(arr: 06.00 Mon, dep: 17.00 Mon)* – Hamina *(arr: 06.00 Thu)*, *Circuit 2* Hamina *(dep: 18.00)* – Tilbury *(06.00 Fri, 17.00 Fri)* – Hamina *(arr: 10.00 Mon)*, *Circuit 3* – Rauma *(dep: 18.00 Fri)* – Antwerp *(arr: 08.00 Mon, dep: 10.00 Mon)* – Tilbury *(arr: 08.00 Tue, dep: 16.00 Tue)* – Rauma *(arr: 07.00 Fri)*, *Circuit 4* – Rauma *(dep: 18.00 Mon)* – Tilbury *(arr: 10.00 Thu, dep: 16.00 Thu)* –

Antwerp *(arr: 07.00 Fri, dep: 10.00 Fri)* – Rauma *(arr: 07.00 Mon); (1,2,3,4)*. Note: 'dep' times are closure times for freight. Ship will actually leave a little later. Ships will often arrive at Tilbury before scheduled time – sometimes the night before if coming from Finland.

1	CAROLINE RUSS	10471t	99	21.0k	153.5m	12P	-	120T	A2	AT
2	ELISABETH RUSS	10471t	99	21.0k	153.5m	12P	-	120T	A2	AT
3	PAULINE RUSS	10471t	99	21.0k	153.5m	12P	-	120T	A2	AT
4	SEAGARD	10471t	99	21.0k	153.5m	12P	-	134T	A2	FI

CAROLINE RUSS, ELISABETH RUSS, PAULINE RUSS Built at Hamburg, Germany for *Ernst Russ* of Germany and chartered to *Transfennica*.

SEAGARD Built at Hamburg, Germany for *Bror Hussel* of Finland and chartered to *Transfennica*.

Ostend Inner Harbour *(Mike Louagie)*

section **4** chain, cable etc ferries
gb & ireland

In addition to the ferries listed above, there are a number of short chain ferries, cable ferries and ferries operated by unpowered floats.

BOURNEMOUTH-SWANAGE MOTOR ROAD AND FERRY COMPANY

Address *Company* Shell Bay, Studland, Swanage, Dorset BH19 5BA. **Tel** +44 (0)1929 450203, **Fax** +44 (0)1929 450498), *Ferry* Floating Bridge, Ferry Way, Sandbanks, Poole, Dorset BH13 7QN. **Tel** +44 (0)1929 450203.

Route Sandbanks – Studland (Dorset).

1	BRAMBLE BUSH BAY	93	74.4m	400P	48C	BA

BRAMBLE BUSH BAY chain ferry, built at Hessle, UK for the *Bournemouth-Swanage Motor Road and Ferry Company.*

CUMBRIA COUNTY COUNCIL

Address Community, Economy & Environment Department, Lower Gaol Yard, The Courts, Carlisle CA3 8NA. **Tel** +44 (0)1228 606744, **Fax** +44 (0)1228 606577.

Internet Email john.robinson@cumbriacc.gov.uk

Route Bowness-on-Windermere – Far Sawrey.

1	MALLARD	90	25.9m	140P	18C	BA

MALLARD Chain Ferry built at Borth, Dyfed for *Cumbria County Council.*

DARTMOUTH – KINGSWEAR FLOATING BRIDGE CO LTD

Address Dart Marina, Sandquay Road, Dartmouth, Devon TQ6 9PH. **Tel** +44 (0)1803 833351.

Route Dartmouth – Kingswear (Devon) across River Dart (higher route) (forms part of A379).

1	HIGHER FERRY	60	42.7m	136P	18C	BA

HIGHER FERRY Built by *Philip Ltd* at Dartmouth UK. Diesel electric paddle propelled vessel guided by cross-river cables.

ISLE OF WIGHT COUNCIL (COWES FLOATING BRIDGE)

Address Ferry Office, Medina Road, Cowes, Isle of Wight PO31 7BX. **Tel** +44 (0)1983 293041.

Route Cowes – East Cowes.

1	NO 5	76	33.5m	-	15C	BA

NO 5 Chain ferry built at East Cowes for *Isle of Wight County Council,* now *Isle of Wight Council.*

KING HARRY STEAM FERRY COMPANY

Address Feock, Truro, Cornwall TR3 6QJ. **Tel** +44 (0)1872 862312, **Fax** +44 (0)1872 863355.

Internet Email info@kingharry.fq.co.uk **Website** www.kingharry-info.co.uk *(English)*

Route Across River Fal, King Harry Ferry (Cornwall).

1	KING HARRY FERRY	74	44.2m	100P	28C	BA

KING HARRY FERRY Chain ferry built at Falmouth, UK for *King Harry Steam Ferry Company*.

REEDHAM FERRY

Address Reedham Ferry, Reedham, Norwich NR13 3HA. **Tel** +44 (0)1493 700429, **Fax** +44 (0)1493 700999.

Route Acle – Reedham – Norton (across River Yare, Norfolk).

1	REEDHAM FERRY	84	11.3m	12P	3C	BA

REEDHAM FERRY Chain ferry built at Oulton Broad, UK for *Reedham Ferry*. Maximum weight, 12 tons.

SOUTH HAMS DISTRICT COUNCIL

Address Lower Ferry Office, The Square, Kingswear, Dartmouth, Devon TQ6 0AA. **Tel** +44 (0)1803 752342, **Fax** +44 (0)1803 752227.

Route Dartmouth – Kingswear (Devon) across River Dart (lower route).

1	THE TOM AVIS	94	33.5m	50P	8C	BA
2	THE TOM CASEY	89	33.5m	50P	8C	BA

THE TOM AVIS Float propelled by tugs built at Fowey, UK for *South Hams District Council*.

THE TOM CASEY Float propelled by tugs built at Portland, UK for *South Hams District Council*.

TORPOINT FERRY

Address 2 Ferry Street, Torpoint, Cornwall PL11 2AX. Tel +44 (0)1752 812233, Fax +44 (0)1752 816873.

INTERNET Website www.torpointferry.org.uk *(English)*

Route Devonport (Plymouth) – Torpoint (Cornwall) across the Tamar. Pre-booking is not possible and the above number cannot be used for that purpose.

1	LYNHER	61	70.7m	350P	48C	BA
2	PLYM	68	70.7m	350P	54C	BA
3	TAMAR	60	70.7m	350P	48C	BA

LYNHER, PLYM, TAMAR Chain ferries built at Southampton, UK (PLYM built at Bristol) for the *Torpoint Ferry*. The three ferries operate in parallel, each on its own 'track'.

Under construction

4	NEWBUILDING 1	04	73.0m	350P	73C	BA
5	NEWBUILDING 2	05	73.0m	350P	73C	BA
6	NEWBUILDING 3	05	73.0m	350P	73C	BA

NEWBUILDING 1, NEWBUILDING 2, NEWBUILDING 3 Under construction at Port Glasgow, UK for *Torpoint Ferry*. To be delivered between October 2004 and June 2005.

WATERFORD CASTLE HOTEL

Address The Island, Waterford, Irish Republic. Tel +353 (0)51 78203.

Internet Email info@waterfordcastle.com **Website** www.waterfordcastle.com *(English (mainly about hotel; little about ferry))*

Route Grantstown – Little Island (in River Suir, County Waterford).

1	LITTLE ISLAND FERRY	68	-	24P	6C	BA

LITTLE ISLAND FERRY Chain ferry built at Cork, Irish Republic for *Waterford Castle Hotel*.

Lynher *(Miles Cowsill)*

Spirit of Gosport *(Miles Cowsill)*

section **5** *major passenger only ferries*

gb & ireland

There are a surprisingly large number of passenger only ferries operating in the British Isles, mainly operated by launches and small motor boats. There are, however, a few 'major' operators who operate only passenger vessels (of rather larger dimensions) and have not therefore been mentioned previously.

6° West (trading name of West Highland Seaways) SPIRIT OF SKYE (2004, 36 passengers). **Route operated** Gairloch – Portree (Skye). **Tel** +44 (0)0800 328 6426, **Email** info@overtheseatoskye.com **Website** www.overtheseatoskye.com *(English)*

Clyde Marine Services CRUISER (119t, 1974, 24.4m, 249 passengers (ex POOLE SCENE, 2001), FENCER (18t, 1976, 11.0m, 33 passengers), KENILWORTH (44t, 1936, 18.3m, 97 passengers (ex HOTSPUR II (Southampton – Hythe ferry) 1979)), ROVER (48t, 1964, 19.8m, 120 passengers), THE SECOND SNARK (45t, 1938, 22.9m, 120 passengers). **Routes operated** Gourock – Kilcreggan – Helensburgh (generally the KENILWORTH), Gourock – Kilcreggan – Helensburgh – Dunoon – Rothesay – Millport – Lochranza and other Clyde coast ports (generally THE SECOND SNARK). **Tel** +44 (0)1475 721281, **Fax** +44 (0)1475 888023, **Websites** www.clyde-marine.co.uk www.secondsnark.co.uk *(English)*

Dart Pleasure Craft EDGCUMBE BELLE (35t, 1957, 17.7m, 150 passengers), KINGSWEAR BELLE (43t, 1972, 18.0m, 257 passengers). **Route operated** Dartmouth – Kingswear. Note Pleasure craft owned by this operator are also used for the ferry service on some occasions. **Tel** +44 (0)1803 834488, **Fax** +44 (0)1803 835248, **Email** sales@riverlink.co.uk **Website** www.riverlink.co.uk *(English)*

Doolin Ferry Company/O'Brien Shipping DONEMARK (70t, 1978, 19.8m, 65 pass), HAPPY HOOKER (77t, 1989, 19.8m, 96 passengers), QUEEN OF ARAN (113t, 1976, 20.1m, 96 passengers), ROSE OF ARAN (113t, 1976, 20.1m, 96 passengers), TRANQUILITY (62t, 1988, 15.8m, 96 passengers). **Route operated** Doolin – Inishere, Doolin – Inishmaan, Doolin – Inishmore. OILEAN ARANN (416t, 1992, 39.6m, 190 passengers). **Route operated** Galway – Inishere, Galway – Inishmaan, Galway – Inishmore. **Tel** +353 (0)65 7074455, **Fax** +353 (0)65 7074417, **Email** doolinferries@eircom.net **Web Site** www.doolinferries.com *(English)*

G&T Ferries (trading name of Lower Thames & Medway Passenger Boat Co Ltd) DUCHESS M (71t, 1956, 23.8m, 124 passengers) (ex VESTA 1979), PRINCESS POCAHONTAS (180t, 1962, 33.5m, 207 passengers (ex FREYA II 1989, LABOE I 1985, LABOE 1984 (excursion vessel)). **Route operated** Gravesend (Kent) – Tilbury (Essex), **Tel** +44 (0)1732 353448, **Direct Line to Ferry** +44 (0)7973 390124, **Email** enquiry@princess-pocahontas.com **Web Site** www.princess-pocahontas.com *(English)*

Gosport Ferry GOSPORT QUEEN (159t, 1966, 30.5m, 250 passengers), PORTSMOUTH QUEEN (159t, 1966, 30.5m, 250 passengers), SOLENT ENTERPRISE (274t, 1971, 32.0m, 250 passengers (ex GAY ENTERPRISE 1979), (mainly used on excursion work), SOLENT PRINCE (12t, 1981, 43m, 60 passengers) (ex JENNY ANN, ex WATER WYTCH) (mainly used on charter work), SPIRIT OF GOSPORT (250t, 2001, 32.6m, 247 passengers). **Under construction** SPIRIT OF PORTSMOUTH (2005, 32.6m, 300 passengers). **Route operated** Gosport – Portsmouth. **Tel** +44 (0)23 9252 4551, **Email** info@gosportferry.co.uk **Web Site** www.gosportferry.co.uk *(English)*

Hovertravel FREEDOM 90 (1990, 25.4m, 98 passengers) (BHC AP1-88/100S hovercraft (converted from AP1-88/100 in 2000)), ISLAND EXPRESS (1985, 25.4m, 98 passengers) (BHC AP1-88/100S hovercraft (converted from BHC AP1-88/100 in 2001)) (ex FREJA VIKING 2002). **Route operated** Southsea – Ryde. **Tel** +44 (0)1983 811000, **Fax** +44 (0)1983 812859, **Email** info@hovertravel.co.uk, **Website** www.hovertravel.co.uk *(English)*

Hugo Express (trading name of Société de Navigation de Normandie (Connex)) VICTOR HUGO (ex SALTEN 2003) (387t, 1997, 35.0m, 190 passengers) (catamaran), **Routes operated** Portbail or Carteret – Jersey, Guernsey and Sark, Dielette – Alderney – Guernsey, MARIN MARIE (ex AREMETI 3 2003) (608t, 1994, 40.0m, 356 passengers), **Route operated** Granville – Jersey. **Tel:** +44(0) 1534 880576, **Email:** info@hugoexpress.com,**Website:** www.hugoexpress.com *(English).*

Island Ferries ARAN EXPRESS (117t, 1984, 27.4m, 180 passengers), ARAN FLYER (170t, 1988, 33.5m, 208 passengers), ARAN SEABIRD (164t, 1976, 27.7m, 181 passengers), CEOL NA FARRAIGE (200t, 2001, 35.4m, 294 passengers), DRAÍOCHT NA FARRAIGE (200t, 1999, 35.4m, 294 passengers). **Routes operated** Rossaveal (Co Galway) – Aran Islands. **Tel** +353 (0)91 568903 (572273 after 19.00), **Fax** +353 (0)91 568538, **Email** island@iol.ie, **Website** www.aranislandferries.com *(English)*

John O'Groats Ferries PENTLAND VENTURE (186t, 1987, 29.3m, 250 passengers). **Route operated** John O'Groats – Burwick (Orkney). **Tel** +44 (0)1955 611353, **Email** Office@jogferry.co.uk **Website** www.jogferry.co.uk *(English)*

Lundy Company OLDENBURG (288t, 1958, 43.6m, 267 passengers). **Routes operated** Bideford – Lundy Island, Ilfracombe – Lundy Island. Also North Devon Coastal Cruises. **Tel** +44 (0)1271 863636, **Fax** +44 (0)1237 477779, **Email** info@lundyisland.co.uk **Web Site** www.lundyisland.co.uk *(English)*

Mersey Ferries ROYAL DAFFODIL (ex OVERCHURCH 1999) (468t, 1962, 46.6m, 860 passengers), ROYAL IRIS OF THE MERSEY (ex MOUNTWOOD 2002) (464t, 1960, 46.3m, 750 passengers), WOODCHURCH (464t, 1960, 46.6m, 750 passengers). **Routes operated** Liverpool (Pier Head) – Birkenhead (Woodside), Liverpool – Wallasey (Seacombe). Also regular summer cruises from Pier Head to Salford along Manchester Ship Canal. **Tel** *Admin* +44 (0)151 639 0609, *Reservations* +44 (0)151 330 1444, **Fax** +44 (0)151 639 0578, **Email** info@merseyferries.co.uk **Website** www.merseyferries.co.uk *(English)*

Nexus (trading name of Tyne & Wear PTE) PRIDE OF THE TYNE (222t, 1993, 24.0m, 350 passengers), SHIELDSMAN (93.2t, 1976, 24.0m, 350 passengers). **Route operated** North Shields – South Shields. Also cruises South Shields – Newcastle. **Tel** +44 (0)191 454 8183, **Fax** +44 (0)191 427 9510, **Web Site** www.nexus.org.uk *(English)*

Strathclyde Passenger Transport (trading name of Strathclyde PTE) RENFREW ROSE (65t, 1984, 21.9m, 50 passengers), YOKER SWAN (65t, 1984, 21.9m, 50 passengers). **Route operated** Renfrew – Yoker. **Note** although this a passenger only service, the vessels are built as small front loading car ferries and are able to convey one vehicle if necessary. This facility is sometimes used for the conveyance of ambulances. **Tel** +44 (0)141 885 2123, **Fax** +44 (0)141 432 1025, **Email** liz.parkes@spt.co.uk **Website** www.spt.co.uk/Travel/ferries.html *(English)*

Thames Clippers (part of Collins River Enterprises) ABEL MAGWITCH (25.6t, 1999, 18.3m, 60 passengers (tri-maran)), HURRICANE CLIPPER (181t, 2002, 37.8m, 27.5k, 220 passengers), SKY CLIPPER (60t, 1992, 25.0m, 62 passengers) (ex VERITATUM 1995, SD10 2000), STORM CLIPPER (60t, 1992, 25.0m, 62 passengers) (ex DHL WORLDWIDE EXPRESS 1995, SD11 2000). **Routes operated** Savoy Pier (Embankment) – Canary Wharf, Canary Wharf – Rotherhithe (Hilton Hotel) (usually the ABEL MAGWITCH). **Tel** +44 (0)20 7977 6892, **Fax** +44(0) 20 7481 8300, **Email** sean@thamesclippers.com **Website** www.thamesclippers.com *(English)*

Waverley Excursions BALMORAL (735t, 1949, 62.2m, 800 passengers), WAVERLEY (693t, 1947, 73.2m, 950 passengers). **Routes operated** Excursions all round British Isles. However, regular cruises in the Clyde, Bristol Channel, South Coast and Thames provide a service which can be used for transport purposes and therefore both vessels are, in a sense, ferries. The WAVERLEY is the only seagoing paddle steamer in the world. **Tel** +44 (0)141 221 8152, **Fax** +44 (0)141 248 2150, **Email** info@waverleyexcursions.co.uk **Website** www.waverleyexcursions.co.uk *(English)*

White Horse Ferries GREAT EXPECTATIONS (66t, 1992, 21.3m, 162 passengers) (catamaran), HOTSPUR IV (50t, 1946, 19.5m, 125 passengers). **Route operated** Southampton – Hythe (Hants). *Head Office* **Tel.** +44 (0)1793 618566, **Fax** +44 (0)1793 488428, *Local Office* **Tel** +44 (0)23 8084 0722, **Fax** +44 (0)23 8084 6611, **Email** post@hytheferry.co.uk **Website** www.hytheferry.co.uk *(English)*

Romantika *(Mike Louagie)*

section **6** *major passenger ferries*

northern europe

BASTØ FOSEN

THE COMPANY *Bastø Fosen* is a Norwegian private sector company, a subsidiary of *Fosen Trafikklag* of Trondheim.

MANAGEMENT Managing Director Olav Brein, **Operations Manager** Kirsti Been Tofte.

ADDRESS PO Box 94, 3191 Horten, Norway.

TELEPHONE Administration +47 33 03 17 40, **Reservations** not applicable.

FAX Administration & Reservations +47 33 03 17 49.

INTERNET Email basto@fosen.no **Website** www.basto-fosen.no *(Norwegian)*

ROUTE OPERATED Moss – Horten (across Oslofjord, Norway) (30 mins; *(1,2)*; up to every 45 mins).

| 1 | BASTØ I | 5505t | 97 | 14.0k | 109.0m | 550P | 200C | 18L | BA | NO |
| 2 | BASTØ II | 5505t | 97 | 14.0k | 109.0m | 550P | 200C | 18L | BA | NO |

BASTØ I, BASTØ II Built at Frengen, Norway for *Bastø Fosen.*

Under Construction

| 2 | BASTØ III | c6000t | 05 | 18.0k | 116.2m | 550P | 212C | 18L | BA | NO |

BASTØ III Under construction at Gdansk Poland for *Bastø Fosen.* She will enable a 30 minute service to be operated.

BORNHOLMSTRAFIKKEN

THE COMPANY *BornholmsTrafikken* is a Danish state owned company.

MANAGEMENT Managing Director Mads Kofod, **Sales and Marketing Manager** Ole B Larsen.

ADDRESS Havnen, DK-3700 Rønne, Denmark.

TELEPHONE Administration +45 56 95 18 66, **Reservations** +45 56 95 18 66.

FAX Administration & Reservations +45 56 91 07 66.

INTERNET Email info@bornholmstrafikken.dk **Website** www.bornholmstrafikken.dk *(Danish, Swedish, English)*

ROUTES OPERATED Conventional Ferries Rønne (Bornholm, Denmark) – Copenhagen (7 hrs; *(1,2)*; 1 or 2 per day). **Fast Ferry** Ystad (Sweden) – Rønne (1 hr 20 mins; *(3)*; up to 6 per day). **Freight Ferry** Rønne – Køge (7 hrs; *(4)*; 1 per day).

1	JENS KOFOED	12131t	79	19.5k	121.0m	1500P	262C	26T	BA	DK
2	POVL ANKER	12131t	78	19.5k	121.0m	1500P	262C	26T	BA	DK
3»	VILLUM CLAUSEN	6402t	99	40.0k	86.6m	1000P	180C	-	BA	DK
4F	VILJA	9698t	78	16k	152.3m	12P	-	95T	A	NO

JENS KOFOED, POVL ANKER Built at Aalborg, Denmark for *BornholmsTrafikken.* Used on the Rønne – Copenhagen, Rønne – Ystad and (until December 2002) Rønne – Sassnitz services.

Povl Anker *(FotoFlite)*

Visby *(Destination Gotland)*

VILLUM CLAUSEN Austal Auto-Express 86 catamaran built at Fremantle, Australia for *BornholmsTrafikken*. Used on the Rønne – Ystad service.

VILJA Built at Krimpen an der IJssel, Rotterdam, Netherlands as the ANZERE for *Keller Shipping* and chartered to *Nautilus Line* for services between Europe and West Africa. In 1991 she was sold to *AS Tiderø* of Norway and renamed the TIDERØ STAR. She was initially chartered to *Fred. Olsen Lines* and later to *Arimure Line* for service in the Far East. In 1994 chartered to *Fred. Olsen Lines* again. In early 1996 she was briefly chartered to *North Sea Ferries* for their Hull – Rotterdam service and then chartered to *Pandoro* and placed on the Liverpool – Dublin service. In 1997, chartered to *P&O Ferrymasters* operating between Middlesbrough and Gothenburg. Later in 1997 she was chartered again to *P&O North Sea Ferries* and placed on the Middlesbrough – Rotterdam service. The charter ended in 1999. After that she undertook a number of short term charters including *Lineas Suardiaz* and NATO. In early 2002 she was renamed the VILJA and entered service with *Ferryways* on their Zeebrugge – Killingholme service. In 2003 chartered to *BornholmsTrafikken* and placed on the Rønne – Køge service.

Under construction

| 5 | NEWBUILDING 1 | - | 05 | 18.5k | 124.9m | 400P | - | 88T | A | DK |
| 6 | NEWBUILDING 2 | - | 05 | 18.5k | 124.9m | 400P | - | 88T | A | DK |

NEWBUILDING 1, NEWBUILDING 2 Under construction at Hardinxveld-Giessendam, Netherlands. To operate a passenger/freight service between Rønne and Køge and Rønne and Ystad replacing the JENS KOFOED, POVL ANKER and chartered freighter.

COLOR LINE

THE COMPANY *Color Line ASA* is a Norwegian private sector stock-listed limited company. The company merged with *Larvik Scandi Line* of Norway (which owned *Larvik Line* and *Scandi Line*) in 1996. *Larvik Line's* operations were incorporated into *Color Line* in 1997; *Scandi Line* continued as a separate subsidiary until 1999, when it was also incorporated into *Color Line*. The marketing name *Color Scandi Line* was dropped at the end of 2000.

MANAGEMENT Managing Director Trond Kleivdal, **Marketing Manager** Elisabeth Anspach.

ADDRESS *Commercial* Postboks 1422 Vika, 0115 OSLO, Norway, *Technical Management* Color Line Marine AS, PO Box 2090, N-3210 Sandefjord, Norway.

TELEPHONE Administration +47 22 94 44 00, **Reservations** +47 810 00 811.

FAX Administration +47 22 83 04 30, **Reservations** +47 22 83 07 76.

INTERNET Website www.colorline.com *(Norwegian, Danish, English, Swedish, German)*

ROUTES OPERATED Conventional Ferries *All year* Oslo (Norway) – Kiel (Germany) (19 hrs 30 mins; *(6,8)*; 1 per day), Oslo – Hirtshals (Denmark) (8 hrs 30 mins; *(3)*; 1 per day), Kristiansand (Norway) – Hirtshals (4 hrs 30 mins; *(2)*; 2 per day), Larvik (Norway) – Frederikshavn (Denmark) (6 hrs 15 mins; *(4 (summer peak only). 7)*; up to 3 per day), Sandefjord (Norway) – Strömstad (Sweden) (2 hrs 30 mins; *(1,5)*; up to 6 per day), *Not peak summer period* Larvik (Norway) – Hirtshals (5 hrs 30 mins; *(4)*; 1 per day). **Fast Ferry (under the name 'Color Line Express') Summer only** Kristiansand – Hirtshals (2 hrs 30 mins; *(9)*; 3 per day).

1	BOHUS	8772t	71	19.5k	122.7m	1480P	280C	34T	BA	NO
2	CHRISTIAN IV	21699t	82	20.0k	153.1m	1860P	480C	56T	BAS2	NO
3	COLOR FESTIVAL	34314t	85	22.0k	168.0m	2000P	330C	80T	BA	NO
4	COLOR TRAVELLER	17046t	81	19.0k	140.8m	1500P	730C	84T	BA2	NO
5	COLOR VIKING	19763t	85	17.0k	134.0m	2000P	320C	40T	BA2	NO
6	KRONPRINS HARALD	31914t	87	21.5k	166.3m	1432P	700C	90T	BA	NO
7	PETER WESSEL	29704t	81	19.0k	168.5m	2100P	570C	136T	BA	NO
8	PRINSESSE RAGNHILD	35855t	81	21.0k	205.3m	1875P	770C	70T	BA	NO
9»	SILVIA ANA L	7895t	96	41.0k	125.0m	1043P	238C	4L	A	BS

10•	SKAGEN	12333t	75	20.0k	129.8m	1200P	430C	28Tr	BA2	NO

BOHUS Built at Aalborg, Denmark as the PRINSESSAN DESIREE for *Rederi AB Göteborg-Frederikshavn Linjen* of Sweden (trading as *Sessan Linjen*) for their service between Gothenburg and Frederikshavn. In 1981 the company was taken over by *Stena Line* and she became surplus to requirements. During 1981 she had a number of charters including *B&I Line* of Ireland and *Sealink UK*. In 1982 she was chartered to *Sally Line* to operate as second vessel on the Ramsgate – Dunkerque service between June and September. She bore the name VIKING 2 in large letters on her hull although she was never officially renamed and continued to bear the name PRINSESSAN DESIREE on her bow and stern. In September 1982 she returned to *Stena Line* and in 1983 she was transferred to subsidiary company *Varberg-Grenaa Line* for their service between Varberg (Sweden) and Grenaa (Denmark) and renamed the EUROPAFÄRJAN. In 1985 she was renamed the EUROPAFÄRJAN II. In 1986, following a reorganisation within the *Stena Line* Group, ownership was transferred to subsidiary company *Lion Ferry AB* and she was named the LION PRINCESS. In 1993 she was sold to *Scandi Line* and renamed the BOHUS. In 1999 *Scandi Line* operations were integrated into *Color Line*.

CHRISTIAN IV Built at Bremerhaven, Germany as the OLAU BRITANNIA for *Olau Line* of Germany for their service between Vlissingen (Netherlands) and Sheerness (England). In 1989 sold to *Nordström & Thulin* of Sweden for delivery in spring 1990. She was subsequently resold to *Fred. Olsen Lines* of Norway and, on delivery, renamed the BAYARD and used on their service between Kristiansand and Hirtshals. In December 1990 she was acquired by *Color Line* and in 1991 renamed the CHRISTIAN IV. She continues to operate on that route.

COLOR FESTIVAL Built at Helsinki, Finland as the SVEA for *Johnson Line* for the *Silja Line* Stockholm – Mariehamn – Turku service. During winter 1991/92 she was extensively rebuilt and in 1991 renamed the SILJA KARNEVAL; ownership was transferred to *Silja Line*. In 1993 she was sold to *Color Line* and renamed the COLOR FESTIVAL. She is used on the Oslo – Hirtshals service.

COLOR TRAVELLER Built at Helsinki, Finland as the TRAVEMÜNDE for *Gedser-Travemünde Ruten* of Denmark for their service between Gedser (Denmark) and Travemünde (Germany). In 1986 the company's trading name was changed to *GT Linien* and in 1987, following the take-over by *Sea-Link AB* of Sweden, it was further changed to *GT Link*. The vessel's name was changed to the TRAVEMÜNDE LINK. In 1988 she was purchased by *Rederi AB Gotland* of Sweden, although remaining in service with *GT Link*. Later in 1988 she was chartered to *Sally Ferries* and entered service in December on the Ramsgate – Dunkerque service. She was renamed the SALLY STAR. In 1997 she was transferred to *Silja Line*, to operate between Vaasa and Umeå during the summer period and operated under the marketing name WASA EXPRESS (although not renamed). She returned to *Rederi AB Gotland* in autumn 1997, was renamed the THJELVAR and entered service with *Destination Gotland* in January 1998. Withdrawn and laid up in December 2003. In 2004 chartered to *Color Line* to inaugurate a new service between Larvik and Hirtshals. Renamed the COLOR TRAVELLER. Operates in reduced passenger mode on this service but in summer peak period operates between Frederikshavn and Larvik in full passenger mode.

COLOR VIKING Built at Nakskov, Denmark as the PEDER PAARS for *DSB (Danish State Railways)* for their service between Kalundborg (Sealand) and Århus (Jutland). In 1990 purchased by *Stena Line* of Sweden for delivery in 1991. In 1991 renamed the STENA INVICTA and entered service on the *Sealink Stena Line* Dover – Calais service. She was withdrawn from the route in February 1998, before the formation of *P&O Stena Line* but ownership was transferred to that company. In summer 1998, she was chartered to *Silja Line* to operate between Vaasa and Umeå under the marketing name 'WASA JUBILEE'. In autumn 1998 she was laid up at Zeebrugge. She remained there until autumn 1999 when she was chartered to *Stena Line* to operate between Holyhead and Dublin. In 2000 chartered to *Color Line* and renamed the COLOR VIKING and in April entered service on the Sandefjord – Strömstad service. In 2002 purchased by *Color Line*.

KRONPRINS HARALD Built at Turku, Finland for *Jahre Line* of Norway for the Oslo – Kiel service. In 1991 ownership was transferred to *Color Line*.

PETER WESSEL Built at Landskrona, Sweden for *Rederi AB Gotland* of Sweden. A sister vessel of the VISBY (see *Destination Gotland*), it was intended that she should be named the GOTLAND.

However, she was delivered as the WASA STAR and chartered to *Vaasanlaivat* of Finland and used on their Vaasa – Sundsvall service. In 1982 she was chartered to *Karageorgis Line* of Greece for service between Patras (Greece) and Ancona (Italy). This charter was abruptly terminated in 1983 following a dispute over payment of charter dues. She returned the Baltic and was laid up until February 1984 when she was sold to *Larvik Line*. She was renamed the PETER WESSEL. In 1988 she was lengthened. In 1996 acquired by *Color Line*. She remains on the Larvik – Moss – Frederikshavn route.

PRINSESSE RAGNHILD Built at Kiel, Germany for *Jahre Line* of Norway for the Oslo – Kiel service. In 1991 ownership transferred to *Color Line*. In 1992 rebuilt in Spain with an additional mid-ships section and additional decks.

SILVIA ANA L Bazan Alhambra monohull vessel built at San Fernando, Spain for *Buquebus* of Argentina. Initially operated between Buenos Aires (Argentina) and Piriapolis (Uruguay). In 1997 chartered to *Color Line* to operate between Kristiansand and Hirtshals. During winter 1997/98 she again operated in South America but returned to *Color Line* in spring 1998. This was repeated during winters 1998/9 and 1999/2000 but during winter 2000/2001 she remained laid up in Europe. In 2001 she was sold to *MDFC Aircraft* of the Irish Republic and chartered to *Color Line* for four years.

SKAGEN Vehicle/train ferry built at Aalborg, Denmark as the BORGEN for *Fred. Olsen Lines* of Norway for Norway – Denmark services. In December 1990 acquired by *Color Line* and in 1991 renamed the SKAGEN. Until 1997 she operated mainly between Hirtshals and Kristiansand although in later years rail wagons were longer conveyed. In recent years she also operated between Hirtshals and Moss but this service ceased in 2000 and she then served Kristiansand only. In spring 2001 she was transferred to the Larvik – Frederikshavn service. Although mainly operated for freight, the service was also available to car passengers and a special lower rate is available on most sailings. In 2004 replaced by the new COLOR TRAVELLER between Larvik and Hirtshals and became spare vessel.

Under Construction

11	COLOR FANTASY	74600t	04	22.0k	224.0m	2770P	750C	90T	BA2	NO

COLOR FANTASY Under construction at Turku Finland for *Color Line* to replace the PRINSESSE RAGNHILD on the Oslo – Kiel service. Enters service in December 2004.

DESTINATION GOTLAND

THE COMPANY *Destination Gotland AB* is a Swedish private sector company owned by *Rederi AB Gotland*. It took over the operations of services to Gotland from 1st January 1998 on a six-year concession. Originally jointly owned by *Rederi AB Gotland* and *Silja Line*, *Silja Line* involvement in the company ceased at the end of 1998.

MANAGEMENT Managing Director Sten-Crister Forsberg, **Marketing Manager** Per-Erling Evensen.

ADDRESS PO Box 1234, 621 23 Visby, Gotland, Sweden.

TELEPHONE Administration +46 (0)498-20 18 00, **Reservations** +46 (0)771-22 33 00.

FAX Administration & Reservations +46 (0)498-20 13 90.

INTERNET Email info@destinationgotland.se **Website** www.destinationgotland.se *(Swedish, English)*

ROUTES OPERATED Fast Conventional Ferries Visby (Gotland) – Nynäshamn (Swedish mainland) (3 hrs 10 mins; *(1,3)*; 1/2 per day), Visby – Oskarshamn (Swedish mainland) (2 hrs 50 mins; *(1,3)*; 1/2 per day). **Fast Ferry (summer only)** Visby – Nynäshamn (2 hrs 50 mins; *(2)*; up to 2 per day), Visby – Oskarshamn (Swedish mainland) (2 hrs 30 mins; *(2)*; occasional).

1	GOTLAND	29000t	03	28.5k	195.8m	1500P	500C	118T	BA	SW
2»	GOTLANDIA	5632t	99	35.0k	112.5m	700P	140C	-	A	SW
3	VISBY	29000t	03	28.5k	195.8m	1500P	500C	118T	BA	SW

GOTLAND Built at Guangzhou, China for *Rederi AB Gotland* for use on *Destination Gotland* services.

GOTLANDIA Alstom Leroux Corsair 11500 monohull vessel built at Nantes, France as the GOTLAND for *Rederi AB Gotland* and chartered to *Destination Gotland*. In 2003 renamed the GOTLANDIA.

VISBY Built at Guangzhou, China for *Rederi AB Gotland* and used on *Destination Gotland* services.

DFDS SEAWAYS

THE COMPANY *DFDS Seaways* is the passenger division of *DFDS A/S*, a Danish private sector company.

MANAGEMENT **Managing Director DFDS A/S** Ole Frie, **Director DFDS Seaways** Thor Johannesen.

ADDRESS Sundkrogsgåde 11, DK-2100, Copenhagen Ø, Denmark.

TELEPHONE Administration +45 33 42 33 42, **Reservations** +45 33 42 30 00.

FAX Administration & Reservations +45 33 42 33 41.

INTERNET Website www.dfdsseaways.com *(Danish, Dutch, English, German, Norwegian, Swedish)*

ROUTE OPERATED Copenhagen – Helsingborg (Sweden) – Oslo (Norway) (16 hrs; *(1,2)*; 1 per day). See Section 1 for services operating to Britain.

1	CROWN OF SCANDINAVIA	35498t	94	21.5k	170.9m	1940P	450C	70T	BA	DK
2	PEARL OF SCANDINAVIA	40039t	89	21.0k	178.4m	2100P	350C	70T	BA	DK

CROWN OF SCANDINAVIA Launched at Split, Croatia for *Euroway* for their Lübeck – Travemünde – Malmö service as the THOMAS MANN. However, political problems led to serious delays and, before delivery, the service had ceased. She was purchased by *DFDS*, renamed the CROWN OF SCANDINAVIA and introduced onto the Copenhagen – Oslo service.

PEARL OF SCANDINAVIA Built at Turku, Finland as the ATHENA for *Rederi AB Slite* of Sweden (part of *Viking Line*) and used on 24 hour cruises from Stockholm to Mariehamn (Åland). In 1993 the company went into liquidation and she was sold to *Star Cruises* of Malaysia for cruises in the Far East. She was renamed the STAR AQUARIUS. Later that year she was renamed the LANGKAPURI STAR AQUARIUS. In February 2001 sold to *DFDS* and renamed the AQUARIUS. After rebuilding, she was renamed the PEARL OF SCANDINAVIA and introduced onto the Copenhagen – Oslo service.

DFDS TOR LINE

THE COMPANY *DFDS Tor Line SIA* is a Latvian Company, a subsidiary of *DFDS A/S* of Denmark. The company traded as *Latlines* until 2004.

MANAGEMENT Director Zigmunds Jankovskis, **Marketing Manager** Aivars Oss.

ADDRESS 1 Zivju street, Riga, LV-1015, Latvia.

TELEPHONE Administration *Latvia* +371 7519880, *Germany* +49 (0)451 7099697, **Reservations** *Latvia* +371 7353523, *Germany* +49 (0)451 7099685.

FAX *DFDS* **Administration** *Latvia* +371 7353066, *Germany* +49 (0)451 7099687, **Reservations** *Latvia* +371 7353071, *Germany* +49 (0)451 7099687.

INTERNET Email *Administration* office.riga@dfdstorline.com

Reservations passenger.riga@dfdstorline.com **Website** www.dfdstorline.lv *(Latvian, English, Russian)*

ROUTE OPERATED Lübeck (Germany) – Riga (Latvia) (32 hrs; *(1,3)*; 4 per week).

1	KAUNAS	25606t	89	15.8k	190.9m	235P	460C	108Tr	A2	LT
3	VILNIUS	22341t	87	15.8k	190.9m	120P	460C	108Tr	A2	LT

Finnfellow *(Pekka Ruponen)*

Mercandia VIII *(Matthew Punter)*

KAUNAS train ferry built at Wismar, Germany (DDR) for *Lisco* of the former Soviet Union and used by to operate between Klaìpeda and Mukran in Germany (DDR). This was part of series of vessels built to link the USSR and Germany (DDR), avoiding Poland. In 1994 she was modified to increase passenger capacity in order to offer limited passenger facilities and placed on Klaìpeda – Kiel service. In 2003 transferred to the Klaìpeda – Karlshamn route. Early in 2004 chartered to *DFDS Tor Line* to operate between Lübeck and Riga.

VILNIUS train ferry as KAUNAS. Operated on the Klaìpeda – Kiel service until June 2003. Later chartered to *DFDS Tor Line* to operate between Lübeck and Riga.

REDERIJ DOEKSEN

THE COMPANY *Rederij G Doeksen & Zonen bv* is a Dutch public sector company. Ferries are operated by subsidiary *Terschellinger Stoomboot Maatschappij*, trading as *Rederij Doeksen*.

MANAGEMENT Managing Director P Melles, **Marketing Manager** C Dekker.

ADDRESS Willem Barentskade 21, Postbus 40, 8880 AA West Terschelling, Netherlands.

TELEPHONE Administration +31 (0)562 442141, **Reservations** +31 (0)562 446111.

FAX Administration & Reservations +31 (0)562 443241.

INTERNET Email info@rederij-doeksen.nl **Website** www.rederij-doeksen.nl *(Dutch)*

ROUTES OPERATED Conventional Ferries Harlingen (Netherlands) – Terschelling (Frisian Islands) (2 hrs; *(1,3)* (up to 6 per day), Harlingen – Vlieland (Frisian Islands) (1 hr 45 mins; *(5)*; 3 per day). **Fast Passenger Ferries** Harlingen – Terschelling (50 mins; *(2,4)*; 2 to 3 per day), Harlingen – Vlieland (50 mins; *(2,4)*; 2 per day), Vlieland – Terschelling (30 mins; *(2,4)*; 2 per day).

1	FRIESLAND	3583t	89	14.0k	69.0m	1750P	122C	12L	BA	NL
2»p	KOEGELWIECK	439t	92	33.0k	36.7m	317P	0C	0L	-	NL
3	MIDSLAND	1812t	74	15.5k	77.9m	1200P	55C	6L	BA	NL
4»p	NAJADE	164t	99	32.0k	31.8m	184P	0C	0L	-	NL
5	OOST-VLIELAND	1350t	70	15.0k	62.6m	1100P	45C	4L	BA	NL
6F	NOORD-NEDERLAND	-	02	14.0k	48.0m	12P	-	9L	BA	NL

FRIESLAND Built at Krimpen aan den IJssel, Rotterdam, Netherlands for *Rederij Doeksen*. Used on the Harlingen – Terschelling route.

KOEGELWIECK Harding 35m catamaran built at Rosendal, Norway for *Rederij Doeksen* to operate between Harlingen and Terschelling, Harlingen and Vlieland and Terschelling and Vlieland.

MIDSLAND Built at Emden, Germany as the RHEINLAND for *AG Ems* of Germany. In 1993 purchased by *Rederij Doeksen* and renamed the MIDSLAND. Used mainly on the Harlingen – Terschelling route but also used on the Harlingen – Vlieland service. She is now a reserve vessel.

NAJADE SBF Shipbuilders 31m monohull built at Henderson, Australia for *Rederij Doeksen* to operate between Harlingen and Terschelling, Harlingen and Vlieland and Terschelling and Vlieland.

OOST-VLIELAND Built at Emden, Germany as the OSTFRIESLAND for *AG Ems* of Germany. In 1981 purchased by *Rederij Doeksen* and renamed the SCHELLINGERLAND. In 1994 renamed the OOST VLIELAND. Now mainly used on the Harlingen – Vlieland service.

NOORD-NEDERLAND Catamaran built at Harwood, New South Wales, Australia for *Rederij Doeksen*. Used on freight services from Harlingen to Terschelling and Vlieland.

Under Construction

7»	NEWBUILDING	-	04	15.0k	64.0m	1300P	58C	-	BA	NL

NEWBUILDING FBMA Babcock Marine catamaran under construction at Cebu, Philippines for *Rederij Doeksen* to operate between Harlingen and Vlieland.

ECKERÖ LINE

THE COMPANY *Eckerö Line Ab Oy* is a Finnish company, 100% owned by *Eckerö Linjen* of Åland, Finland. Until January 1998, the company was called *Eestin-Linjat*.

MANAGEMENT Managing Director Jarl Danielsson, **Marketing Director** Håkan Nordström.

ADDRESS Hietalahdenranta 13, FIN-00180 Helsinki, Finland.

TELEPHONE Administration +358 (0)9 22885421, **Reservations** +358 (0)9 2288544.

FAX Administration & Reservations +358 (0)9 22885222.

INTERNET Email info@eckeroline.fi **Website** www.eckeroline.fi *(Swedish, Finnish, English, German)*

ROUTE OPERATED Helsinki – Tallinn (Estonia) (3 hrs 30 mins; *(1,2)*; up to 4 per day).

1	NORDLANDIA	21473t	81	21.0k	153.4m	2048P	530C	40T	BA	FI
2	TRANSLANDIA	13700t	76	17.0k	135.8m	100P	280C	115T	A	FI

NORDLANDIA Built at Bremerhaven, Germany as the OLAU HOLLANDIA for *Olau Line* of Germany for the service between Vlissingen (Netherlands) and Sheerness (England). In 1989 she was replaced by a new vessel of the same name and she was sold to *Nordström & Thulin*. She was renamed the NORD GOTLANDIA and introduced onto *Gotlandslinjen* services between Gotland and the Swedish mainland. In 1997 she was purchased by *Eckerö Linjen* of Åland for delivery in early 1998, following the ending of *Nordström & Thulin's* concession to operate the Gotland services. She was renamed the NORDLANDIA and placed on the *Eckerö Line* Helsinki – Tallinn service, operating day trips. From May 2004 on some days to operate two round trips per day.

TRANSLANDIA Built at Hamburg, Germany as the TRANSGERMANIA for *Poseidon Schiffahrt OHG* of Germany interests for *Finncarriers-Poseidon* services between Finland and West Germany. In 1991 chartered to *Norse Irish Ferries* and used on their freight service between Liverpool and Belfast. In 1992 she was returned to *Finncarriers* and in 1993 sold to Cypriot interests for use in the Mediterranean and renamed the ROSEBAY. In 1994 chartered to *Stena Line* to inaugurate a new service between Harwich and Rotterdam (Frisohaven). In 1995 the service was switched to Hoek van Holland following the construction of a new linkspan. She also, during the summer, carried cars towing caravans, motor caravans and their passengers. In 1997 she was chartered to *Sally Freight* and renamed the EUROSTAR, operating between Ramsgate and Ostend. Later in 1997 she was renamed the EUROCRUISER. In 1998 she returned on charter to *Stena Line* and resumed the name ROSEBAY. In 1999 she was temporarily transferred to the Irish Sea. In autumn 2000 she was transferred to the Killingholme – Hoek van Holland service but was withdrawn in 2001 when the delivery of the new STENA HOLLANDICA enabled the STENA SEARIDER to replace her. She was then sold to *Rederi AB Engship* of Sweden, renamed the TRANSPARADEN and chartered to *Botnia Link*. In 2002 chartered to *DFDS Tor Line* to operate between Kiel and Riga. In January 2003 transferred to the *Latlines* Lübeck – Riga route. Later in 2003 chartered to *SCF St Petersburg Line*. In May 2004 sold to *Eckerö Line* and operated between Helsinki and Tallinn. Renamed the TRANSLANDIA.

ECKERÖ LINJEN

THE COMPANY *Eckerö Linjen* is an Åland Islands company.

MANAGEMENT Managing Director Jarl Danielsson, **Marketing Director** Christer Lindman.

ADDRESS Torggatan 2, Box 158, AX-22100 Mariehamn, Åland.

TELEPHONE Administration +358 (0)18 28000, **Reservations** +358 (0)18 28300.

FAX Administration & Reservations +46(0)175 30820.

INTERNET Website www.eckerolinjen.fi *(Swedish, Finnish, English, German)*

ROUTE OPERATED Eckerö (Åland) – Grisslehamn (Sweden) (2 hrs; *(1,2)*; 5 per day).

| 1 | ALANDIA | 6754t | 72 | 17.0k | 108.7m | 1320P | 225C | 32T | BA | AL |
| 2 | ROSLAGEN | 6652t | 72 | 18.7k | 109.3m | 1320P | 225C | 32T | BA | AL |

ALANDIA Built at Papenburg, Germany as the DIANA for *Rederi AB Slite* of Sweden for *Viking Line* services. In 1979 she was sold to *Oy Vaasa-Umeå Ab* of Finland, renamed the BOTNIA EXPRESS and operated between Vaasa and Umeå. In 1982 she was sold to *Sally Line* of Finland; later that year she was sold to *Suomen Yritysrahoitus Oy* and chartered back. 1989 she was chartered to *Jacob Lines* for the route Skellefteå – Jakobstad under the marketing name 'Polar Princess' and in March 1990 she was placed on Helsinki-Tallinn cruises, but due to some customs/visa problems she never called at Tallinn. In 1992 she was sold to *Eckerö Linjen* and renamed the ALANDIA. She has also been used by subsidiary company *Eckerö Line*.

ROSLAGEN Built at Papenburg, Germany as the VIKING 3 for *Rederi AB Sally* and used on *Viking Line* Baltic services. In 1976 she was sold to *Vaasanlaivat* of Finland for their service between Vaasa (Finland) and Umeå/Sundsvall (Sweden) and renamed the WASA EXPRESS. In 1982 *Vaasanlaivat* was taken over by *Rederi AB Sally* and in April 1983 she resumed the name VIKING 3, was transferred to *Sally Line* and used on the Ramsgate – Dunkerque service. She remained in the Channel during winter 1983/4 on freight-only services. However, in early 1984 she returned to *Vaasanlaivat* and resumed the name WASA EXPRESS. In 1988 she was sold to *Eckerö Linjen* and renamed the ROSLAGEN. During winter 1992/3 she operated between Helsinki and Tallinn for *Estonia New Line* and returned to *Eckerö Linjen* in the spring.

AG EMS

THE COMPANY *AG Ems* is a German public sector company.

MANAGEMENT Managing Director & Chief Executive B W Brons, **Marine Superintendent** J Alberts, **Marketing Manager & Assistant Manager** P Eesmann, **Operating Manager** Konrad Huismann.

ADDRESS Am Aussenhafen, Postfach 1154, 26691 Emden, Germany.

TELEPHONE Administration & Reservations +49 (0)4921 8907-400 or +49 (0)4921 8907-406.

FAX Administration & Reservations +49 (0)4921 8907-405.

INTERNET Email info@ag-ems.de **Website** www.ag-ems.de *(German, Dutch)*

ROUTES OPERATED Conventional Ferries Emden (Germany) – Borkum (German Frisian Islands) (2 hrs; *(1,3,6)*; up to 4 per day), Eemshaven (Netherlands) – Borkum (55 mins; *(1,3,6)*; up to 4 per day). **Fast Ferries** Emden – Borkum (1 hr; *(2,4)*; up to 4 per day), Eemshaven – Borkum (30 mins; *(2,4)*; 1 per week in summer).

1	MÜNSTERLAND	1859t	86	15.5k	78.7m	1200P	70C	10L	BA	GY
2p»	NORDLICHT	435t	89	33.0k	38.8m	272P	0C	0L	-	GY
3	OSTFRIESLAND	1859t	85	15.5k	78.7m	1200P	70C	10L	BA	GY
4p»	POLARSTERN	636t	00	40.0k	45.0m	405P	0C	0L	-	GY
5p	WAPPEN VON BORKUM	287t	76	11.5k	42.8m	358P	0C	0L	-	GY
6	WESTFALEN	1812t	72	15.5k	77.9m	1200P	65C	10L	BA	GY

MÜNSTERLAND, OSTFRIESLAND Built at Leer, Germany for *AG Ems*.

NORDLICHT Fjellstrand 38m passenger only catamaran built Mandal, Norway for *AG Ems*.

POLARSTERN Oceanfast Ferries (Australia) 45m passenger only catamaran built at Henderson, Australia for another operator as the CARAIBE JET. This order was cancelled before delivery and she was sold to *AG Ems* after a period of lay-up, arriving in 2001.

WAPPEN VON BORKUM Built at Oldersum, Germany as the HANNOVER for *Friesland Fahrlinie* of Germany. In 1979 sold to *AG Ems* and renamed the STADT BORKUM. In 1988 sold to *ST-Line* of Finland, operating day trips from Rauma. In 1994 returned to *AG Ems* and renamed the WAPPEN VON BORKUM.

WESTFALEN Built at Emden, Germany for *AG Ems*. Rebuilt in 1994.

FINNLINES

THE COMPANIES *Finnlines plc* is a Finnish private sector company.

MANAGEMENT President Asser Ahleskog, **Vice-President** Simo Airas.

ADDRESS PO Box 197, Salmisaarenkatu 1, FIN-00180 Helsinki, Finland. *Sales and marketing of Finnlines Passenger Services* Nordic Ferry Center Oy, Lönnrotinkatu 21, FIN-00120 Helsinki, Finland.

TELEPHONE Administration +358 (0)10 34350. **Reservations** *(Nordic Ferry Center Oy)* +358 (0)9-2510 200.

FAX Administration +358 (0)10 3435200, **Reservations** +358 (0)9-2510 2022.

INTERNET *Finnlines* **Email** info@finnlines.fi *Nordic Ferry Center* info@ferrycenter.fi

Website *Finnlines* www.finnlines.fi *(English, Finnish, German)*

Nordic Ferry Center www.ferrycenter.fi/finnlines/en/index.shtml *(English)*

ROUTES OPERATED All year Helsinki – Travemünde (33 hrs; *(1,2,3,4)*; 1/2 per day) **Note** frequencies refer to services which convey passengers.

1	FINNHANSA	32531t	94	21.3k	183.0m	90P	-	236T	A2	FI
2	FINNPARTNER	32534t	94	21.3k	183.0m	90P	-	236T	A2	FI
3	FINNTRADER	32534t	95	21.3k	183.0m	90P	-	236T	A2	FI
4	TRANSEUROPA	32534t	95	21.3k	183.0m	90P	-	236T	A2	GY

FINNHANSA, FINNPARTNER, FINNTRADER 'Ro-pax' vessels built at Gdansk, Poland for *Finnlines Oy* of Finland to provide a daily service conveying both freight and a limited number of cars and passengers on a previously freight-only route.

TRANSEUROPA 'Ro-pax' vessel built at Gdansk, Poland for *Poseidon Schiffahrt* of Germany to operate on a joint service between Lübeck and Helsinki. In 1997 *Poseidon Schiffahrt* was acquired by *Finnlines* and in 2001 renamed *Finnlines Deutschland AG.*

Under Construction

5	NEWBUILDING 1	42000t	05	25.0k	216.0m	500P	-	300T	A2	FI
6	NEWBUILDING 2	42000t	06	25.0k	216.0m	500P	-	300T	A2	FI
7	NEWBUILDING 3	42000t	06	25.0k	216.0m	500P	-	300T	A2	FI

NEWBUILDING 1, NEWBUILDING 2, NEWBUILDING 3 Under construction at Ancona, Italy to operate between Helsinki and Travemünde.

FINNLINK

FinnLink Oy operates a service between Kapellskär (Sweden) and Naantali (Finland). Until spring 2002 the service was freight only. However passengers were conveyed on some sailings from summer 2002.

THE COMPANY is a subsidiary of *Finnlines.*

MANAGEMENT Managing Director Christer Backman.

ADDRESS Satamatie 11, FIN-21100, Naantali, Finland.

TELEPHONE Administration & Reservations +358 (0)10 436 7620.

FAX Administration & Reservations 358 (0)10 436 7660.

INTERNET Email finnlink@finnlink.fi **Website** www.finnlink.fi *(English, Finnish, Swedish)*

ROUTE OPERATED Kapellskär (Sweden) – Naantali (Finland) (6 hrs; *(8,9,10)*; 3 per day). **Note** car passengers are now conveyed on all sailings.

8	FINNCLIPPER	30500t	99	22.0k	188.3m	440P	-	184T	BA	FI
9	FINNEAGLE	30500t	99	22.0k	188.3m	440P	-	176T	BA2	FI
10	FINNFELLOW	33796t	00	22.0k	188.3m	452P	-	216T	BA	FI

FINNCLIPPER 'Ro-pax' vessel built at Cadiz, Spain. Ordered by *Stena Ro-Ro* of Sweden and launched as the STENA SEAPACER 1. In 1998 sold, before delivery, to *Finnlines* and renamed the FINNCLIPPER. Entered service on the Helsinki – Travemünde route in 1999. During winter 1999/2000 she was converted to double-deck loading. In late 2002 transferred to *FinnLink*.

FINNEAGLE 'Ro-pax' vessel built at Cadiz, Spain. Ordered by *Stena Ro-Ro* of Sweden and launched as the STENA SEAPACER 2. In 1998 sold, before delivery, to *Finnlines* and renamed the FINNEAGLE. Although expected to join her sister on the Helsinki – Travemünde route, on delivery in late 1999 she entered service with *FinnLink*. During winter 1999/2000 she was modified for two deck loading.

FINNFELLOW Ro-pax ferry built as the STENA BRITANNICA at Cadiz Spain for *Stena RoRo* and chartered to *Stena Line bv* to operate between Hoek van Holland and Harwich. In 2003 replaced by a new STENA BRITANNICA, sold to *Finnlines*, renamed the FINNFELLOW and placed on the Helsinki – Travemünde route. In 2004 transferred to *FinnLink*.

FJORD LINE

THE COMPANY *Fjord Line* is 100% owned by *Bergen-Nordhordland Rutelag AS (BNR)*, a Norwegian company.

MANAGEMENT Managing Director Ove Solem, **Marketing Manager** Nils Henrik Geitle.

ADDRESS Skoltegrunnskaien, PO Box 6020, N-5020 Bergen, Norway.

TELEPHONE Administration +47 55 54 87 00, **Reservations** +47 55 54 88 00.

FAX Administration & Reservations +47 55 54 86 01.

INTERNET Email fjordline@fjordline.com **Website** www.fjordline.com *(Norwegian, Danish, English)*

ROUTE OPERATED Bergen – Egersund (Norway) – Hanstholm (Denmark) (15 hrs 30 mins; *(1)*; 3 per week), Egersund – Hanstholm (6 hrs 45 mins; *(1)*; 7 per week in summer). Also UK route – see Section 1.

| 1 | FJORD NORWAY | 31356t | 86 | 21.0k | 161m | 1800P | 600C | 100T | BA | NO |

FJORD NORWAY Built at Bremerhaven, Germany as the PETER PAN for *TT-Line* for the service between Travemünde and Trelleborg. In 1992 sold to *TT Line* of Australia (no connection) for use on their service between Port Melbourne (Victoria) and Hobart (Tasmania) and renamed the SPIRIT OF TASMANIA. In 2002 sold to *Nordsjøferger K/S* of Norway and renamed the SPIR. After modification work she was renamed the FJORD NORWAY and chartered to *Fjord Line*.

HH-FERRIES

THE COMPANY *HH-Ferries* is a Danish/Swedish private sector company. In 2002 it was acquired by *Steneo AB* of Sweden, part of the *Stena Group*.

MANAGEMENT Managing Director Lars Meijer, **Marketing Manager** Jon Cavalli-Björkman.

ADDRESS Atlantgatan 2, S-252 25 Helsingborg, Sweden.

TELEPHONE Administration +46 (0)42-26 80 00, **Reservations Denmark** +45 49 26 01 55, **Sweden** +46 (0)42-19 8000.

FAX Administration & Reservations Denmark +45 49 26 01 56, **Sweden** +46 (0)42-28 10 70.

INTERNET Email admin@hhferries.se **Website** www.hhferries.se *(Swedish, Danish)*

ROUTE OPERATED Helsingør – Helsingborg (20 mins; *(1,2)*; every 30 minutes).

| 1 | GITTE 3 | 4296t | 87 | 12.7k | 95.0m | 300P | 170C | 20T | BA | DK |

| 2 | MERCANDIA IV | 4296t | 89 | 13.0k | 95.0m | 420P | 170C | 18L | BA | DK |
| 3 | MERCANDIA VIII | 4296t | 87 | 13.0k | 95.0m | 420P | 170C | 18L | BA | DK |

GITTE 3 Built at Sunderland, UK as the SUPERFLEX DELTA for *Vognmandsruten*. In 1990 this company was taken over by *DIFKO* and she was renamed the DIFKO STOREBÆLT. In 1998, following the opening of the Great Belt fixed link, the service ceased and she was laid up. In 1999 she was chartered to *Easy Line* renamed the GITTE 3 and operated between Gedser and Rostock. Laid up after August 1999 except for brief periods on charter to *HH-Ferries*. In 2003 sold to *HH-Ferries*.

MERCANDIA IV Built at Sunderland, UK as the SUPERFLEX NOVEMBER for *Vognmandsruten* of Denmark. In 1989 sold to *Mercandia* and renamed the MERCANDIA IV. In 1990 she began operating on their *Kattegatbroen* Juelsminde – Kalundborg service. In 1996 she was transferred to their *Sundbroen* Helsingør – Helsingborg service. In 1997 the service and vessel were leased to *HH-Ferries*. In 1999 she was purchased by *HH-Ferries*. She has been equipped to carry dangerous cargo.

MERCANDIA VIII Built at Sunderland, UK as the SUPERFLEX BRAVO for *Vognmandsruten* of Denmark and used on their services between Nyborg and Korsør and Copenhagen (Tuborg Havn) and Landskrona (Sweden). In 1991 she was chartered to *Scarlett Line* to operate on the Copenhagen and Landskrona route. In 1993 she was renamed the SVEA SCARLETT but later in the year the service ceased and she was laid up. In 1996 she was purchased by *Mercandia*, renamed the MERCANDIA VIII and placed on their *Sundbroen* Helsingør – Helsingborg service. In 1997 the service and vessel was leased to *HH-Ferries*. In 1999 she was purchased by *HH-Ferries*.

HURTIGRUTEN

SERVICE The 'Hurtigruten' is the 'Norwegian Coastal Express Service'. It is part cruise, part passenger ferry, part cargo line and part car ferry (although this is a fairly minor part of the operation). In recent years the service has been operated by a consortium of two operators – *Ofotens og Vesteraalen Dampskibsselskab* and *Troms Fylkes Dampskibsselskap*. Plans to merge in 2002 to form a new company called *Nord Norges Dampskipselskap* were dropped.

ADDRESS *Ofotens og Vesteraalen Dampskibsselskab* Postboks 43, 8501 Narvik, Norway. *Troms Fylkes Dampskibsselskap* 9005 Tromsø, Norway.

TELEPHONE Administration *Ofotens og Vesteraalen D/S* +47 76 96 76 96, *Troms Fylkes D/S* +47 77 64 82 00, **Reservations Norway** 810 30 000, *UK* +44 (0)20 7371 4011.

FAX Administration & Reservations *Ofotens og Vesteraalen D/S* +47 76 96 76 11, *Troms Fylkes D/S* +47 77 64 82 40, *Reservations (UK)* +44 (0)20 7371 4070.

INTERNET Email booking@ovds.no booking@tfds.no **Website** www.hurtigruten.no *(English, Norwegian)*

ROUTE OPERATED Bergen – Kirkenes with many intermediate calls. Daily departures throughout the year. The round trip takes just under 11 days.

1	FINNMARKEN	14000t	02	18.0k	133.0m	647P	50C	0L	SC	NO
2	KONG HARALD	11204t	93	18.0k	121.8m	691P	50C	0L	SC	NO
3	LOFOTEN	2621t	64	16.0k	87.4m	410P	4C	0L	C	NO
4	MIDNATSOL	14000t	03	18.0k	135.7m	626P	50C	-	SC	NO
5•	MIDNATSOL II	6167t	82	18.0k	108.6m	550P	40C	0L	SC	NO
6	NARVIK	6257t	82	18.0k	108.6m	550P	40C	0L	SC	NO
7	NORDKAPP	11386t	96	18.0k	123.3m	691P	50C	0L	SC	NO
8	NORDLYS	11204t	94	18.0k	121.8m	691P	50C	0L	SC	NO
9	NORDNORGE	11384t	97	18.0k	123.3m	691P	50C	0L	SC	NO
10	POLARLYS	11341t	96	18.0k	123.0m	691P	50C	0L	SC	NO
11	RICHARD WITH	11205t	93	18.0k	121.8m	691P	50C	0L	SC	NO
12	TROLLFJORD	14000t	02	18.0k	135.7m	626P	50C	0L	SC	NO
13	VESTERÅLEN	6261t	83	18.0k	108.6m	550P	40C	0L	SC	NO

FINNMARKEN Built at Ulsteinvik, Norway for *Ofotens og Vesteraalen D/S* to replace the LOFOTEN.

KONG HARALD Built at Stralsund, Germany for *Troms Fylkes D/S*.

LOFOTEN Built at Oslo, Norway for *Vesteraalens D/S*. In 1988 she was sold to *Finnmark Fylkesrederi og Ruteselskap*. In 1996 she was sold to *Ofotens og Vesteraalen D/S*. In 2002 she was replaced by the FINNMARKEN but continued to operate cruises and she substituted for the NORDNORGE during winter 2002/3 when she went to South America to operate cruises. This was repeated during winter 2003/4.

MIDNATSOL Built at Rissa, Norway for *Troms Fylkes D/S*. To replace the existing MIDNATSOL, renamed the MIDNATSOL II.

MIDNATSOL II Built at Ulsteinvik, Norway for *Troms Fylkes D/S* at the MIDNATSOL. Withdrawn in 2003 and renamed the MIDNATSOL II. Laid up.

NARVIK Built at Trondheim, Norway for *Ofoten D/S*. Since 1987 owned by *Ofotens og Vesteraalen D/S*.

NORDKAPP Built at Ulsteinvik, Norway for *Ofotens og Vesteraalen D/S*.

NORDLYS Built at Stralsund, Germany for *Troms Fylkes D/S*.

NORDNORGE Built at Ulsteinvik, Norway for *Ofotens og Vesteraalen D/S*. During winter 2002/3 operated cruises down the coast to Chile and to Antarctica.

POLARLYS Built at Ulsteinvik, Norway for *Troms Fylkes D/S*.

RICHARD WITH Built at Stralsund, Norway for *Ofotens og Vesteraalen D/S*. In 2002 sold to Norwegian interests and chartered back.

TROLLFJORD Built at Rissa, Norway for *Troms Fylkes D/S*.

VESTERÅLEN Built at Harstad, Norway for *Vesteraalens D/S*. Since 1987 owned by *Ofotens og Vesteraalen D/S*.

KYSTLINK

THE COMPANY *KystLink AS* is a Norwegian private sector company.

MANAGEMENT Managing Director *not known,* **Marketing Manager** *not known.*

ADDRESS Kongshavn 8, NO-3970 Langesund, Norway.

TELEPHONE Administration & Reservations +47 35 96 68 00.

FAX Administration & Reservations +47 35 96 68 01.

INTERNET Email post@kystlink.de **Website** www.kystlink.no *(Norwegian, English)* www.kystlink.de *(German)*

ROUTE OPERATED Langesund – Hirtshals (6 hours; *(1)*; 1 per day).

1	BOA VISTA	4078t	73	16k	143.3m	100P	-	72T	BA	BS

BOA VISTA Built at Crepelle a/d IJssel, Netherlands as the UNION WELLINGTON. In 1977 chartered to *Aghiris Navigation* of Greece and renamed the ALPHA EXPRESS. In 1980 sold to *Stena Line,* renamed the STENA SHIPPER. In 1981 chartered to *Sealink UK;* rail tracks were fitted and she was operated on the Harwich – Zeebrugge train ferry service, being renamed the SPEEDLINK VANGUARD. In 1987 the charter was terminated, rail tracks were removed and, after a brief period as the CARIBE EXPRESS, she was renamed the STENA SHIPPER. In 1988 she was chartered to *Kirk Line* of the USA for service in the Caribbean and renamed the KIRK SHIPPER. In 1989 she had additional passenger accommodation added and was chartered to *Truckline Ferries,* renamed the NORMANDIE SHIPPER and inaugurated a Caen – Portsmouth freight service. In 1996 she was laid up. In 1999 was sold to Canadian interests and renamed the BONAVISTA. She was not moved to

Canada; she was laid up in Swinoujscie, Poland awaiting sale or charter. In 2001 she was sold to *KystLink* and renamed the BOA VISTA. Passengers began to be carried in 2004.

LISCO BALTIC SERVICE

THE COMPANY *AB Lisco Baltic Service* is a Lithuanian company, 76% owned by *DFDS A/S of Denmark*; they purchased this holding from Lithuanian Government in 2001. Passenger and cargo services are marketed by *AB Lisco Baltic Service* and ticket sales in Lithuania by *Krantas Shipping*.

ADDRESS 24 J Janonio Str, Klaìpeda LT-5813, Lithuania.

TELEPHONE Administration *LISCO Baltic Service (Klaìpeda)* + 370 46 393101, Reservations *LISCO (Klaìpeda):* + 370 46 393288, *Krantas (Klaìpeda)* + 370 46 395050, *DFDS Tor Line/LISCO Baltic Service (Karlshamn)* + 46 (0)45433680, *LISCO Baltic Service GmbH (Kiel)* + 49 (0)431 2097 6444 – cargo, + 49 (0)43120976420 – passengers.

FAX Administration *LISCO Baltic Service (Klaìpeda)* + 370 46 393601, Reservations *LISCO (Klaìpeda)* + 370 46 393287, *Krantas (Klaìpeda):* + 370 46 395052, *DFDS Tor Line/LISCO Baltic Service (Karlshamn)* + 46 (0)45433689, *LISCO Baltic, Service GmbH (Kiel)*: + 49 (0)431 2097 6555.

INTERNET Email – Administration ml5@lisco.lt **Reservations *LISCO (Klaìpeda)*** booking@lisco.lt *Krantas (Klaìpeda)* Cargo.de@krantas.lt *DFDS Tor Line/LISCO Baltic Service (Karlshamn)* Karlshamn@dfdstorline.com, *LISCO Baltic Service GmbH (Kiel)*: cargo@lisco-baltic-service.de passage@lisco-baltic-service.de **Website:** www.lisco.lt *(English, German)*

ROUTES OPERATED Klaìpeda (Lithuania) – Kiel (Germany) (21 hrs; *(2)*; 6 per week) (joint with *Scandlines Euroseabridge* under the 'Kiel-Klaìpeda-Express' name), Klaìpeda – Karlshamn (Sweden) (15 hrs *(3,4)*; 6 per week), Klaìpeda – Sassnitz (Germany) (18 hrs; *(1)*; 3 per week (joint with *Scandlines Euroseabridge*)).

1F	KLAÌPEDA	21890t	87	15.8k	190.9m	12P	250C	110Tr	A	LT
2	LISCO GLORIA	20600t	02	22.0k	199.4m	308P	316C	180T	A	LT
3	MERMAID II	13730t	72	17.5k	137.3m	69P	170C	84T	AS	PA
4	PALANGA	11630t	79	19.0k	126.5m	126P	300C	70T	A	LT

KLAÌPEDA Train ferry as KAUNAS – but not converted to full ro-pax format (although she does carry more than the normal 12 for a ro-ro). Operates on the Klaìpeda –Sassnitz route.

LISCO GLORIA Built in Szczecin, Poland for *Lloyd Sardegna* of Italy as the GOLFO DEI CORALLI for operating between Italy and Sardinia. However, due to late delivery the order was cancelled. In 2002 purchased by *DFDS Tor Line*, renamed the DAN GLORIA and, in Autumn 2002 placed on the Esbjerg – Harwich service. In June 2003 replaced by modified sister vessel DANA SIRENA (see Section 1) and sold to *Lisco Baltic Service* and renamed the LISCO GLORIA. Operates between Klaìpeda and Kiel.

MERMAID II Built at Turku, Finland as the HANZ GUTZEIT and chartered to *Finncarriers* for Finland – Germany service. In 1982 she was sold to *EFFOA* of Finland and renamed the CAPELLA. She continued to be chartered to *Finncarriers* and this charter continued under a number of subsequent owners. In 1986 she was renamed the CAPELLA AV Stockholm. In 1988 she was renamed the FINNMAID. In 1989 she was placed on the *FinnLink* service between Uusikaupunki (Finland) and Hargshamn (Sweden). In 1997, this service was transferred to the Kapellskär – Naantali route. In 1998 she was replaced by the FINNARROW and, after service on *Finncarriers'* Finland – Germany routes, was laid up. In 2000 she was chartered to *VV-Line*. Passenger capacity was raised from 48 to 69. She was owned by *Rederi AB Gustaf Erikson* of Åland but in 2001 purchased by *VV-Line* and renamed the MERMAID II. In 2003 chartered to *DFDS Tor Line* to operate between Kiel and Riga. In March service transferred to Lübeck. In 2003 sold to *Skandia Liv Ab* of Panama. In 2004 chartered to *LISCO* and placed on the Klaìpeda – Karlshamn route.

PALANGA Built at Le Havre, France; rebuilt at in 1992 to increase passengers capacity. In 1996 sold to *Lisco*, renamed the PALANGA; used on a Klaìpeda – Stockholm route (later Klaìpeda –

Maren Mols *(FotoFlite)*

Baltic Jet *(Pekka Ruponen)*

Karlshamn). In 2003 briefly operated the Klaìpeda – Kiel route but returned to the Karlshamn when the LISCO GLORIA entered service.

AB Lisco Baltic Service also own the TOR NERINGA which is currently on charter to *DFDS Tor Line*. It is shown under *DFDS Tor Line* in Section 3.

MOLS-LINIEN

THE COMPANY *Mols-Linien A/S* is a Danish private sector company; previously a subsidiary of *J Lauritzen A/S*, it was, in 1988 sold to *DIFKO No LXII (Dansk Investeringsfond)*. Since 1994 shares in the company have been traded on the stock exchange. In January 1999 a 40% share in the company was acquired by *Scandlines Danmark A/S*. Their *Scandlines Cat-Link* Århus – Kalundborg service became part of *Mols-Linien* in February 1999 and the service was switched from Kalundborg to Odden in April 1999. The Ebeltoft – Odden ro-pax vessels were transferred to the Århus – Kalundborg route in January 2000.

MANAGEMENT Managing Director Preben Wolff, **Marketing Manager** Christian Hingelberg.

ADDRESS Færgehavnen, DK-8400 Ebeltoft, Denmark.

TELEPHONE Administration +45 89 52 52 00, **Reservations** +45 70 10 14 18.

FAX Administration +45 89 52 52 90, **Reservations** +45 89 52 52 92.

INTERNET Email administration@mols-linien.dk **Website** www.mols-linien.dk *(Danish)*

ROUTES OPERATED Ro-pax Ferries Århus (Jutland) – Kalundborg (Sealand) (2 hr 40 mins; *(3,5)*; 7 per day). **Fast Ferries** Århus – Odden (Sealand) (1 hr 5 mins; *(1)*; every 3 hrs), Ebeltoft (Jutland) – Odden (45 mins; *(2,4)*; two hourly).

1»	MADS MOLS	5619t	98	43.0k	91.3m	800P	220C	-	A	DK
2»	MAI MOLS	3971t	96	43.4k	76.1m	450P	120C	-	BA	DK
3	MAREN MOLS	14221t	96	19.0k	136.4m	600P	344C	82L	BA2	DK
4»	MIE MOLS	3971t	96	43.4k	76.1m	450P	120C	-	BA	DK
5	METTE MOLS	14221t	96	19.0k	136.4m	600P	344C	82L	BA2	DK

MADS MOLS InCat 91 metre catamaran, built speculatively at Hobart, Tasmania, Australia. In spring 1998, following *InCat's* acquisition of a 50% share in *Scandlines Cat-Link A/S*, she was chartered to that company, operating between Århus and Kalundborg and named the CAT-LINK V. She is the current holder of the Hales Trophy for fastest crossing of the Atlantic during her delivery voyage between the USA and Falmouth, UK. In 1999 the charter was transferred to *Mols-Linien*, she was renamed the MADS MOLS and operated between Århus and Odden.

MAI MOLS Danyard SeaJet 250 catamaran built at Aalborg, Denmark for *Mols-Linien*.

MAREN MOLS, METTE MOLS Ro-pax vessels built at Frederikshavn, Denmark for *Mols-Linien*. Initially operated on the Ebeltoft – Odden route. In January 2000 switched to the Århus – Kalundborg route.

MIE MOLS Danyard SeaJet 250 catamaran built at Aalborg, Denmark for *Mols-Linien*.

REEDEREI NORDEN-FRISIA

THE COMPANY *Aktiengesellschaft Reederei Norden-Frisia* is a German public sector company.

MANAGEMENT President/CEO Dr Stegmann, **Managing Director/CFO** Prok. Graw.

ADDRESS Postfach 1262, 26534 Norderney, Germany.

TELEPHONE Administration +49 (0)4932 9130.

FAX Administration +49 (0)4932 9131310.

INTERNET Email info@reederei-frisia.de **Website** www.reederei-frisia.de *(German)*

ROUTES OPERATED *Car Ferries & Passenger Ferries* Norddeich (Germany) – Norderney (German Frisian Islands) (1 hr; *(2,4,5)*; up to 15 per day), Norddeich – Juist (German Frisian Islands) (1 hr 20 mins; *(3,6)*; up to 15 per day), *Passenger only fast ferry* Norderney – Helgoland (1 hr 30 mins; *(1)*), Langeoog – Helgoland (1 hr 15 min; *(1)*), Wangerooge – Helgoland (1 hr 15 min; *(1)*), Hooksiel-Außenhafen – Sylt (2 hrs 30 mins; *(1)*), Hooksiel-Außenhafen – Amrum/Föhr (2 hrs; *(1)*).

1p»	CAT NO 1	963t	99	40.0k	52.6m	432P	-	-	-	GY
2	FRISIA I	1020t	70	12.3k	63.7m	1500P	53C	-	BA	GY
3	FRISIA II	1125t	78	12.0k	63.3m	1340P	53C	-	BA	GY
4	FRISIA IV	1600t	02	12.0k	71.7m	1342P	60C	-	BA	GY
5	FRISIA V	1007t	65	11.0k	63.8m	1442P	53C	-	BA	GY
6	FRISIA VI	768t	68	12.0k	54.9m	1096P	35C	-	BA	GY
7F	FRISIA VII	363t	84	12.0k	53.0m	12P	30C	-	BA	GY
8p	FRISIA IX	571t	80	11.0k	57.0m	785P	-	-	-	GY
9p	FRISIA X	187t	72	12.0k	36.3m	290P	-	-	-	GY

CAT NO I Built at Fremantle, Western Australia for *Reederei Norden-Frisia* to inaugurate new services to Helgoland and other North Sea Islands.

FRISIA I, FRISIA II, FRISIA V, FRISIA VI Built at Papenburg, Germany for *Reederei Norden-Frisia*. Passenger capacities relate to the summer seasons. Capacity is reduced during the winter.

FRISIA IV Built at Emden, Germany for *Reederei Norden-Frisia* to replace the FRISIA VIII.

FRISIA VII Built at Papenburg, Germany for *Reederei Norden-Frisia*. Conveys ro-ro freight to Norderney and Juist.

FRISIA IX, FRISIA X Built at Oldersum, Germany for *Reederei Norden-Frisia*. The FRISIA IX was built at to convey 9 cars at the bow end but is now used mainly in passenger only mode. These ships are generally used for excursions.

NORDIC JET LINE

THE COMPANY *Nordic Jet Line* is an international company, registered in Estonia. Main shareholders are *Förde Reederei Seetouristik* of Germany, *Finnmark Fylkesrederi og Ruteselskap* of Norway and *Kværner Investments* of Norway.

MANAGEMENT Managing Director Mikael Granrot, **Deputy Managing Director** Hans Jonasson.

ADDRESS *Estonia* Sadama 25-4, 15051 Tallinn, Estonia, *Finland* Kanavaterminaali K5, 00160 Helsinki, Finland.

TELEPHONE Administration *Estonia* +372 (0)6 137200, *Finland* +358 (0)9 68177150, **Reservations** *Estonia* +372 (0)6 137000, *Finland* +358 (0)9 681770.

FAX Administration & Reservations *Estonia* +372 (0)6 137222, *Finland* +358 (0)9 6817111.

INTERNET Email marketing@njl.fi **Website** www.njl.fi *(English, Estonian, Finnish)*

ROUTE OPERATED Helsinki (Finland) – Tallinn (Estonia) (1 hr 30 mins; *(1,2)*; up to 6 per day (all year except during winter ice period)).

1»	BALTIC JET	2273t	99	36.0k	60.0m	430P	52C	-	A	NO
2»	NORDIC JET	2273t	98	36.0k	60.0m	430P	52C	-	A	NO

BALTIC JET, NORDIC JET Kværner Fjellstrand JumboCat 60m catamarans built at Omastrand, Norway for *Nordic Jet Line*. Alternative traffic mix is 38 cars and 2 buses.

NORDÖ LINK

THE COMPANY *Rederi AB Nordö-Link* is a Swedish private sector company, a subsidiary of *Finnlines* of Finland.

MANAGEMENT Managing Director Rüdiger Meyer.

ADDRESS PO Box 106, S-201 21 MALMÖ, Sweden.

TELEPHONE Administration +46 (0)40 72417, **Reservations** +46 (0)40 79603, **Fax:** +46 (0)40 6119849.

INTERNET Website www.nordoe-link.se *(Swedish, German)*

ROUTES OPERATED Malmö – Travemünde (9 hrs; *(1,2,3,4)*; up to 4 per day but passengers are not carried on all departures).

1	FINNARROW	25996t	96	21.0k	168.0m	200P	800C	154T	BA2	SW
2	FINNSAILOR	20783t	87	20.3k	157.6m	119P	-	146T	A	SW
3	LÜBECK LINK	33163t	80	19.0k	194.1m	240P	-	250T	BS	SW
4	MALMÖ LINK	33163t	80	19.0k	194.1m	240P	-	250T	BS	SW

FINNARROW Built at Kodja, Indonesia as the GOTLAND for *Rederi AB Gotland* for charter. In 1997 briefly chartered to *Tor Line* and then to *Nordic Trucker Line*, to operate between Oxelösund and St Petersburg (a ro-ro service). In June 1997 she was chartered to *SeaWind Line*, enabling a twice daily passenger service to be operated. In late 1997 she was sold to *Finnlines* and renamed the FINNARROW. She started operating twice weekly between Helsinki and Travemünde. During summer 1998 she was transferred to *FinnLink*; a bow door was fitted and she was modified to allow for two level loading. In 2003 transferred to *Nordö Link*.

FINNSAILOR Built at Gdansk, Poland for *Finnlines* of Finland for freight service between Finland and Germany. In 1996 converted to ro-pax format to inaugurate a new passenger/freight service between Helsinki to Norrköping (Sweden) for subsidiary *FinnLink*. In 1997, this service was transferred to the Kapellskär – Naantali route and passengers (other than lorry drivers) ceased to be conveyed. Later in 1997 she was transferred to the Helsinki – Lübeck route. In 2000 she was chartered to *Nördo Link* to operate between Travemünde and Malmö. In 2002 she returned to *FinnLink*. In 2004 transferred to *Nordö Link*.

LÜBECK LINK Built at Oskarshamn, Sweden as the FINNROSE for *Finncarriers* of Finland and used on deep sea services. In 1990 sold to *Sea Link AB*, converted to ro-pax format with passenger accommodation and rail tracks, and placed on the Malmö – Travemünde service.

MALMÖ LINK Built as the FINNHAWK; otherwise as the LÜBECK LINK.

POLFERRIES

THE COMPANY *Polferries* is the trading name of *Polska Zegluga Baltycka SA (Polish Baltic Shipping Company)*, a Polish state owned company.

MANAGEMENT General Director & President of the Board Jan Warchol, **Shipping Policy Director and Board Member** Grazyna Bak, **Financial Director** Wojciech Rogowski, **Technical Director** Wlodzimierz Miadowicz.

ADDRESS ul Portowa 41, PL 78-100 Kolobrzeg, Poland.

TELEPHONE Administration +48 (0)94 35 52 103, +48 (0)94 35 52 102, **Passenger Reservations** *Swinoujscie* +48 (0)91 32 26 140, *Gdansk* +48 (0)58 34 31 887, **Freight Reservations** *Swinoujscie* +48 (0)91 32 26 104, *Gdansk* +48 (0)58 34 30 212.

FAX Administration +48 (0)94 35 52 208, **Passenger Reservations** *Swinoujscie* +48 (0)91 32 26 168, *Gdansk* +48 (0)58 34 36 574, **Freight Reservations** *Swinoujscie* +48 (0)91 32 26 169, *Gdansk* +48 (0)58 34 30 975.

INTERNET Email info@polferries.pl **Passenger Reservations** *Swinoujscie* boas.pax@polferries.pl
Gdansk pax.gdansk@polferries.pl **Freight Reservations** *Swinoujscie* boas.cargo@polferries.pl,
Gdansk cargo.gdansk@polferries.pl **Website** www.polferries.pl *(Polish, English, Danish, Swedish)*

ROUTES OPERATED Swinoujscie – Ystad (8 hrs; *(1,4)*; 2 per day), Swinoujscie – Copenhagen (9 hrs
45 mins; *(2)*; 5 per week), Swinoujscie – Rønne (6 hrs; *(2)*; 1 per week (seasonal)), Gdansk –
Nynäshamn (Sweden) (19 hrs; *(3)*; 3 per week).

1	KAHLEBERG	10271t	83	14.5k	140.1m	79P	-	45L	AS	LB
2	POMERANIA	12087t	78	15.4k	127.7m	1000P	273C	26L	BA	BS
3	SCANDINAVIA	23775t	80	20.0k	146.1m	1800P	510C	38L	BA2	BS
4	SILESIA	10553t	79	17.0k	127.6m	755P	250C	22L	BA	BS

KAHLEBERG Built at Wismar, Germany (DDR) for *DSR* of Germany (DDR). In 1991 chartered to *TR
Line* (joint venture between *TT-Line* and *DSR*) for service between Rostock and Trelleborg. In 1995
DSR pulled out of the venture and the service became *TT-Line*. In 1997 she returned to *DSR* to
operate for *Euroseabridge* (later *Scandlines Euroseabridge*). She initially operated on the
Travemünde – Klaìpeda service. In 1999 she was transferred to the formerly freight only Rostock –
Liepaja service. In 2000 transferred to the *Amber Line* Karlshamn – Liepaja route as a ro-pax vessel.
In 2003 chartered to *Polferries* to operate between Swinoujscie and Ystad.

POMERANIA Built at Szczecin, Poland for *Polferries*. In 1978 and 1979 she briefly operated between
Felixstowe and Swinoujscie via Copenhagen. In recent years she was the regular vessel on the
Gdansk – Helsinki service before that service was withdrawn. She was rebuilt in 1997. Currently
used on the Swinoujscie – Copenhagen and Swinoujscie – Rønne routes.

SCANDINAVIA Built at Landskrona, Sweden as the VISBY for *Rederi AB Gotland* of Sweden for their
services between the island of Gotland and the Swedish mainland. In 1987, the franchise to operate
these services was lost by the company and awarded to *Nordström & Thulin* of Sweden. A subsidiary
called *N&T Gotlandslinjen AB* was formed to operate the service. The VISBY was chartered to this
company and managed by *Johnson Line*, remaining owned by *Rederi AB Gotland*. In early 1990 she
was chartered to *Sealink* and renamed the FELICITY. After modifications at Tilbury, she was, in
March 1990, introduced onto the Fishguard – Rosslare route. Later in 1990 she was renamed the
STENA FELICITY. In summer 1997 she was returned to *Rederi AB Gotland* for rebuilding, prior to
her entering service with *Destination Gotland* in January 1998. She was renamed the VISBY. In late
2002 she was renamed the VISBORG. In March 2003 replaced by the new VISBY and laid up for sale
or charter. In July sold/chartered to *Polferries*, renamed the SCANDINAVIA and placed on the
Gdansk – Nynäshamn route.

SILESIA Built at Szczecin, Poland for *Polferries*. rebuilt during winter 1997/98, although not as
extensively as the POMERANIA. Currently used on the Swinoujscie – Ystad route.

RG-LINE

THE COMPANY *RG-Line Oy/Ab* is a Finnish private sector company, named after its owner, Rabbe
Grönblom.

ADDRESS Hovioikeudenpuistikko 11, 65100 Vaasa, Finland.

TELEPHONE Administration & Reservations +358 (0)6-3200 300.

FAX Administration & Reservations +358 (0)6-3104 551.

INTERNET Email marketing@rgline.com **Website** www.rgline.com *(Finnish, Swedish)*

ROUTE OPERATED Vaasa (Finland) – Umeå (Sweden) (4 hrs; *(1)*; 1/2 per day).

1	CASINO EXPRESS	10542t	66	18.0k	128.9m	1200P	265C	32T	BA	SW

CASINO EXPRESS Built at Landskrona, Sweden as the FENNIA for *Siljavarustamo-Siljarederiet* of
Finland to operate *Silja Line* services between Sweden and Finland. In 1970 she was transferred to
Stockholms Rederi AB Svea, when *Silja Line* became a marketing organisation. In 1983 she was
withdrawn and operated for a short period with *B&I Line* of Ireland between Rosslare and Pembroke

Dock. In 1984 she was sold to *Jakob Lines*. In 1985 she was sold to *Vaasanlaivat*. In 1992 she was returned to *Jakob Lines*. During winter 1992/3 she operated for *Baltic Link* between Norrköping (Sweden) and Riga (Latvia), but returned to *Silja Line* in summer 1993 and was used on the Vaasa – Umeå and Pietarsaari – Skellefteå services. The latter service did not operate in 1999 and, on 1st July, she was transferred to the new *Wasa Line*, a *Silja Line* subsidiary formed to operate the Vaasa – Umeå link. In September 1999 she was replaced by the WASA QUEEN and withdrawn. During summer 2000 she operated freight only services between Stockholm and Turku. In 2001 sold to *RG-Line*, renamed the CASINO EXPRESS and in May re-opened the Vaasa – Umeå route which had been closed by *Silja Line* subsidiary *Vaasanlaivat* in December 2000.

RIGA SEA LINES

THE COMPANY *Riga Sea Lines (Rigas Juras Linija)* is a Latvian company, largely owned by the city of Riga.

MANAGEMENT Managing Director Egils Rozinskis, **Marketing Manager** Galina Fomenko.

ADDRESS A/s Rigas Juras Linija, Eksporta iela 3a, Riga LV – 1010, Latvia.

TELEPHONE Administration +371 7205454, **Reservations** *Passenger* +371 7205460, *Cargo* +371 7205464.

FAX Administration +371 7205457, **Reservations** +371 7205461.

INTERNET Email Administration office@rigasealine.lv **Reservations** booking@rigasealine.lv

Website www.rigasealine.lv *(Latvian, English, Russian, Swedish)*

ROUTE OPERATED Riga (Latvia) – Stockholm (Sweden) (17 hrs 30 mins; *(1)*; 3 per week).

1	BALTIC KRISTINA	12281t	73	19.0k	128.0m	512P	50C	30T	BA2	LV

BALTIC KRISTINA Built at Turku, Finland as the BORE 1 for *Ångfartygs AB Bore* of Finland for *Silja Line* services between Turku and Stockholm. In 1980, *Bore Line* left the *Silja Line* consortium and disposed of its passenger ships. She was acquired by *EFFOA* of Finland and continued to operate on *Silja Line* service, being renamed the SKANDIA. In 1983 she was sold to *Stena Line* and renamed the STENA BALTICA. She was then resold to *Latvia Shipping* of the USSR, substantially rebuilt, renamed the ILLICH and introduced onto a Stockholm – Leningrad (now St Petersburg) service trading as *ScanSov Line*. In 1986 operations were transferred to *Baltic Shipping Company*. In 1992 she inaugurated a new service between Stockholm and Riga but continued to also serve St Petersburg. In 1995 the Swedish terminal was changed to Nynäshamn. In late 1995 arrested and laid up in Stockholm. In 1997, services were planned to restart between Kiel and St Petersburg under the auspices of a German company called *Baltic Line*, with the vessel renamed the ANASTASIA V. However, this did not materialise and she was sold to *Windward Line* of Barbados and renamed the WINDWARD PRIDE. In 1997, she was chartered to *ESCO*, and renamed the BALTIC KRISTINA. In late 1997 she sailed for *EstLine* between Stockholm and Tallinn in a freight-only role. Following a major refurbishment, she entered service with *EstLine* in May 1998, allowing a daily full passenger service to be operated. In 2000 the charter was transferred to *Tallink*. Placed on the Paldiski – Kapellskär service. In late 2002 chartered to *Riga Sea Lines* to inaugurate a service between Riga and Stockholm.

RÖMÖ-SYLT LINIE

THE COMPANY *Römö-Sylt Linie GmbH* is a German company, a subsidiary of *FRS (Förde Reederei Seetouristik)* of Flensburg.

MANAGEMENT Managing Director P Rathke.

ADDRESS *Germany* Am Fähranleger, D-25992 List, Germany, *Denmark* Kilebryggen, DK-6792 Rømø, Denmark.

TELEPHONE Administration (Germany) +49 (0)4651 870475, **Reservations (Denmark)** +45 73 75 53 03.

FAX Administration (Germany) +49 (0)4651 871446, **Reservations (Denmark)** +45 73 75 53 05.

INTERNET Email romo-sylt@post12.tele.dk **Website** www.romo-sylt.dk *(Danish, German)*

ROUTE OPERATED List (Sylt, Germany) – Havneby (Rømø, Denmark) (45 mins; *(1,2)*; variable – half hourly at peaks). **Note** the island of Rømø is linked to the Danish mainland by a road causeway; the island of Sylt is linked to the German mainland by a rail-only causeway on which cars are conveyed on shuttle wagons.

| 1 | VIKINGLAND | 1963t | 74 | 11.0k | 68.3m | 420P | 60C | 8L | BA | GY |
| 2 | WESTERLAND | 1509t | 71 | 11.0k | 58.3m | 400P | 40C | 5L | BA | GY |

VIKINGLAND, WESTERLAND Built at Husum, Germany for *Römö-Sylt Linie*.

SAAREMAA LAEVAKOMPANII

THE COMPANY *Saaremaa Laevakompanii* is an Estonian company, founded in 1992.

MANAGEMENT General Director Tõnis Rihvk.

ADDRESS AS Kohtu, 93812 Kuressaare, Estonia.

TELEPHONE Administration +372-45-24350, **Reservations** +372-45-24444.

FAX Administration +372-45-24355, **Reservations** +372-45-24373.

INTERNET Email slk@laevakompanii.ee **Website** www.laevakompanii.ee *(Estonian, English)*

ROUTE OPERATED Kuivastu – Virtsu (30 mins; *(3,6,8,10)*; up to 12 per day), Heltermaa (Hiiumaa) – Rohuküla (1 hr 30 mins; *(2,4,5,6)*; 5 per day), Rohuküla – Sviby (45 mins; *(1,4)*; up to 3 per day), Triigi – Sõru (1 hr 5 mins; *(9)*; up to 2 per day).

1	HARILAID	1028t	85	9.9k	49.9m	120P	35C	0L	BA	ES
2	HIIUMAA	1549t	66	10.0k	53.8m	175P	28C	0L	BA	ES
3	KOGUVA	1305t	79	10.6k	55.5m	204P	41C	0L	BA	ES
4	KÖRGELAID	1028t	87	9.9k	49.9m	200P	35C	0L	BA	ES
5	OFELIA	3638t	68	14.4k	74.4m	600P	110C	12L	BA	ES
6	REGULA	1157t	71	14.5k	71.2m	580P	105C	12L	BA	ES
7	SCANIA	3474t	72	14.5k	74.2m	400P	80C	12L	BA	ES
8	ST OLA	4833t	71	16.0k	85.9m	500P	140C	12L	BA	ES
9	VARDO	116t	62	9.0k	27.1m	47P	17C	0L	BA	ES
10	VIIRE	4101t	88	12.7k	95.8m	469P	140C	36L	BA	ES

HARILAID Built at Riga, Latvia (USSR) for *ESCO* of Estonia. In 1992 transferred to *Saaremaa Laevakompanii*.

HIIUMAA Built at Kristiansand, Norway as the TAARS for *Sydfyenske Dampskibsselskab A/S* of Denmark. Initially used on the Spodsbjerg – Nakskov route. In 1975 transferred to the Spodsbjerg – Taars route. Withdrawn in 1984 and in 1985 sold to *ESCO* of Estonia and renamed the HIIUMAA; she was placed on the Heltermaa – Rohuküla route. In 1992 renamed the HIIUMAA 2. In 1992 transferred to *Saaremaa Laevakompanii*. In 1996 renamed the HIIUMAA.

KOGUVA Built at Riga, Latvia (USSR) for *ESCO* of Estonia. In 1992 transferred to *Saaremaa Laevakompanii*.

KÖRGELAID Built at Riga, Latvia (USSR) for *ESCO* of Estonia. In 1992 transferred to *Saaremaa Laevakompanii*.

OFELIA Built at Rendsburg, Germany for *Svenska Rederi-AB Öresund* of Sweden and used on the Limhamn – Dragør service. In 1980 sold to *Scandinavian Ferry Lines*. In 1990 transferred to *SweFerry* and later to *Scandlines AB*. In 1997 sold to *Saaremaa Laevakompanii*.

REGULA Built at Papenburg, Germany for *Stockholms Rederi AB Svea* of Sweden for the service between Helsingborg and Helsingør operated by *Linjebuss International AB* (a subsidiary company).

In 1980 she was sold to *Scandinavian Ferry Lines*. During winter 1984/85 she was rebuilt to increase vehicle and passenger capacity. In 1991 ownership was transferred to *SweFerry* and operations to *ScandLines* on the Helsingborg – Helsingør service. Ownership later transferred to *Scandlines AB*. In 1997 sold to *Saaremaa Laevakompanii*.

SCANIA Built at Aalborg, Denmark for *Svenska Rederi-AB Öresund* of Sweden and used on the Limhamn – Dragør service. In 1980 sold to *Scandinavian Ferry Lines*. In 1990 transferred to *SweFerry* and later to *Scandlines AB*. In 1999 sold to *Saaremaa Laevakompanii*.

ST OLA Built at Papenburg Germany as the SVEA SCARLETT for *Stockholms Rederi AB Svea* of Sweden and used on the *SL (Skandinavisk Linjetrafik)* service between Copenhagen (Tuborg Havn) and Landskrona (Sweden). In 1980 she was sold to *Scandinavian Ferry Lines* of Sweden and *Dampskibsselskabet Øresund A/S* of Denmark (jointly owned). Initially she continued to serve Landskrona but later that year the Swedish terminal became Malmö. In 1981 she operated on the Helsingborg – Helsingør service for a short while, after which she was withdrawn and laid up. In 1982 she was sold to *Eckerö Linjen* of Finland, renamed the ECKERÖ and used on services between Grisslehamn (Sweden) and Eckerö (Åland Islands). In 1991 she was sold to *P&O Scottish Ferries* and renamed the ST OLA. In March 1992 she replaced the previous ST OLA (1345t, 1974) on the Scrabster – Stromness service. In September 2002 withdrawn and sold to *Saaremaa Laevakompanii*. Used on the Kuivastu – Virtsu route.

VIIRE Built as the SUPERFLEX CHARLIE for *Vognmandsruten* of Denmark to establish a new service between Korsør (Fyn) and Nyborg (Sjælland). In 1990 this company was taken over by DIFKO and the renamed the DIFKO KORSØR. In 1998, following the opening of the Great Belt fixed link, the service ceased and she was laid up. In 1999 chartered to *Saaremaa Laevakompanii* and renamed the VIIRE. In 2000, the charter ended and she returned to lay-up in Denmark. In 2001 she was again chartered to *Saaremaa Laevakompanii*. Used on the Kuivastu – Virtsu route.

VARDO Built at Rauma, Finland *ESCO* of Estonia. In 1992 transferred to *Saaremaa Laevakompanii*.

SAGA LINE

THE COMPANY *Saga Line* is a Norwegian Company.

MANAGEMENT Managing Director Lars Helminsen.

ADDRESS PO Box 47, N-1684 Vesteroy, Norway.

PHONE Administration & Reservations +47 69 20 69 40.

FAX Administration & Reservations +47 69 20 69 40.

INTERNET Email booking@sagaline.no **Website** www.sagaline.dk *(Danish)* www.sagaline.no *(Norwegian)*

ROUTE OPERATED Moss (Norway) – Skagen (Denmark) (6 hrs; *(1)*; 1 per day). Operations opened at Easter 2004.

| 1 | SAGAFJORD | 5678t | 65 | 17.8k | 99.5m | 1100P | 145C | 30T | BA | NO |

SAGAFJORD Built at Lübeck, Germany as the VIKING III for *Otto Thoresen* of Norway for the *Thoresen Car Ferries* Southampton (England) – Cherbourg and Southampton – Le Havre services. During the winter, until 1970/71, she was chartered to *Lion Ferry* of Sweden for their Harwich – Bremerhaven service. In 1967 the service was acquired by *European Ferries* of Great Britain, trading as *Townsend Thoresen*. She was chartered to this organisation and retained Norwegian registry. During winter 1971/72 and 1972/73 she was chartered to *Larvik Line*. She became surplus to requirements following the delivery of the 'Super Vikings' in 1975 and was the subject of a number of short term charters until 1982 when she was sold to *Da-No Linjen* of Norway, renamed the TERJE VIGEN and used on their Fredrikstad (Norway) – Frederikshavn (Denmark) service. In 1986 she was sold to *KG Line* to operate between Kaskinen (Finland) and Gävle (Sweden) and renamed the SCANDINAVIA. In 1990 she was sold *Johnson Line* and used on *Jakob Line* service, being renamed the FENNO STAR. In 1991 she was sold to *Scandi Line* and renamed the SANDEFJORD but served briefly as the FENNO STAR on the *Corona Line* service between Karlskrona and Gdynia before being

Mecklenburg-Vorpommern *(FotoFlite)*

Spodsbjerg *(FotoFlite)*

introduced onto the Sandefjord – Strömstad service in 1992. In 1999 *Scandi Line* operations were integrated into *Color Line*. In she was 2000 withdrawn and in 2001 sold to *Buquebus Los Cipreses* of Uruguay. However, she was not moved to South America and remained laid up in Norway. In 2003 she was sold to *Saga Line* and renamed the SAGAFJORD. The service started in spring 2004.

SCANDLINES (DENMARK & GERMANY)

THE COMPANY *Scandlines AG* is a German company, 50% owned by *DB Cargo AG*, a subsidiary of *Deutsche Bahn AG (German Railways)* (which is owned by the Federal Government) and 50% owned by the Kingdom of Denmark. In 1998 it took over *DFO (Deutsche Fährgesellschaft Ostsee mbH)* of Germany (renamed *Scandlines Deutschland GmbH*) and *Scandlines A/S* of Denmark (renamed *Scandlines Danmark A/S*). A 50% share in *Euroseabridge GmbH* was acquired in 1998 (by *Scandlines A/S* of Denmark before the merger with *DFO*) and the remaining 50% in 1999; the name was changed to *Scandlines Euroseabridge GmbH*.

Scandlines A/S was formerly *DSB Rederi A/S* and before that the Ferries Division of *DSB (Danish State Railways)*. *DFO* was formed in 1993 by the merging of the Ferries Divisions of *Deutsche Bundesbahn (German Federal Railways)* (which operated in the Federal Republic of Germany) and *Deutsche Reichsbahn (German State Railways)* (which operated in the former DDR).

Stena Line owned *Scandlines AB* of Sweden also trades under this name but remains a separate company. Danish domestic routes are operated by subsidiary company *Scandlines Sydfyenske A/S*, and are marketed as part of the *Scandlines* network.

MANAGEMENT **Chairman** Bernd Malmström, **Managing Director** Peter Grønlund, **Finance Director** Uwe Bakosch.

ADDRESS *Denmark* Dampfærgevej 10, DK-2100 Copenhagen Ø, Denmark. *Germany* Hochhaus am Fährhafen, D-18119 Rostock-Warnemünde, Germany.

TELEPHONE Administration *Denmark* +45 33 15 15 15, *Germany* +49 (0)381 5435-0, **Reservations** *Denmark* +45 33 15 15 15, *Germany* +49 (0)1805-7226 354637.

INTERNET Email scandlines@scandlines.dk

Websites www.scandlines.dk *(Danish)* www.scandlines.com *(German, English)*

ROUTES OPERATED

Helsingør (Sealand, Denmark) – Helsingborg (Sweden) (25 mins; *(7,27)*; every 20 mins) (joint with *Scandlines AB* of Sweden), Rødby (Lolland, Denmark) – Puttgarden (Germany) (45 mins; *(2,8,17,18,21 (8 road freight only))*; half hourly train/vehicle ferry + additional road freight only sailings), Gedser (Falster, Denmark) – Rostock (Germany) (2 hrs; *(3,9,16)*; every 2 hours (less frequent Dec – Feb), Rostock (Germany) – Trelleborg (Sweden) (5 hrs 45 mins (7 hrs night); *(12)*; 3 per day) (joint with *Scandlines AB* of Sweden), Sassnitz (Germany) – Trelleborg (3 hrs 45 mins; *(20)*; 4-5 per day) (joint with *Scandlines AB* of Sweden), **Summer only** Sassnitz – Rønne (Bornholm, Denmark) (3 hrs 45 mins; *(19)*; 1/2 per day).

**Danish domestic services operated by subsidiary *Scandlines Sydfyenske A/S (formerly Sydfyenske Dampskibsselskab (SFDS))* and forming part of *Scandlines* network Fynshav (Als) – Bøjden (Fyn) (50 mins; *(26)*; 6-8 per day), Esbjerg (Jutland) – Nordby (Fanø) (12 mins; *(5,13,23)*; every 20-40 mins), Spodsbjerg (Langeland) – Tårs (Lolland) (45 mins; *(6,14,24)*; hourly).

Germany – Latvia & Lithuania routes operated by subsidiary *Scandlines Euroseabridge GmbH* Kiel – Klaìpeda (Lithuania) (20 hrs; *(25, Lisco vessel)*; 6 per week (joint with *Lisco Baltic Service* of Lithuania under the *Kiel-Klaìpeda-Express* name)), Sassnitz (Mukran) (Germany) – Klaìpeda (Lithuania) (18 hrs; *(Lisco vessel)*; 3 per week (joint with *Lisco Baltic Service* of Lithuania)), Rostock (Germany) – Liepaja (Latvia) (24 hrs; *(28)*; 2 per week).

Denmark – Lithuania freight route operated by *Scandlines Balticum Seaways division* Århus (Denmark) – Aabenraa (Denmark) – Klaìpeda (Lithuania) (from 30 hrs; *(22)*; 2 per week from Aabenraa (1 westbound via Århus), 1 per week from Århus via Aabenraa).

Sweden – Latvia routes operated by *Scandlines Amber Line* Karlshamn (Sweden) – Liepaja (Latvia) (17 hrs; *(15)*; 3 per week), Nynäshamn (Sweden) – Ventspils (Latvia) (12 hrs; *(4)*; 5 per week).

Germany – Finland – Estonia freight route operated by Scandlines Estonia AS Rostock (Germany) – Muuga (Estonia) – Helsinki (Finland) – (32 hrs to Muuga, 40 hrs to Helsinki; *(1,10,11)*; 2/3 per week).

#	Name	Tonnage	Year	Speed	Length						
1	AURORA	20391t	82	18.5k	155.0m	12P	-	160T	A	NO
2	DEUTSCHLAND	15187t	97	19.0k	142.0m	900P	294C	30Lr	BA2	GY
3	DRONNING MARGRETHE II	10850t	73	16.5k	144.6m	400P	195C	20Lr	BA2	DK
4	FELLOW	14297t	73	18.0k	137.3m	64P	170C	84T	AS	FI
5	FENJA	751t	98	11.5k	49.9m	396P	34C	4L	BA	DK
6	FRIGG SYDFYEN	1676t	84	12.5k	70.1m	338P	50C	8L	BA	DK
7	HAMLET	10067t	97	14.0k	111.2m	1000P	244C	34L	BA	DK
8F	HOLGER DANSKE	2779t	76	14.5k	86.8m	12P	55C	12L	BA	DK
9	KRONPRINS FREDERIK	16071t	81	19.5k	152.0m	1082P	210C	46T	BA	DK
10	LEHOLA	7800t	98	17k	122.3m	12P	-	86T	A	ES
11	LEMBITU	7800t	98	17k	122.3m	12P	-	86T	A	ES
12	MECKLENBURG-VORPOMMERN	36185t	96	20.0k	199.9m	600P	90C	230Tr	A2	GY
13	MENJA	751t	98	11.5k	49.9m	396P	34C	4L	BA	DK
14	ODIN SYDFYEN	1698t	82	12.5k	70.4m	338P	50C	8L	BA	DK
15	PETERSBURG	25353t	86	16k	190.8m	144P	329C	110T	A2	LB
16	PRINS JOACHIM	16071t	80	19.5k	152.0m	1080P	-	46Lr	BA	DK
17	PRINS RICHARD	14621t	97	19.0k	142.0m	900P	294C	36Lr	BA	DK
18	PRINSESSE BENEDIKTE	14621t	97	19.0k	142.0m	900P	294C	36Lr	BA	DK
19	RÜGEN	12289t	72	17.5k	152.2m	850P	235C	30Lr	A2	GY
20	SASSNITZ	21154t	89	19.0k	171.5m	1000P	390C	50Tr	BA2	GY
21	SCHLESWIG-HOLSTEIN	15187t	97	19.0k	142.0m	900P	294C	30Lr	BA2	GY
22F	SEA CORONA	12110t	72	17.0k	137.5m	12P	-	106T	A	NO
23p	SØNDERHO	93t	62	10.0k	26.3m	199P	0C	0L	-	DK
24	SPODSBJERG	958t	72	13.0k	67.3m	225P	40C	9L	BA	DK
25	SVEALAND	25026t	99	21.5k	186.0m	327P	164C	170T	A	MA
26	THOR SYDFYEN	1479t	78	12.0k	71.0m	292P	48C	9L	BA	DK
27	TYCHO BRAHE	11148t	91	14.0k	111.2m	1250P	240C	35Lr	BA	DK
28	URD	13144t	81	17.0k	171.0m	100P	-	104T	AS	DK

AURORA Built at Rauma, Finland as the ARCTURUS for *EFFOA* of Finland and chartered to *Finncarriers*. In 1991 renamed the AURORA. In 2003 chartered to *Scandlines Estonia* to operate between Rostock and Helsinki.

DEUTSCHLAND Train/vehicle ferry built at Krimpen aan den IJssel, Rotterdam, Netherlands for *DFO* for the Puttgarden – Rødby service. During winter 2003/4 extra mezzanine deck added for cars.

DRONNING MARGRETHE II Train/vehicle ferry built at Nakskov, Denmark for *DSB* for the Nyborg – Korsør service. In 1981 transferred to the Rødby – Puttgarden service. An additional vehicle deck was added in 1982. Withdrawn in 1997. In 1998 became a back-up freight-only vessel on the Rødby – Puttgarden and Gedser – Rostock routes. In 1999 she replaced the fast ferry BERLIN EXPRESS (4675t, 1995) as regular vessel on the Gedser – Rostock route.

FELLOW Built in Turku, Finland for *Finncarriers* as the FINNFELLOW. In 1989 transferred to *FinnLink*. In 2002 chartered to *VV-Line* and renamed the FELLOW. In 2003 *VV-Line* went into liquidation and she was chartered to *Scandlines*, who took over the service.

FENJA Vehicle ferry built at Svendborg, Denmark for *SFDS A/S* for the Esbjerg – Nordby service.

FRIGG SYDFYEN Vehicle ferry built at Svendborg, Denmark for *Sydfyenske Dampskibsselskab (SFDS)* of Denmark for the service between Spodsbjerg and Tårs. In 1996, this company was taken over by *DSB Rederi* and the company is now *Scandlines Sydfyenske A/S.*

HAMLET Road vehicle ferry built Rauma, Finland for *Scandlines* (50% owned by *Scandlines AG* and 50% owned by *Scandlines AB* of Sweden) for the Helsingør – Helsingborg service. Sister vessel of the TYCHO BRAHE but without rail tracks.

HOLGER DANSKE Built at Aalborg, Denmark as a train/vehicle ferry for *DSB* for the Helsingør – Helsingborg service. In 1991 transferred to the Kalundborg – Samsø route (no rail facilities). In 1997, transferred to subsidiary *SFDS A/S.* Withdrawn at the end of November 1998 when the service passed to *Samsø Linien.* In 1999 began operating between Rødby and Puttgarden as a road freight only vessel, carrying, among others, loads which cannot be conveyed on passenger vessels.

KRONPRINS FREDERIK Train/vehicle ferry built at Nakskov, Denmark for *DSB* for the Nyborg – Korsør service. Withdrawn in 1997. After conversion to car/lorry ferry, she was transferred to the Gedser – Rostock route (no rail facilities).

LEHOLA Built at Huelva, Spain as the LEMBITU for *Estonian Shipping Company.* Initially used on *ESCO* Baltic services. In 1998 chartered to *Czar Peter Line* to operate between Moerdijk (Netherlands) and Kronstadt (Russia). In 1999 chartered to *Delom* of France to operate between Marseilles and Sete and Tunis. In 2000 she returned to *ESCO,* operating between Kiel and Tallinn. In 2003 purchased by *Scandlines AG* and transferred to subsidiary *Scandlines Estonia AS.* Operates Rostock – Helsinki – Muuga.

LEMBITU Built at Huelva, Spain as the LEMBITU for *Estonian Shipping Company.* On completion chartered to *P&O European Ferries (Irish Sea)* and placed on their Liverpool Dublin route. In Autumn 1998 she was chartered to *Dart Line* and placed on the Dartford – Vlissingen route. In 1999 she was renamed the DART 7. In Autumn 1999 the charter was ended and she was chartered to *Cetma* of France, resumed the name LEMBITU and used on services between Marseilles and Tunis. In 2000 she was chartered to *P&O European Ferries (Irish Sea)* and renamed the CELTIC SUN; she operated between Liverpool and Dublin. In 2001 the chartered ended; she then reverted to the name LEMBITU and was chartered to *NorseMerchant Ferries* and placed on the Heysham – Dublin service. In late 2001 charter ended and returned to *ESCO* service in the Baltic. In 2003 purchased by *Scandlines AG* and transferred to subsidiary *Scandlines Estonia AS.* Operates Rostock – Helsinki – Muuga.

MECKLENBURG-VORPOMMERN Train/vehicle ferry built at Bremerhaven, Germany for *DFO* for the Rostock – Trelleborg service. During winter 2002/3 modified to increase freight capacity and reduce passenger capacity.

MENJA Built at Svendborg, Denmark for *SFDS A/S* for the Esbjerg – Nordby service.

ODIN SYDFYEN Vehicle ferry built at Svendborg, Denmark for *Sydfyenske Dampskibsselskab (SFDS)* of Denmark for the service between Spodsbjerg and Tårs.

PETERSBURG Built at Wismar, Germany (DDR) as the MUKRAN for *DSR* of Germany (DDR). In 1995 she was rebuilt to introduce road vehicle and additional passenger capacity and was renamed the PETERSBURG. She inaugurated the Travemünde service in 1995 but is now used on the Sassnitz – Klaìpeda service. This service was operated jointly with the *Lisco* vessel KLAIPEDA, a sister vessel which has not been converted to ro-pax format. In 2001 she was transferred to the Kiel – Klaìpeda service, replacing the sister vessel GREIFSWALD whose charter was ended. In 2003 replaced by the SVEALAND and transferred to the *Amber Line* Karlshamn – Liepaja route.

PRINS JOACHIM Train/vehicle ferry, built at Nakskov, Denmark for *DSB* for the Nyborg – Korsør service. Withdrawn in 1997 and laid up. During winter 2000/2001 modified in same way as KRONPRINS FREDERIK and transferred to the Gedser – Rostock route.

PRINS RICHARD, PRINSESSE BENEDIKTE Train/vehicle ferries, built at Frederikshavn, Denmark for *DSB Rederi* for the Rødby – Puttgarden service. During winter 2003/4 extra mezzanine deck added for cars.

RÜGEN Train/vehicle ferry built at Rostock, Germany (DDR) for *Deutsche Reichsbahn* of Germany (DDR) for services between Trelleborg and Sassnitz. In 1993 ownership was transferred to *DFO*. Since 1989 she has been used on the summer only Sassnitz – Rønne service. In 1998 and 1999 she also operated between Ystad and Rønne but this has not been repeated.

SASSNITZ Train/vehicle ferry built at Frederikshavn, Denmark for *Deutsche Reichsbahn*. In 1993 ownership transferred to *DFO*. Used on the Sassnitz – Trelleborg service.

SCHLESWIG-HOLSTEIN Train/vehicle ferry built at Krimpen aan den IJssel, Rotterdam, Netherlands for *DFO* for the Puttgarden – Rødby service. During winter 2003/4 extra mezzanine deck added for cars.

SEA CORONA Built at Rauma, Finland as the ANTARES for *Finska Ångfartygs A/B* of Finland and used on services between Finland and Germany. In 1975 she was chartered to *DG Hansa* of Germany and renamed the RHEINFELS. In 1977 she was sold to *Nedlloyd* of the Netherlands and renamed the NEDLLOYD ROCKANJE. In 1977 she was chartered to *Constellation Line* of the USA for services between the USA and Europe. In 1983 she was sold to *Kotka Line* of Finland, renamed the KOTKA LILY and used on their services between Finland, UK and West Africa. In 1985 she was chartered to *Jahre Line* of Norway, renamed the JALINA and operated freight services between Oslo and Kiel. Two years later, she returned to Baltic waters, being chartered to *Finncarriers* and renamed the FINNROVER. In 1988 she was chartered to *Kent Line*, renamed the SEAHORSE and used on their Dartford – Zeebrugge service. In 1991 she was chartered to *DFDS* and in 1992 she was renamed the DANA CORONA. She was initially used on the service between the Immingham and Cuxhaven (Germany) but in 1995 she was transferred to the Fredericia – Copenhagen – Klaìpeda (Lithuania) service. In 2001 the charter was ended and she returned to owners, being renamed the SEA CORONA. She was chartered to *Scandlines AG* and placed on the *Scandlines Balticum Seaways* Århus – Aabenraa – Klaìpeda route.

SØNDERHO Passenger only ferry built at Esbjerg, Denmark for *Post & Telegrafvæsenet* (Danish Post Office). In 1977 taken over by *DSB*. Used on extra peak sailings and late night and early morning sailings between Esbjerg and Nordby.

SPODSBJERG Vehicle ferry built at Husum, Denmark as the ÆRØ-PILEN for *Øernes D/S* of Denmark for services to the island of Ærø. In 1974 sold to *Sydfyenske Dampskibsselskab (SFDS)* for the service between Spodsbjerg and Tårs.

SVEALAND Ro-pax vessel built at Donada, Italy as the ALYSSA for *Levantina Transporti* of Italy for charter. She was initially chartered to *CoTuNav* of Tunisia for service between Marseilles, Genoa and Tunis and in 2000 to *Trasmediterranea* of Spain for service between Barcelona and Palma de Majorca. In 2001 chartered to *Stena Line Scandinavia AB*, renamed the SVEALAND and placed as second vessel on the *Scandlines AB* freight only Trelleborg – Travemünde service. In 2003 sub-chartered to *Scandlines AG* and placed on the Kiel – Klaìpeda route, replacing the ASK and PETERSBURG.

THOR SYDFYEN Vehicle ferry built at Århus, Denmark for *Sydfyenske Dampskibsselskab (SFDS)* of Denmark (now *Scandlines Sydfyenske A/S*) for the service between Spodsbjerg and Tårs. In 1998 she was transferred to the Fynshav – Bøjden route.

TYCHO BRAHE Train/vehicle ferry, built at Tomrefjord, Norway for *DSB* for the Helsingør – Helsingborg service.

URD Built at Venice, Italy as the EASY RIDER, a ro-ro freight ferry, for *Delpa Maritime* of Greece and used on Mediterranean services. In 1985 she was acquired by *Sealink British Ferries* and renamed the SEAFREIGHT HIGHWAY to operate freight-only service between Dover and Dunkerque. In 1988 she was sold to *SOMAT* of Bulgaria for use on *Medlink* services in the Mediterranean and renamed the BOYANA. In 1990 she was sold to *Blæsbjerg* of Denmark, renamed the AKTIV MARINE and chartered to *DSB*. In 1991 she was converted into ro-pax vessel, renamed the URD and introduced onto the Århus – Kalundborg service. Purchased by *Scandlines* in 1997. Withdrawn at the end of May 1999 and, after modification, transferred to the *Balticum Seaways* (later *Scandlines Balticum Seaways*) Århus – Aabenraa – Klaìpeda route. In 2001 lengthened moved to the Rostock – Liepaja route.

SCANDLINES (SWEDEN)

THE COMPANY *Scandlines AB* (formerly *SweFerry*) is a Swedish company, a subsidiary of *Stena Line Scandinavia AB* of Sweden.

MANAGEMENT Managing Director Gunnar Blomdahl.

ADDRESS Knutpunkten 43, S-252 78 Helsingborg, Sweden.

TELEPHONE Administration +46 (0)42-18 60 00, **Reservations *Helsingborg*** +46 (0)42-18 61 00, ***Trelleborg*** +46 (0)410-65 000.

FAX Administration +46 (0)42-18 60 49, **Reservations *Helsingborg*** +46 (0)42-18 74 10, ***Trelleborg*** +46 (0)410-65 001.

INTERNET Email kundservice@scandlines.se **Website** www.scandlines.se *(Swedish, English)*

ROUTES OPERATED Conventional Ferries Helsingborg (Sweden) – Helsingør (Denmark) (25 mins; *(2)*; every 20 mins), Trelleborg (Sweden) – Rostock (Germany) (6 hrs; *(4)*; 4 per day), Trelleborg – Sassnitz (Germany) (3 hrs 30 mins; *(5)*; 3 per day), Trelleborg (Sweden) – Travemünde (Germany) (8 hrs; *(1,3)*; 2 per day – freight-only). All routes are joint with *Scandlines AG* except Trelleborg – Travemünde.

1	ASK	13294t	82	18.0k	171.0m	186P	-	104T	AS	DK
2	AURORA AF HELSINGBORG	10918t	92	14.9k	111.2m	1250P	240C	535r	BA	SW
3	GÖTALAND	18060t	73	18.5k	183.1m	400P	118C	94Tr	AS2	SW
4	SKÅNE	42558t	98	21.0k	200.2m	600P	-	240Tr	AS2	SW
5	TRELLEBORG	20028t	82	21.0k	170.2m	900P	108C	48Tr	A2	SW

ASK Built at Venice, Italy as the LUCKY RIDER, a ro-ro freight ferry, for *Delpa Maritime* of Greece. In 1985 she was acquired by *Stena Line* and renamed the STENA DRIVER. Later that year she was acquired by *Sealink British Ferries* and renamed the SEAFREIGHT FREEWAY to operate freight-only services between Dover and Dunkerque. In 1988 she was sold to *SOMAT* of Bulgaria for use on *Medlink* services in the Mediterranean and renamed the SERDICA. In 1990 she was sold and renamed the NORTHERN HUNTER. In 1991 she was sold to *Blæsbjerg* of Denmark, renamed the ARKA MARINE and chartered to *DSB*. She was then converted into a ro-pax vessel, renamed the ASK and introduced onto the Århus – Kalundborg service. Purchased by *Scandlines AS* of Denmark in 1997. In 1999 she was, after some modification, transferred to *Scandlines Euroseabridge* and placed on the Travemünde – Klaìpeda route. In 2000 she was transferred to the Rostock – Liepaja route. Lengthened by 20m in 2001 and, in late 2001, chartered to *Nordö Link* to operate between Travemünde and Malmö. In late 2002 replaced by the FINNARROW and returned to *Scandlines*. She was transferred to the Rostock – Trelleborg route whilst the MECKLENBURG-VORPOMMERN was being rebuilt. She was then transferred to the Kiel – Klaìpeda route. In 2003 chartered to *Scandlines AB* to operate on the Trelleborg – Travemünde route.

AURORA AF HELSINGBORG Train/vehicle ferry built at Tomrefjord, Norway for *SweFerry* for *ScandLines* joint *DSB/SweFerry* service between Helsingør and Helsingborg. Owned by *Aurora 93 Trust* of the USA and chartered to *Scandlines*.

GÖTALAND Train/vehicle ferry built at Nakskov, Denmark for *Statens Järnvägar (Swedish State Railways)* for freight services between Trelleborg and Sassnitz. In 1990 transferred to *SweFerry*. In 1992 modified to increase passenger capacity in order to run in passenger service. She is was on the Trelleborg – Rostock service until autumn 1998 when she was replaced by the SKÅNE. She then inaugurated a new freight-only Trelleborg – Travemünde service.

SKÅNE Train/vehicle ferry built at Cadiz, Spain for an American trust and chartered to *Scandlines*. She is used on the Trelleborg – Rostock service.

TRELLEBORG Train/vehicle ferry built at Landskrona, Sweden for *Svelast* of Sweden (an *SJ* subsidiary). In 1990 ownership transferred to *SweFerry*. She is used on the Trelleborg – Sassnitz service.

Tallink AutoExpress *(Mike Louagie)*

Silja Symphony *(Mike Louagie)*

SCF ST PETERSBURG LINE

THE COMPANY *SCF St Petersburg Line* is a Russian company, a subsidiary of *Sovcomflot*.

ADDRESS *Kiel* Renaissance Shipping Agency GmbH, Ostuferhafen 15, 24149 Kiel, Germany.

TELEPHONE Reservations (Kiel) +49 (0)431 990-7611.

FAX Reservations (Kiel) +49 (0)431990-7631.

INTERNET Email petersburg@rsagency.de **Website** www.scflines.com *(English)*

ROUTE OPERATED St Petersburg (Russia) – Kiel (Germany) (61 hours; *(1)*; 2 per week).

The TRANSPARADEN served the route December 2003 - May 2004 but has been sold to *Eckerö Line*. Replaced by the HAMBURG (see *Mann Lines*). No passenger service at present.

SEA ADMINISTRATION OF ST PETERSBURG

THE COMPANY *Sea Administration of St Petersburg* is an agency of the Russian government.

ADDRESS St Petersburg (agents) Port Authority, Port of Saint Petersburg, Gapsalskaya str, 10, Saint Petersburg, 198035, Russia. **Kaliningrad (agents)** Baltfinn-Kaliningrad Maritime Agency, Suvorova str, 45, Kaliningrad, 236039, Russia.

TELEPHONE St Petersburg (agents) +7 (812) 380-7094, **Kaliningrad (agents)** +7 0112 728-401 – agency dept (English speaking), +7 0112 728-404 – booking/ticket office (Russian speaking only), +7 0112 756-803 – cargo/truck forwarder (Russian speaking only).

FAX St Petersburg (agents) +7 (812) 380-7095, **Kaliningrad (agents)** +7 0112 728402.

INTERNET Email Saint Petersburg povg@mail.pasp.ru maai@mail.pasp.ru **Kaliningrad** office@baltfinn **Website** www.baltfinn.ru *(English)*

ROUTE OPERATED St Petersburg (Russia) – Baltijsk (Kaliningrad, Russia) (36 hrs; *(1)*; 1 per week).

1	GEORG OTS	12549t	80	17.0k	136.8m	250P	107C	15T	BA	RU

GEORG OTS Built at Gdansk, Poland for *Estonian Shipping Company (ESCO)*, then of the USSR, to operate between Tallinn and Helsinki. Later chartered to *Tallink* (which was at the time partly owned by *ESCO*). Rebuilt in 1993 to increase car capacity from 14 to 110 and bring up to modern standards. In 2000 charter ended and she was returned to *ESCO*. In 2002 sold to *Sea Administration St Petersburg* and placed on the St Petersburg – Baltijsk service.

SEAWIND LINE

THE COMPANY *SeaWind Line* is a Swedish private sector company owned by *Silja Service Oy*.

MANAGEMENT Managing Director Mats Rosin **Sales Manager** Anders Levin.

ADDRESS Linnankatu 84, FIN-20100 Turku, Finland.

TELEPHONE Administration & Reservations +358 (0)2 2102 800.

FAX Administration & Reservations +358 (0)2 2102 810.

INTERNET Website www.seawind.fi *(English, Swedish, Finnish)*

ROUTE OPERATED Stockholm (Sweden) – Långnäs (Åland) – Turku (Finland) (10 hrs 45 mins; *(1,2)*; 2 per day), Helsinki – Tallinn) (3 hrs 15 mins; *(3)*; 2/3 per day).

1	SEA WIND	15879t	71	18.0k	154.9m	260P	60C	88Tr	BAS	SW
2	SKY WIND	16925t	86	15.0k	188.4m	-	-	130Tr	A	SW
3	STAR WIND	13788t	77	18.0k	158.6m	119P	100C	66Tr	A	SW

SEA WIND Train/vehicle ferry built at Helsingør, Denmark as the SVEALAND for *Stockholms Rederi AB Svea* and used on the *Trave Line* Helsingborg (Sweden) – Copenhagen (Tuborg Havn) – Travemünde freight service. In 1981 she was sold to *TT-Saga Line* and operated between Travemünde and Malmö. In 1984 she was rebuilt to increase capacity and renamed the SAGA WIND. In 1989 she was acquired by *SeaWind Line*, renamed the SEA WIND and inaugurated a combined rail freight, trailer and lower priced passenger service between Stockholm and Turku.

SKY WIND Train/vehicle ferry built at Moss, Norway as the ÖRESUND for *Statens Järnvägar* (*Swedish State Railways*) for the 'DanLink' service between Helsingborg and Copenhagen. Has 817 metres of rail track. Service ceased in July 2000 and vessel laid up. In 2001 sold to *Sea Containers Ferries* and, in 2002 is being converted at Gdansk, Poland to passenger ferry. She was chartered to *SeaWind Line* and, in autumn 2002, replaced the STAR WIND on the Stockholm – Turku service.

STAR WIND Train/vehicle ferry built at Bergen, Norway as the ROSTOCK for *Deutsche Reichsbahn* of Germany (DDR). Used on freight services between Trelleborg and Sassnitz. In 1992 modified to increase passenger capacity in order to run in passenger service. In 1993 ownership transferred to *DFO* and in 1994 she opened a new service from Rostock to Trelleborg. In 1997 she was used when winds preclude the use of the new MECKLENBURG-VORPOMMERN. Following modifications to this vessel in late 1997, the ROSTOCK continued to operate to provide additional capacity until the delivery of the SKÅNE of *Scandlines AB*, after which she was laid up. In 1999 she was sold to *SeaWind Line*, renamed the STAR WIND and operated in freight-only mode. Initial plans to bring her passenger accommodation up to the standards required for Baltic night service were dropped. Later in 2002 replaced by the SKY WIND and transferred to the Helsinki – Tallinn route. She now carries a limited number of ordinary passengers on some sailings.

SILJA LINE

THE COMPANY *Silja Oyj Abp*, based in Finland, is a wholly owned subsidiary of *Sea Containers Ltd*. The company has marketing organisations in Sweden, Estonia and Germany.

MANAGEMENT President Antti Pankakoski, **Senior Vice-President, Passenger Services** Pekka J Helin, **Senior Vice President Cargo Services** Sören Lindman, **Senior Vice President, Ship Management** Christian Grönvall, **Senior Vice President, Corporate Communications** Tuomas Nylund, **CFO** Steven G Robson, **Senior Vice President, Business Development** Tuomas Roufa.

ADDRESS Silja Oyj Abp, FIN-02060 SILJA, Finland.

TELEPHONE Administration *Finland* +358 (0)9 18041, **Reservations** *Finland* +358 (0)9 1804 422, *Sweden* +46 (0)8-222 140.

FAX Administration & Reservations *Finland* +358 (0)9 1804 279, *Sweden* +46 (0)8-667 8681.

INTERNET Email info@silja.com **Website** www.silja.com *(English, Finnish and Swedish)*

ROUTES OPERATED Conventional Ferries *All year* Helsinki (Finland) – Mariehamn (Åland) – Stockholm (Sweden) (16 hrs; *(5,6)*; 1 per day), Turku (Finland) – Mariehamn (Åland) (day)/Långnäs (Åland) (night) – Stockholm (11 hrs; *(2,3)*; 1 or 2 per day), St Petersburg (Russia) – Tallinn (Estonia) – Rostock (Germany) (38 hrs (St Petersburg – Tallinn, 12-15 hrs, Tallinn – Rostock, 24 hrs)); *(1)*; every 4 days (summer), ever 5 days (winter)). *Winter, Spring and Autumn only* Turku (Finland) – Mariehamn (day)/Långnäs (night) – Kapellskär (Sweden) (11 hrs; *(2)*; 1 per day). **Fast Ferry** Helsinki – Tallinn (1 hr 30 mins; *(7,8)*; up to 7 per day). **Cruise Service** Helsinki – Tallinn – Visby (Gotland), Helsinki – Riga (Latvia), Helsinki – St Petersburg and other destinations *(4)*.

1	FINNJET	32940t	77	31.0k	214.9m	1790P	374C	44T	BA	FI
2	SILJA EUROPA	59912t	93	21.5k	201.8m	3000P	400C	68T	BA	FI
3	SILJA FESTIVAL	34414t	85	22.0k	170.7m	2000P	400C	80T	BA	SW
4p	SILJA OPERA	25076t	92	21.0k	158.9m	1400P	0C	0T	-	SW
5	SILJA SERENADE	58376t	90	21.0k	203.0m	2641P	450C	70T	BA	FI
6	SILJA SYMPHONY	58377t	91	21.0k	203.0m	2641P	450C	70T	BA	SW
7»	SUPERSEACAT THREE	4697t	99	38.0k	100.0m	800P	175C	-	A	IT
8»	SUPERSEACAT FOUR	4697t	99	38.0k	100.0m	752P	164C	-	A	IT

FINNJET Built at Helsinki, Finland for *Finnlines* to operate between Helsinki and Travemünde, replacing several more vessels with intermediate calls. Her exceptionally fast speed was achieved by the use of gas turbine engines. During winter 1981/82 she was equipped with diesel engines for use during periods when traffic did not justify so many crossings per week. Later the trading name was changed to *Finnjet Line*. In 1986 the company was acquired by *EFFOA* and the trading name changed to *Finnjet Silja Line*. In winter 1997/98 she operated between Helsinki and Tallinn (Muuga Harbour). In summer 1998 she operated a weekly Travemünde – Tallinn – Helsinki – Travemünde triangular service in addition to two weekly Travemünde – Helsinki round trips. In autumn 1998 she resumed operating between Helsinki and Tallinn and since summer 1999 she operated Helsinki – Tallinn – Rostock during the summer and Helsinki – Tallinn in the winter. From June 2004 to operate Rostock – Tallinn – St Petersburg all year.

SILJA EUROPA Built at Papenburg, Germany. Ordered by *Rederi AB Slite* of Sweden for *Viking Line* service between Stockholm and Helsinki and due to be called EUROPA. In 1993, shortly before delivery was due, *Rederi AB Slite* went into liquidation and the order was cancelled. A charter agreement with her builders was then signed by *Silja Line* and she was introduced onto the Stockholm – Helsinki route as SILJA EUROPA. In early 1995 she was transferred to the Stockholm – Turku service. During the off peak period she operates between Turku and Kapellskär.

SILJA FESTIVAL Built at Helsinki, Finland as the WELLAMO for *EFFOA* for the *Silja Line* Stockholm – Mariehamn – Turku service. In 1990, following the sale of the FINLANDIA to *DFDS*, she was transferred to the Stockholm – Helsinki service until the SILJA SERENADE was delivered later in the year. During winter 1991/92 she was extensively rebuilt and in 1991 renamed the SILJA FESTIVAL; ownership was transferred to *Silja Line*. In 1993 she was transferred to the Malmö – Travemünde service of *Euroway*, which was at this time managed by *Silja Line*. This service ceased in 1994 and she was transferred to the Vaasa – Sundsvall service. In 1994 and 1995 she operated on this route during the peak summer period and on the Helsinki – Tallinn route during the rest of the year. The Vaasa – Sundsvall service did not operate in summer 1996 and she continued to operate between Helsinki and Tallinn. In 1997 she was transferred to the Stockholm – Turku route replacing the SILJA SCANDINAVIA (see the GABRIELLA, *Viking Line*).

SILJA OPERA Built as the SALLY ALBATROSS at Rauma, Finland for *Rederi AB Sally* of Finland, a subsidiary of *EffJohn International* to operate cruises from Helsinki. She was built on the lower portions of the previous SALLY ALBATROSS, which had been declared a total constructive loss following a fire when being refitted at a Stockholm shipyard in 1990. (This vessel had been built in 1980 at Turku for *Rederi AB Sally* (at that time part of *Viking Line*) as the VIKING SAGA and was used on the Helsinki – Stockholm service. In 1986 she was replaced by the OLYMPIA (now PRIDE OF BILBAO), modified to a cruising role and renamed the SALLY ALBATROSS). In spring 1994 she grounded whilst on a winter cruise and was badly damaged. Her cruise programme was cancelled and, when she had been repaired and modified, she was renamed the LEEWARD and chartered to *Norwegian Cruise Line* for Caribbean cruising. In 1999 she was chartered to *Star Cruises* of Singapore and renamed the SUPERSTAR TAURUS. She was used on cruises in the Far East. In 2002 returned to *Silja Line* and renamed the SILJA OPERA. She is used on cruises from Helsinki to various destinations, including Tallinn, Visby (Gotland), Riga (Latvia) and St Petersburg.

SILJA SERENADE, SILJA SYMPHONY Built at Turku, Finland for *Silja Line* for the Stockholm – Helsinki service. In 1993, SILJA SERENADE was transferred to the Stockholm – Turku service but in early 1995 she was transferred back to the Helsinki route.

SUPERSEACAT THREE Fincantieri MDV1200 monohull vessel built at La Spézia, Italy. In 1999 operated on the Liverpool – Dublin service, operated by *Sea Containers Ferries Scotland*, replacing the SUPERSEACAT TWO. In 2000 she also operated on the Liverpool – Douglas service. In summer 2001 she operated between Dover and Calais and Dover and Ostend; in summer 2002 she operated from Liverpool to Dublin and Douglas. In 2003 she operated between Helsinki and Tallinn.

SUPERSEACAT FOUR Fincantieri MDV1200 monohull vessel built at Riva Trigoso, Italy. Laid-up following delivery. In 2000 transferred to an Estonian subsidiary of *Sea Containers* to operate between Helsinki and Tallinn under the *Silja Line SeaCat* branding. The service was marketed by *Silja Line*. She operates on the route during the ice free season.

STENA LINE

THE COMPANY *Stena Line Scandinavia AB* is a Swedish private sector company.

MANAGEMENT Managing Director & Chief Operational Officer Gunnar Blomdahl, **Ship Management Director** Robert Åuerlund, **Communication Director** Joakim Kenndal.

ADDRESS S-405 19 Gothenburg, Sweden (**Visitors' address** Danmarksterminalen, Masthuggskajen).

TELEPHONE Administration +46 (0)31-85 80 00, **Reservations** +46 (0)31-704 00 00.

FAX Administration & Reservations +46 (0)31-24 10 38.

INTERNET Email info@stenaline.com **Website** www.stenaline.com *(English, Swedish)*

ROUTES OPERATED Conventional Ferries Gothenburg (Sweden) – Frederikshavn (Denmark) (3 hrs 15 mins; *(4,7)*; up to 6 per day), Gothenburg – Kiel (Germany) (14 hrs; *(6,11)*; 1 per day), Frederikshavn – Oslo (Norway) (8 hrs 45 mins; *(10)*; 1 per day), Varberg (Sweden) – Grenaa (Denmark) (4 hrs; *(7)*; 2 per day), Karlskrona (Sweden) – Gdynia (Poland) (10 hrs 30 mins; *(1,9)*; 2 per day). **Fast Ferry** Gothenburg – Frederikshavn (2 hrs; *(2)*; 4 per day). **Freight Ferries** Gothenburg – Frederikshavn (Train Ferry) (3 hrs 45 mins; *(12)*; 2 per day), Gothenburg – Travemünde (15 hrs; *(3,5)*; 1 per day).

1	STENA BALTICA	31189t	86	20.0k	161.8m	1800P	500C	72T	BA	SW
2»	STENA CARISMA	8631t	97	40.0k	88.0m	900P	210C	-	A	SW
3F	STENA CARRIER	21104t	04	22.0k	182.6m	12P	-	200T	A	SW
4	STENA DANICA	28727t	83	19.5k	154.9m	2274P	555C	120T	BAS2	SW
5F	STENA FREIGHTER	21104t	04	22.0k	182.6m	12P	-	200T	A	SW
6	STENA GERMANICA	38772t	87	20.0k	175.4m	2400P	550C	120T	BAS2	SW
7	STENA JUTLANDICA	29691t	96	21.5k	183.7m	1500P	550C	156T	BAS2	SW
8	STENA NAUTICA	19763t	86	19.4k	134.0m	700P	330C	70T	BA2	SW
9	STENA NORDICA	24500t	01	25.0k	169.8m	405P	375C	122T	BA2	SW
10	STENA SAGA	33750t	81	22.0k	166.1m	2000P	510C	76T	BA	SW
11	STENA SCANDINAVICA	38756t	88	20.0k	175.4m	2400P	550C	120T	BAS2	SW
12F	STENA SCANRAIL	7504t	73	16.5k	142.4m	65P	-	64Tr	A	SW

STENA BALTICA Built at Krimpen aan den IJssel, Rotterdam, Netherlands as the KONINGIN BEATRIX for *Stoomvaart Maatschappij Zeeland* of The Netherlands for their Hoek van Holland – Harwich service (trading as *Crown Line*). In 1989 transferred to *Stena Line bv*. In June 1997 chartered by *Stena Line bv* to *Stena Line Ltd* and used on the Fishguard – Rosslare service. In August 1997, transferred to the British flag. In 2002 renamed the STENA BALTICA and transferred to the Karlskrona – Gdynia service.

STENA CARISMA Westamarin HSS 900 craft built at Kristinsand, Norway for *Stena Line* for the Gothenburg – Frederikshavn service. Work on a sister vessel, approximately 30% completed, was ceased.

STENA CARRIER Laid down in 1998 at Viagreggio Italy for *Stena RoRo*. In 1999 the builders went bankrupt and work ceased. The hull was purchased by *Enrico Bugazzi Shipmanagement*, named the ARONTE and in 2003 she was towed to Marina di Carrara, Italy for work to be completed. In 2003 she was sold to *Stena RoRo* and, in 2003, she was renamed the STENA CARRIER II. After further work at Gothenburg she entered service on the Gothenburg – Travemünde route. To be renamed the STENA CARRIER.

STENA DANICA Built at Dunkerque, France for *Stena Line* for the Gothenburg – Frederikshavn service. Sister vessel STENA JUTLANDICA was transferred to the Dover – Calais service in July 1996 and renamed the STENA EMPEREUR (now the PRIDE OF PROVENCE of *P&O Ferries*). This vessel is listed in Section 1.

STENA FREIGHTER Laid down in 1998 at Viagreggio Italy for *Stena RoRo*. Due to be called the SEA CHIEFTAIN for charter to the *British MoD*. In 1999 the builders went bankrupt and work ceased. In 2003 the incomplete vessel was purchased at auction by *Stena RoRo* and she was renamed the STENA SEAFREIGHTER and towed to Kraljevica, Croatia for work to be completed. In 2004 she was renamed the STENA FREIGHTER and entered service with *Stena Line* between Gothenburg and Travemünde.

STENA GERMANICA, STENA SCANDINAVICA Built at Gdynia, Poland for *Stena Line* for the Gothenburg – Kiel service. Names were swapped during construction in order that the STENA GERMANICA should enter service first. There were originally intended to be four vessels. Only two were delivered to *Stena Line*. The third (due to be called the STENA POLONICA) was sold by the builders as an unfinished hull to *Fred. Olsen Lines* of Norway and then resold to *ANEK* of Greece who had her completed at Perama and delivered as EL VENIZELOS for service between Greece and Italy. The fourth hull (due to be called the STENA BALTICA) was never completed. During the summer period on some days, the vessel arriving in Gothenburg overnight from Kiel operates a round trip to Frederikshavn before departing for Kiel the following evening. During winter 1998/99 they were modified to increase freight capacity and reduce the number of cabins.

STENA JUTLANDICA Train/vehicle 'ro-pax' vessel built at Krimpen aan den IJssel, Rotterdam, Netherlands for *Stena Line* to operate between Gothenburg and Frederikshavn. She was launched as the STENA JUTLANDICA III and renamed on entry into service.

STENA NAUTICA Built at Nakskov, Denmark as the NIELS KLIM for *DSB (Danish State Railways)* for their service between Århus (Jutland) and Kalundborg (Sealand). In 1990 she was purchased by *Stena Rederi* of Sweden and renamed the STENA NAUTICA. In 1992 she was chartered to *B&I Line*, renamed the ISLE OF INNISFREE and introduced onto the Rosslare – Pembroke Dock service, replacing the MUNSTER (8093t, 1970). In 1993 she was transferred to the Dublin – Holyhead service. In early 1995 she was chartered to *Lion Ferry*. She was renamed the LION KING. In 1996 she was replaced by a new LION KING and renamed the STENA NAUTICA. During summer 1996 she was chartered to *Trasmediterranea* of Spain but returned to *Stena RoRo* in the autumn and remained laid up during 1997. In December 1997 she was chartered to *Stena Line* and placed on the Halmstad – Grenaa route. This route ended on 31st January 1999 and she was transferred to the Varberg – Grenaa route. During winter 2001/2 rebuilt to heighten upper vehicle deck and allow separate loading of load vehicle decks; passenger capacity reduced. On 16 February 2004 hit by the coaster JOANNA and holed. Due to return to service at the end of May 2004 after repairs at Gothenburg and Gdansk.

STENA NORDICA Built at Shimonoeki, Japan as the EUROPEAN AMBASSADOR for *P&O Irish Sea* for the Liverpool - Dublin service. Service transferred to Mostyn in November 2001. Also operated between Dublin and Cherbourg once a week. In 2004 the Mostyn route closed and she was sold to *Stena RoRo*. Chartered to *Stena Line* to operate between Karlskrona and Gdynia and renamed the STENA NORDICA.

STENA SAGA Built at Turku, Finland as the SILVIA REGINA for *Stockholms Rederi AB Svea* of Sweden. She was registered with subsidiary company *Svea Line* of Turku, Finland and was used on *Silja Line* services between Stockholm and Helsinki. In 1981 she was sold to *Johnson Line* and in 1984 sold to a Finnish Bank and chartered back. In 1990 she was purchased by *Stena RoRo* of Sweden for delivery in 1991. In 1991 she was renamed the STENA BRITANNICA and took up service on the Hoek van Holland – Harwich service for Dutch subsidiary *Stena Line bv*, operating with a British crew. In 1994 she was transferred to *Stena Line's* Oslo – Frederikshavn route and renamed the STENA SAGA. During winter 2002/3 rebuilt to increase passenger capacity by 200.

STENA SCANRAIL Built at Capelle an der IJssel, Rotterdam, Netherlands. Launched as the STENA SEATRADER for *Stena AB* and entered service as the SEATRADER. In 1976 she was lengthened and then demise chartered to *Bahjah Navigation* of Cyprus and renamed the BAHJAN. In 1981 charter ended and she was renamed the STENA SEARIDER. In 1983 chartered to *Snowdrop Shipping* of Cyprus and renamed the SEARIDER. The charter ended the following year and she renamed the name STENA SEARIDER. Later in 1984 she was renamed the TRUCKER and in 1985 again reverted to the name STENA SEARIDER. In 1987 she was converted to a train ferry to operate between Gothenburg and Frederikshavn, chartered to *Stena Line* and renamed the STENA SCANRAIL.

Stena Germanica *(Philippe Holthof)*

Huckleberry Finn *(FotoFlite)*

SUPERFAST FERRIES

THE COMPANY *SuperFast Ferries* is a Greek company, owned by *Attica Enterprises*.

MANAGEMENT Managing Director Alexander P Panagopulos, **Corporate Marketing Director** Yannis B Criticos, **General Manager, Germany of Attica Premium SA** Jens-Peter Berg.

ADDRESS *Greece* 157 Alkyonidon Avenue, Voula, GR-16673 Athens, Greece, *Northern Europe* Hermann-Lange-Strasse 1, DE-23558 Lübeck, Germany.

TELEPHONE Administration (Greece) +30 (0)210 891 9500, **Administration (Germany)** +49 (0)451 88006130, **Reservations** +49 (0)451 88006130.

FAX Administration (Greece) +30 (0)210 891 9509, **Administration & Reservations (Germany)** +49 (0)451-8800629.

INTERNET Email criticos@superfast.com **Website** www.superfast.com *(English, German, Finnish, Swedish)*

ROUTES OPERATED Rostock (Germany) – Hanko (Finland) (21 hrs; *(1,2)*; 1 per day).

| 1 | SUPERFAST VII | 29800t | 01 | 29.2k | 203.3m | 626P | 1000C | 140T | BA2 | GR |
| 2 | SUPERFAST VIII | 29800t | 01 | 29.2k | 203.3m | 626P | 1000C | 140T | BA2 | GR |

SUPERFAST VII, SUPERFAST VIII Built at Kiel, Germany for *Attica Enterprises* for use by *SuperFast Ferries* between Rostock and Hanko.

TALLINK

THE COMPANY *AS Tallink Grupp*, (formerly *AS Hansatee Grupp* trading as *Tallink*), is an Estonian company owned by the *AS Infortar (*86.0%) and others. Services are marketed outside Estonia by *Tallink Finland Oy*.

MANAGEMENT Director, Tallink Finland Oy Keijo Mehtonen.

ADDRESS PO Box 195, 00181 Helsinki, Finland.

TELEPHONE Administration +358 (0)9 228211, **Reservations** +358 (0)9 228311.

FAX Administration & Reservations +358 (0)9 228 21242.

INTERNET Email keijo.mehtonen@tallink.fi **Website**s www.tallink.ee *(Estonian)*

www.tallink.se *(Swedish)* www.tallink.fi *(Finnish, English)*.

ROUTES OPERATED Conventional Ferries Helsinki – Tallinn (3 hrs 30 mins; *(3,6)*; up to 3 per day), Helsinki – Tallinn – St Petersburg – Helsinki (Helsinki – St Petersburg – 16 hrs; *(1)*; alternate days), Stockholm – Långnäs (Åland) – Tallinn (14 hrs; *(5,12)*; daily), Kapellskär – Paldiski (9 hrs – 11 hrs; *(11)*; 1 per day). **Freight Ferries** Helsinki – Tallinn (3 hrs 30 mins; *(2)*; 1 per day), Kapellskär – Paldiski (9 hrs – 11 hrs; *(4)*; 1 per day). **Fast Ferries** Helsinki – Tallinn (1 hr 30 mins; *(7,8,9,10)*; up to 10 per day).

1	FANTAASIA	16630t	79	21.3k	136.1m	1700P	549C	46T	BA2	ES
2F	KAPELLA	‡2794t	74	14.5k	110.1m	50P	-	42T	A	ES
3	MELOODIA	17955t	79	21.0k	138.8m	1500P	480C	52T	BA2	ES
4F	REGAL STAR	15281t	00	17.5k	156.6m	100P	-	-	A	ES
5	REGINA BALTICA	18345t	80	21.3k	145.2m	1450P	500C	68T	BA	ES
6	ROMANTIKA	40000t	02	22.0k	193.8m	2178P	300C	83T	BA	ES
7»	TALLINK AUTOEXPRESS	4859t	95	32.0k	78.6m	586P	150C	-	BA	ES
8»	TALLINK AUTOEXPRESS 2	5419t	97	37.0k	82.3m	700P	175C	-	A	ES
9»	TALLINK AUTOEXPRESS 3	4000t	97	36.0k	95.0m	600P	155C	-	A	ES
10»	TALLINK AUTOEXPRESS 4	3750t	96	36.0k	95.0m	580P	155C	-	A	ES
11	VANA TALLINN	10002t	74	18.0k	153.7m	1500P	300C	44L	BAS	ES

12	VICTORIA I	40000t	04	22.0k	193.8m	2500P	300C	83T	BA	ES

FANTAASIA Built at Turku, Finland as the TURELLA for *SF Line* of Finland for the *Viking Line* Stockholm – Mariehamn – Turku service and later moved to the Kapellskär – Mariehamn – Naantali service. In 1988 she was sold to *Stena Line*, renamed the STENA NORDICA and placed onto the Frederikshavn – Moss (night) and Frederikshavn – Gothenburg (day) service. In 1996 the Frederikshavn – Moss service ceased and she was transferred to subsidiary *Lion Ferry* and renamed the LION KING. She operated between Halmstad and Grenaa. In December 1997 she was sold to *Tallink Line Ltd* of Cyprus and renamed the FANTAASIA. In February 1998, after substantial modification, she was placed on the *Tallink* service between Helsinki and Tallinn. In June 2002 moved to the Tallinn – Stockholm route, enabling a daily service to be reinstated. In 2004 inaugurated a new Helsinki – Tallinn – St Petersburg – Helsinki service.

KAPELLA Built at Kristiansand, Norway for *A/S Larvik-Frederikshavnferjen* of Norway as DUKE OF YORKSHIRE. In 1978 she was chartered to (and later purchased by) *CN Marine* of Canada (from 1986 *Marine Atlantic*) and renamed the MARINE EVANGELINE. She was used on services between Canada, USA and Newfoundland. In 1992 she was chartered to *Opale Ferries* of France and inaugurated a new Boulogne – Folkestone freight service. In 1993 the company went into liquidation and the service and charter were taken over by *Meridian Ferries*, a British company. She was renamed the SPIRIT OF BOULOGNE. In spring 1995, *Meridian Ferries* went into liquidation and she returned to her owners, resuming the name MARINE EVANGELINE. After a period of lay up she was chartered to *Stena Sealink Line*. She spent the summer on the Newhaven – Dieppe service and was then transferred to the Stranraer – Larne (from November 1995 Stranraer – Belfast) route. She returned to Newhaven in summer 1996 but was laid up during most of 1997. In late 1997 she was chartered to *Hansatee* and inaugurated a new ro-pax service between Paldiski and Kapellskär. She was renamed the KAPELLA. In 2004 transferred to the Helsinki – Tallinn route.

MELOODIA Built at Papenburg, Germany as DIANA II for *Rederi AB Slite* for *Viking Line* services between Stockholm and Turku, Mariehamn, Kapellskär and Naantali. In 1992 sold to a *Nordbanken* and, in 1993, chartered to *TR-Line* of Germany (joint venture between *TT-Line* and *DSR*) for service between Trelleborg and Rostock. In 1994 sold to *ESCO* and chartered to *EstLine* and renamed the MARE BALTICUM. During winter 1994/95 she was completely renovated. In 1996, following the delivery of the REGINA BALTICA, she was chartered to *Tallink*, renamed the MELOODIA and placed on the Tallinn – Helsinki service.

REGAL STAR Initially built at St Petersburg. Work started in 1993 (as a deep sea ro-ro) but was never completed. In 1999 the vessel was purchased, taken to a shipyard in Naples and completed as a short-sea ro-ro with accommodation for 80 drivers. In 2000 she was delivered to *MCL* of Italy and placed on a route between Savona and Catonia. In September of that year she was chartered to *Grimaldi Ferries* and operated on a route Salerno – Palermo – Valencia. In late 2003 she was sold to *Hansatee Shipping* of Estonia and, in 2004, placed on the Kapellskär – Paldiski route, replacing the KAPELLA.

REGINA BALTICA Built at Turku, Finland as the VIKING SONG for *Rederi AB Sally* of Finland and used on the *Viking Line* service between Stockholm and Helsinki. In 1985 replaced by the MARIELLA of *SF Line* and sold to *Fred. Olsen Lines*. She was named BRAEMAR and used on services between Norway and Britain as well as Norway and Denmark. Services to Britain ceased in June 1990 and she continued to operate between Norway and Denmark. She was withdrawn in 1991 and sold to *Rigorous Shipping* of Cyprus (a subsidiary of *Fred. Olsen Lines*). She was chartered to the *Baltic Shipping Company* of Russia, renamed the ANNA KARENINA and inaugurated a service between Kiel and St Petersburg. In 1992 a Nynäshamn call was introduced. In 1996 the service ceased and she was returned to her owners and renamed the ANNA K. Later in 1996 she was sold to *Empremare Shipping Co Ltd* of Cyprus (a company jointly owned by *Nordström & Thulin* and *Estonian Shipping Company*), chartered to *EstLine* and renamed the REGINA BALTICA. In 2000 charter transferred to *Tallink*. Continues to operate between Stockholm and Tallinn. Purchased by *Tallink* in 2002.

ROMANTIKA Built at Rauma, Finland for *Tallink Grupp* to operate for *Tallink* between Tallinn and Helsinki.

TALLINK AUTOEXPRESS Austal Ships Auto Express 79 catamaran ordered by *Sea Containers* and launched at Fremantle, Western Australia as the AUTO EXPRESS 96. On completion she was renamed the SUPERSEACAT FRANCE. However, due to a dispute between *Sea Containers* and the builders, delivery was not taken and it was announced that she was to be sold to *Stena Rederi* of Sweden, renamed the STENA LYNX IV and chartered to *Stena Line (UK)*, Inaugurating a Newhaven – Dieppe service in February 1996. This did not happen and she was instead sold to *DSB Rederi* (now *Scandlines Danmark A/S*) and, in summer 1996, she was chartered to *Cat-Link* and renamed the CAT-LINK III. In 1999 she was sold to *Tallink* and renamed the TALLINK AUTOEXPRESS. Operates between Tallinn and Helsinki.

TALLINK AUTOEXPRESS 2 Austal Ships Auto Express 82 catamaran built at Fremantle, Western Australia as the BOOMERANG for *Polferries* and used on the Swinoujscie – Malmö route. In autumn 1999 she withdrawn and it was anticipated that she would no longer operate for *Polferries*. However in summer 2000 she returned to the Swinoujscie – Malmö route. She was laid up again in the autumn and in May 2001 was sold to Tallink and renamed the TALLINK AUTOEXPRESS 2. Operates between Tallinn and Helsinki.

TALLINK AUTOEXPRESS 3 Fincantieri MDV1200 monohull vessel. Built as the PEGASUS TWO at La Spezia, Italy for *Ocean Bridge Investments* and, in summer 1997 and summer 1998, chartered to *Color Line* to operate between Larvik and Skagen. In 1999 chartered to *Plonin Linija* of Croatia to operate a Venedig – Ravemma – Plomin service. In 2000 sold to *African & Affairs SAL* of Spain and placed on a route between Malaga (Spain) and Nador (Morocco) until arrested in Gibraltar later in the year. In December purchased by *DMF Investments* of Gibraltar and in 2001 renamed the SHANNON ALEXIS. Laid up during 2001 and 2002. In 2003 briefly chartered to the *US Military*. In 2004 sold to *Tallink* and renamed the TALLINK AUTOEXPRESS 3.

TALLINK AUTOEXPRESS 4 Fincantieri MDV1200 monohull vessel. Built at La Spezia, Italy for *Ocean Bridge Investments*. Entered service as the STENA PEGASUS for *Stena Line* between Newhaven and Dieppe. In autumn 1996 she was laid up and later named the PEGASUS ONE. In 1997 she was chartered to *Conferrys* of Venezuela and operated between Puerto la Cruz and Punta de Piedras. In 1999 she was laid up in Greece. In 2002 she was moved to Gibraltar and renamed the ST MATTHEW. In 2004 she was sold to *Tallink* and renamed the TALLINK AUTOEXPRESS 4.

VANA TALLINN Built at Helsingør, Denmark as the DANA REGINA for *DFDS* and used on their Esbjerg – Harwich service until 1983 when she was moved to the Copenhagen – Oslo route. In 1990 she was sold to *Nordström & Thulin* of Sweden, renamed the NORD ESTONIA and used on the *EstLine* Stockholm – Tallinn service. In 1992 she was chartered to *Larvik Line* to operate as a second vessel between Larvik and Frederikshavn and renamed the THOR HEYERDAHL. In 1994 she was sold to *Inreko Ships Ltd*, chartered to *Tallink* and renamed the VANA TALLINN. In November 1996 she was withdrawn and in December 1996 she was chartered to a new company called *TH Ferries* and resumed sailings between Helsinki and Tallinn. In January 1998 she was sold to *Hansatee* subsidiary *Vana Tallinn Line Ltd* of Cyprus and placed on *Tallink* service between Helsinki and Tallinn. *TH Ferries* then ceased operations. In autumn 2002 moved to the Paldiski – Kapellskär route, replacing the BALTIC KRISTINA.

VICTORIA I Built at Rauma, Finland for *Tallink* to operate between Tallinn and Stockholm.

TESO

THE COMPANY *TESO* is a Dutch public sector company. Its full name is *Texels Eigen Stoomboot Onderneming.*

MANAGEMENT Managing Director R Wortel.

ADDRESS Pontweg 1, 1797 SN Den Hoorn, Texel, Netherlands.

TELEPHONE Administration +31 (0)222 369600, **Reservations** n/a.

FAX Administration & Reservations +31 (0)222 369659.

INTERNET Email info@teso.nl **Website** www.teso.nl *(Dutch, English, German, French)*

ROUTES OPERATED Den Helder (Netherlands) – Texel (Dutch Frisian Islands) (20 minutes; *(1,2)*; hourly).

1	MOLENGAT	6170t	80	13.0k	88.8m	1200P	126C	19L	BA2	NL
2	SCHULPENGAT	8311t	90	13.6k	110.4m	1750P	156C	25L	BA2	NL

MOLENGAT, SCHULPENGAT Built at Heusden, Netherlands for *TESO.*

Under Construction

3	DOKTER WAGEMAKER	c10500t	05	15.0k	130.0m	1750P	300C	-	BA2	NL

DOKTER WAGEMAKER Under construction at Galatz, Romania (hull and superstructure) and Vlissingen (fitting out) for *TESO* to replace the MOLENGAT.

TRANSRUSSIAEXPRESS

THE COMPANY *TransRussiaExpress* is jointly operated by *Finnlines Deutschland AG*, of Germany (wholly owned by *Finnlines* of Finland) and *JSC Baltic Transport Systems* of Russia.

ADDRESS Einsiedelstrasse 43-45, 23554 Lübeck, Germany.

TELEPHONE Administration & Reservations +49 (0) 451 15 070.

FAX Administration & Reservations +49 (0) 451 15 07-139.

INTERNET Email info@finnlines.de **Website** www.tre.de *(German, English)*

ROUTE OPERATED Lübeck – Sassnitz – Baltijsk (Kaliningrad) – St Petersburg (57/60 hours; *(1,2)*; 2 per week (one sailing does not call at Baltijsk southbound)). Normally only the TRANSLUBECA conveys ordinary passengers.

1F	FINLANDIA	8110t	81	19k	157.5m	24P	-	164T	A	GE
2	TRANSLUBECA	24727t	90	20.5k	157.0m	84P	-	152T	A	GE

FINLANDIA Built as the TRANSFINLANDIA for *Poseidon Schiffahrt OHG* of Germany (now *Finnlines Deutschland AG*) and used on *Poseidon-Finncarriers* (later *Finnlines*) service in the Baltic. In 2003 transferred to *TransRussiaExpress*. Later in 2003 sold to Norwegian interests and chartered back. Renamed the FINLANDIA.

TRANSLUBECA Built for *Poseidon Schiffahrt OHG* of Germany and used on *Poseidon-Finncarriers* service in the Baltic. In 1999 chartered to *DFDS Tor Line* and operated between Harwich and Gothenburg. In 2001 transferred to *TransRussiaExpress*.

TT-LINE

THE COMPANY *TT-Line GmbH & Co* is a German private sector company.

MANAGEMENT Managing Director Hans Heinrich Conzen & Dr Arndt-Heinrich von Oertzen, **Sales Manager** Dirk Lifke.

ADDRESS Mattentwiete 8, D-20457 Hamburg, Germany.

TELEPHONE Administration *Hamburg* +49 (0)40 3601 372, *Rostock* +49 (0)381 6707911, **Reservations** *Hamburg* +49 (0)40 3601 442, *Rostock* +49 (0)381 670790.

FAX Administration & Reservations *Hamburg* +49 (0)40 3601 407, *Rostock* +49 (0)381 6707980.

INTERNET Email info@TTLine.com **Website** www.TTLine.com *(German, English)*

ROUTES OPERATED Passenger Ferries Travemünde (Germany) – Trelleborg (Sweden) (7 hrs; *(3,4)*; 2/3 per day). **Ro-pax Ferries** Travemünde (Germany) – Trelleborg (Sweden) (7 hrs 30 mins; *(2,5)*; 2 per day), Rostock (Germany) – Trelleborg (Sweden) (6 hrs; *(1,6)*; 3 per day), Travemünde – Helsingborg (Sweden) (10 hrs; *(2,5)*; 1 per week). **Fast Ferry** Rostock (Germany) – Trelleborg

(Sweden) (2 hrs 45 mins; *(7)*; up to 3 per day). **Note** the Travemünde – Helsingborg service is freight only.

1	HUCKLEBERRY FINN	30740t	88	20.0k	177.2m	400P	280C	146T	BAS	SW
2	NILS DACKE	26790t	95	21.0k	179.6m	308P	-	157T	BA	BS
3	NILS HOLGERSSON	36468t	01	22.0k	190.0m	744P	-	174T	BA2	GY
4	PETER PAN	36468t	01	22.0k	190.0m	744P	-	174T	BA2	SW
5	ROBIN HOOD	26800t	95	21.0k	179.6m	308P	-	157T	BA	GY
6	TOM SAWYER	30740t	89	20.0k	177.0m	400P	280C	146T	BAS	GY
7»	TT-DELPHIN	5333t	96	37.5k	82.3m	600P	175C	-	A	SW

HUCKLEBERRY FINN Built at Bremerhaven, Germany as the NILS DACKE, a ro-pax vessel. During summer 1993 rebuilt to transform her into a passenger/car ferry and renamed the PETER PAN, replacing a similarly named vessel (31356t, 1986). On arrival of the new PETER PAN in autumn she was renamed the PETER PAN IV. She was then converted back to ro-pax format, renamed the HUCKLEBERRY FINN and, in early 2002, transferred to the Rostock -Trelleborg route.

NILS DACKE, ROBIN HOOD Ro-pax vessels built at Rauma, Finland for *TT-Line*. Primarily freight vessels but accompanied cars – especially camper vans and cars towing caravans – are conveyed. They operate on the Travemünde – Trelleborg and Travemünde – Helsingborg routes.

NILS HOLGERSSON, PETER PAN Built at Bremerhaven, Germany for *TT-Line* for the Travemünde – Trelleborg route.

TOM SAWYER Built at Bremerhaven, Germany as the ROBIN HOOD, a ro-pax vessel. During winter 1992/93 rebuilt to transform her into a passenger/car ferry and renamed the NILS HOLGERSSON, replacing a similarly named vessel (31395t, 1987) which had been sold to *Brittany Ferries* and renamed the VAL DE LOIRE. In 2001 converted back to ro-pax format and renamed the TOM SAWYER. Transferred to the Rostock – Trelleborg route.

TT-DELPHIN Austal Ships Auto Express 82 catamaran built as the DELPHIN at Fremantle, Western Australia for *TT-Line* to operate between Rostock and Trelleborg. In 2002 renamed the TT-DELPHIN.

UNITY LINE

THE COMPANY *Unity Line* is a Polish company, jointly owned by *Polish Steamship Company* and *Euroafrica Shipping Lines*.

MANAGEMENT Chairman of the Board Krzysztof Rodzoch, **Managing Director** Ronald Stone.

ADDRESS 70-419 Szczecin, Plac Rodla 8, Poland,

TELEPHONE Administration +48 (0)91 35 95 795, **Reservations** +48 (0)91 35 95 692, (0)91 35 95 755.

FAX Administration +48 (0)91 35 95 885, **Reservations** +48 (0)91 35 95 673.

INTERNET Email unity@unityline.pl **Website** www.unityline.pl *(Polish, Swedish)*

ROUTE OPERATED Swinoujscie (Poland) – Ystad (Sweden) (6 hrs 30 mins (day), 9 hrs (night); *(1)*; 1 per day).

1	POLONIA	29875t	95	17.2k	169.9m	920P	860C	160Tr	BA	BS

POLONIA Train/vehicle ferry built at Tomrefjord, Norway for *Polonia Line Ltd* and chartered to *Unity Line*.

VENTLINES

THE COMPANY *VentLines* is a subsidiary of *Latvian Shipping Company*, a Latvian private sector company.

ADDRESS 51 Elizabetes str, Riga LV-1010, Latvia.

TELEPHONE Administration & Reservations +371 7 285628.

FAX Administration & Reservations +371 7 820463.

INTERNET Email ventlines@latfinn.com **Website** www.ventlines.lv *(English, German, Latvian, Russian)*

ROUTE OPERATED Travemünde (Germany) – Ventspils (Latvia) (30 hrs; *(1)*; 2 per week).

1	KAPTAN BURHANETTIN ISIM	18653t	91	17k	158m	120P	-	130T	BA	TU

KAPTAN BURHANETTIN ISIM Built at Fevag, Norway for *Turkish Cargo Lines* of Turkey to operate between Trieste (Italy) and Derince (Turkey). In 2002 chartered to *Latlines* to operate between Lübeck and Riga (Latvia). In 2003 chartered to *VentLines* to inaugurate a new service between Travemünde and Ventspils.

VIKING LINE

THE COMPANY *Viking Line AB* is an Åland (Finland) company (previously *SF Line*, trading (with *Rederi AB Slite* of Sweden) as *Viking Line*). Services are marketed by subsidiary company *Viking Line Marketing AB OY* of Finland and Sweden; this dates from the time that *Viking Line* was a consortium of three operators.

MANAGEMENT Managing Director *(Viking Line AB)* Nils-Erik Eklund, **Managing Director** *(Viking Line Marketing AB OY)* Boris Ekman.

ADDRESS *Viking Line AB* Norragatan 4, FIN-22100 Mariehamn, Åland, *Viking Line Marketing AB OY* PO Box 35, FIN-22101 Mariehamn, Åland.

TELEPHONE Administration +358 (0)18 26011, **Reservations** +358 (0)9 12351.

FAX Administration & Reservations +358 (0)9 1235292.

INTERNET Email incoming@vikingline.fi **Websites** www.vikingline.fi *(Finnish, Swedish, English)* www.vikingline.se *(Swedish, English)* www.vikingline.de *(German)*

ROUTES OPERATED Stockholm (Sweden) – Mariehamn (Åland) – Helsinki (Finland) (14 hrs; *(3,5)*; 1 per day), Stockholm – Mariehamn (day)/Långnäs (Åland) (night) – Turku (Finland) (9 hrs 10 mins; *(2,4)*; 2 per day), Kapellskär (Sweden) – Mariehamn (Åland) (2 hrs 15 mins; *(1)*; up to 3 per day), Helsinki – Tallinn (3 hrs; *(6)*; 2 per day), Cruises from Stockholm to Mariehamn (21 hrs – 24 hrs round trip (most 22 hrs 30 mins); *(7)*; 1 per day).

1	ÅLANDSFÄRJAN	6172t	72	17.0k	104.6m	1004P	185C	26T	BA	SW
2	AMORELLA	34384t	88	21.5k	169.4m	2480P	450C	70T	BA	FI
3	GABRIELLA	35492t	92	21.5k	171.0m	2420P	420C	70T	BA	FI
4	ISABELLA	34386t	89	21.5k	169.4m	2480P	364C	70T	BA	FI
5	MARIELLA	37799t	85	22.0k	177.0m	2500P	480C	82T	BA	FI
6	ROSELLA	16850t	80	21.3k	136.2m	1700P	340C	52T	BA	FI
7	VIKING CINDERELLA	46398t	89	21.5k	190.9m	2500P	340C	82T	BA	SW

ÅLANDSFÄRJAN Built at Helsingør, Denmark as the KATTEGAT for *Jydsk Færgefart* of Denmark for the Grenaa – Hundested service. She was used on this route until 1978 when the service became a single ship operation. She was then sold to *P&O Ferries*, renamed the N F TIGER and introduced as the second vessel on the Dover – Boulogne service. Sold to *European Ferries* in 1985 and withdrawn in June 1986. In 1986 sold to *Finlandshammen AB*, Sweden, renamed the ÅLANDSFÄRJAN and used on *Viking Line* summer service between Kapellskär and Mariehamn. This service now operates all year round.

AMORELLA Built at Split, Yugoslavia for *SF Line* for the Stockholm – Mariehamn – Turku service.

GABRIELLA Built at Split, Croatia as the FRANS SUELL for *Sea-Link AB* of Sweden to operate for subsidiary company *Euroway AB*, who established a service between Lübeck, Travemünde and Malmö. In 1994 this service ceased and she was chartered to *Silja Line*, renamed the SILJA SCANDINAVIA and transferred to the Stockholm – Turku service. In 1997 she was sold to *Viking Line* to operate between Stockholm and Helsinki. She was renamed the GABRIELLA.

ISABELLA Built at Split, Yugoslavia for *SF Line*. Used on the Stockholm – Naantali service until 1992 until she was switched to operating 24 hour cruises from Helsinki and in 1995 she was transferred to the Stockholm – Helsinki route. During 1996 she additionally operated short cruises to Muuga in Estonia during the 'layover' period in Helsinki. In 1997 she was transferred to the Stockholm – Turku route.

MARIELLA Built at Turku, Finland for *SF Line*. Used on the Stockholm – Helsinki service. During 1996 additionally operated short cruises to Muuga in Estonia during the 'layover' period in Helsinki but this has now ceased.

ROSELLA Built at Turku, Finland for *SF Line*. Used mainly on the Stockholm – Turku and Kapellskär – Naantali services until 1997. Since 1997 operated 21-24 hour cruises from Stockholm to

Mariehamn under the marketing name 'The Dancing Queen', except in the peak summer period when she operated between Kapellskär and Turku. In autumn 2003 transferred to a new twice daily Helsinki – Tallinn ferry service.

VIKING CINDERELLA Built at Turku, Finland for *SF Line*. Until 1993 provided additional capacity between Stockholm and Helsinki and undertook weekend cruises from Helsinki. In 1993 she replaced the OLYMPIA (a sister vessel of the MARIELLA) as the main Stockholm – Helsinki vessel after the OLYMPIA had been chartered to *P&O European Ferries* and renamed the PRIDE OF BILBAO. In 1995 switched to operating 20 hour cruises from Helsinki to Estonia in the off peak and the Stockholm – Mariehamn – Turku service during the peak summer period (end of May to end of August). Since 1997 she remained cruising throughout the year. In autumn 2003 transferred to Swedish flag, renamed the VIKING CINDERELLA and transferred to Stockholm – Mariehamn cruises. She operates these cruises all year round.

WAGENBORG PASSAGIERSDIENSTEN

THE COMPANY *Wagenborg Passagiersdiensten BV* is a Dutch public sector company.

MANAGEMENT Managing Director G van Langen.

ADDRESS Postbus 70, 9163 ZM Nes, Ameland, Netherlands.

TELEPHONE Administration & Reservations +31 (0)519 546111.

FAX Administration & Reservations +31 (0)519 542905.

INTERNET Email info@wpd.nl **Website** www.wpd.nl *(Dutch, German, English)*

ROUTES OPERATED Ameland (Netherlands) – Holwerd (Frisian Islands) (45 minutes; *(3,5)*; up to 14 per day), Lauwersoog (Netherlands) – Schiermonnikoog (Frisian Islands) (45 minutes; *(2,4)*; up to 6 per day).

1	BRAKZAND	450t	67	10.5k	50.0m	1000P	20C	-	A	NL
2	MONNIK	1121t	85	12.2k	58.0m	1000P	46C	9L	BA	NL
3	OERD	2286t	03	11.2k	73.2m	1200P	72C	22L	BA	NL
4	ROTTUM	1121t	85	12.2k	58.0m	1140P	46C	9L	BA	NL
5	SIER	2286t	95	11.2k	73.2m	1200P	72C	22L	BA	NL

BRAKZAND Built at Hoogezand, Netherlands for *Wagenborg Passagiersdiensten BV*. Now a spare vessel.

MONNIK Built at Hoogezand, Netherlands for *Wagenborg Passagiersdiensten BV* as the OERD. In 2003, on delivery of the new OERD she was renamed the MONNIK. Used on the Lauwersoog – Schiermonnikoog route.

OERD Built at Lemmer, Netherlands for *Wagenborg Passagiersdiensten BV*. Used on the Ameland – Holwerd route.

ROTTUM Built at Hoogezand, Netherlands for *Wagenborg Passagiersdiensten BV* as the SIER and used on the Holwerd – Ameland route. In 1995 renamed the ROTTUM and transferred to the Lauwersoog – Schiermonnikoog route.

SIER Built at Wartena, Netherlands for *Wagenborg Passagiersdiensten BV*. Used on the Ameland – Holwerd route.

section **7**

others

The following vessels are, at the time of going to print, not operating and are owned by companies which do not currently operate services. They are therefore available for possible re-deployment, either in the area covered by this book or elsewhere. Withdrawn vessels not yet disposed of owned by operating companies are shown under the appropriate company and marked '•'.

Rederi AB Gotland (Sweden)

1F	GUTE	6643t	79	15.0k	118.5m	52P	-	50T	BA	SW

GUTE Built at Falkenburg, Sweden for *Rederi AB Gotland* of Sweden. Used on service between Gotland and the Swedish mainland. In 1988 chartered to *Brambles Shipping* of Australia and used between Port Melbourne (Victoria) and Burnie (Tasmania). In 1992 she was renamed the SALLY SUN and chartered to *Sally Ferries*, operating between Ramsgate and Dunkerque. In 1994 she inaugurated a Ramsgate – Vlissingen service, which was later changed to Dartford – Vlissingen. In 1995 she was chartered to *SeaWind Line*, renamed the SEAWIND II and operated between Stockholm and Turku. In 1997 she was chartered to *Nordic Trucker Line* for the Oxelösund – St Petersburg service and in 1998 she returned to *SeaWind Line*. In 1998, after *Rederi AB Gotland* owned *Destination Gotland* regained the franchise to operate to Gotland, she was renamed the GUTE and resumed her summer role of providing summer freight back up to the passenger vessels, but with a number of short charters during the winter. In autumn 2002 chartered to *Amber Lines* for the Karlshamn – Liepaja service. In 2003 chartered to *NATO* for the Iraq crisis. Returned to *Destination Gotland* in summer 2003. In autumn 2003 chartered to *Scandlines Amber Lines* to operate between Karlshamn and Liepaja. In to be 2004 lengthened by 20.3m in Gdynia, Poland. Like to be chartered out or inaugurate a new route between Gotland and Latvia or Lithuania. She is unlikely to operate for *Destination Gotland* again.

Stena RoRo

1	STENA ENVOY	18653t	79	18.2k	150.0m	107P	-	142T	A	BD
2	STENA TRAVELLER	18332t	92	18.0k	153.6m	250P	-	132T	BA2	SW

STENA ENVOY Built at Tamano, Japan as the IBEX for *P&O* for *Pandoro* Irish sea services. In 1980 chartered to *North Sea Ferries*, renamed the NORSEA and used on the Ipswich – Rotterdam service. In 1986 she was renamed the NORSKY. In 1995 she returned to *Pandoro* and was re-registered in Bermuda. Later in 1995 she resumed her original name of IBEX. An additional deck was added in 1996. In late 1997 she was renamed the EUROPEAN ENVOY. In November 2001 transferred to the Mostyn – Dublin service. In 2004 the Mostyn route closed and she was sold to *Stena RoRo and renamed* STENA ENVOY.

STENA TRAVELLER Built at Fevaag, Norway for *Stena RoRo*. After a short period with *Stena Line* on the Hoek van Holland - Harwich service, she was chartered to *Sealink Stena Line* for their Southampton - Cherbourg route. At the end of the 1992 summer season she was chartered to *TT-Line* to operate between Travemünde andTrelleborg and was renamed the TT-TRAVELLER. In late 1995, she returned to *Stena Line*, resumed the name STENA TRAVELLER and inaugurated a new service between Holyhead and Dublin. In early 1997 she was again chartered to *TT-Line* and renamed the TT-TRAVELLER. She operated on the Rostock - Trelleborg route. Passenger capacity increased to 250. In early 2002 the charter ended and she was renamed the STENA TRAVELLER, chartered to *Stena Line* and placed on their Karlskrona - Gdynia service. Charter ended May 2003. Sold to *Lisco Baltic Service* and renamed the LISCO PATRIA.

European Ambassador and **European Envoy** *(Gordon Hislip)*

PO Kent *(Miles Cowsill)*

section **8** changes since ferries 2003
british isles and
northern europe

DISPOSALS

The following vessels, listed in the *Ferries 2003 – British Isles and Northern Europe* have been disposed of – either to other companies listed in this book or others. Company names are as used in that publication.

CLARE *(Smyril Line)* In September 2003 charter ended. In December 2004 chartered to *NorthLink*.

DIFKO FYN *(DIFKO)* In 2003 sold to *Transbordadores del Caribe SA* of Mexico and renamed the SUPERFLEX TRADER.

DOUBLE O SEVEN *(Hovertravel)* In 2003 sold to *Diamond Airlines* of Sierra Leone, West Africa for their route connecting Lungi International airport and the country's capital, Freetown.

EILEAN BHEARNARAIGH *(Comhairle Nan Eilean Siar)* In 2003 sold to *Transalpine Redemptorists Inc,* a community of monks who live on Papa Stronsay, Orkney. Used for conveying supplies to the island – not a public service.

EILEAN NA H-OIGE *(Comhairle Nan Eilean Siar)* In 2003 sold to *Bere Island Ferries* and renamed the OILEAN NA H-OIGE.

EUROPEAN AMBASSADOR *(P&O Irish Sea)* In 2004 sold to *Stena RoRo.* Renamed STENA NORDICA.

EUROPEAN ENVOY *(P&O Irish Sea)* In 2004 sold to *Stena RoRo.* Now listed in section 7.

EUROPEAN LEADER *(P&O Irish Sea)* In 2004 sold to *Stena Line* and renamed the STENA LEADER.

EUROPEAN PIONEER *(P&O Irish Sea)* In 2004 sold to *Stena Line* and renamed the STENA PIONEER.

EUROPEAN SEAFARER *(P&O Irish Sea)* In 2004 sold to *Stena Line* and renamed the STENA SEAFARER.

FINNARROW *(FinnLink)* In 2003 chartered to *Nordö Link.*

GITTE 3 *(DIFKO)* In 2003 sold to *HH-Ferries.*

GREIFSWALD *(Reederei F Laeisz (Germany))* Chartered to *UkrFerry,* of the Ukraine. Operates between Batumi and Ilyichevsk.

HOBURGEN *(Cobelfret Ferries)* In 2003 charter terminated. Chartered to *DFDS Tor Line* to operate between Immingham and Esbjerg. In 2004 chartered to *Isle of Man Steam Packet Company* to operate between Douglas and Heysham during the BEN-MY-CREE'S rebuilding. Later chartered to *SOL Shipping* of Latvia.

LANGLAND *(Foegeruten Langeland-Keil)* Service ended autumn 2004. Chartered to *SEM-Marina* of Crooatia.

LIV VIKING *(Hovertravel)* In 2003/4 converted to an AP188 Dash 100S, refitted and converted to *Canadian Coastguard* specification. In 2004 sold to the *Canadian Coastguard,* and operated from the Vancouver hovercraft Search and Rescue base.

MAX MOLS *(Mols-Linien)* In 2004 chartered to *P&O Ferries* to operate between Portsmouth and Caen. Operates under the marketing name 'Caen Express'.

MERCHANT VENTURE *(Norse Island Ferries)* In 2003 sold to *Ivory Marine Lines* of Dubai and renamed the WARSAN.

MISNEACH *(Bere Island Ferries)* In 2004 sold to *Rex Lines (Offshore Work Boats)* of Renfrew, Scotland.

NORDHAV *(BornholmsTrafikken)* In 2003 charter ended.

NORRÖNA I *(Smyril Line)* In January 2004 she was reactivated following damage caused to the new NORRÖNA. She was withdrawn again in March 2004 and sold to *OM Ships International* and renamed the LOGOS HOPE. She is expected to begin active service during 2005.

NORSE MERSEY *(NorseMerchant Ferries)* In 2003 charter ended.

NORTHERN STAR *(Dart Line)* In 2003 charter ended.

PANEVEZYS *(DFDS Tor Line)* In 2004 sold to Dutch interests.

PO CANTERBURY *(P&O Ferries)* In 2003 sold to *GA Ferries* of Greece and renamed the ALKMINI A. She operates between Piraeus and the Dodecannese islands of Kos and Rhodes.

PO KENT *(P&O Ferries)* In 2003 sold to *GA Ferries* of Greece and renamed ANTHI MARINA. To operate between Piraeus and the Dodecannese islands of Kos and Rhodes.

PRINCE OF SCANDINAVIA *(DFDS Seaways)* In 2003 sold to *Moby Lines* of Italy and renamed the MOBY DREA. Operates between Livorno and Olbia.

PURBECK *(Channel Island Ferries)* In 2003 chartered to *TransRail* of New Zealand to operate between Wellington and Picton.

ROGALIN *(Polferries)* In 2003 sold for scrap in India.

ROSEANNE *(TransEuropa Ferries)* In 2004 sold to *Sea Witch Maritime* of Malta and renamed the SEA WITCH.

RUSS *(Far Eastern Shipping)* Now operating between Russia and Japan.

SEA TRADER *(Scandlines (Denmark & Germany))* In 2003 charter ended.

SEACAT DANMARK *(Sea Containers Ferries)* In 2004 transferred to a *SNAV/Sea Containers* joint venture between Pescara (Italy) and Split (Croatia) and renamed the PESCARA JET.

SEAHAWK *(Cobelfret Ferries)* In 2003 charter ended. Briefly chartered to Dart Line. Later sold to Aegean Cargo of Greece and renamed the AEGEAN SUN.

SIAULIAI *(Lisco Baltic Services)* In 2004 sold to Dutch interests.

SOLIDOR 4 *(Emeraude Lines)* In 2003 renamed the ALINE. In 2004 sold to the Government of Senegal.

SOLIDOR 5 *(Emeraude Lines)* Not transferred to new owners of company. In 2004, due to dispute, not overhauled. Laid up.

SPEED ONE *(Speedferries)* Charter and renaming did not happed as expected. She remained with *Mols Linien* as MADS MOLS.

ST ROGNVALD *(Norse Island Ferries)* In 2003 service ceased. Chartered to *NorthLink* and continued to operate on the same route. Later in 2003 sold to Middle East owners. In 2004 sold to Indian breakers for scrap.

STENA CARRIER *(Stena Line)* In late 2003 sold to *Lillbacka Oy* of Finland and chartered back. In 2004 renamed the GLOBAL CARRIER. Operated for *Power Line* between Travemünde and Turku.

STENA FREIGHTER *(Stena Line)* In late 2003 sold to *Lillbacka Oy* of Finland and chartered back. In 2004 renamed the GLOBAL FREIGHTER. Charter back continued for a brief period and then operated on *Power Line* service between Travemünde and Turku.

TEHUMARDI *(Saaremaa Laevakompanii)* In 2004 sold for scrap.

THJELVAR *(Destination Gotland)* In 2004 chartered to *Color Line* and renamed the COLOR TRAVELLER.

European Causeway *(Colin Smith)*

TRADEN *(Mann Lines)* In 2003 charter ended. In 2004 sold to *Golden Anchor Line* and renamed the TRADER I.

TRANSFINLANDIA *(Finnlines)* In 2003 transferred to *TransRussiaExpress*. Later sold to Norwegian interests and renamed the FINLANDIA.

TRANSPARADEN *(Eckero Lines)* In 2004 sold to Eckerö Line and renamed TRANSLANDIA

TREKRONER *(Scandlines AG)* In 2004 sold to *Alyans Chartering & Shipping* of Turkey. Operates between the Black Sea ports of Erdemir and Zonguldak.

VISBORG *(Destination Gotland)* In 2003 sold to *Polferries* and renamed the SCANDINAVIA.

ZERAN *(Seawheel)* In 2003 charter ended.

NAME CHANGES

The following ships have been renamed without change of operator:

AMANDINE *(Cobelfret Ferries)* In 2003 sold and chartered back; renamed the AMANDA.

CINDERELLA *(Viking Line)* In 2003 renamed the VIKING CINDERELLA.

FINNMERCHANT *(Finnlines)* In 2003 sold to Norwegian interests and chartered back; renamed the MERCHANT.

FINNRIDER *(Finnlines)* In 2003 sold to Norweigian interests and charted back. In 2004 renamed the RIDER.

FINNRUNNER *(Finnlines)* In 2003 sold Norwegian interests and chartered back. In 2004 renamed the RUNNER.

GOTLAND *(Destination Gotland)* In 2003 renamed the GOTLANDIA.

OERD (1985) *(Wagenborg)* In 2003 renamed the MONNIK.

SEA CRUSADER *(Cobelfret Ferries)* In 2003 charter ended. Returned to *Cobelfret Ferries* and renamed the CELESTINE.

SOLIDOR 4 *(Emeraude Lines)* In 2004 renamed the ALINE.

TRANSBALTICA *(Finnlines)* In 2003 sold to Norwegian interests and chartered back; renamed the BALTICA.

COMPANY CHANGES

Ånedin Line No longer listed as a cruise operator.

Birka Cruises No longer listed as a cruise operator.

CETAM This service has now ceased.

Foergeruten Langeland-Keil^ This operation has ceased trading.

Lat Lines From the start of 2004 name changed to *DFDS Tor Line SIA*.

Norse Island Ferries This operator has ceased trading.

Smyril Line (Section 3) This operator no longer operates a dedicated freight ferry. All traffic is carried on the passenger ferry listed in Section 1.

VV-Line This operator ceased trading in 2003. Service and vessel transferred to *Scandlines AG*.

LATE NEWS

STENA TRAVELLER *(Stena RoRo)* In May 2004 sold to *AB Lisco Baltic Service* and renamed the LISCO PATRIA. Replaced the MERMAID II on the Klaìpeda - Karlshamn route.

index I

ferries illustrated

BALTIC JET	183	SEAFRANCE MANET	87
BEN-MY-CHREE	30	SEAFRANCE NORD PAS-DE-CALAIS	156
COMMODORE CLIPPER	74	SEAFRANCE RODIN	22
COMMODORE GOODWILL	135	SILJA FESTIVAL	169
COUTANCES	129	SILJA SYMPHONY	197
DANA SIRENA	61	SOUND OF SANDA	108
DART 2	135	SPIRIT OF GOSPORT	163
DAWN MERCHANT	100	SPODSBJERG	191
DUKE OF SCANDINAVIA	79	ST CATHERINE	125
EUROPEAN AMBASSADOR	213	STENA ADVENTURER	44, 51
EUROPEAN ENVOY	213	STENA EXPLORER	29
EVA ODEN	129	STENA FREIGHTER	41
FINNFELLOW	174	STENA GERMANICA	203
FINNHANSA	37	STENA TRANSFER	156
GARDENIA	126	SUPERFAST X	99
GOD MET ONS III	118	SUPERSEACAT TWO	79
HAMNAVOE	113	TALLINK AUTOEXPRESS	197
HASCOSAY	140	THORSVOE	113
HUCKLEBERRY FINN	203	TOM SAWYER	2
ISLE OF CUMBRAE	103	TOR NERINGA	140
LINGA	118	TOR PETUNIA	41
LOCH TARBERT	108	ULYSSES	44, 74
LYNHER	163	VAL DE LOIRE	224
MAERSK ANGLIA	147	VISBY	170
MAREN MOLS	183		
MAX MOLS	87		
MECKLENBURG-VORPOMMERN	191		
MERCANDIA VIII	174		
MONT ST MICHEL	29		
NORBANK	147		
NORMANDY	30		
PETER PAN	37		
PO KENT	213		
PONT-AVEN	5, 10, 16		
POVL ANKER	169		
PRIDE OF BILBAO	22		
PRIDE OF CANTERBURY	59		
ROMANTIKA	166		
SATURN	103		

index 2
ferries a to z

ABEL MAGWITCH	165	BRETAGNE	68	CROWN OF	
ALANDIA	177	BRITTA ODEN	132	SCANDINAVIA	173
ÅLANDSFÄRJAN	210	BRUERNISH	105	CRUISER	164
ALI CAT	105	CAEDMON	124	CYMBELINE	132
ALINE	75	CAILIN AN AISEAG	111	DAGALIEN	120
AMANDA	131	CALEDONIAN ISLES	105	DAGGRI	120
AMORELLA	210	CALIBUR	141	DANA SIRENA	72
ANGLIAN WAY	141	CANNA	105	DART 2	134
ANNA ODEN	131	CAROLINE RUSS	160	DART 3	134
ANTARES	143	CARRIGALOE	110	DART 4	134
ANVIL POINT	128	CASINO EXPRESS	187	DART 8	134
ÁRAINN MHÓR	104	CAT NO 1	185	DART 9	134
ARAN EXPRESS	165	CATHERINE	132	DAWN MERCHANT	82
ARAN FLYER	165	CELANDINE	132	DEUTSCHLAND	193
ARAN SEABIRD	165	CELESTINE	132	DIAMANT	90
ASK	196	CENRED	124	DIEPPE	99
ASTREA	143	CENWULF	124	DOKTER	
AURORA	193	CEOL NA FARRAIGE	165	WAGEMAKER	207
AURORA AF		CFF SEINE	130	DONEMARK	164
HELSINGBORG	196	CFF SOLENT	130	DRAÍOCHT	
BALMORAL	165	CHODZIEZ	154	NA FARRAIGE	165
BALTIC EIDER	143	CHRISTIAN IV	170	DRONNING	
BALTIC JET	185	CLANSMAN	105	MARGRETHE II	193
BALTIC KRISTINA	188	CLARE	149	DUC DE NORMANDIE	68
BALTICA	143	CLAYMORE	117	DUCHESS M	164
BARFLEUR	68	CLEMENTINE	132	DUCHESS OF	
BASTØ I	168	COLL	104	SCANDINAVIA	72
BASTØ II	168	COLOR FANTASY	172	DUKE OF	
BASTØ III	168	COLOR FESTIVAL	170	SCANDINAVIA	72
BEACHY HEAD	128	COLOR TRAVELLER	170	EARL SIGURD	115
BEGONIA	158	COLOR VIKING	170	EARL THORFINN	115
BELNAHUA	102	COMETA	153	EASDALE	102
BEN-MY-CHREE	81	COMMODORE		EDDYSTONE	128
BERGEN CASTLE	119	CLIPPER	70	EDGCUMBE BELLE	164
BIGGA	120	COMMODORE		EDMUND D	116
BIRKA CARRIER	143	GOODWILL	134	EGLANTINE	132
BIRKA EXPRESS	143	CONDOR 10	70	EIGG	105
BIRKA TRADER	143	CONDOR EXPRESS	70	EILEAN DHIURA	102
BOA VISTA	181	CONDOR VITESSE	70	ELISABETH RUSS	160
BOHUS	170	CORRAN	111	ERNEST BEVIN	125
BRAKZAND	211	CORUISK	105	ESTRADEN	146
BRAMBLE BUSH BAY	161	COUTANCES	130	EUROPEAN	
BRAVE MERCHANT	83	CROMARTY ROSE	110	CAUSEWAY	88
BRAYE SPIRIT	112			EUROPEAN DIPLOMAT	151

Name	Page	Name	Page	Name	Page
EUROPEAN		FYLGA	120	ISLE OF INISHMORE	78
HIGHLANDER	88	GABRIELLA	210	ISLE OF LEWIS	105
EUROPEAN MARINER	151	GARDENIA	158	ISLE OF MULL	105
EUROPEAN SEAWAY	150	GEIRA	120	JAMES NEWMAN	125
EUROVOYAGER	158	GELLAN	122	JENACK	122
EVA ODEN	132	GEORG OTS	198	JENS KOFOED	168
EXPRESS	85	GITTE 3	179	JOHN BURNS	125
EYNHALLOW	115	GLENACHULISH	111	JONATHAN SWIFT	78
F.B.D. DUNBRODY	104	GLENBROOK	110	JUNO	106
FANTAASIA	204	GOD MET ONS III	122	JUPITER	76
FASTCAT RYDE	124	GOLDEN MARIANA	116	JUPITER	106
FASTCAT SHANKLIN	124	GOOD SHEPHERD IV	120	KAHLEBERG	187
FELLOW	193	GOSPORT QUEEN	164	KAPELLA	204
FENCER	164	GÖTALAND	196	KAPTAN	
FENJA	193	GOTLAND	172	BURHANETTIN ISIM	209
FILLA	120	GOTLANDIA	172	KAUNAS	173
FINLANDIA	207	GRAEMSAY	116	KENILWORTH	164
FINNARROW	186	GREAT		KING HARRY FERRY	162
FINNBIRCH	143	EXPECTATIONS	165	KINGSWEAR BELLE	164
FINNCLIPPER	179	GRIMA	120	KLAÌPEDA	182
FINNEAGLE	179	GRY MARITHA	112	KOADA	120
FINNFELLOW	179	GUTE	212	KOEGELWIECK	175
FINNFOREST	143	GYLEN LADY	114	KOGUVA	189
FINNHANSA	178	HAMBURG	146	KONG HARALD	180
FINNHAWK	144	HAMLET	193	KÖRGELAID	189
FINNJET	199	HAMNAVOE	115	KRONPRINS	
FINNKRAFT	144	HAPPY HOOKER	164	FREDERIK	193
FINNMARKEN	180	HARILAID	189	KRONPRINS HARALD	170
FINNMASTER	144	HARTLAND POINT	128	LADY OF MANN	81
FINNMILL	144	HASCOSAY	149	LAGAN VIKING	83
FINNOAK	144	HEBRIDEAN ISLES	105	LAIG BAY	110
FINNPARTNER	178	HEBRIDES	105	LARKSPUR	158
FINNPULP	144	HENDRA	120	LEHOLA	193
FINNREEL	144	HIGHER FERRY	161	LEIRNA	120
FINNSAILOR	186	HIIUMAA	189	LEMBITU	193
FINNTRADER	178	HJALTLAND	115	LINDA ROSA	148
FIVLA	120	HOLGER DANSKE	193	LINGA	120
FJORD NORWAY	179	HOTSPUR IV	165	LISCO GLORIA	182
FLANDERS WAY	141	HOVERSPEED		LISMORE	102
FOYLE RAMBLER	114	GREAT BRITAIN	75	LITTLE ISLAND	
FOYLE VENTURE	114	HOY HEAD	116	FERRY	162
FREEDOM 90	164	HROSSEY	115	LOCH ALAINN	106
FRIESLAND	175	HUCKLEBERRY FINN	208	LOCH BHRUSDA	106
FRIGG SYDFYEN	193	HUMBER WAY	141	LOCH BUIE	106
FRISIA I	185	HURRICANE CLIPPER	165	LOCH DUNVEGAN	106
FRISIA II	185	HURST POINT	128	LOCH FYNE	106
FRISIA IV	185	IKOM K	114	LOCH LINNHE	106
FRISIA V	185	IPSWICH WAY	141	LOCH PORTAIN	106
FRISIA VI	185	ISABELLA	210	LOCH RANZA	106
FRISIA VII	185	ISLAND EXPRESS	164	LOCH RIDDON	106
FRISIA IX	185	ISLE OF ARRAN	105	LOCH STRIVEN	106
FRISIA X	185	ISLE OF CUMBRAE	105	LOCH TARBERT	106

LOCHNEVIS	106	NAJADE	175	PIONEER	106
LOFOTEN	180	NARVIK	180	PLYM	162
LONGSTONE	128	NEW ADVANCE	120	POLARIS	144
LORD OF THE ISLES	106	NILS DACKE	208	POLARLYS	180
LOUISE RUSS	132	NILS HOLGERSSON	208	POLARSTERN	177
LÜBECK LINK	186	NO 4	122	POLONIA	208
LYNHER	162	NO 5	161	POMERANIA	187
LYONESSE LADY	112	NOORD-NEDERLAND	175	PONT-AVEN	68
MADS MOLS	184	NORBANK	151	PORTAFERRY II	122
MAERSK ANGLIA	146	NORBAY	151	PORTSMOUTH QUEEN	164
MAERSK DOVER	82	NORCAPE	150	POVL ANKER	168
MAERSK DUNKERQUE	82	NORCLIFF	144	PRIDE OF AQUITAINE	85
MAERSK EXPORTER	146	NORDIC JET	185	PRIDE OF BILBAO	85
MAERSK FLANDERS	146	NORDKAPP	180	PRIDE OF BRUGES	85
MAERSK IMPORTER	146	NORDLANDIA	176	PRIDE OF BURGUNDY	85
MAI MOLS	184	NORDLICHT	177	PRIDE OF CALAIS	85
MAID OF GLENCOUL	111	NORDLYS	180	PRIDE OF	
MALLARD	161	NORDNORGE	180	CANTERBURY	85
MALMÖ LINK	186	NORKING	150	PRIDE OF	
MARABOU	132	NORMANDIE	68	CHERBOURG	85
MAREN MOLS	184	NORMANDY	78	PRIDE OF DOVER	85
MARIELLA	210	NORQUEEN	150	PRIDE OF HULL	85
MARIN MARIE	165	NORRÖNA	93	PRIDE OF KENT	85
MASSILIA	134	NORSKY	150	PRIDE OF	
MAX MOLS	85	NORSTREAM	150	LE HAVRE	85
MECKLENBURG-		NORTHERN		PRIDE OF	
VORPOMMERN	193	MERCHANT	82	PORTSMOUTH	85
MELOODIA	204	OBBOLA	152	PRIDE OF	
MELUSINE	132	ODIN SYDFYEN	193	PROVENCE	85
MENJA	193	OERD	211	PRIDE OF	
MERCANDIA IV	180	OFELIA	189	ROTTERDAM	85
MERCANDIA VIII	180	OILEAN ARANN	164	PRIDE OF THE TYNE	165
MERCHANT	144	OILEAN NA H-OIGE	104	PRIDE OF YORK	85
MERCHANT BRAVERY	148	OLDENBURG	165	PRIMROSE	158
MERCHANT		OLEANDER	158	PRINCESS OF	
BRILLIANT	148	OOST-VLIELAND	175	SCANDINAVIA	72
MERMAID II	182	ORTVIKEN	152	PRINCESS	
MERSEY VIKING	83	OSTEND WAY	141	POCAHONTAS	164
METTE MOLS	184	OSTFRIESLAND	177	PRINS JOACHIM	193
MIDNATSOL	180	ÖSTRAND	152	PRINS RICHARD	193
MIDNATSOL II	180	OUR LADY PAMELA	124	PRINSESSE	
MIDNIGHT MERCHANT	82	OUR LADY PATRICIA	124	BENEDIKTE	193
MIDSLAND	175	PALANGA	182	PRINSESSE	
MIE MOLS	184	PAULINE RUSS	160	RAGNHILD	170
MIRANDA	144	PEARL OF		QUEEN OF ARAN	164
MOLENGAT	207	SCANDINAVIA	173	QUEEN OF	
MONNIK	211	PENTALINA B	117	SCANDINAVIA	72
MONT ST MICHEL	68	PENTLAND VENTURE	165	RAASAY	106
MOONDANCE	154	PESCARA JET	90	RAPIDE	90
MORVERN	104	PETER PAN	208	RED EAGLE	119
MUIRNEAG	130	PETER WESSEL	170	RED FALCON	119
MÜNSTERLAND	177	PETERSBURG	193	RED JET 1	119

RED JET 2	119	SEAWHEEL HUMBER	154	STENA EUROPE	94
RED JET 3	119	SEAWHEEL RHINE	154	STENA EXPLORER	94
RED JET 4	119	SHANNON BREEZE	120	STENA FREIGHTER	201
RED OSPREY	119	SHANNON DOLPHIN	120	STENA GERMANICA	201
REEDHAM FERRY	162	SHAPINSAY	116	STENA HOLLANDICA	94
REGAL STAR	204	SHIELDSMAN	165	STENA JUTLANDICA	201
REGINA BALTICA	204	SIER	211	STENA LEADER	155
REGULA	189	SILESIA	187	STENA LYNX III	94
RENFREW ROSE	165	SILJA EUROPA	199	STENA NAUTICA	201
RHUM	104	SILJA FESTIVAL	199	STENA NORDICA	201
RICHARD WITH	180	SILJA OPERA	199	STENA PARTNER	155
RIDER	144	SILJA SERENADE	199	STENA PIONEER	155
RIVER LUNE	148	SILJA SYMPHONY	199	STENA SAGA	201
RIVERDANCE	154	SILVIA ANA L	170	STENA SCANDINAVICA	201
ROBIN HOOD	208	SKAGEN	171	STENA SCANRAIL	201
ROMANTIKA	204	SKÅNE	196	STENA SEAFARER	155
ROSE OF ARAN	164	SKY CLIPPER	165	STENA SEARIDER	155
ROSELLA	210	SKY WIND	198	STENA SEATRADER	155
ROSLAGEN	177	SLINGEBORG	132	STENA SHIPPER	137
ROTTUM	211	SNOLDA	120	STENA TRANSFER	155
ROVER	164	SOLENT ENTERPRISE	164	STENA TRANSPORTER	155
ROYAL DAFFODIL	165	SOLENT PRINCE	164	STENA TRAVELLER	212
ROYAL IRIS		SOLIDOR 5	75	STENA VOYAGER	94
OF THE MERSEY	165	SØNDERHO	193	STORM CLIPPER	165
RÜGEN	193	SOUND OF SANDA	123	STRANGFORD FERRY	122
RUNNER	144	SOUND OF SCALPAY	123	SUPERFAST VII	204
SAGA MOON	148	SOUND OF SCARBA	123	SUPERFAST VIII	204
SAGAFJORD	190	SOUND OF SHUNA	123	SUPERFAST IX	98
SARDINIA VERA	99	SOUND OF SLEAT	123	SUPERFAST X	98
SASSNITZ	193	SPAARNEBORG	132	SUPERFERRY	98
SATURN	106	SPEED ONE	94	SUPERSEACAT ONE	90
SC ABERDEEN	153	SPIRIT OF GOSPORT	164	SUPERSEACAT TWO	81
SCANDINAVIA	187	SPIRIT OF		SUPERSEACAT THREE	199
SCANIA	189	PORTSMOUTH	164	SUPERSEACAT FOUR	199
SCHIEBORG	132	SPIRIT OF SKYE	164	SUPERSTAR EXPRESS	88
SCHLESWIG-		SPODSBJERG	193	SVEALAND	193
HOLSTEIN	193	ST CATHERINE	124	SYMPHORINE	132
SCHULPENGAT	207	ST CECILIA	124	TALLINK	
SCILLONIAN III	112	ST CLARE	124	AUTOEXPRESS	204
SEA CORONA	193	ST FAITH	124	TALLINK	
SEA WIND	198	ST HELEN	124	AUTOEXPRESS 2	204
SEACAT FRANCE	90	ST OLA	189	TALLINK	
SEACAT ISLE OF MAN	81	STAR WIND	198	AUTOEXPRESS 3	204
SEACAT SCOTLAND	90	STENA ADVENTURER	94	TALLINK	
SEAFRANCE BERLIOZ	93	STENA BALTICA	201	AUTOEXPRESS 4	204
SEAFRANCE CEZANNE	92	STENA BRITANNICA	94	TAMAR	162
SEAFRANCE MANET	92	STENA CALEDONIA	94	THE PRINCESS ANNE	90
SEAFRANCE NORD PAS-DE-		STENA CARISMA	201	THE PRINCESS	
CALAIS	153	STENA CARRIER	201	MARGARET	90
SEAFRANCE RENOIR	92	STENA DANICA	201	THE SECOND SNARK	164
SEAFRANCE RODIN	92	STENA DISCOVERY	94	THE TOM AVIS	162
SEAGARD	160	STENA ENVOY	212	THE TOM CASEY	162

THOR SYDFYEN	193	TOR PRIMULA	137	VASALAND	144
THORA	120	TOR SCANDIA	137	VESTERÅLEN	180
THORSVOE	116	TOR SELANDIA	137	VICTOR HUGO	165
TOM SAWYER	208	TOR SUECIA	137	VICTORIA I	205
TOR ANGLIA	137	TRANQUILITY	164	VICTORINE	132
TOR BALTICA	137	TRANS CARRIER	153	VIIRE	189
TOR BEGONIA	141	TRANSEUROPA	178	VIKING CINDERELLA	210
TOR BELGIA	137	TRANSLANDIA	176	VIKINGLAND	189
TOR BRITANNIA	137	TRANSLUBECA	207	VILJA	168
TOR CIMBRIA	137	TRELLEBORG	196	VILLUM CLAUSEN	168
TOR DANIA	137	TROLLFJORD	180	VILNIUS	173
TOR FLANDRIA	137	TT-DELPHIN	208	VISBY	172
TOR FRESIA	141	TYCHO BRAHE	193	WAPPEN VON	
TOR FUTURA	137	ULYSSES	78	BORKUM	177
TOR GOTHIA	137	UNDINE	132	WAVERLEY	165
TOR HOLLANDIA	137	URD	193	WESTERLAND	189
TOR HUMBRIA	137	VAL DE LOIRE	68	WESTFALEN	177
TOR MAGNOLIA	137	VALENTINE	132	WOODCHURCH	165
TOR MAXIMA	137	VANA TALLINN	205	YOKER SWAN	165
TOR MINERVA	137	VARAGEN	116		
TOR NERINGA	137	VARBOLA	148		
TOR PETUNIA	137	VARDO	189		

Val de Loire *(Miles Cowsill)*